Richard Pryor
in Hollywood

ALSO BY ANTHONY BALDUCCI
AND FROM MCFARLAND

---

*I Won't Grow Up! The Comic Man-Child
in Film from 1901 to the Present* (2016)

*The Funny Parts: A History
of Film Comedy Routines and Gags* (2012)

*Lloyd Hamilton: Poor Boy Comedian
of Silent Cinema* (2009)

Richard Pryor in Hollywood

The Narrative Films, 1967–1997

ANTHONY BALDUCCI

McFarland & Company, Inc., Publishers
Jefferson, North Carolina

LIBRARY OF CONGRESS CATALOGUING-IN-PUBLICATION DATA

Names: Balducci, Anthony, 1958– author.
Title: Richard Pryor in Hollywood : the narrative films, 1967–1997 / Anthony Balducci.
Description: Jefferson, North Carolina : McFarland & Company, Inc., Publishers, 2018. | Includes bibliographical references and index.
Identifiers: LCCN 2018023832 | ISBN 9781476673820 (softcover : acid free paper) ∞
Subjects: LCSH: Pryor, Richard, 1940–2005—Criticism and interpretation.
Classification: LCC PN2287.P77 B35 2018 | DDC 792.702/8092—dc23
LC record available at https://lccn.loc.gov/2018023832

BRITISH LIBRARY CATALOGUING DATA ARE AVAILABLE

ISBN (print) 978-1-4766-7382-0
ISBN (ebook) 978-1-4766-3279-7

© 2018 Anthony Balducci. All rights reserved

No part of this book may be reproduced or transmitted in any form or by any means, electronic or mechanical, including photocopying or recording, or by any information storage and retrieval system, without permission in writing from the publisher.

Front cover: Richard Pryor and Margot Kidder in the 1982 film *Some Kind of Hero* (Paramount Pictures/Photofest)

Printed in the United States of America

McFarland & Company, Inc., Publishers
Box 611, Jefferson, North Carolina 28640
www.mcfarlandpub.com

For my mother,
Jennie Balducci

Acknowledgments

It was my priority in writing this book to understand the creative process behind Richard Pryor's films. This meant it was vital for me to talk to the screenwriters who worked at ground zero to conceive the characters, the situations, and the jokes. I was fortunate to be able to talk to a number of those writers, including Denis Hamill, Kenneth Vose, Lawrence DuKore, David Taylor, Hal Barwood, Peter Seaman, and Bruce Jay Friedman. I am grateful for their recollections and insights.

My biggest thrill in writing this book was my interview with Mr. Friedman, the author of *Stir Crazy*. I have been a fan of his since my adolescent years. It turns out that besides being wonderfully talented, he is wonderfully good-natured.

Harry Northup contributed a great deal to my chapters on *Which Way Is Up?* and *Blue Collar*. I was so impressed by Harry's stories that I spent a day watching several of his films, including *Taxi Driver* (1976), *Fighting Mad* (1976), *Kansas* (1988), and *Silence of the Lambs* (1991). Harry has a scene in *Taxi Driver* where he tries to sell Robert De Niro a piece of Errol Flynn's bathtub. This was a clever bit of business that Harry invented on the set. Harry is a good man. I thank him for his help.

A special thanks to Jacque Roethler, who provided me with the "Double Whoopee" script from the Gene Wilder Papers at the University of Iowa.

Table of Contents

Acknowledgments vi
Introduction 1

The Busy Body (1967)	5
Wild in the Streets (1968)	14
Uncle Tom's Fairy Tales: The Movie for Homosexuals (1969)	18
Carter's Army (1970)	20
The Phynx (1970)	23
You've Got to Walk It Like You Talk It or You'll Lose That Beat (1971)	25
Lady Sings the Blues (1972)	26
The Mack (1973)	30
Some Call It Loving (1973)	37
Hit! (1973)	40
Uptown Saturday Night (1974)	42
Adiós Amigo (1976)	47
The Bingo Long Traveling All-Stars & Motor Kings (1976)	52
Car Wash (1976)	57
Silver Streak (1976)	58
Greased Lightning (1977)	65
Which Way Is Up? (1977)	73
Blue Collar (1978)	85
The Wiz (1978)	102
California Suite (1978)	104
The Muppet Movie (1979)	108

Wholly Moses! (1980)	109
In God We Tru$t (or Gimme That Prime Time Religion) (1980)	111
Stir Crazy (1980)	114
Bustin' Loose (1981)	123
Some Kind of Hero (1982)	136
The Toy (1982)	142
Superman III (1983)	151
Brewster's Millions (1985)	160
Jo Jo Dancer, Your Life Is Calling (1986)	168
Critical Condition (1987)	173
Moving (1988)	180
Harlem Nights (1989)	182
See No Evil, Hear No Evil (1989)	186
Another You (1991)	190
The Three Muscatels (1991)	194
Mad Dog Time (1996)	195
Lost Highway (1997)	196

Epilogue   201

Notes   203

Bibliography   217

Index   219

Introduction

Richard Pryor had a major impact on stand-up comedy in the 1970s and 1980s. Damon Wayans said, "There are many different kinds of comedians ... the observational humorist, the impressionist, the character creator, the physical comedian, the self-depreciator, and the dirty-joke teller. What made Richard Pryor so brilliant is he was able to incorporate all these styles at once."[1]

Before I undertook writing this book, I had only one of Pryor's films in my DVD collection. It was *Richard Pryor: Live on the Sunset Strip* (1982), which features the comedian in a stand-up performance at the Hollywood Palladium. This film never fails to make me laugh. Pryor talks intimately of his childhood, reflecting on events with humor and insight. He acts out stories, playing the different roles. He talks about his grandmother whipping him with a switch for misbehaving. In the course of the story, he alternates between depicting the formidable grandmother and the terrified child. He expresses a wide range of emotions while never forgetting his main purpose for being on the stage that night is to make people laugh.

The switch becomes a diabolical instrument in his tale. He speaks about the rage he once felt when he saw a young tree sprouting branches that might one day be used as switches. He describes stopping his car so that he could throttle the tree (which he demonstrates by throttling his microphone stand). "You ain't never gonna grow up," he roars. "You won't be beating nobody's ass.'"

Lily Tomlin remembered the first time she saw Pryor on *The Ed Sullivan Show*.

> I was mesmerized by his heartbreaking wit, full of hurt and truth. Even then, his expression of personal experiences was unique—blending chaos and compassion, vulnerability and bravado, attitude and insight.... The last time I saw Richard, I was in the audience at the Santa Barbara film festival honoring him for his work. For almost two hours, I watched the greatest pioneering comic artist of the last three generations at the top of his genius—this gifted, raging, soaring, plummeting, deeply human man with the tender boy inside. I wept and I laughed....[2]

Pryor is not, as many critics claim, only thundering, scathing, and explosive in his concert performances. He expresses an easy confidence. He is often playful and joyous. He does, as Tomlin says, occasionally reveal "the tender boy inside."

He doesn't limit his characters to humans. He uses his adroit pantomimic skills to parody the gazelles, water buffaloes, and lions on the African plains. He plays the role of a cocaine pipe, which urges him in a seductively evil voice to get high. His sharpness and versatility on stage is mesmerizing.

Charlie Chaplin is one of the greatest comic artists in motion picture history. After more than one hundred years, his films continue to attract the interest of people who recognize the importance of cinema and the importance of laughter in one's life. Chaplin's fans, who span many generations, have found the comedian's work to be a source of endless fascination. At present, Amazon lists six dozen books about the comedian/director. Pryor is another of the rare comedians who inspires endless fascination among his fans. At present, Amazon lists eleven biographies about Pryor. But these books, unlike those devoted to Chaplin, do not focus on the comedian's artistry. They focus instead on the traumas of his childhood, his struggles with race, and his addiction to drugs and alcohol. With this book, I set out to disentangle the funnyman from the tragic issues that dominated his personal life.

A comedian possesses special attributes that are part of his basic human composition. It doesn't matter where he was raised, it doesn't matter the color of his skin, and it doesn't matter what drugs he abused in his lifetime. A comedian's ability to connect with an audience is something natural. A comedian has an innate ability to deliver a funny line, make a silly face, or move his body in ways that elicit laughter. Journalists always wanted Pryor to tell them what made him funny. The comedian had a simple answer: "God made me funny."[3] Experience shapes and refines these abilities, but these abilities exist in the DNA and they lay dormant even as an individual lies as a baby in a cradle. Comedy is, in this way, a pure essence. It is my objective to distinguish Pryor's natural comic abilities, which were too often obscured in the chaos of his life.

The two most revolutionary stand-up comedians of the 1970s were Richard Pryor and George Carlin. But neither man started out wanting to be shocking or groundbreaking. They just wanted to be funny. Carlin said, "I loved Danny Kaye.... I thought *funny* was great."[4] He explained to *Playboy*: "By the age of six or seven, I was already doing voices and faces, making my friends and my mother laugh. Then I saw Danny Kaye in a movie, and he was doing voices and faces on that big, big screen and making whole audiences laugh. It was just an instant hookup."[5] He wanted to be Kaye.[6] "Danny Kaye," he said, "was very influential in terms of physical humor—face and hands."[7] You couldn't find an entertainer with less edge than Kaye, who had cultivated a comic persona that was gentle and agreeable.

In his autobiography, Pryor described his comedy style as "profane and profound."[8] But he wasn't initially interested in being profane or profound. David and Joe Henry, the authors of *Furious Cool: Richard Pryor and the World That Made Him*, wrote: "His family had just bought their first television set, so he mimicked the antics of comics like Red Skelton and Jerry Lewis."[9] Wayne Federman of Vulture wrote: "A breakthrough moment occurred at age twelve, when he saw the Martin & Lewis feature *Sailor Beware* at the Rialto Theater. Jerry Lewis immediately jumped to the top of his list of comedy heroes. Years later, he called Lewis 'the God of comedy.'"[10]

Carlin was another fan of Lewis. He said, "I liked Jerry Lewis' early work. His abandon. That's what I've always admired. The ability to let go."[11]

Scott Saul, author of *Becoming Richard Pryor*, wrote:

> As he groped toward his own style, Richard did not aspire to be a comedian in the mold of Bob Hope, who chose his lines from an overstuffed catalog of gags (most of them written by jokesmiths in his employ). In sensibility, he leaned toward his idol Sid Caesar and his fellow Midwesterner Jonathan Winters, two comics who submerged their real selves beneath the outlandish characters they created. Both Caesar and Winters were averse to jokes; they were performers, not commentators. They were interested in the absurdity of so-called normal life. Caesar specialized in nutty professors and squabbling husbands; Winters, in squares and hayseeds. Richard had his own body of material—

the people he'd observed in Peoria's pulpits, used-car lots, and working-class bars—and his comedy inclined to the off-kilter and the zany.[12]

David and Joe Henry wrote: "Once upon a time a lanky and loose-limbed Richard had bounded onto the stage with acrobatic grace, shape-shifting himself into all manner of people and things: pious preachers, rum-soaked raconteurs, white guys on acid, drunken brawlers, drooling junkies, angry black militants, bullet-punctured automobile tires, an infant at the moment of birth, a deer alerted by the sounds of hunters crunching leaves in the forest, copulating monkeys, police dogs...."[13]

His early stand-up material included surreal pantomime routines. He might pretend to be a baby being born or show what it would be like for the first man to walk on the Sun. Pryor managed in his portrayal of the baby to mostly convey fear. Joan Acocella of *The New Yorker* wrote: "The baby tries and tries and pushes and pushes. Finally, he pops his head out, looks around, and begins shrieking."[14] Pryor's astronaut, his feet touching the fiery surface of the Sun, hops around with extreme pain and fear. From the start, pain and fear formed the basis of his act. Pryor remembered often feeling scared as a child and it was this feeling that he was now channeling into his work. Pryor once said, "Anything you want to know about fear, you got the right person."[15]

The pantomime routines became more and more elaborate as time went on. Actor Harry Northup saw Pryor at the Improv in the mid–1960s, performing a routine about the evolution of man. He wrote: "He transformed from this simple amoeba-like creature into a fish-like creature, then a being with hands and legs, and then into a human standing upon two legs."[16]

Early on, Pryor wanted to ingratiate himself to his audiences. He couldn't be confident or easygoing in the same way as Bill Cosby. Federman wrote: "The college-graduated Cosby was everything the twenty-two-year-old 'Richie' (as he was known at the time) Pryor wasn't: smooth, confident, and urbane."[17] At first, he developed a shy, nervous, vulnerable persona that audiences found endearing. But he had more forceful emotions that refused to be contained. It was only a matter of time before he relinquished his timid, endearing persona and exposed his raw self in front of an audience. Colin Beckett of the *Brooklyn Rail* wrote: "The dynamic interplay between vicious self-loathing and furious pride, righteous anger and wounded empathy ... animated his stand-up material."[18]

Pryor's film acting has inspired far less acclaim than his stand-up performances. His fans were, for the most part, disappointed with his narrative films, especially misfires like *The Toy* and *Superman III*. How could a comedian who could be so funny and profound on a bare stage not be funny and profound when flanked by the vast resources of a major Hollywood film studio? Could it be that the bad reputation of Pryor's films is undeserved? This book is designed to address these questions in a comprehensive film-by-film analysis.

The Busy Body (1967)

Production: William Castle Productions.
Distribution: Paramount Pictures.
Producer: William Castle.
Associate Producer: Dona Holloway.
Director: William Castle.
Screenplay: Ben Starr, from the Donald Westlake novel.
Photography: Harold Stine.
Editor: Edwin H. Bryant.
Music: Vic Mizzy.
Release date: March 12, 1967.
Running time: 101 minutes
Cast: Sid Caesar (George Norton), Robert Ryan (Charley Barker), Anne Baxter (Margo Foster Kane), Kay Medford (Ma Norton), Jan Murray (Murray Foster), Richard Pryor (Whittaker), Arlene Golonka (Bobbi Brody), Charles McGraw (Fred Harwell), Ben Blue (Felix Rose), Dom DeLuise (Kurt Brock), Bill Dana (Archie Brody), Godfrey Cambridge (Mike), Marty Ingels (Willie), George Jessel (Mr. Fessel).

The Busy Body was adapted from a novel by Donald Westlake. Westlake was attracting much interest from studio executives at the time. In 1967, three film adaptations of Westlake novels were released to theatres. The first was a French film, *Mise à sac*, which was based on *The Score*. The film involves a criminal gang that plots a hit-and-run raid on a mining town to steal payroll money from a copper-processing plant. The second was *Point Blank*, which was based on *The Hunter*. The film involves a professional criminal who is double-crossed by a partner in an armed robbery. He is shot and left for dead while his partner takes off with the money, but he (astonishingly) survives his gunshot wounds and sets out to hunt down his traitorous accomplice. *Mise à sac* and *Point Blank* are tense, grim, violent crime-dramas that involve revenge, theft, and murder. Both films involve a homicidal, criminal-looking man out to satisfy a deadly vendetta. *The Busy Body* is different: it is a comedy. Its protagonist, George Norton, is not on a quest for retribution or restitution. He is neither cool nor competent.

The Busy Body was part of a tradition of Westlake novels that started with *The Fugitive Pigeon* (1965), which involves a lazy young man who is given a job by his gangster uncle to run a mob-owned bar. Westlake novels in which the protagonist was modeled after the gangster's nephew in *The Fugitive Pigeon* became known as the "Nephew" books. Fred Fitch of the *Westlake Review* wrote: "The 'Nephew' books … feature a fairly befuddled but likable young man who has delayed maturity in some way, and is a bit of a slacker, a deadbeat, a bum, a loser—but, it must be said, a loser with potential. But if there's one rule of the Nephew stories that holds true book after book, it's this—the hero will end up in trouble for something he didn't do."[1]

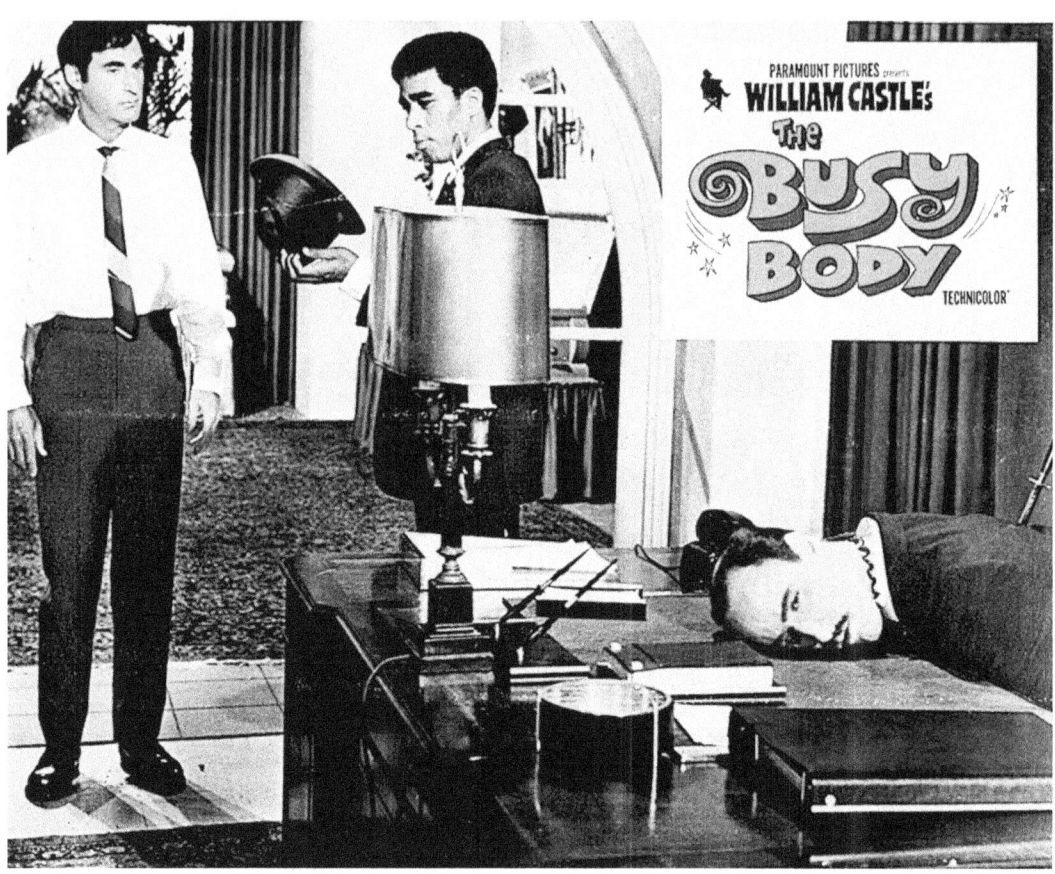

Pryor (center) questions Sid Caesar about a murder in *The Busy Body* (1967).

The Busy Body used the outline of the novel. Let's discuss the novel. Mob boss Nick Rovito pays for a big send-off for a drug courier, Charlie Brody, who suffers a heart attack while boiling water for a cup of instant coffee. Brody's death means something to Rovito because Brody was the first active member of the organization to die in three years. But Rovito realizes—after Brody has been laid to rest—that his widow had dressed him in the same blue suit he had worn on his recent return from a drug pick-up in Baltimore— the same blue suit that has $250,000 worth of uncut heroin neatly sewn into the jacket lining. Rovito summons Aloysius Eugene Engel (the book's version of Norton) to recover the blue suit.

Rovito suspects that one of his underlings, Willy Menchik, snitched to the cops about their activities. He orders Menchik to go with Engel to dig up the dead body. He tells Engel that, once they have the body, he needs to knock Willy unconscious with the shovel and bury him in the grave. But the job doesn't work out as planned. To start, the coffin is empty. No body. No suit. No heroin. Engel cannot even manage to knock off Menchik. Westlake wrote: "He dropped the flashlight, took a two-handed grip on the shovel, swung wildly, missed the departing Willy by two feet, lost his balance, fell into the hole, landed on the white plush, and the lid slammed down."[2]

Engel quickly realizes that his boss does not forgive failure. He will be dead soon unless he can track down the missing cache of heroin. Fitch wrote: "Bad enough he had

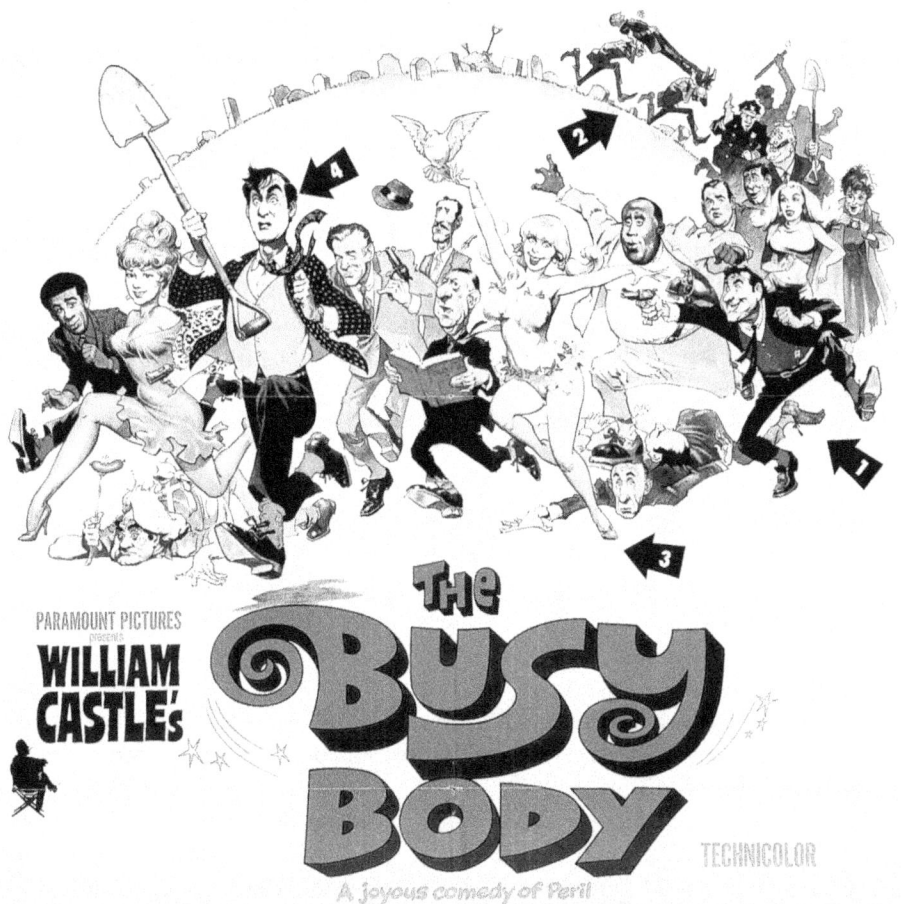

Frank Frazetta's poster for *The Busy Body*.

to play grave robber, but now he's got to play detective, solve the case of the missing corpse, and retrieve the drugs—or at least find out what happened."[3]

Engel has an extensive backstory that never made it into the script. His father worked as a messenger for the New York Syndicate. It was at the urging of the man's overbearing, ambitious wife that he maneuvered to get his son a job with the criminal organization.

From the start, Engel is content with his job. He never questions the morality of his profession. Fitch wrote: "Here, [Westlake]'s writing about an older guy (over thirty, I think) who has chosen to be somebody's flunky for life—a second generation mobster—an organization man practically from the cradle to the grave—almost literally, in fact. His protagonist is an empty suit, with lots of money, and no real self-understanding. He feels no strong attachment to anybody in his life, or to his job."[4]

Engel is given information by his father on Conelly, Rovito's right hand man, who is planning to betray the crime boss and take his place in the organization. All hell breaks loose when Rovito and Engel confront Conelly.

> Conelly got purple in the face, said, "*Gahhh!*" and made a run for Engel, his hands out to take Engel apart.
> Nick Rovito reached into a desk drawer, took out a gun and tossed it casually to Engel. It was the first time in his career Engel had even *held* a gun, but there was no time to think, what with Conelly and those hands getting rapidly closer, so Engel just closed his eyes and pulled the trigger five times, and when he opened his eyes again Conelly was lying on the floor.

Rovito holds onto the murder weapon, which has Engel's fingerprints on it, to use against Engel if he ever fails to follow orders. Other Westlake protagonists find themselves in an odd situation in which they have to solve a mystery to save their own lives. But Engel, who complains and broods a lot, is not as sympathetic as those other protagonists.

Rovito mistakenly believes that Engel has double-crossed him and sends out a pair of hit men to rub him out. Engel repeatedly runs from the police and the hit men while managing to cleverly solve the mystery. He ties everything up neatly in a nice bow for Rovito, who offers Engel his old job back. Engel, who would rather pursue a less lethal career, politely turns down the offer. As Fitch puts it, "[He] extracts himself bloodlessly from his employers.[5] He decides working for people you can never trust is for the birds. He's going to try being his own man—and part of that means telling his mother goodbye—she's been pestering him to have dinner with her all through the book—this woman who wanted him to be a big career man with the mob, but never could process what this would actually mean for him."[6]

The Busy Body novel in no way lent itself to a formulaic 1960s comedy. Fitch noted that, with this novel, Westlake had come up with a storyline that was essentially serious and that permeated the action with straight-faced humor. The producer, William Castle, did not want serious. He did not want straight-faced humor. He wanted the type of slapstick lunacy that had drawn ticket buyers to *It's a Mad, Mad, Mad, Mad World* (1963) and *The Pink Panther* (1964).

The Pink Panther, no doubt, was on Castle's mind when the producer proclaimed Caesar "the American Peter Sellers."[7] Castle assigned the adaptation duties to veteran sitcom scribe Ben Starr, who had written for *Bachelor Father*, *My Favorite Martian*, *Petticoat Junction*, and his most prolific stretch (forty episodes) for *Mr. Ed*. Besides his television work, he had been busy lately writing feature films. Within the preceding year, he had turned out scripts for three 1966 releases: *Our Man Flint*, *Texas Across the River*,

The Busy Body (1967)

and *The Pad and How to Use It*. Starr did everything he could to play up Westlake's comic angles and make the story come out as an outright comedy. Other Hollywood producers would follow the same strategy when it came to adapting Westlake's comic novels. Fitch observed that, because filmmakers never took Westlake's plots seriously, the movie adaptations were "almost never funny."[8]

Shooting for *The Busy Body* began in Chicago on September 26, 1966. Castle and Caesar had already collaborated on *The Spirit Is Willing* (which went into production in May but would not be released until 1967, after *The Busy Body*).

Starr worked hardest to make his main character a nice guy. Norton is a well-meaning fellow who has little control in his life. He is a man-boy dominated by his mother. He is a mob flunky afraid of his boss. In the book, Engel is a mid-level officer in the criminal organization, but he is given a lower rank in the film to make him less consequential in the organization and less likely to have direct involvement in the organization's nefarious deeds.

The courier is played by comedian Bill Dana. His character's name is now Archie Brody, maybe because Archie is a funnier name than Charlie. Brody no longer has heroin hidden inside his suit. Sewn into the suit, instead, is five hundred thousand dollars in cash. The novel's dry, dark humor is not reflected by the film's method for disposing of Brody—he is blown to pieces when his barbeque grill explodes in a freak accident.

The book lacks a real love interest. Fitch wrote: "There are girls, but there is not The Girl."[9] Engel has a girlfriend who works as an exotic dancer. He also has dealings with Brody's grieving widow, who is a former call girl. Starr combined the exotic dancer and the former call girl into a single character that could serve as Engel's love interest. So, now, the film had The Girl—Brody's widow and former exotic dancer Bobbi, played charmingly by Arlene Golonka.

Engel has a cold relationship with his mother, but Norton's relationship with his mother in the film is sweet and funny. Ma Norton, played by Kay Medford, spends the entire film trying to get her boy to come to dinner.

In the novel, Engel runs into trouble with a hard-headed police detective, Deputy Inspector Callahan. Rovito refers to Callahan as a "rotten bastard"[10] because he refuses to accept bribes. Westlake wrote: "[Callahan] threw a hammerlock on the boy and double-timed him over to Nick Rovito's office and threw him over Nick Rovito's desk into Nick Rovito's lap and said, 'This is yours. But I'm not.'"[11]

Richard Pryor was cast as the detective, now named Lt. Whitaker. The way he got the role came down to good, old-fashioned networking. In 1966, Pryor performed as the opening act for Bobby Darin at the Flamingo Hotel in Las Vegas. Darin became so fond of Pryor that he arranged a posh party in Beverly Hills to introduce his new friend to Hollywood producers and agents. One person Pryor met at the party was Caesar, who was getting ready to star in *The Busy Body*. On the spot, Caesar offered Pryor the role of the detective.

Norton encounters Whitaker at a funeral home, where a group of police officers are gathered for a police officer's service. The scene came straight out of the novel, except it turned out to be surprisingly restrained on screen. Fitch describes Westlake's scene as something "right out of Buster Keaton."[12] He wrote: "Engel flee[s] what seems to be roughly half the NYPD … and negotiate[s] a series of obstacles to evade them—and by dint of desperation-fueled ingenuity, mak[es] those obstacles work in his favor—he ends by plugging an alleyway with a handy truck, leaving them all stuck in there, while he walks nonchalantly back into the funeral parlor to ask more questions."[13] Caesar and Pryor play out an extended scene with various dialogue exchanges in a visitation room, a hallway, and a mortician's office. The police never chase Norton. In general, the dialogue-heavy film skimps on action.

Whitaker is befuddled by the idea of having to solve a murder mystery. In his one other key scene in the film, he becomes rattled when having to interrogate Norton's overbearing mother.

Some of the character's discomfort may have actually been the actor's. Pryor admitted to being uneasy about taking on his first film role. David and Joe Henry wrote: "The prospect of acting alongside Sid Caesar made him jittery enough. Richard had idolized Caesar as a skit comic on the NBC variety series *Your Show of Shows* since he was ten years old. Adding to his nervousness was the fact that he didn't have a clue how movies were made. He'd performed in front of cameras on television, of course, but had never acted for a camera in a movie before, and he knew enough to know there was a difference."[14] Pryor later said, "I faked it. Tried a little of this, a little of that. Some Steve McQueen, some Humphrey Bogart. Bless my confused heart. But it was hard because I didn't have my own thing to do."[15]

Whether confused or not, the strategy was useful. The script allowed Pryor roughly five minutes to showcase his talents. In that time he produces a character with some dimension. It is obvious that he is nervous and confused in his efforts to break the case, but he does everything he can to look tough and knowing. His fidgety manner exposes a man who fears failing at his job and coming out looking stupid. Ma Norton sees through his bluff. In her eyes, he is just a frail and vulnerable young man who needs a good meal.

Engel coldly abandons his controlling mother at the end of the book. He phones her and tells her, "Goodbye forever." But Norton ends up bringing his new girlfriend, Bobbi, to the dinner that his mother has been arranging from the start of the film.

Robert Ryan is appropriately menacing as the crime boss. The film has the distinction of presenting his only comedy work in a feature film. The actor would provide a similarly gruff performance when he played Walter Burns in a Broadway revival of *The Front Page*, in 1969.

The *Pittsburgh Press* referred to *The Busy Body* as "a spoof on American mobsters on the trail of an elusive corpse and a vanished cache of loot."[16] The plot was well encapsulated by the film's poster, which was designed by fantasy artist Frank Frazetta to resemble Jack Davis's classic poster for *It's A Mad, Mad, Mad, Mad World*, which was also about a vanished cache of loot.

Westlake was understandably unhappy with *The Busy Body*. Critics were even less happy. *Time* reported: "*The Busy Body* comes not to praise Sid Caesar but to bury him, and surrounding him in this tasteless Runyonesque rehash are such borscht belt holdovers as Murray, Dana, Jessel, and Mickey Deems."[17]

Castle went on a press tour to promote the film. He told the *Pittsburgh Press*, "Sid is just great to work with…. [He's] willing to take direction, but at the same time contributing some good ideas of his own."[18] Castle spoke further about Sid Caesar to columnist Barbara Bladen. He said, "[He's] not temperamental but fighting within himself to be perfect. He's very moody and I had to keep telling him to let the comedy come to you, it's a wide screen and you can't be larger than life. He fought me on comedy timing and he turned out to be right."[19]

Of course, Caesar was not the only comedian Castle had to direct in the film. He said, "The most difficult thing in the world is working with a lot of comedians in the same film. They go insane when left alone in a simple scene. It's complicated by the fact that the crew and technicians are laughing at them cutting up. Then I have to play God and decide what is funny within the context of the story."[20] He continued, "It's such a temptation to print a cut-up scene and use it. But it's bad picture making if it isn't pertinent to the story. Otherwise you're making Abbott and Costello films if you don't hold to that ideal that the play is the thing."[21]

Caesar said at the time, "In a movie, you have time to think about the role, and you can talk over each scene with a director. In TV, you walk in, say, 'You want to do it this way?' and *bang*—you do it."[22] Years later, the comedian admitted that he preferred the "*bang*—you do it" method because, he said, comedy was best produced through spontaneity.

Many parallels can be drawn between Caesar and Pryor. Like Caesar, Pryor disliked doing multiple takes and believed he was at his best when he was spontaneous. He, too, was at his most confident when he was breaking up the crew. Castle's statements about the moodiness of his comedy star and his need to control his improvisations were issues that would later have to be addressed by the directors who presided over Pryor's vehicles.

Pryor could have learned important life lessons from Caesar. Dick Cavett wrote: "Sid Caesar is a mysterious and complex man who seems to have been singled out by the gods to set two all-time records, one of dubious and unenviable distinction: to have set the high-water-mark for sustained comic brilliance over a long period of years, and to have ingested enough booze and pills to kill the Lippizaner stallions. The twin mysteries of how anyone gets so talented and how anyone could abuse himself so disastrously remain unsolved."[23]

It was explained in the press release for Caesar's autobiography: "The combination of devastating insecurity and the pressure of success led to a dependence on alcohol and pills that soon became an addiction. Periods of despair alternated with uncontrollable rages and violent behavior; work was sporadic and his family relationships were under tremendous strain."[24]

At the peak of his success, Caesar displayed self-destructive tendencies and a schizoid personality. He became notorious for the acts of rage that he inflicted on co-workers. Yet, the comedian was able to make anger funny. Neil Simon said of his days with Caesar, "There was an enormous amount of anger, but it would all come out in comedy. When he was angry, he could be very funny about it." David Zurawik of the *Baltimore Sun* wrote: "I was fascinated by the angry, manic energy of Caesar sweating through suit after suit on live TV looking as if he was going to explode right through the box into our living room."[25] Caesar admitted that he often became angry while working on *Your Show of Shows* and *Caesar's Hour*. He said, "The time pressures were so great I took the telephone out of the room. I literally ripped it out of the wall and threw it in the hallway."[26]

Jeff Simon of the *Buffalo News* wrote in 2014:

> Caesar was big and beefy back then and, by anecdote, almost as strong as a middle linebacker. [In a parody of the popular television program *This Is Your Life*] he ran around the audience, chased by TV studio ushers pretending to try to trap him and force him up on the stage so that his life story could be told to early TV's sentimental watchers. Caesar's sweaty pushings and shovings of those extras were actually terrifying to watch. His genius, in those years, was that he was a comic who seemed genuinely violent and scary.[27]

Cavett wrote: "[It] reminds me of an anecdote Mel Brooks tells hilariously about crossing a street in New York with Sid when a cabbie shouted something insulting at him. The window was closed but the wing was open. After asking him to repeat the slur, Sid asked the man if he remembered his birth. In response to, 'Yeah, what of it?' Sid said, 'Because you're about to re-enact it,' grabbed the cabbie by the lapels and had him partway out the narrow aperture before cooler heads prevailed."[28]

Caesar said that learning to play the saxophone saved his life. He said, "It helped me blow off some steam and get rid of some of the anger."[29] The saxophone was not the only instrument that Caesar adopted to calm his nerves. He became a gun enthusiast because, he found, firing guns is also a good way to relieve anger. Jack Carter said, "We became very close. We'd shoot skeet. He had violence on his mind. Guns. He's calm now."[30] His rehabilitation had a calming effect, but it left him a shadow of his former self. Fans were bewildered and frustrated to find that, after years of making them laugh, Caesar had lost his comic spark. In his rehabilitation, he drew away from his career, which had always created more stress than he could bear. He spent the final years of his life away from the spotlight.

The subject of Caesar's anger was prominent in his obituaries. Dennis McLellan wrote:

> His drinking at the time, Caesar later wrote, caused his underlying anger and violence to emerge. Most famously, after a day of doing nine performances at a theater in Chicago, a drunk Caesar angrily lifted Brooks and rushed him to the open window of an 18th floor hotel room after Brooks kept insisting they go out.
>
> "You want out? I'll show you out," Caesar yelled, dangling Brooks halfway out the window before Caesar's brother, Dave, grabbed him and Brooks was pulled back into the room.

Caesar addressed some of his emotional issues and his entry into psychoanalysis in a 1956 *Look* magazine article he wrote: "On stage, I could hide behind the characters and inanimate objects I created. Off stage, with my real personality for all to see, I was a mess. It was difficult for me to establish a normal, healthy relationship with anyone. I couldn't believe that anyone could like me for myself."[31] Caesar realized that he was being self-destructive in the way he abused his body with pills and alcohol. The aggressive, high-energy comedian had, in the end, been left dissipated by his substance addictions.

Several reporters interviewed Caesar about *The Busy Body*. None of them failed to notice his weight loss. Cavett wrote: "I used to hear rumors in the early 1970s that Sid was 'in trouble' and there was the mysterious weight loss and the change in appearance that were said to be part of a new exercise regime, but very few people even in 'the biz' had any notion of what he was going through."[32]

The amount of weight that the comedian had lost varied from report to report. It was noted in one article that he was down from 196 pounds to 183. Norma Lee Browning of the *Chicago Tribune* said that he had lost twenty pounds. It was estimated by yet another journalist that the actor had lost thirty. Whatever the exact figure, it was not something the press was willing to ignore. It was the general assumption that the actor was ill. This was something that had to be addressed by Castle and Caesar because people were unlikely to go to a movie to laugh at a sick actor.

"Let's get this straight," said Castle, "he's not sick. He lost those pounds by sensible dieting and he's as strong as ever. He always was a physically powerful man and still is."[33]

Caesar told Ken Barnard of the *Detroit Free Press*, "People on the street don't recognize me so easily anymore."[34] He said that his weight loss and new style of clothing were meant to change his look for motion pictures; he wanted to look modern to the young people who represented the majority of theatregoers. But, more than that, he thought his new look was appropriate for his new leading man status. He said, "In motion pictures you always have to wind up with the girl at the end, and if you're going to get the girl, you should look the part. You have to make audiences believe it." Norma Lee Browning of the *Chicago Tribune* made Caesar's "Sebring hair-do and Carnaby street Mod look"[35] the focus of her article.

Castle supported Caesar's "new look" narrative. He explained that he could not depend on Caesar's longstanding television fans to abandon their livings rooms for a night at the picture show. Teenagers had become a powerful force at the box office and he had to find a way to market the comedian to them. So, the solution was the new wardrobe. He told Kaspar Monahan of the *Pittsburgh Press*, "Teen-agers are wild about him for his mod look."[36]

The reporters remained suspicious. Barnard wrote: "[Caesar] insists that he feels great. Yet, though he is still a friendly man, he struck this reporter as somewhat more tense and reserved than a few years ago."[37] Simon wrote: "He wasn't the same, of course. The great critic Pauline Kael's theory was that he was never the same after he had lost the excess weight. His autobiography describes the offstage 'violent drunk' and drug abuser he was—a man, in effect, who couldn't help but burn himself out."[38]

Cavett remembered seeing Caesar at a time when he was "alarmingly thin." He said, "Somehow the vital spark was missing."[39] Cavett wrote that Caesar's autobiography, *Where Have I Been?*, "probably will revive the old hoary argument about the link between neurosis and talent: if you cure the one, do you cripple the other? More than one learned volume has been written on the subject. Some artists fear that, analyzed, they will no longer feel the compulsion to work and, further, that their talent is somehow bound up with, if not caused by, the neurosis. Where the idea came from that neurosis is anybody's guess. If true, with half the world neurotic, why isn't there more talent?" In Cavett's view, the idea that a comedian cured of his neurosis loses his ability to be funny is no more true than "a man cured of migraines loses his hair."[40]

Pryor underwent a personal and professional conversion not long after his film debut in *The Busy Body*. Jason Bailey, author of *Richard Pryor: American Id*, wrote: "[Pryor] walked away from his lucrative career … because he'd grown bored with his tame, uninspired material. His reinvention of his onstage persona dovetailed with a political rebirth that recast his philosophy closer to Malcolm X and Huey P. Newton than Martin Luther King."[41]

Gerald Nachman said of postwar comedians, "[They] had little to say about society, much less about their own real lives. They were, in the purest sense, entertainers who had no public worldview; they presumed the world wasn't interested."[42] But then Lenny Bruce came along. Richard Zoglin wrote: "[Bruce] held back nothing. Everything got tossed into the performance Mixmaster: social criticism, political commentary, pop culture satire, snatches of autobiography, sexual confessions, personal gripes, public hectoring, today's headlines, and yesterday's trip to the laundry."[43]

Pryor moved from Jonathan Winters to Lenny Bruce. Bailey wrote:

> And in those venues, there was no tolerance for bullshitters. "People don't talk about nothin' real," Richard complains on his breakthrough album, *Craps (After Hours)*; for him, talking about what was real was his golden rule, his guiding principle, his mission statement…. It was the raw material [from personal tragedy] from which his comedy was built: the child of a broken marriage, raised in his

grandmother's brothel, sexually abused, time in an army prison, time in L.A. County Jail, several failed marriages, two heart attacks, and a lifetime of drug use, culminating in that horrible thing—that "accident." But Pryor talked about all of it, spun his pain into his act—all of the fear and anger and bitterness and resentment and embarrassment, he used it all, gave it a voice, put it all on the line. And he was complicated, needy, and self-destructive enough that he would never want for material.[44]

He was on stage to share personal experiences and blow off steam. He liked to be bold and shocking. It made him feel liberated.

Bailey wrote:

After Pryor's self-imposed exile from mainstream show business and his resetting stint in Berkeley, California, it took some time to find an audience. But he eventually did, particularly among young African-Americans who were looking for entertainment that reflected their more militant worldview.... He'd spent the 1960s hedging his bets, draining his routines of color to appeal to white audiences; now, with an act that was tougher and coarser and "blacker" than ever before, white audiences had come to him—often to hear themselves ridiculed.[45]

Zoglin wrote: "The black comics who reached out to white audiences before him tried to foster racial understanding by stressing how much alike we are. Pryor rubbed our noses in the differences—and yet made us feel their universality."[46] Joan Rivers explained that Pryor used humor to take audiences through the pain and ugliness of his life.

It is unknown if Pryor had serious ambitions for a film career at this point. His new stand-up act offered, in Bailey's estimation, blackness, coarseness, and pain. It would be difficult to translate this sort of comedy into feature films.

Wild in the Streets (1968)

Production and Distribution: American International Pictures.
Producer: Burt Topper.
Director: Barry Shear.
Screenplay: Robert Thom, from his short story "The Day It All Happened, Baby" (published in *Esquire* in December 1966).
Photography: Richard Moore.
Editor: Fred Feitshans Jr. and Eve Newman.
Music: Les Baxter
Release date: May 29, 1968.
Running time: 97 minutes.
Cast: Shelley Winters (Daphne Flatow), Christopher Jones (Max Frost), Diane Varsi (Sally Leroy), Hal Holbrook (Johnny Fergus), Millie Perkins (Mary Fergus), Richard Pryor (Stanley X), Bert Freed (Max Jacob Flatow Sr.), Kevin Coughlin (Billy Cage), Larry Bishop (The Hook), Michael Margotta (Jimmy Fergus), Ed Begley (Senator Amos Allbright), May Ishihara (Fuji Elly).

Wild in the Streets grew out of the paranoia about the youth culture that fermented among the establishment in the 1960s. Pauline Kael of *The New Yorker* described *Wild in the Streets* as a "crudely made" film "slammed together with spit, hysteria, and opportunism."[1] Kael thought that the film was a feature-length comic strip, except that it occasionally defied comic strip conventions with a number of surprising and witty elements. She wrote: "There's not a trace of sensitivity in the drawing or in the ideas, and there's

Wild in the Streets (1968) 15

Pryor is part of rock star Max Frost's diverse entourage in *Wild in the Streets* (1968).

something rather specially funny about wit without *any* grace at all; it can be enjoyed in a particularly crude way—as Pop wit. The basic idea is corny—*It Can't Happen Here* with the freaked-out young as a new breed of fascists—but it's treated in the paranoid style of the editorials about youth (it even begins by blaming everything on the parents)."[2] But Kael found that the idea had "an almost lunatic charm"[3] and a "nightmare gaiety."[4]

The film's narrative brings together the elite of Washington, D.C., with the elite of Hollywood. Johnny Fergus (Holbrook), a California congressman who is running for the Senate, seeks an endorsement from a rock star phenomenon, Max Frost. Senator Allbright, Fergus's mentor, advises him against this shameless effort to court the youth vote. Allbright says, "Youth has become a disease."

Erich Kuersten, of *Academic*, wrote: "Between 1967 and '70, the establishment was seriously concerned about being overrun by its own children. The suits were scared, the politicians saw the size of the crowds at Woodstock, the small cities' worth of people who would appear within a week of some rock star announcing a free concert, and they knew no army could stand in their way. And we have *Wild in the Streets* to prove it."[5]

Frost agrees to perform at a television rally on Fergus's behalf. Frost incites his multitude of fans to mount a widespread protest to pressure the government to lower the voting age to fourteen. Politicians become fearful of the protesters, which they see as the beginning of a powerful trend that could topple the government. They negotiate with

Frost to end the protests. Once the voting age is lowered, Frost is able to use the country's youth as a voting bloc to get himself elected president.

The ultimate goal of the new president is to create, in his words, "the most hedonistic society the world has ever known." Frost makes it clear in his inaugural address that the older generations must be "neutralized" to stop wars, poverty, racism, and sexism. It is to serve his interests that his first official act is to require citizens over the age of thirty-five to be sent to "rehabilitation camps." "We're gonna psyche them all out on LSD," he declares. Just as he intended, prisoners of the camps are forced to take daily doses of LSD to keep them compliant. It isn't long before Frost's radical administration causes the country to devolve into druggie anarchy.

Kuersten wrote: "This is the film that made good on the ever-looming urban myth, that the hippies wanted to spike the water supply with LSD, lower the voting age ... and send everyone over thirty off to camps for 're-grooving.'"[6] Kael observed: "There's a relish that people have for the idea of drug-taking kids as monsters threatening them—the daily papers merging into *Village of the Damned*."[7]

Senator Fergus forms a band of rebels, but the rebels are rounded up and brought to a camp. Fergus retains enough self-control to end his life. The most memorable image in the film is Fergus's limp and colorless corpse hanging nightmarishly from a tree.

Frost finds that running the country is too much work. He is in an LSD stupor as he drives off into the countryside. He comes to a wooded area, where he climbs a tree and rolls around in the grass. He keeps thinking about a little girl who told him he was "old." He knows that, in this new world he has created, it won't be long before *he* turns thirty and is locked away in a camp.

A film similar to *Wild in the Streets* had been released in England the year before. That film, *Privilege*, was also about a pop singer who becomes a messianic leader. People were undoubtedly fearful of this idea throughout the Western world. Folk singer Phil Ochs turned down the role of Frost as he saw the script as an unfair indictment of the youth counterculture. Glenn Erickson, of *DVD Savant*, wrote:

> *Wild in the Streets* actually promotes conservative values. The movie is about The Generation Gap, all right, but its message is anti-youth. The Kids Aren't Alright, they're just sheep waiting to be led. There's no hope of a new Youth Movement being sincere. The sixties generation is just an unseen mob following whatever dictates are laid down by the manipulative rock icon. Max Frost is a right-winger's idea of Beatle John Lennon crossed with Hitler, a charismatic rock 'n' roll dictator, a low grade reboot of Lonesome Rhodes from ten years before.... Max Frost isn't a legit teen emancipator, but a cynical operator from the start—the whole group laughs at the thought of gaming the system to put Max in power ... far out![8]

English writer Alan Moore referred to Frost's form of government as "hippy fascism."[9]

Sam Tweedle of the "Confessions of a Pop Culture Addict" blog wrote:

> *Wild in the Streets* is disguised as a counter culture cult film, but actually plays out as a battle of the generation gap with absolutely no winners.... The glorification of youth culture and the hippie movement scared the older generation who could no longer recognize nor relate to their kids, while their children embraced new freedom of expression in an attempt not to be pigeon holed like their parents were, creating a battle of ideologies right in the home.... Jones brings Frost from being a dissatisfied youth to megalomaniac zealot with each of his well-planned actions being more disturbing than the next.[10]

Shelley Winters, who received top billing for playing Frost's opportunistic mother, had a close and perhaps sexual relationship with the film's leading man, Christopher

Kevin Coughlin, Christopher Jones, and Pryor in *Wild in the Streets* (1968).

Jones. Frank Corsaro, a teacher at the Actors Studio, said, "Shelley kind of took an interest in [Jones] and she really gave him his boost."[11] Insight into the relationship may be found in Winters's semi-autobiographical play *One Night Stands of a Noisy Passenger*, the third act of which involves a middle-aged, Oscar-winning actress who uses her wealth and influence to lure a gruff, sullen young actor into a turbulent affair. The play was staged at the Actors' actress with Diane Ladd as the actress, and Robert De Niro as her lover.

Yet again, Pryor's talent for networking earned him a film role. Winters, who saw Pryor open for Miles Davis at the Village Gate, used her clout with producer Burt Topper to get him cast in the film. Allegedly, Winters engaged in a sexual liaison with Pryor. David Henry and Joe Henry wrote: "Richard was more than happy to pay the price of admission, according to [Paul] Mooney, getting 'Wild in the Sheets' with Miss Winters, 'the most cock-hungry actress in Hollywood.'"[12]

Pryor's character, Stanley X, is a member of Frost's inner circle. Stanley X is introduced by a narrator as "anthropologist, guitarist, and author of *The Aborigine Cook Book*." Pryor plays the coolest of fools to a mad king. Saul wrote: "Richard was a trivial, token presence in the white rock star's entourage—the black militant there to balance out the gay guitarist, the vegetarian acidhead, and the teenage Japanese masseuse."[13] He has dialogue in two scenes, but he otherwise remains a silent background player (Saul describes him as being "part of the scenery"[14]). He is oddly missing from Frost's entourage for many of the later scenes. The comedian had now entered a period of his career in which his specialty was to play pretentious black hipsters in underground, counterculture films.

With *Wild in the Streets*, Pryor began a trend in which his bad behavior on the set overshadowed his work in front of the cameras. A story has long persisted that Pryor urinated on Winters's head from a platform during filming. According to actor Max Julien, producer Harvey Bernhard later resisted casting Pryor in *The Mack* because he had heard about the incident.

Aaron Hillis, a film critic on the IFC website, asked Larry Bishop, who played Frost's bass player, if the incident was true. Bishop replied: "No, he didn't piss on her head. Well, maybe [Julien] knows something I don't know, but I've never heard that, truthfully. But for one of the scenes, where Shelley was waiting down below and six of us had to come out, [Pryor] said, 'Let's all walk out naked.' To which all of us replied, 'Yeah, let's do it!' Until it came time to do it, and then he was the only one who did it. Shelley just about fainted."[15]

Wild in the Streets is an overwrought teen exploitation film with an excess of dark, political satire. The film absurdly incorporates a variety of social issues, including the youth culture, riots, assassination, and the draft. Erickson wrote: "[The film] is a fast-paced political satire, pitched almost at the level of a *Mad* magazine parody."[16] Greg Ferrara of the TCM website wrote: "If the plot sounds utterly ridiculous, that's because it is. It's the kind of satirical movie that makes *Network* look like a subtle, under the radar, gentle critique of television. *Wild in the Streets* is many things but realistic and measured it is not."[17] The most overdone element of the film is Jones's performance, which is irritating from the first scene to the last.

The film's message is lost in the chaos. Tweedle wrote: "Even days after watching it I'm still not sure exactly who the intended audience of the film was, and if it is supposed to be a black comedy, a political satire or a nightmarish dystopia and a warning to 1960s era America."[18]

Pryor later said that he was disappointed with the project.

Uncle Tom's Fairy Tales: The Movie for Homosexuals (1969)

Director: Penelope Spheeris.
Screenplay: Richard Pryor.
Cast: Richard Pryor, Franklyn Ajaye.

This is Pryor's mysterious, unfinished film. It is questionable if it even belongs in a listing of his films: it was not completed and has been lost for decades. The single print that was assembled from the feverish shoot will, if found, show damage from the comedian's cocaine-fueled attempt to destroy it.

David and Joe Henry wrote: "Nobody ever saw a script, although they did see Richard from time to time consulting a spiral notebook of frayed, handwritten pages."

Saul wrote:

The production gradually took shape over the course of 1968 and early 1969. In its first outline, *Uncle Tom's Fairy Tales* was propaganda pure and simple. When art director Gary Burden visited Richard's home in June 1968 for the cover shoot of Richard's first album, he observed that Richard was brainstorming "a documentary ... of black people taking over the world, and he had all these storyboards on the wall of black warriors mowing down the white pigs." But the project took a surprising turn in the wake of the [murder] trial of Huey Newton, cofounder of the Black Panther Party. That trial was the major Black Power media event of 1968, a political shocker in a summer of shockers, and Richard's creative imagination was jolted by its electricity.[1]

The Newton murder trial took place in 1968, from July 15 to September 8.

David and Joe Henry wrote: "In Pryor's own telling, the film, which he recalled shooting in March 1969, tells the story of a wealthy white man abducted by a group of Black Panther–type militants who hold him prisoner in a basement and put him on trial for all the racial crimes in U.S. history."[2] David and Joe Henry knew of one comedy bit that Pryor performed in the film. "Each time he tried to say the word *white*, Richard's proud, defiant poet was reduced to a wincing, stammering mess, contorting his entire body as he struggled to expel the word. 'Now, a lot of you out there, you're sayin' to yourselves right now, "Well, if you feel that way about wh-wh-wh-white people, how come you married a wh-wh-wh-wh-white woman?" That ain't got nothin' to do with it.'"[3]

Saul wrote:

[Pryor, as the defense attorney,] pled his case in a basement courtroom, in front of a black judge and a jury stocked with pimps, prostitutes, winos, and drug addicts. The judge had a plate of cocaine and a bottle of liquor in front of him; the jury was similarly well furnished....

Uncle Tom's Fairy Tales was half lurid, half loopy, and fully avant-garde. In one scene, the white man was stripped to his underwear and made to lie on the floor in the courtroom. A gang of black men arrived with sponges and buckets of water. They soaped him up and rinsed him off—an event billed as a "car wash." When the time came for the jury to reach its verdict, it didn't deliberate over the man's fate but yelled out his sentence like members of a lynch mob: "Kill the motherfucker!," "Hang him!," "Shoot him!" In his cocaine-whirred imagination, Richard had conceived a vision of revolution as a travesty of justice, a kangaroo court. Blacks were granted a fantastic power, only to abuse it.[4]

Pryor argued with his wife, Shelley, while working with Penelope Spheeris to edit the film. In a fit of rage, he attacked footage that Spheeris had worked long and hard to assemble from the dailies. He wrestled with the strips of film, ripping and mangling as much as he could.

David and Joe Henry wrote: "Penelope spent days splicing the pieces of the film back together like a jigsaw puzzle. She reconstructed the forty-some minutes of film by arduously piecing together the mangled pieces, some only a few frames long."[5]

Pryor was disappointed with the film. He stored the footage away and refused to release it. He later claimed that he destroyed the only print.

In 2005, scenes from Spheeris's dailies were screened at the 57th Directors Guild of America Awards as part of a tribute to Pryor. His wife, Jennifer Lee-Pryor, presumed that Pryor's daughter Rain had smuggled the footage out of her father's home. She filed a suit against Spheeris and Rain. But Jennifer was wrong. These were discarded outtakes that Spheeris had possessed for decades. The footage reportedly remains in the archives of the Academy of Motion Picture Arts and Sciences.

Carter's Army (1970)

Production: Thomas/Spelling Productions.
Distribution: American Broadcasting Company.
Producers: Shelley Hull, Aaron Spelling, and Danny Thomas.
Director: George McCowan.
Screenplay: Aaron Spelling and David Kidd.
Photography: Archie R. Dalzell,
Editor: George W. Brooks.
Music: Fred Steiner.
Release date: January 27, 1970.
Running time: 72 minutes.
Cast: Stephen Boyd (Captain Beau Carter), Robert Hooks (Lieutenant Edward Wallace), Susan Oliver (Anna), Rosey Grier (Big Jim), Moses Gunn (Doc), Richard Pryor (Jonathan Crunk), Glynn Turman (George Brightman), Billy Dee Williams (Lewis), Paul Stewart (General Clark), Bobby Johnson (Robinson), Napoleon Whiting (Fuzzy).

Aaron Spelling, the producer of the television hit *The Mod Squad*, befriended Pryor while the two were teammates in an amateur baseball league. Spelling believed that Pryor had potential as an actor and had a role created for him in *Carter's Army*, a television

Stephen Boyd (second left) is skeptical about leading black soldiers on a crucial mission in *Carter's Army* (1970). The other cast members are (from left to right) Rosey Grier, Pryor, and Glynn Turman.

film that was to serve as a series pilot. Spelling's idea was to fashion a World War II combat unit in the style of *The Mod Squad*. Again, disaffected social outcasts would come together to defeat the bad guys.

Captain Carter (Boyd), a drawling Southerner, is assigned a dangerous covert mission to capture a dam that the Germans intend to destroy. The captain expects to have a combat unit assigned to him, but he is instead put in command of a sanitation unit that is close enough to the dam to reach it before the Germans blow it up.

Carter is surprised to find that his new unit is comprised entirely of black men. Lieutenant Edward Wallace, the commanding officer of the unit, greets Carter while taking a hearty swig out of a bottle of wine. The other men are throwing down cash in a lively craps game. The next morning, Carter has the men line up. Not one is wearing a complete uniform and not one demonstrates the slightest understanding of military form. Carter barks, "This isn't a company—it's a *circus*!" Wallace insists that the men enlisted to fight, but three years of digging latrines, picking up garbage, and burying bodies has caused them to lose their dignity, their direction, and their discipline. Wallace is sure that, if given the chance, the men will perform the duties that are demanded of them. Carter makes no secret of the fact that he has a low opinion of black men: "Take a look. Tell me again they're soldiers. It's black men doing what black men know how to do."

The film is a simple-minded, heavy-handed anti-racism parable in which racial tensions are largely expressed by Boyd and Hooks glowering at each other. The DVD box explains everything you need to know about the film with the following line: "Despite seething racial tensions, everyone pulls together to destroy an enemy dam." Carter's racism and shit-kicking attitude is overstated, making the character overbearing, cartoonish, and irredeemable. But, at the same time, Wallace's men are presented as grossly incompetent. An IMDb critic was appalled that one of the "buffoonish 'soldiers' has cigarettes in his belt in lieu of ammunition!"[1]

The unit's march to the dam gives Carter a chance to get to know his new men better. He observes the men's skills closely to know how best to use them to fulfill his mission. He can see that Doc Hayes is intelligent. He is surprised to learn that Hayes is a physics professor. Lewis, a street tough from Harlem, impresses Carter with his ability to throw a knife. But he has serious doubts that Crunk (Pryor's character), who comes across as lazy and undisciplined, can do his part in the mission. (Pryor is paired with Rosey Grier, who plays the good-natured giant Big Jim. The disheveled Mutt and Jeff soldiers had been a stock element of military comedies since the time that *What Price Glory?* (1926) introduced audiences to Captain Flagg and Sergeant Quirt.)

Fuzzy (Whiting), a deaf soldier, fails to hear a plane that's patrolling the area. He is standing in full view when the plane swoops down on him and strafes him with bullets. The unit is shaken by Fuzzy's death. Carter explains that they have no time to bury him. Wallace asks, "Would there be time if he was white?"

Crunk remains on edge after Fuzzy's death. He grows increasingly fearful, knowing that he is about to go behind enemy lines and confront German soldiers in a life-or-death battle. While walking through a forest, he becomes paranoid that snipers are hiding in the trees and getting ready to fire on them. "I don't want to die, Big Jim," he says. He suddenly panics. "LOOK," he cries, "I SEE ONE—IN THE TREE!" He loses control, wildly firing his rifle. Then, he runs off and jumps into a hole. Carter finds him whimpering and curled up into a fetal position. Crunk claims that he is too frightened to move. Big Jim tells him that if he doesn't get up and continue with the mission, "I'll leave you. And

I'll tell Carter to come back with his pistol and he can tell all his white friends, 'Man, I knew those niggers couldn't cut the mustard. They just curled up in a hole and let me shoot 'em in the head.' And, in a hundred years, black men will be cleaning latrines like you and me." Big Jim's speech convinces Crunk to rejoin the other men.

The first half of the film focuses on the relationship of Carter and Wallace. The story follows an obvious character arc with these men. For the mission to succeed, the white captain and the black lieutenant have to learn to respect each other despite the difference in their skin color. But then, abruptly, the filmmakers abandon Carter and Wallace and turn their attention instead to Crunk and Big Jim.

The soldiers rendezvous at a farmhouse, where an Ally partisan gives them access to a radio. They next move on to an abandoned winery, where Big Jim is fatally shot by a German sniper. His death devastates Crunk.

Hayes and Lewis are sent to handle reconnaissance. On their way back to the other men, Lewis steps on a mine and is killed. Lewis is injured, but he is still able to return to Carter with his report. He tells him that the detonator the Germans plan to use to trigger the explosives is being stored in the back of a truck. Crunk abandons the combat unit while everyone else is preoccupied.

The remaining three soldiers make it to the bridge. While surveying the scene, the soldiers are surprised to see Crunk suddenly emerge from under the hay in the back of a farmer's wagon. Crunk is shot by German soldiers as he snatches the detonator out of the back of a truck. But the brave soldier, who has only been wounded, is not out of the action yet. He uses his remaining strength to toss the detonator over the side of the bridge. Finally, he drags himself to cover before the German soldiers have a chance to open fire on him again.

Carter leads an assault on the German soldiers. They are wiped out, mostly by Carter's relentless machine gun fire.

Carter and Wallace come to Crunk's aid. He tells them, "I had to decide if I was gonna be a something or a nothing."

The film's ending is faithful to the shooting script. A white soldier throws a shovel at Crunk and rudely demands that he dig a latrine. The script reads:

> 343 ANGLE ON WALLACE as he picks up one of the shovels. He holds it in his hand for a beat. A hand comes INTO THE SHOT and grabs the shovel. Wallace looks up. It is Carter. Carter takes to shovel and throws it off the dam [*sic*] into the lake. He hands Wallace his rifle. In a beat, Wallace smiles quietly.
> 344 MED. SHOT—CARTER, WALLACE, CRUNK
> Crunk has picked up the other shovel. He looks at it for a beat, drops it. The three men start walking in the direction the troops are going, as we
> FADE OUT.
> The End.

Carter's Army is, in the end, Crunk's story. His outburst of cowardice is the film's most crucial dramatic scene. Big Jim cares greatly about his friend and helps him work through his fears. This creates an emotional impact when Big Jim is later shot and Crunk holds his dying friend in his arms. In the end, Crunk honors Big Jim's memory by playing a crucial role in the final mission.

It is inevitable, with Crunk's abrupt coward-to-hero character arc overshadowing the original character arc, that Pryor would play an inconsistent role in the film. He provides comic relief in the first act, is largely absent during the second, and plays a major dramatic role in the third. But, in the script's defense, the message remains the same in either plot thread. The filmmakers tell us that we can never truly know what a man has on the inside unless we give him an opportunity to prove himself.

The film is poor in other, more significant, ways. It suffers from low production values (most evident in the battle scenes) and a cliché script. It is too short and slapdash to adequately develop its characters or themes. The point of the story gets lost at times. The scene in which Big Jim lectures Crunk about black soldiers being able to perform their duties is quickly followed by a scene with the two men coming upon an abandoned winery, where they break out bottles and get drunk. They are engaged in drunken clowning, in fact, when the sniper shoots Big Jim.

The world's greatest directors have deeply affected audiences with their dramatizations of war missions. This war mission, however, stirs very little feeling. It is the actors who make the film occasionally compelling.

Pryor got along well with his co-stars. "There was a great feeling of togetherness," he said. "At one point in the picture, one of the men in the unit is killed en route to the dam. When the actor who played him didn't come into work the day after that scene was filmed, I think we all thought that he had really died. It was one of the most unusual experiences I've ever been through."[2]

Pryor said of his role: "I play a coward and that was the hardest thing I've ever done. My natural instinct is to be funny and I really had to fight with myself not to make the character a lampoon." Pryor, who was not a trained actor, had no acting technique to bring to his performance. Hooks and Gunn were highly respected New York stage actors who had founded the Negro Ensemble Company. The two men furnished performances that were, in contrast, natural. Gunn is believable in his depiction of a physics teacher. He expresses emotions through carefully used small gestures. In contrast, Pryor's performance is raw and messy, uneven, and, at times, unconvincing. For better or worse, he lacked the discipline and refinement of a trained actor. In retrospect, Pryor should have been comfortable playing a fearful soldier. Fear had been part of his stage persona when he was the shy, vulnerable young man performing stand-up in nightclubs. It remained part of his act for the remainder of his career. Hilton Als of *The New Yorker* wrote: "Pryor was the first image we'd ever had of black male fear. Not the kind of Stepin Fetchit noggin-bumpin'-into-walls fear that turned Buckwheat white when he saw a ghost in the 'Our Gang' comedies popular in the twenties, thirties, and forties…. Pryor was filled with dread and panic—an existential fear, based on real things…."[3] Saul similarly wrote: "Richard's fear had little in common with the eye-popping, teeth-chattering, 'feets-don't-fail-me-now' cowardice of earlier black and blackface comedians. It was immense but not cartoonish, and hinted at something tragic and new from a black male actor in the age of Black Power: a near-total vulnerability."[4]

ABC did not give Spelling the green light to turn *Carter's Army* into a series. The question remains if Pryor would have continued with *Carter's Army* if it had become a weekly series.

The Phynx (1970)

Production: Cinema Organization.
Distribution: Warner Brothers/Seven Arts.

Producer: Bob Booker and George Foster.
Director: Lee H. Katzin
Screenplay: Stan Cornyn (story by Bob Booker and George Foster).
Photography: Michel Hugo.
Editor: Dann Cahn.
Music: Mike Stoller.
Release date: May 6, 1970.
Running time: 81 minutes.
Cast: The Phynx—Michael A. Miller, Ray Chipperway, Dennis Larden and Lonny Stevens (Themselves), Lou Antonio (Corrigan), Mike Kellin (Bogey), Michael Ansara (Colonel Rostinov), George Tobias (Markevitch), Joan Blondell (Ruby), Martha Raye (Foxy), Larry Hankin (Philbaby), Pat McCormick (Father O'Hoolihan), Ultra Violet (Felice), Rich Little (Voice in Box), Susan Bernard (London Belly), Sally Struthers (World's Number 1 Fan).
Cameos: Patty Andrews, Rona Barrett, Edgar Bergen and Charlie McCarthy, Busby Berkeley, James Brown, Dick Clark, Xavier Cugat, Cass Daley, Andy Devine, Fritz Feld, Leo Gorcey, Huntz Hall, John Hart (as The Lone Ranger), Louis Hayward, George Jessel, Ruby Keeler, Patsy Kelly, Dorothy Lamour, Guy Lombardo, Trini Lopez, Joe Louis, Marilyn Maxwell, Butterfly McQueen, Pat O'Brien, Maureen O'Sullivan, Richard Pryor, Harold Sakata, Colonel Harland Sanders, Jay Silverheels (as Tonto), Ed Sullivan, Rudy Vallee, Clint Walker, Johnny Weissmuller.

David and Joe Henry called the film "incomprehensible camp."[1] This is obvious from the plot. An Albanian dictator kidnaps dozens of old-time Hollywood celebrities and holds them captive in a secluded castle. The U.S. Government recruits four young men to go undercover as a chart-topping pop band and pretend to be on a concert tour of Europe while searching various cities for the captive luminaries.

Pryor plays one of the military officers in charge of training the band. His appearance in the film is so brief and insignificant that it isn't worth developing an in-depth discussion of the film's production or its plot.

Nathan Rabin of *A.V. Club* wrote: "*The Phynx* eventually makes it to the castle where the luminaries are being held, and after a spirited musical performance, smuggle the elderly guest stars back to freedom, all in time for a climactic ditty so rocking, it causes the walls of the castle where the stars were being held captive to come down and bring the world one rocking step closer to ending the Cold War."[2]

Bailey called *The Phynx* a "strained, unfunny, would-be counterculture farce." He perfectly summed up Pryor's role thusly:

> A whistle blows, and we see the four men in the mess hall with Pryor. The counter between them is covered in soul food. "Gentlemen," he says, "my name is Richard Pryor, and I'm here to teach you soul."
> One of the men, the token black member of the group, asks, "Hey, man, you don't eat this stuff, do you?" Richard looks away, a soldier steps in front of the camera, the whistle blows again, and the scene is over. Pryor is onscreen for all of thirteen seconds.[3]

Jeff Rovin, author of *Richard Pryor: Black and Blue*, said that Pryor was discouraged that this was the only film role to come his way at the time.[4]

You've Got to Walk It Like You Talk It or You'll Lose That Beat (1971)

Production and Distribution: J. E. R. Pictures.
Producer: Peter Locke.
Director: Peter Locke.
Screenplay: Peter Locke.
Photography: Stephen Bower.
Editors: Wes Craven, David Finfer, Lana Jokel, and Peter Locke.
Music: Walter Becker, Donald Fagin, and Billy Cunningham.
Release date: September 19, 1971.
Running time: 85 minutes.
Cast: Zalman King (Carter Fields), Allen Garfield (Herby Moss), Suzette Green (Susan), Paula Frankle (Corinna), Karen Ludwig (Erika), Richard Pryor (Wino), Bob Downey (Ad Agency Head), Liz Torres (Singer in Men's Room), Roz Kelly (Girl in Park), Billy Cunningham (Fat Lady), Steve Landesberg (Men's Room Attendant), Michael Sullivan (Man on Toilet), Eric Krupnik (Hood in Group Therapy), John Fodor (Revolutionary), Ruth Locke (Carter's Mother), Daisy Locke (Old Woman), Stan Gottlieb (Mr. Fellestrio).

The film has been lost in the mist of time. We must rely on contemporary reviews to understand its minimal plot. A naïve, glazed-eyed young man (King) quits his job on Wall Street to roam through Central Park in search of the meaning of life. *Box Office Booking Guide* described King's character as "a twenty-five-year-old nobody who can't seem to find his place."[1] *Filmfacts* describes him as being "stymied by both his domineering mother and the overall lunacy of New York City."[2] In his wanderings, he has encounters with revolutionaries, radical feminists, and, according to A. H. Weiler of the *New York Times*, "a crazy old lady."[3] No one he encounters can be trusted. The crazy old lady turns out to be a professional shoplifter. A group of convent schoolgirls turn out to be a ring of pickpockets.

Filmfacts provided the most extensive description of the plot:

> While strolling through Central Park, [Carter] is molested by a fat black girl and then watches in disbelief as a young hippie exposes his bare behind to an obscenity-shouting old woman; seeking refuge in the men's room, he is badgered by a garrulous drunk and a singing woman dressed in black lace who sings "Going Out of My Head"; and his attempts to find sexual and emotional fulfillment in the beds of various girls are ruined when he suffers nosebleeds during intercourse. Realizing that he is a helpless neurotic misfit, Carter tries to commit suicide by hanging himself, but he fails in this, too; and upon seeking help in a group therapy session, he only manages to meet another assortment of bizarre characters…. Eventually, Carter believes he has found happiness when he marries a lovely and seemingly understanding girl named Susan, becomes a father, and gets a job at a posh Madison Avenue ad agency. A short time later, however, he is fired for incompetency, and Susan leaves him. Taking his baby to Central Park, Carter forlornly sits on a park bench, still vowing to seek "meaning" in the mindless world that surrounds him.[4]

The film was clearly influenced by Robert Downey's *Putney Swope* (1969) and Brian De Palma's *Hi, Mom!* (1970). Judith Crist of *New York Magazine* described the film as an example of "poverty-program pseudo-Downeyism,"[5] based on "the notion that urinals and bare behinds are the top stuff of comedy and mama the source of all else."[6]

Weiler described the film as "the wacky saga of Carter Fields, his young, confused middle-class hero, who's anxious to achieve a 'meaningful' career but is judged a freaked-out flop by his girl and a succession of far-out characters he encounters in his quest."[7] He wrote: "As a genial put-down of the Establishment, *You've Got to Walk It Like You Talk It or You'll Lose That Beat* … is the latest example of youthful, charming iconoclasm that appears to be losing some of its charm…. The results are sporadically comic and only rarely trenchant or meaningful."[8] He dismissed the film as "a plethora of sight gags and surface philosophies."[9] He identified two cast members as stand-outs: Allen Garfield, who is as "crazily apoplectic as a group therapy fiend,"[10] and Robert Downey as a "doubletalking ad executive."[11] A number of critics singled out Garfield for praise. *Variety* described him as "humorously greasy and lecherous."[12] None of these critics mentioned Pryor, who played the "garrulous drunk" in the men's room. Rovin simply described Pryor as "babbling bitterly."[13]

Ann Guarino of the (New York) *Daily News* gave the film zero stars. She insisted that this "sophomoric and absolutely dull" comedy" only proved that "the films of bright young men are not so bright these days."[14]

Constance Clarke of *Applause* wrote: "It has the same crazily irreverent attitude toward just about everything established in the world. It is a take-off in a put-on. It is often funny, sometimes just looney, and sometimes just gross. This art form (?) might be described as Protest Pornography."[15]

Variety reported:

> Although some of the screwball dialogue, preposterous sight gags and bit character roles are hilarious, the film suffers from a weak storyline, comic situations that are overdone and tasteless, sloppy editing and color, and camera work that is often blurred and shaky…. [The actors] all seem participants in a comedy review. Use of silent movie titles, mock-melodramatic narration, soap-opera organ music and other stylistic gimmicks are amusing for a while, but it all suffers from chaotic excess. Locke includes anything for a laugh and doesn't seem to care where or how often he uses it. Consequently, the film moves in spurts of hilarity with too many lags between them.[16]

Leo Mishkin of the *Morning Telegraph* wrote: "The search is conducted in such a heavy-handed style, and just what is meant by a 'meaningful existence' is left so high in the air, that almost all common sense and justification seems to disappear…. If it's a serious attack on current manners and mores, Mr. Locke should have his camera washed out with soap."[17] One gag may say a lot about Locke's manners and mores. Mishkin wrote that a "young man in Central Park takes down his pants to bear his exotically painted derrière to the gaze of a little old lady walking along just behind."[18] As it turns out, the little old lady is played by Locke's grandmother.

Archer Winsten of the *New York Post* wrote: "The main weakness is that the script lacks clarity and incisiveness. The attack is all-inclusive, the burlesque vicious, but it fails to add up to anything other than a mound of obscenity, for the comedy is not funny."[19]

Lady Sings the Blues (1972)

Production: Motown Productions.
Distribution: Paramount Pictures.
Producers: Brad Dexter, Jay Weston, James S. White, and Berry Gordy.
Director: Sidney J. Furie.

Lady Sings the Blues (1972)   27

Screenplay: Terence McCloy, Chris Clark, and Suzanne De Passe, from the book *Lady Sings the Blues* by Billie Holiday and William Dufty.
Photography: John A. Alonzo.
Editor: Argyle Nelson.
Music: Michel Legrand.
Release date: October 12, 1972.
Running time: 144 minutes
Cast: Diana Ross (Billie Holiday), Billy Dee Williams (Louis McKay), Richard Pryor (Piano Man), Paul Hampton (Harry), Sid Melton (Jerry), Virginia Capers (Mama Holiday), Isabel Sanford (The Madame), Ned Glass (The Agent), Milton Selzer (The Doctor), Scatman Crothers (Big Ben), Jayne Kennedy (Louis's Date).

Lady Sings the Blues dramatizes the triumphs and hardships of legendary jazz singer Billie Holiday, beginning with her childhood. Her father abandons the family, leaving her mother to raise her on her own. Left with her grandparents while her mother works as a maid, the young girl is regularly beaten by an older cousin. Despite this, Holiday is determined to achieve independence and find her own path in the world.

Jesse Hamlin of the *San Francisco Chronicle* wrote: "Holiday scrubbed white people's doorsteps for nickels and ran errands for the prostitutes at Alice Dean's brothel in exchange for being allowed to listen and sing along to Louis Armstrong and Bessie Smith records on the whorehouse Victrola. The swinging sound and feeling of Armstrong's trumpet and voice made a deep impression on Holiday, an untrained singer with a great

Pryor and Diana Ross in *Lady Sings the Blues* (1972).

ear and a gift for creating melodic lines that floated and danced around the beat in a beguiling new way."[1] A man in the neighborhood sexually molested her when she was ten years old. Hamlin wrote: "The abuser went to jail and she was sent to a Catholic home for wayward girls."[2]

At fourteen, Holiday turned to prostitution to earn a living. It wasn't long after that the brothel at which she was working was raided by police. She was arrested, convicted, and spent four months in jail.

Holiday pursued a singing career once she was released. She swiftly rose to stardom on the New York nightclub circuit. At the age of eighteen, she was brought into a recording studio to lay down a couple of songs. One of these, "Riffin' the Scotch," became her first hit. Holiday went on to have her biggest success in 1939 with the sad song "Strange Fruit." According to biographer David Margolick, this recording changed Holiday from "exuberant jazz singer to chanteuse of lovelorn pain and loneliness."[3]

Holiday's struggle with heroin came to dominate her life. She wrote in her autobiography that her husband, Jimmy Monroe, brought her "white junk" on a nightly basis. Holiday was forty-four years old when she died from cirrhosis of the liver.

Holiday wrote in her autobiography about her first audition, which was at a Harlem cabaret and jazz club called Pod's and Jerry's.

> Finally, when I got to Pod's and Jerry's, I was desperate. I went in and asked for the boss. I think I talked to Jerry. I told him I was a dancer and I want to try out. I knew exactly two steps, the time step and the crossover. I didn't even know the word "audition" existed, but that was what I wanted.
>
> So Jerry sent me over to the piano player and told me the dance. I started, and it was pitiful. I did my two steps over and over until he barked at me and told me to quit wasting his time.
>
> They were going to throw me out on my ear, but I kept begging for the job. Finally the piano player took pity on me. He squashed out his cigarette, looked up at me, and said, "Girl, can you sing?"
>
> I said, "Sure I can sing, what good is that?" I had been singing all my life, but I enjoyed it too much to think I could make any real money at it. Besides, those were the days of the Cotton Club and all those glamorous pussies who didn't do nothing but look pretty, shake a little, and take money off tables.
>
> I thought that was the only way to make money, and I needed forty-five bucks by morning to keep Mom from getting set out in the street. Singers were never heard of, unless it was Paul Robeson, Julian Bledsoe, or someone legit like that.
>
> So I asked him to play "Trav'lin' All Alone." That came closer than anything to the way I felt. And some part of it must have come across. The whole joint quieted down. If someone had dropped a pin, it would've sounded like a bomb. When I finished, everybody in the joint was crying in their beer, and I picked thirty-eight bucks up off the floor. When I left the joint that night I split with the piano player and still took home fifty-seven dollars.[4]

It was important to the filmmakers to recreate the scene and make sure that it stood out. They needed an actor who could make a strong impression in the role of the pianist, who was to appear in only one scene. Pryor came in to audition for the role. He wrote: "Given the word on the street, I wasn't surprised Motown founder Berry Gordy and director Sydney Furie assumed a lot of shit about me when I audition[ed] for *Lady Sings the Blues*. From the questions they asked, I realize[d] they thought I was a junkie. They thought I shot up heroin. I never had."[5] Despite the rumors about Pryor, Gordy and Furie decided to take a chance on him.

Pryor found his improv experience to be useful on the film. Henry Jaglom, a Pryor confidant, said, "He was surprised and delighted that Sidney Furie not only let him [improvise], but actually *encouraged* him to do it, whereas other directors had openly discouraged it up to that point."[6] Furie was so uncertain of what Pryor might do that he always made a point to shoot him in a long take. Ross, who was usually jittery on the set, felt calm working with Pryor and enjoyed his performance. Bailey wrote: "Richard came on like a hurricane, his hat cocked, talking out of the side of his mouth, bullshitting the boss—a real operator."[7] The producer, Jay Weston, wrote: "[Pryor's] delivery was so wryly amusing that we decided to bring him back the next day for another scene. That night, we all huddled … and Suzanne DePasse had a brilliant idea. Why not create a character called 'Piano Man' and add him to scenes in the rest of the script. Done … and another star was born."[8]

Pryor's best scene in the film comes in the final act. On a beach, Billie persuades Piano Man to pawn her ring to buy drugs. Piano Man keeps the ring and tries to get away without paying. The dealers track him down to Billie's beachside bungalow and coldly beat him to death. Moments earlier, he was acting playful with Billie as the two friends got high. Now, he emits terrified screams and desperate gurgles as the life is pounded out of him. It is a chilling scene—but a fictitious one. Piano players had important roles in Holiday's life. Bobby Henderson was one the first pianists to accompany the singer. Henderson was later replaced by Bobby Tucker, who played for the singer from 1946 to 1949. But Holiday didn't have a piano player who did drugs with her at a beach bungalow. For sure, neither Henderson nor Tucker was murdered by drug dealers (Henderson lived until 1969 and Tucker until 2008).

Pryor modeled his character after a piano player he knew in Peoria named Jimmy Brinkley. Pryor realized that he wouldn't be able to manage the challenges of the role if he was high all the time. He wrote: "I tried not to get high as we shot the movie. It seemed to let me hold my own. Diana Ross was great, mysterious, gorgeous. Billy Dee [Williams]'s self-assurance in front of the camera made me jealous, though I thought he took himself way too seriously. At the end I felt like I opened a new door."[9]

Williams had not wanted Pryor in the film. He said, "Richard's kind of so-called 'ghetto humor' was never really something I had much interest in. I wanted the movie to be a totally brand-new experience, devoid of stereotypes."[10]

Furie acknowledged that the film was not historically accurate. Ross was not even made to approximate Holiday's singing style. She was directed to create, in Kremer's words, "an impressionistic outline of Billie Holiday."[11] He added:

> The filmmakers never permitted Diana Ross at any point to parrot the inimitable style of the iconic jazz chanteuse she portrays, although both Furie and Berry Gordy had noted Ross's uncanny ability to impersonate the trembling, dulcetly quivering voice of the real-life Holiday. That Ross's voice is her own means that her Billie functions more as an interpretation and evocation of the real-life figure, wisely avoiding claims toward "gospelship" on Holiday's life and career. Therefore, accusations made against the film because of its blatant, unapologetic fictionalization are both knee-jerk and nearsighted. The release of *Lady Sings the Blues* did not mark the first time that historical purists and biographical scholars had bones to pick with Hollywood, and it was not the last. But this admittedly ultraliberal reading of recorded fact is part and parcel of the film's objective and, as a result, the film feels less constricted and more alive than most biopics, which are more often than not rigidly sober when claiming gospelship—a gospelship that is still doubtful despite all efforts.[12]

The book *Lady Sings the Blues* was written by journalist William Dufty, Holiday's close friend. William's wife, Maely, and son Bevan (who was Holiday's godson) expressed their thoughts about Furie's "impressionistic outline" of Holiday to Hamlin, who wrote:

> Like others who knew Holiday, the Duftys hated the 1972 film *Lady Sings the Blues*, which starred svelte Diana Ross as the tough, buxom Billie Holiday. Bevan Dufty and his mother saw the picture at

the old Varsity Theater in Palo Alto.... His mother was angered by the portrayal of Holiday as weak, and the singer's husband, Louis McKay, played by Billy Dee Williams, as a Good Guy; Maely referred to him in real life as Louis Decay because of what she saw as his corrosive influence. She cursed the screen and walked out.

"It's just not who Holiday was," Bevan Dufty said. "She was a very strong person who lived a vibrant, tough life. She never felt sorry for herself."[13]

Absolute truth in a biopic is not possible, but relative truth is something that a filmmaker should make every effort to achieve. A fairly accurate interpretation of a historical figure is more substantial and meaningful than a filmmaker's unbounded impressionistic outline of a historical figure. Conveying the power of a person who left a lasting impression on the world can only come from a respectful portrayal of that person. The power of a subject cannot be conveyed if the portraitist is more concerned about conveying his own power.

The fact that the filmmakers were unwilling to at least be faithful to Holiday's music casts serious doubts on what Furie and his cohorts achieved with this film. Hamlin wrote: "[Her] subtle artistry, with its rhythmic freedom and bare emotion, changed the sound of jazz and pop singing, and continues to seduce and move people who listen to her records."[14] But the filmmakers decided to leave that out. It's would be like making a new version of *Lady Sings the Blues* with Beyoncé and letting Beyoncé be Beyoncé. But Holiday was defined by her voice throughout her career. Hamlin wrote: "After her Decca contract ended, [Holiday] signed with Norman Granz's Verve Records, for which she recorded throughout the '50s. Her voice was weaker and frayed from hard living, and her work was uneven. But her late-period interpretations were often richer, the feeling even deeper."[15] That voice, in all its variations, should have been at the center of the film.

The Mack (1973)

Production: Harbor Productions.
Distribution: Cinerama Releasing Corporation.
Producer: Harvey Bernhard.
Director: Michael Campus.
Screenplay: Robert J. Poole.
Photography: Ralph Woolsey.
Editor: Frank C. Decot.
Music: Willie Hutch.
Release date: April 4, 1973.
Running time: 110 minutes.
Cast: Max Julien (Goldie), Don Gordon (Hank), Richard Pryor (Slim), Carol Speed (Lulu), Roger E. Mosley (Olinga), Dick Williams (Pretty Tony), William Watson (Jed), George Murdock (Fatman), Juanita Moore (Mother).

Bobby Poole wrote the script, originally titled "Black Is Beautiful," while incarcerated in San Quentin State Prison for forgery. The likely inspiration for the script was a 1967 novel, *The Pimp*. An independent producer, Harvey Bernhard, took an immediate interest in Poole's saga. He was fascinated by the Svengali-like power a pimp exerts over women. He agreed to film the script and set out to find financing.

The poster for *The Mack* (1973).

The film opens with a big action scene. Drug dealers Goldie (Julien) and Slim (Pryor), get into a gun battle with the members of a rival gang. Slim is fired upon as he takes cover in his car and drives off at full speed. The car is sprayed with bullets, including one that shatters the back window. Slim loses control of the vehicle, which crashes and overturns. Corrupt cops Hank and Jed arrive on the scene and see that Goldie is bleeding and barely conscious. They laugh and leave without calling an ambulance. Goldie later learns that he had been set up by the cops, who tipped off the rival gang.

Goldie returns home to Oakland after serving time in jail. He meets up with his brother Olinga (Mosley), who has become a militant black nationalist. Goldie is encouraged by his brother to join his organization, but he has no interest in political activism. A crime boss, The Fatman, wants Goldie to work the drug trade for him and stop his brother's activities, which are interfering with his business. Goldie refuses The Fatman, too. He has clear ambitions to get into the highly profitable pimp trade.

Bernhard had selected Oakland as the shooting location. At the time, Oakland had become a war zone due to territorial disputes between the criminal underworld, led by the Ward brothers, and the Black Panthers, led by Huey Newton and Bobby Seale. Frank Ward, a brutal and flamboyant underworld kingpin, controlled the area's drug and prostitution trade with his brothers Ted, Willie, and Andrew. Richard Harland Smith of the TCM website wrote that the Ward brothers "distinguished themselves by the cut of their fur-lined coats and the shine of their gold-plated Cadillacs."[1] Campus approached Ward to get his permission to film in Oakland. He put the kingpin on the payroll. Ward acted as a technical consultant and also provided the film crew with protection in the city's violent neighborhoods.

Julien wanted to create a character that was unique and complex. "I can't play Goldie as a fop," Julien told Campus. "He has to be a real person." He was real and he was real flamboyant. Saul described Goldie as "preening in a maxi-length white fur coat."[2]

Goldie enjoys great success as a pimp. At the Players Ball, he is happy to win the Pimp of the Year award. Ward, who plays himself in the scene, wanted the script changed to make himself declared the Player of Year at the ball. Campus and Julien had to convince him that, for the purpose of the story, Goldie had to win.

Goldie is elated by his success until he learns that his girlfriend, Diane, has died from a drug overdose. In his grief, he vows to stop The Fatman from poisoning his community with drugs. He plots with Slim to murder The Fatman. Slim catches The Fatman's bodyguards unawares by disguising as an old, blind street musician. He pulls out a gun and shoots the bodyguards. Goldie and Slim drag The Fatman out of his car and inject him with battery acid, which sends the crime boss into painful convulsions and quickly brings about his death.

Pryor (right) and Mack Julien in *The Mack* (1973).

Goldie has no hesitation to threaten or injure rival pimps who wish to get him out of the way. His viciousness reaches new heights when his mother is beaten to death and he suspects his chief rival, Pretty Tony, of having arranged the attack. Goldie and Slim chase Pretty Tony into an abandoned warehouse. At first, they hold a gun on him and force him to stab himself. Then, they tie the pimp to a chair and tape a stick of dynamite in his mouth. They make sure to be safely outside the warehouse when the fiery explosion occurs.

Later, Goldie goes to meet Slim, but finds him dead. Hank and Jed come out of the shadows and brag about killing Slim and Goldie's mother. Olinga, who has been following Goldie, suddenly comes out of hiding behind the cops. Enraged, he strangles Jed to death. Goldie forces Hank to drop to his knees before shooting him in the head.

Goldie regrets that his pimp life has gotten people he loved killed. He decides to leave town and start a new life. He hugs his brother at the bus station and boards a bus to an unspecified destination.

Newton was angry to see that the production company had become aligned with Ward. He demanded an immediate meeting with Bernhard, but he had no interest in involving himself with a political militant. Newton sent men to Bernhard's hotel room. When they kicked down the door, Bernhard assumed that they had come to kill him. But, as it turned out, the objective of the brutish visitors was simply to take Bernhard to see Seale.

Bernhard obtained the Black Panthers' cooperation by writing Seale a check for five thousand dollars. This arrangement did not work out as planned. Seale attempted to cash the check before Bernhard's financing agent had the opportunity to put up the money. That the check bounced infuriated Seale, who had the Panthers set up picket lines at filming locations and stand on roofs, throwing bottles and trash cans at the crew.

Bernhard was deeply unsettled by his dealings with the Panthers. For the remainder of the production, he made sure that he was protected by bodyguards.

The cast and crew came together before Campus or Julien had settled on the shooting script. Saul wrote: "Julien insisted that his friend Richard Pryor play Goldie's partner, Slim, and Pryor in turn demanded that he be able to write all the dialogue for his character."[3]

Bernhard knew that Pryor had a bad reputation. "Richard's too crazy!" he said. But Julien convinced him that the film would benefit from the comedian's input.

As expected, Pryor was difficult. Julien said that, before they even got in the front of the cameras, his co-star became obsessed with the idea that Bernhard was "ripping [them] off."[4]

Campus had problems with Pryor on their first meeting. The comedian was angry as soon as he entered the room. Campus remembered him saying, "You're not going to direct this film, are you? The last time I looked, you is white. Not only that, you're Jewish." Campus said, "[Richard] walked into the other room and slammed the door. And I had no idea what to make of it. And then he came back in and grabbed me and hugged me."[5]

Julien said that Pryor could be as shy and sensitive as child. He said, "I have never been around a human being like [Richard].... He was like an open nerve." But, he added, "If he had not been on the film, the film would not have worked."[6]

Pryor proved invaluable to the script revision process. "I was born into this," Pryor told Campus. "This was my childhood. These people—the players, the pimps and the women—that was my world."[7] Saul wrote:

Julien inflected Goldie with his verbal bravado and the sensitivity that peeked out from underneath it. Richard gave the film his ear and his feeling for black street life. In his handwritten notes from the time, Campus described how Richard's creativity erupted in the rewrite sessions. Campus said, "Richie says nothing. He just doesn't talk, then suddenly, he says everything. The words tumble out, a river. Overlapping, caustic, furious, tough, sloppy, myopic, visionary, crude and always, always real. His life is chaos. But in the core, constant discovery. Realization."[8]

"We wrote the last five drafts together," Campus said. "Richie was brilliant, he was extraordinary."[9]

Slim was originally written as tough and confident, but Pryor wasn't interested in playing the character that way. He wanted Slim to be as insecure, apprehensive, and tormented as the comedian himself had been when his father tried to force him into the pimp trade. Slim conveys his nervousness by talking incessantly and furiously. Saul wrote:

> In one [scene], he refuses to walk away from two dirty cops who ask him and Goldie to beat it. Slim is perceptive enough to know that as soon as he and Goldie turn their backs, they might be shot for "resisting arrest," and bold enough to defy a shotgun pointed at him by a cop. But Slim isn't as collected as he is perceptive. He sucks in his mouth; his eyes widen with fear. "I ain't runnin' no fucking place," he says. "I ain't no track star." As Slim raves on alone, … the camera gradually pulls back to reveal a new detail of his outfit: along with a pink floral shirt and gray satin vest, he's wearing a pair of crimson knee pants that seem designed for a child. Neither the pimping game nor these brave words have made a man of Slim….[10]

Pryor expresses a fragility that makes Slim more sympathetic. Saul described the character as a "wobbly sidekick, macho in theory if not in practice."[11] Julien believed that Pryor's confrontation with the dirty cops was his best scene in the film. Viewers, he said, have always responded strongly to the scene.

Saul wrote: "Through Richard's suggestions, he also became a more stylish sadist, injecting battery acid into the veins of a drug kingpin, forcing a rival to stick himself with his own dagger-tipped cane, or locking a 'rat' into the trunk of a car that was teeming with the real thing."[12]

Conflict in Oakland quickly escalated. While the film was still in production, Ward and one of his prostitutes were murdered while sitting in Ward's Rolls Royce.

Ward had become romantically involved with Carol Speed, who played a prostitute named Lulu. Speed was traumatized when Ward was murdered and left town soon after. The actress later spoke badly of her experience working on *The Mack*. She believed that she had been exploited by the filmmakers. In 1974, Speed wrote *Inside Black Hollywood*, a novel based on that intense experience. The memoir expresses nothing but contempt for the story's colorful cast of characters. Even the character based on Speed, herself, is depicted as contemptible.

Pryor became friendly with Annazette Chase, who played comely hooker China Doll. Chase said that Pryor protected her like a big brother. The local pimps were looking to turn out the actresses that were working on the film. A pimp approached Chase, but Pryor quickly came forward to intervene. "You can't talk to her," he said. The pimp went away. One day, Chase told Pryor that she wanted to find a way to stand out in a scene. Pryor recommended that she play the scene holding a Chihuahua. The next day, Pryor drove Chase around Oakland to find a camera-ready canine, but failed to do so. They finally settled on an overweight poodle.

Pryor was not as kind to his other co-workers. He would show up late if he showed up at all. Don Gordon said, "He was on coke. He was just fucked up. He wouldn't listen to anybody."[13] Pryor spent much of the production partying with hookers. He drank champagne. He consumed vast quantities of coke. He barely slept. One morning, he came staggering out of his trailer with three prostitutes who had partied with him all night. He approached Campus and introduced the prostitutes as his cousins. Saul wrote: "Richard was so wasted on booze and coke that Michael Campus needed to prop him up during filming. If Campus lost his grip for a moment, Richard hit the floor."[14]

Pryor had pitched in on the script without discussing compensation. Later, when the script was finished, he became angry because Campus didn't appear willing to provide him with credit or remuneration. Saul wrote: "The irony … wasn't lost on Richard: Wasn't he writing a movie *about* getting paid? Who was 'the mack' but an expert in squeezing the last nickel from anyone who owed him?"[15]

"You're gonna pay me for doin' all this shit," Pryor told Campus. Campus explained that, as a director, he had no authority to pay a writer. Pryor recited a line that Goldie says in the script: "Get me my money."

Saul wrote: "Richard continued to simmer over his unpaid work on the film's script, his anger spilling out on set and off."[16] Pryor and Campus were angry about production delays that had them working into the early hours. Pryor shouted at Campus, demanding that he let him go in front of the cameras to finish a scene. Campus shouted back at Pryor. Saul wrote:

> Richard charged at the director and clocked him so hard on the jaw that Campus reeled and fell to the ground, unconscious.
>
> "How'd you like that blow?" Richard asked the limp body on the ground. Then, to everyone: "Did I get him? Did I really get him?"
>
> The security crew trained their guns on Richard, and Max Julien rushed to grab and protect him.[17]

Julien remembered Pryor as being furious. He said that, while Campus was lying on the floor, Pryor repeatedly kicked him.

The comedian remained unrepentant. He decided that it was Bernhard's fault that he had lost his temper and he believed he had no choice but to beat up the man. So, he filled a sock with coins and marched down to Bernhard's room. He said he loved him, but that he had come to kill him. Then, he swung the sock at him. Bernhard had been using a knife to peel almonds and was prepared to use it to cut Pryor's throat. But Bernhard's wife rushed into the room and was able to get Pryor to calm down. She defended Bernhard to Pryor, insisting that her husband had a good heart. "I can't take this shit," said Pryor. Then, he left.

Julien has told a more dramatic version of the story in which Bernhard pulled a gun on Pryor and that the producer's bodyguards came rushing into the room.

Pryor refused to finish the film. He flew back to Los Angeles the next morning. The hotel manager showed Bernhard the damage that Pryor has done to his room. Saul wrote: "It looked as if a hurricane had torn through it: broken lamps, broken chairs; a total shambles."[18]

Bernhard was not as willing as Julien and others to talk about Pryor's behavior on set. He simply said, "[Richard] was good, he was great, but he was difficult."

Campus remained angry at Pryor for years, but he was eventually able to forgive him for his actions. He understood that Pryor was "at a very dark moment … because of the drugs."[19] He stressed, "I will never regret having him in the film."[20]

Goldie's trusted friend, Slim, had to be written out of the remaining scenes. So, we don't see Hank and Jed murder him. We are only shown the aftermath of the murder as the camera pans down to a body lying face-down on the floor. Next to the body is Slim's prized accordion, the keys of which are smeared with blood.

Julien, himself, only became upset with Campus once. It had to do with a scene in which the corrupt cop, Hank (Gordon), is in bed with a large black woman. Hank tells the woman how excited he is by her big body as he roughly fondles her breasts. Julien said, "Michael shot it when I wasn't around. I probably would have broken the camera if I had seen it. I hated that scene with a passion. I thought it was insulting. I thought it was ridiculous."[21] Campus explained to Julien that the scene is meant to show that the cop is decadent. Julien responded, "Because he makes love to a big, dark black woman, it makes him decadent? You don't understand that *that's* insulting?"

The Mack brought the pimp to mainstream America. But Campus and Julien insisted that the film did not glorify the pimp; the message, they insisted, was more profound than that. Elvis Mitchell, curator of Film Independent at LACMA, said, "[*The Mack* is] about a guy who sort of struggles with maturity and gets his comeuppance. He finds out he's not meant for this. I think it's a movie that is really about these questions of black masculinity: Do you take the easy way out and become this horrible kind of mutation of free enterprise, or do you try to sort of stand up and take the nationalist route and help your people?"[22]

A proposed sequel, to be titled "Goldie," was never produced.

Julien is proud of the film's continuing popularity. He said that, in black communities, no DVD collection is complete without *The Godfather*, *Scarface*—and *The Mack*.

In the end, *The Mack* does not promote the pimp's life. Ward's death, which was acknowledged in the opening dedication, underscores the film's final downbeat message. Saul wrote: "All told, the arc of the film became more melancholy, less triumphant, its radical politics tempered by the disenchantment of 1972. The dirty cops were still righteously dispatched, but Goldie was left with nothing. At the beginning of the film, he came empty-handed to Oakland on a bus, and now he departed the film seemingly on the same bus, again empty-handed."[23]

The Mack is elevated by the performances. Julien brings his own intelligence, morality, and sensitivity to the role, which gives Goldie more depth as a character and makes him sympathetic. The sympathy that Julien engenders is important in maintaining the viewer's interest. If Goldie is just a homicidal criminal who makes his living selling women, the bad events that befall him would seem pointless.

The pain and vulnerability that Pryor expresses in *The Mack* made him intense and sympathetic to audiences. Joe Henry did not believe the comedian could have provided the raw performances he gave on stage and screen without drugs or alcohol. Henry believed that, without the abuse he suffered as a child, or the drugs he used to cope, Pryor would not have been the "flickering, fragile flame" that made him so endearing and fascinating to his fans. John A. Williams and Dennis A. Williams, the authors of *If I Stop I'll Die: The Tragedy and Comedy of Richard Pryor*, noted that, for Pryor, "the absence of pain would be the kiss of comic death."[24]

Some Call It Loving (1973)

Production: Two Worlds Films and James B. Harris Productions.
Distribution: Cine Globe, Inc.
Producer: James B. Harris.
Director: James B. Harris.
Screenplay: James B. Harris, from the short story "Sleeping Beauty" by John Collier.
Photography: Mario Tosi.
Editor: Paul Jasiukonis.
Music: Richard Hazard.
Release date: November 16, 1973.
Running time: 103 minutes.
Cast: Zalman King (Robert Troy), Carol White (Scarlett), Tisa Farrow (Jennifer), Richard Pryor (Jeff), Veronica Anderson (Angelica), Logan Ramsey (Carnival Doctor), Brandy Herred (Cheerleader).

Jonathan Rosenbaum of *Sight & Sound* wrote: "Spectators who like to keep their fairy tales innocent, their pornography sordid, their allegories obvious and their dreams intact are bound to be disconcerted by James B. Harris' haunting *Some Call it Loving*, which pursues the improbabilities of dream logic to clarify rather than mystify, and tough-mindedly concerns itself with the processes and consequences of dreaming as well as its objects."[1]

Fantasy dominates the film from the first frame to the last. Robert Troy, a wealthy jazz musician, lives a cloistered, dreamlike existence in a seaside mansion. When we first meet him, he appears to be comforting a widow at a funeral. But the woman's black dress and black veil turn out to be nothing more than a costume. The rich man pays beautiful

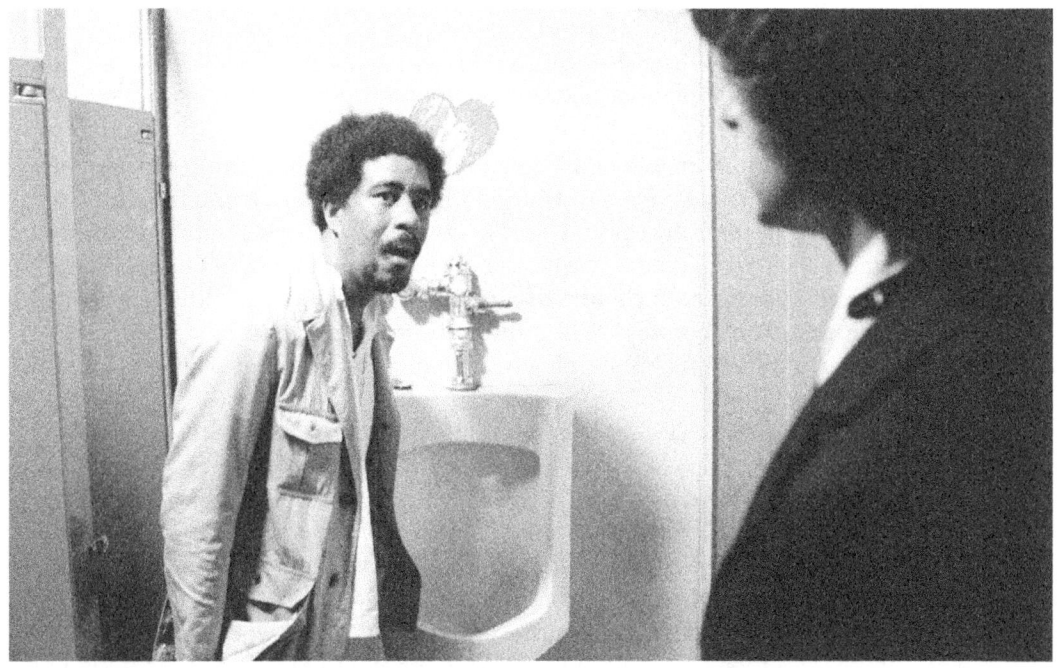

Pryor and Zalman King in *Some Call It Loving* (1973).

young women to participate in role-playing games with him. He has his various concubines act out fantasy scenarios dressed as stock characters, including nuns, maids, and cheerleaders. On this particular day, he has the women pretending to be mourners at a fake funeral.

Troy goes out one evening to visit a carnival. Visitors to a carnival tent are treated to the sight of a real-life Sleeping Beauty. A carny challenges the young men in the group to pay a dollar for the chance to awaken the woman with a kiss. He will, for fifty dollars, leave a man alone with her, presumably to engage in more involved revival methods. Troy is so fascinated by the woman that he offers the carny twenty thousand dollars to buy her. The carny agrees. He provides Troy with a bottle containing the mysterious drug that he has used to keep the woman asleep. Troy takes the woman back to the mansion to play out his latest fantasy.

After a few days, Troy realizes that he has fallen in love with the awakened Jennifer. He decides to leave behind the mansion and his role-playing games to make a real life with her. The couple travels cross-country in a "Sleeping Beauty" van that was included in Troy's purchase of Jennifer. The van was owned (offscreen) by King, who thought the colorfully painted vehicle would further the surreal and fanciful style of the film.

Troy feels uneasy being out in the real world. He is compelled, after less than a day, to return to the mansion. Harris said:

> If you have multiple relationships in your life, you keep moving on from one girl to another, as I had…. Could there be something wrong with all the girls? It had to be something within myself that was causing these abortive relationships. In John Collier's story, the guy who finds the "Sleeping Beauty" figures he's going to have happiness for the rest of his life if he can wake her up, and when he wakes her up, it turns out she's terrible, awful, impossible to get along with, to the extent that he's so unhappy that he puts her back to sleep. I figure that's the wrong way to tell the story. It's too easy to blame somebody else, too easy to blame all the women. Look at yourself and find out if there's something in yourself that's causing the problem. I wanted him to wake the girl up and have her be perfect, have her be everything that he wanted." But Robert couldn't function with a perfect woman. Harris believed that he has been aroused for so long by kinky fantasies that he is unable to "get it up when [he tries] to do it normally." He said, "It turns out that he's so diseased with playing games of this sort that it's all lost."[2]

Troy decides that it is time to end his painful love affair with Jennifer. He secretly pours the sleeping tonic into a glass of wine and has her drink it. Jennifer is surprised when she suddenly becomes groggy. "Gee, I'm so tired," she tells him. "It must have been that wine. I had to drink the whole glass. I don't ever remember feeling this sleepy." She continues to talk as she feels herself succumbing to the tonic. "I'm so happy," she says. "Can we go on this way? Will I always be your jelly bean? So sleepy. I love you." Troy is tearful as he lifts his sleeping beauty into his arms and carries her out of the room.

The final scene shows that the Sleeping Beauty exhibit has been revived, with Troy as the doctor and his mistress Scarlett as his nurse.

At the time of its release, most critics agreed with the *New York Times*' A. H. Weiler, who dismissed the film as "a rambling, contemporary fable that is merely pretentious."[3]

Miriam Bale of *L Magazine* wrote in 2013: "'I bought a Sleeping Beauty! I thought you should know,' says the obscenely wealthy jazz musician to his complicit concubines. He's just returned to his stone palace from a carnival freak show, where he purchased a used and abused beauty who has been slumbering for eight years. Yes, it's that kind of movie—whatever that kind of movie is."[4] Still, Bale liked the film. She wrote: "It's pervy as hell, yet somehow tender and absurd while roughly challenging the taboos that cult movies like this do."[5] Modern-day critics, like Bale, have a more favorable view of the film than critics did in 1973. Martin Wilson of *MUBI's Notebook* wrote: "Unique film. Once seen, never forgotten. For some reason, the image that lingers the most is of the little white sailing boat, bobbing like a toy, out on the hazy sea. It's hard to think of another film quite like it, though *Vertigo* comes to mind. The similar hypnotic mood accompanied by a mesmerizing score, the dream logic and a man trying to control, or at least make real, the very thing he yearns for."[6]

Harris had to make cuts to the film as his two hour-plus print was not well-received by a preview audience. He removed his lead character's backstory, which he hoped would make the plot mysterious, but it only made it confusing. At Cannes, a reporter tried to discuss the plot with Pryor, but the actor admitted he had no idea what the film was about.

Pryor plays Jeff, a simple-minded junkie. Taylor regards Jeff as his best friend and does everything he can to take care of him. Harris said:

> Being a jazz musician, he would be around a certain element of people, and I figured if he performs at a club, the kinds of friends that this character would have would be somebody like the character Pryor played. I wrote the character, Jeff, and gave the script to Zalman, and he suggested we get Richard Pryor, who he had known as a friend from New York. He said: "He fits the character perfectly." Richard's part was practically all improvisation. He was not a major star at that time—in fact he had no money at all. I remember him calling me from Chicago and asking me to advance him some money to get to California to do the film because he didn't have enough money to get there. The only problem was that he was always on drugs, and it wasn't easy to work with, but I think we got what we were looking to get.[7]

Critics had varied ideas about who Jeff is. He has been described as "a black derelict dying of drugs and drink"[8] (Jonathan Rosenbaum), "a strung out graffiti artist"[9] (Nathaniel Drake Carlson), a "wino philosopher"[10] (Miriam Bale), and "a gibbering lush in a men's room"[11] (A. H. Weiler). Is he an artist or a derelict? Is he a philosopher or a gibbering fool? This junkie is a thin shadow of the emotionally rich junkie Pryor portrayed in his "Wino and Junkie" routine. Danny King of *MUBI's Notebook* described Pryor's performance as "soused beyond coherence."[12]

The thinly written character has no real place in this story, which may be the reason Pryor fails to create a character that is coherent or believable. It could be argued that the character's disjointedness is due to mental health issues *or* drug issues. Brandon of *Deeper Into Movies* wrote: "There is something wrong with him. He is either mental[ly ill] or drunk, or just trying to play his scenes way too energetically to make up for the languor around him."[13]

David and Joe Henry wrote: "Richard, for the most part, is wasted as King's drug-addled friend who is insistent in explaining the deeper meaning of a lopsided heart he has painted in glow-in-the-dark red on the wall above a urinal in the men's room of a jazz club where King is performing. Midway through the film, Richard's character dies of an overdose for no apparent reason (story-wise)."[14]

Jeff coughs in the same ominous way that fellow junkie Ratso Rizzo coughed in *Midnight Cowboy* (1969), which means that he isn't going to be alive much longer. In the end, Jeff's death *does* have a reason. His funeral is meant to contrast the mock funeral that opened the film. It is harsh reality intruding on Robert's fantasy world, which is something the dreamy young man finds deeply unsettling. Harris said in his DVD commentary that he had a hard time getting Pryor to lie still in the coffin. He remained restless, even as a corpse.

Hit! (1973)

Production and Distribution: Paramount Pictures.
Producer: Harry Korshak.
Director: Sidney J. Furie.
Screenplay: Alan R. Trustman and David M. Wolf.
Photography: John A. Alonzo.
Editor: Argyle Nelson.
Music: Lalo Schifrin.
Release date: September 18, 1973.
Running time: 134 minutes.
Cast: Billy Dee Williams (Nick Allen), Richard Pryor (Mike Willmer), Paul Hampton (Barry Strong), Gwen Welles (Sherry Nielson), Warren Kemmerling (Dutch Schiller), Janet Brandt (Ida), Sid Melton (Herman).

David and Joe Henry perfectly summarized the plot in two sentences: "[Federal agent Nick Allen] takes it upon himself to recruit, finance, train, and transport to France a small band of private American citizens who have each suffered personal tragedies as a result of illegal drugs. They seek vengeance ... against the nine leaders of a Marseilles drug syndicate who control product and distribution."[1] Critical to the story is the fact that, during training, the group develops into a family.

The script had all of the ingredients for a high-energy action-thriller. Alan Trustman wrote the lead role for Charles Bronson, whom he was sure could mete out bloody revenge in a chillingly stoic manner. This was something proven only a year later with *Death Wish* (1974). But Paramount was not interested in Bronson for the film. The studio intended for the film to be a prestige vehicle for Steve McQueen and expected the violent vendetta that the feverishly obsessed protagonist wages against a French drug cartel to attract the same critical acclaim and box-office profits as *The French Connection* (1971). Trustman could not have been happy with this plan. He nearly quit the business after fighting with McQueen over his script for *Le Mans* (1971). But McQueen never came on board the project and it was decided that a black lead could allow the studio to market the film to fans of blaxploitation, a trend that was then at its peak of popularity.

Pryor plays Mike Willmer, a man whose wife was raped and murdered by a junkie. Allen guarantees that Willmer will join him by driving the man to a low-security prison to confront the junkie responsible for the crime. Pryor gives one of the best dramatic performances of his career in these early scenes. It was, without question, the actor's most subtle performance to date. He is not playing a manic pimp or a drug-addled graffiti artist. Henry Jaglom said, "I remember Richy saying how Sidney Furie was constantly challenging him, and told him to expect greatness in himself as a dramatic performer."[2] Pryor said, "I want to do something to show that I have depth. It's time to branch out, time to stretch my talents as far as they will go. The happy-go-lucky comic—that's an act. I like to do parts. But I don't want to be one-dimensional, to lock myself in."[3]

Unfortunately, Pryor partied every night. The film's executive producer, Gray Fred-

Pryor in *Hit!* (1973).

erickson, said, "Once we got to Marseilles, Richard Pryor wore me out. He was such a wild man."[4]

Pryor's character isn't introduced until forty-two minutes into the film. He later disappears from the storyline for a full twenty minutes. But he makes the most of his time on screen. While piloting a boat, he improvises a blue, off-the-cuff sea shanty—"I gotta get laid, I gotta get laid…." In another scene, he comforts Sherry, an emotionally unstable heroin addict who is distraught over having killed a man. Pryor refers back to a scene in which his character killed a drug lord with a speargun. He says, "You think you got troubles, nigga? I lost a motherfuckin' spear. Cost me forty-seven boxtops. I saved for six months. Shit! Had a gold tip on it and everything."

A common complaint of critics was that the film takes too long to get started and, in the end, doesn't have enough action to satisfy fans of the blaxploitation subgenre. It is, in fact, more a relationship story than an action film. It remains focused on its ensemble of characters and the comradeship they form as they plot their attack.

David and Joe Henry wrote: "The few critics who bothered to give *Hit!* any notice

Pryor readies his speargun for an aquatic hit in *Hit!* (1973).

complained that the film provided a scant twenty minutes of thrills, and only after the audience had endured an hour and fifty minutes of set-up and character development. All true. For audiences expecting a blaxploitation thrill ride, Furie's art-house pacing, often disorienting camera work, and generous attention to character and detail made for slow going."[5]

The film failed at the box office. "We got swept under the rug with *Hit!*," said Furie. "It just opened and closed. It wasn't even abused, just dismissed, nothing you could do."[6] It had to have hurt the film that a similar film, *Gordon's War*, preceded it into theaters by six weeks. However, the film found an audience when it was released on DVD in 2012.

Uptown Saturday Night (1974)

Production: First Artists.
Distribution: Warner Bros.
Producer: Melville Tucker.
Director: Sidney Poitier.
Screenplay: Richard Wesley.
Photography: Fred J. Koenskamp.
Editor: Pembroke J. Herring.
Music: Tom Scott.
Release date: July 26, 1974.
Running time: 104 minutes.
Cast: Sidney Poitier (Steve Jackson), Bill Cosby (Wardell Franklin), Harry Belafonte (Geechie Dan Beauford), Flip Wilson (The Reverend), Calvin Lockhart (Silky Slim), Richard Pryor (Sharp Eye Washington), Rosalind Cash (Sarah Jackson), Roscoe Lee Browne (Congressman Lincoln), Paula Kelly (Leggy Peggy).

Sidney Poitier, as a co-owner of First Artists, was looking to develop a project he could direct. He had an idea to bring together an all-star cast of black comedians for a free-wheeling comedy. He was confident that he had found an ideal candidate to write the script after he saw Richard Wesley's play *Gettin' It Together*. The play, which starred Morgan Freeman and Beverly Todd, involved an auto mechanic who resents his girlfriend pressuring him to get married. The auto mechanic stood out in the play as a compellingly authentic representation of the blue collar black man. Wesley said, "Sidney's assistant called and asked me to come to his office at 1860 Broadway. I was stunned. Sidney was one of the biggest stars in the world."[1]

Wesley thought about a big robbery that occurred in Atlanta on the night that Muhammad Ali and Jerry Quarry fought at Atlanta's Civic Auditorium. Author David Rosen wrote: "After the bout, a jubilant, all-night celebrator party was held at the swank Regency Hyatt Hotel and everyone who was anybody in the African-American community was proudly in attendance, sporting their grandest finery. Boxing historian Bert Sugar later noted, 'It was the greatest collection of black money and black power ever assembled until that time.' He added, 'Right in the heart of the old Confederacy, it was *Gone With the Wind* turned upside-down.'"[2] Rosen noted that between one hundred and two hundred guests left the party at the hotel when they were told that an even more elaborate soirée was to be held at an upscale home. The bigger and better party turned

Uptown Saturday Night (1974)

The robbery that sets the plot into motion in *Uptown Saturday Night* (1974). *Left to right:* two extras, Bill Cosby and Sidney Poitier

out to be a set-up by a gang of bold robbers. Masked men held sawed-off shotguns on the guests, who obligingly stuffed a pillowcase with their cash and jewelry to avoid being shot.

Wesley said, "I based *Uptown Saturday Night* on that robbery. Sidney loved the story, hired me, and flew me down to his house in [the] Bahamas to write the script."[3]

As he had in *Gettin' It Together*, the writer drew his lead characters from the working class. Steve Jackson (Poitier), a factory worker, and Wardell Franklin (Cosby), a taxi driver, aspire to a better life. It is with these aspirations that they pretend to be diamond merchants to gain access to an exclusive gambling parlor. Wardell is on a winning streak at the craps table when masked gunmen burst into the club and rob the clientele.

The next morning, Steve is excited to learn that he purchased a winning lottery ticket worth fifty thousand dollars. The problem is that he put the ticket in his wallet, which was taken by the men who robbed him at the club.

Steve and Wardell need help to track down the robbers and recover the wallet. They visit the Sharp Eye Detective Agency, where they meet a jumpy detective named Sharp Eye Washington (Pryor). Washington tells them that he will take their case if they pay him a fifty dollar advance. Steve no sooner pays the advance than police officers arrive to arrest Washington for fraud.

Poitier and Cosby obligingly step aside to let Pryor take charge of the scene. Sharp Eye Washington was designed to mock the larger-than-life image created by supercool black detective John Shaft. Novotny Lawrence, a media professor at Southern Illinois University, wrote: "Washington's constant twitching and sweaty brow make him appear as if he is on the verge of having a nervous breakdown."[4] Als found that Sharp Eye Washington "makes use of Pryor's ability to convey paranoia with his body: throughout the movie, he looks like a giant exclamation point."[5] Washington tells Steve and Wardell, "In the movies they always got some super nigga killin' them white boys in the Mafia and beatin' up the crooked police. That's not true. And women, black detectives in the movie always got the women. I haven't had a woman in months! That's the real truth of it."

Steve and Wardell continue to search for the robbers on their own. They learn that local gangsters may have been involved in the heist. They are so desperate to retrieve the lottery ticket that it doesn't matter to them if their snooping gets them caught up in an ongoing gang war.

Steve visits a bar to talk to a gang boss, Geechie Dan Beauford (Belafonte, who parodies Brando in *The Godfather*), who is likely to know something about the robbery. Geechie is irritated by Steve's questions and asks his men to throw him out. Just then, gunmen storm into the bar and open fire on Geechie, who avoids being shot by ducking to the floor and scrambling out a back door. He escapes to his hideout, with Steve and Wardell as captives. He interrogates the men, whom he believes fingered him to his rival Silky Slim. Geechie is about to murder Steve and Wardell when Silky Slim and his men

Poitier hangs onto the roof of a gangster's speeding car to retrieve a lottery ticket in *Uptown Saturday Night* (1974).

surround the hideout to finish their hit. Steve and Wardell recognize Silky Slim's voice as belonging to one of the masked robbers. Wardell comes up with an idea to save their lives and retrieve the lottery ticket. He knows that the loot includes a bogus legal letter used to identify them to the club manager as diamond merchants. He quickly tells Geechie about it. He lies that he overheard diamond merchants at the club talking about a $300,000 cache of diamonds. He insists that the letter will lead them to the diamonds. This is enough money to convince Geechie to negotiate with Silky Slim. He assures him that the two stand to make a lot of money if he lets him look through the stolen items he picked up at the club. Silky Slim has the items secured in a suitcase. He agrees to bring the suitcase with him to a meeting at a church social. Steve and Wardell plan to break into Silky Slim's car at the church social, but the trunk in which Slim has placed the suitcase has a lock that Steve and Wardell cannot break despite their most strenuous efforts.

Pryor as panicky sleuth Sharp Eye Washington in *Uptown Saturday Night* (1974).

The gangsters find the letter and send their men to the law office, where they believe the diamonds have been stored. Steve has his wife contact the police, who set up a stakeout at the law office.

The police arrive at the church social to arrest Silky Slim and Geechie. The gangsters jump into their car to make a fast getaway. Steve desperately climbs onto the roof of the car before they speed off. He repeatedly reaches into the car to snatch the suitcase away from Slim, but Slim refuses to let go of it. Steve needs to force them to stop the car. He removes a hammer from his tool belt and smashes the windshield. The car stops at a bridge. Steve wrestles with Silky Slim for the suitcase. When Slim throws it into the river, Steve doesn't hesitate to jump off the bridge to recover it. Wardell shows up in time to follow Steve into the river. The two eventually make it out of the river with the suitcase and find the lottery ticket intact. Geechie and Silky Slim are arrested. (The idea of a protagonist on a desperate chase to retrieve a winning lottery ticket was used several decades earlier in René Clair's 1931 early sound comedy *Le Million*.)

While writing the screenplay, Wesley envisioned Pryor and Redd Foxx in the lead roles. But, as it turned out, Poitier was pressured by financiers to take the lead role in the film. The character intended for Pryor was entirely changed to suit Poitier, who was determined to maintain his upright screen image. The character was, under his control, well-mannered, dignified, proud, and ethical. Donald Bogle, author of *Toms, Coons, Mulattoes, Mammies, and Bucks: An Interpretive History of Blacks in American Films*, wrote: "In all his films, [Poitier] was educated and intelligent. He spoke proper English, dressed conservatively, and had the best of table manners."[6] Cosby was as smooth and mannerly as Poitier. Neither he nor his co-star wanted to offend their fans.

It isn't hard to imagine Pryor and Foxx in the Steve and Wardell roles. Pryor could have been funny panicking while a cruel crime boss threatens to kill him. Foxx could have been cool and sharp in contrast to Pryor's more lively antics. Foxx had developed a laid-back, unapologetic style in his stand-up act. He was smooth, sassy, and streetwise.

Bailey noted that Pryor seems like an afterthought in the film. He wrote: "When he pops up (from behind a desk, screeching 'Whaddaya want!') in the 1974 Sidney Poitier–Bill Cosby comedy, *Uptown Saturday Night*, as hyperparanoid private detective 'Sharp-Eye Washington,' he gives the sleepy picture a jolt of electricity and danger it can't contain; he's barely arrived before he's sent packing."[7]

Pryor was a riotous force that could not be assimilated. In his brief appearance, his wild and cutting comic style provides a sharp contrast to Cosby's carefree approach. The comedy of the film did require the articulate and refined Poitier to surrender his dignity at times. He was, after all, playing a desperate man who must confront homicidal gangsters to retrieve a fifty thousand dollar lottery ticket. So, Poitier tends to bubble over with comic panic as his life is threatened or his chances to recover his lottery ticket slip away. Cosby, who assures Poitier that he has "got [his] back," stands at his friend's side as a cool and faithful straight man. He only panics when Belafonte jams the muzzle of his gun into his face.

Cosby became dismayed when prominent critics attacked the film for depicting black people in a demeaning manner. Jay Cocks of *Time* wrote: "Poitier's idea of comic acting is to bulge his eyes out, as if doing a Mantan Moreland impression."[8] Vincent Canby, senior film critic for the *New York Times*, wrote: "'Uptown Saturday Night' is an exuberant black joke that utilizes many of the stereotypical attitudes that only black writers, directors and actors can decently get away with. You've never seen so much eye-popping fear and unwarranted braggadocio used in the service of laughs. Yet the result is not a put-down comedy but a cheerful jape that has the effect of liberating all of us from our hangups."[9]

Cosby contacted Bob Thomas of the Associated Press to publicly protest the reviews. Thomas went on to convey Cosby's complaints in an article entitled "Cosby Piqued by Criticism of 'Uptown Saturday Night.'" Cosby turned the conversation into a lecture on comedy (Thomas referred to the comedian speaking "in a pedagogical manner"[10]). Cosby was especially offended that critics accused the stars relying on eye-popping antics for laughs. He said, "The color of the skin of a black man gives more prominence to the whiteness of the eyes than does the pinkish tinge of the white man's skin. Watch George Segal or Jack Nicholson or Walter Matthau or Jack Lemmon when they are doing comedy and you will note that their eyes do indeed bug out. It is only natural in comedy to open your eyes wider."[11] Cosby later angered black activists with a radio advertisement in which he said that, by seeing *Uptown Saturday Night*, a person could enjoy the pleasures of Harlem without having to worry about "gettin' [their] head beat in."[12]

Later that year, Pryor was offered a starring role in a feature film. David Picker, the president of United Artists, gave Schultz a script called "Timmons from Chicago," which was about a pimp who becomes president of the United States. Picker sent Schultz to Los Angeles to meet with Pryor about playing the pimp-turned-POTUS. The two men got along well and were eager to work together, but Schultz walked away from the project because he was dissatisfied with the small budget allocated by Picker. Picker responded by canceling the project.

Adiós Amigo (1976)

Production: Po' Boy Productions.
Distribution: Atlas Films.
Producer: Fred Williamson.
Director: Fred Williamson.
Screenplay: Fred Williamson.
Photography: Anthony R. Palmieri
Editors: Eva Ruggiero and Gene Ruggiero.
Music: Blue Infernal Machine.
Release date: January 1976
Running time: 87 minutes.
Cast: Richard Pryor (Sam), Fred Williamson (Big Ben), James Brown, Robert Philips (Notary), Mike Henry (Mary's Husband), Suhalia Farhat, Victoria Jee, Lynn Jackson, Heidi Dobbs, Liz Treadwell, Joy Lober, The Ink Spots, Thalmus Rasulala (Noah), Deborah Chenoweth, Timothy Blake, Victor Rogers, Jon Mercedes, Nick Dimitri, Chuck Duncan, Doyle Baker, Leonard D'John, Richard Brown, Fred W. S. Newton, Neil Summers, Vujka Andrich, Otis Lewellen, Robert L. Lein, Robert L. Lein, Joe Kurtzo, Vince Malone, Bruce Malone, Jonathon Barnes, Emanuel Smith, Robert Jones, Emmett S. Robbins, Sonny Cooper, Willie Chavez, Luther Elmore, John Millhollin, John J. Wallwork Jackson D. Kane Roberto Valentino De Leonm, Phil Mead, Bud Conlan, Henry J. Luck, Herb Robins, John Jarrell, George Cayley, Fred Maio, Raleigh Gardenhire, Ben Yeller, James Sargent, Henry Lente, James Doudna.

Pryor's worst film is not *The Toy*. It is *Adiós Amigo*.
The jumbled patchwork of scenes fail to tell a bona-fide story. The first character introduced is Big Ben (Williamson), a large, brawny, dull-witted gunslinger. A rancher gets his men to rustle Ben's horses. When Ben gets into a gunfight with the men, the rancher tells the sheriff that he tried to rob them.

The sheriff is transferring Ben to prison in a stagecoach when Sam (Pryor) comes along to rob the passengers. Sam frees Ben, only to abandon him in the desert. Ben figures to escape the arid wasteland by stealing a horse from a trapper. He comes upon Sam being robbed by Mexican bandits and gets in a gun battle to rescue him. An ungrateful Sam rides away in the confusion, leaving Ben to fight the bandits on his own.

Sam and Ben meet up again at a boxing match. Sam volunteers Ben to fight the champion. Once he collects the bets and Ben climbs into the ring, Sam leaps on his horse and rides off with the cash. Similarly, the next segment involves Sam enlisting Ben in a knife-throwing contest and sneaking away after he has collected plentiful bets in his hat. Every episode invariably ends with him crying out, "Adiós, amigo!"

Next, Sam meets up with a peddler, whose daughters he deflowers and whose money

The poster for *Adiós Amigo!* (1976).

he pilfers. He hasn't ridden very far before he robs a wagon from a surveyor. Pretending to be a surveyor when he arrives at the next town, he claims to be doing work for a railroad company, and offers to sell information about impending railroad routes. Sam is finally exposed and thrown in jail when the real surveyor shows up. Ben helps Sam escape from jail, but he still does not express the slightest gratitude for his rescuer's continuing aid.

Sam and Ben are captured by a Mexican gang and forced to work in a mine. One night, Sam uses a stick of dynamite that he pilfered from the miners' explosives to blow open a safe in the main office. He rides off with the company's cash before anyone has time to catch him.

The central protagonists are reunited when they are captured by the Mexican bandits who want the money Sam stole from the mining company; he promises to retrieve it from its hiding place and give it to them. But Sam manages to outwit the bandits and get away with the money.

In the final scene, the many people who have been wronged by Sam and Ben confront them on a mountain ridge. Sam gleefully tosses the money in the air as he and Ben ride off. He tells Ben that it was useless Confederate money.

Adiós Amigo was intended as a cross between *The Good, the Bad and the Ugly* and *Blazing Saddles*. The film was, in fact, Pryor's misguided response to the latter. He was angry that he had been denied the lead role in that Mel Brooks–directed megahit. Michael Schultz, who was soon to direct Pryor in *Car Wash*, said, "Richard wrote it and Mel Brooks chased him out. Mel Brooks was trying to get total credit for the picture.... To be outmaneuvered and ripped off at that early stage in his career is something that's a little hard for him to get over. I'd feel the same way."[1] Pryor said, "That movie wasn't funny when I first got there. *I* told Mel Brooks to put in the farting and shit."[2] It was, as he saw it, his film and his film alone. "They used me and that's not fair," he insisted. "And it's a thorn in my heart about it."[3] Pryor spoke about this on many occasions. He wrote in his autobiography: "They were scared of my reputation. Yes, I was funny, nobody could deny that. But they also saw me as a volatile, vulgar, profane black man who wisecracked about getting high and screwing white women. It scared the shit out of their Brooks Brothers sensibilities to think about risking millions of dollars on a movie starring a person like me."[4] He believed for the rest of life that, if Brooks had fought harder for him, he could have gotten him the role of Sheriff Bart, the black lawman.

Let us examine the facts concerning *Blazing Saddles*.

Andrew Bergman wrote a comedy script about a black man who becomes a sheriff in an Old West town. The original title of the script was *Tex X* (a play on Malcolm X), and it was arranged for James Earl Jones to play the sheriff. But then, Mel Brooks came onto the project and wanted to make changes to the script. Brooks got help from Pryor, Bergman, Norman Steinberg, and Alan Uger. David and Joe Henry wrote: "Richard, by all accounts, threw himself into the project with abandon, spinning out gags and situations like an inspired Rumpelstiltskin—even offering up bits from 'Black Stranger,' a cowboy screenplay he'd written while in Berkeley."[5] Schultz said that "The Black Stranger" script was about a black gunslinger who uses occult magic to rid a town of a corrupt magnate. It sounds like the plot of Clint Eastwood's *High Plains Drifter* (1973).

Brooks got the idea of casting Pryor as the sheriff, but Warner Bros. insisted that Brooks find another actor. The studio executives explained plainly that they wouldn't be able to obtain financing for the film if a known drug addict was the star. It wasn't his wisecracks about getting high and sleeping with white women that were the problem; it was the fact that he got high on a daily basis, adversely affecting his behavior on set. Pryor didn't think this was fair, despite the fact that rumors were floating around Hollywood about Pryor urinating on Shelley Winters during filming of *Wild in the Streets*, knocking a director unconscious during filming of *The Mack*, and that he forced his way into the hotel room of *The Mack*'s producer in an attempt to assault him. Pryor never took responsibility for his bad behavior, and many of the people around him were willing to overlook his bad behavior.

It was Brooks's idea to hire Pryor as a writer. It was Brooks's idea to cast Pryor in the leading role. He didn't chase Pryor out of anything. Bryan Thomas of *Night Flight* wrote: "On the commentary track for the *Blazing Saddles* DVD, Brooks talks about going 'on bended knee to every studio executive' to try to convince them to hire Pryor, who he felt was the funniest guy who ever lived, but the rampant rumors about Pryor's mental health and drug use at the time, as well as his controversial reputation at the time as a profane stand-up comic, caused the studio to reject the idea."[6]

Pryor was inconsolable. He said, "I didn't want [the role] originally, but I was told I was going to get it. After that, I wanted it. I didn't think Mel Brooks was the sort of man who would lie. You get your hopes up. That's the thing that hurt me the most. He hurt me ... didn't have the decency to call me up and tell me I was wasn't going to star in *Blazing Saddles*."[7] Pryor especially resented the fact that Brooks informed Pryor's agent of the studio's decision instead of talking to him personally. Rovin wrote: "The director's aide says that Brooks was simply following protocol, allowing Pryor's agent to bear him the bad tidings."[8]

Cleavon Little, who was cast as Black Bart, was Pryor's friend. The two actors had met while working together on an episode of *The Mod Squad*. But Pryor stopped talking to his friend for taking a role that he believed belonged to him.

Williamson, who had been successful directing the blaxploitation crime-drama *Mean Johnny Barrows* (1976), proposed to Pryor that they make a comedy-western themselves. But he said he wanted his film to avoid the silliness of the Brooks film and be "a down and dirty western."[9]

As a child, Pryor was fascinated with B-western star Lash LaRue. "I wanted to be just like him, I wanted to be him,"[10] he said. LaRue dressed in a stylish black outfit and mightily managed a bullwhip against the bad guys. Pryor believed that he had the opportunity with *Adiós Amigo!* to be, according to Martin Weston of *Ebony* magazine, a "riding, blasting fool."[11]

The film is similar to *Buck and the Preacher* (1972), a western that featured Sidney Poitier as a wagon master and Harry Belafonte as a con man. But *Adiós Amigo!* is an embarrassing effort compared to that professionally crafted film.

Not much time or care was lavished on *Adiós Amigo!* The script was only twelve pages long. The fact that the principal photography was completed in nine days meant lighting and camera set-ups had to be done in a hurry. It is the reason that night scenes were muddy, and certain shots were out of focus. The man in charge, Anthony Palmieri, was a camera operator who had never worked as a cinematographer before. Nor did he do so again until 1992, when he was hired to photograph the television series *Dark Justice*. He continued to perform the same duties on many television series, including *Murder One, Providence, ER,* and *Monk*. The film's editor, Gene Ruggiero, was an Oscar winner who had worked at MGM from 1946 to 1961. He worked on many classic films, including *Ninotchka* (1939), *Oklahoma!* (1955), and *Around the World in 80 Days* (1956). It is astonishing that he ended up working on *Adiós Amigo!*

Pryor didn't bother to promote the film. He said in an interview with *Ebony* magazine, "Tell them I apologize. Tell them I needed some money. Tell them I promise not to do it again."[12]

Williamson was made upset by Pryor's comments. He maintained that the comedian was uncooperative during production. He said, "So Richard would nod, and then he would get in front of the cameras—and you got thirty seconds at most. He'd walk off, and I'd be staring at him and say, 'Man, what are you *doing*? I need *more*, go and *do* it.' But he'd stop…. There was no getting him to do what I wanted."[13]

Williamson and Pryor did not work well together on or off screen. Williamson said, "I wanted to be able to maintain my straight-man figure to Richard's con man, still be tough, and do my fight scenes—but just have someone floating around me like a butterfly to provide the comedy."[14] He added in another interview, "I wanted to give [Richard] an idea, a concept, and then just turn the light on him and let him do whatever he wanted. You know what they say about comedians—that you can just open the refrigerator door and the light comes on, the jokes roll on out. Well, Richard's light didn't come on."[15]

It surely didn't help the film that Pryor was uncooperative and didn't put much effort into his performance, but it is not wise to expect a comedian to float around a set with a vague idea of what he's supposed to be doing. Roger Ebert once wrote: "Comic actors, even good ones, are rarely funny in and of themselves. They need characters to play, and they need funny material."[16] This principle, though simple and obvious, is something a filmmaker should never forget.

Adiós Amigo! is so slapdash that it is barely a film; it looks instead like a collection of outtakes. And not even funny outtakes, where people are flubbing lines and breaking up. It is like the sort of outtakes where people are standing around aimlessly, waiting for the director to yell, "Action!"

Tayvis Dunnahoe of the Grindhouse Cinema Database wrote: "What transpires is a string of disjointed encounters between Sam and Ben in which Ben is always left holding some sort of 'bag.' Are they friends? Partners? No one knows. The film never really sets up a context. Billed as a comedy, the funny never really happens with the exception of a few forced chuckles."[17]

It is reasonable to expect your two lead characters to develop a relationship during the course of a film. But that never happens in *Adiós Amigo!* Ben and Sam never become friends. They never become enemies. It would have been engaging if they had developed the sort of uneasy and dysfunctional friendship like those in countless buddy comedies. But the film has no characters and no story, no meaningful interaction. Pryor grins with a manic glee as he robs, fornicates, and flees from one setting to his next. That's not a character. That's a wind-up toy.

David and Joe Henry were generous in their assessment of Pryor's con man character, which they saw as a "classic trickster." They wrote: "[His character] repeatedly thwarts Williamson's plans, squanders his looted cash, and leaves him in the lurch with his life in peril. Each time, Spade pulls off a wily reversal of fortune, securing Williamson's rescue and replenishing their coffers."[18]

Williamson exaggerated the film's budget while selling distribution rights at Cannes.

He made the film for a paltry $75,000, but told distributors that he spent $500,000 to make the film.

The Bingo Long Traveling All-Stars & Motor Kings (1976)

Production: Motown Productions and Universal Pictures.
Distribution: Universal Pictures.
Producer: Rob Cohen.
Director: John Badham.
Screenplay: Hal Barwood and Matthew Robbins; based on the novel by William Brashler.
Photography: Bill Buller.
Editor: David Rawlins.
Music: William Goldstein.
Release date: July 16, 1976.
Running time: 111 minutes.
Cast: Billy Dee Williams (Bingo), James Earl Jones (Leon), Richard Pryor (Charlie Snow), Rico Dawson (Willie Lee), Stan Shaw (Esquire Joe Callaway), DeWayne Jessie (Rainbow), Tony Burton (Isaac), Ted Ross (Sallie Potter), Mabel King (Bertha), Sam Laws (Henry Dunbar, Owner of Baltimore Elite Giants), Alvin Childress (Horace Quigley, Owner of Atlanta Black Crackers), Ken Foree (Honey, Potter's Goon), Carl Gordon (Mack, Potter's Goon), Anna Capri (The Prostitute), Joel Fluellen (Mr. Holland), Sarina C. Grant (Pearline), Jester Hairston (Furry Taylor).

The Bingo Long Traveling All-Stars & Motor Kings involves a team of enterprising ex–Negro League baseball players in 1939, a time when racial segregation existed in baseball. The film was the second feature film for the writing team of Hal Barwood and Matthew Robbins, who had previously written Steven Spielberg's *The Sugarland Express* (1974). Their work on that script earned them a prestigious award at Cannes.

Barwood wrote:

> Sometime in 1975, the producer-director Rob Cohen, a friend who was then running film development at Motown, came to Matthew Robbins and me with the very entertaining William Brashler novel. We had never adapted a story conceived by someone else, and we were energized by the challenge of turning a sprawling novel into a movie. In the process we became fascinated by the history of black professional baseball in the years before Jackie Robinson and eagerly rolled up our sleeves, comforted by the ready-made plot and characters.[1]

Bingo Long, a rubber-armed star pitcher for the St. Louis Ebony Aces, is unhappy with the treatment of players by the team's owner, Sallison Potter. Sallie's lack of empathy for the players becomes obvious when the team owner fires a player, Rainbow, who was struck in the head by a ball and is now unable to talk. Bingo lets Sallie know his opinion on the matter, but Sallie is unwilling to tolerate players questioning his actions and immediately fines Bingo for insubordination. The team owner tells Bingo, "Around me, you ain't got no opinion!" Bingo convinces other players, including Leon Carter, to defect from the league to form their own independent team, The Bingo Long Traveling All-Stars & Motor Kings.

The All-Stars were based on actual players from the Bingham Black Barons, Indianapolis Clowns, and other barnstorming teams in the 1930s. Satchel Paige, a pitcher with a famous fastball, was the inspiration for Bingo. Many characteristics of legendary players carried over to his fictional counterpart. Paige, a true showman, developed a reputation for behaving in a colorful manner on the field. But, in the novel, Carter was a pitcher and Bingo was a catcher. Brashler wrote: "[Bingo Long] was changed from a catcher to a pitcher for the simple reason that Billie Dee Williams was not a star who would abide by a catcher's mask on his chiseled mug."[2] Carter was modeled on Josh Gibson. Esquire Joe Callaway, to be introduced later, was meant to be Willie Mays.

Pryor (left) and Stan Shaw in *The Bingo Long Traveling All-Stars & Motor Kings* (1976).

Bingo recruits Charlie Snow (Pryor) as the team's third baseman only because Snow has a large touring car they can use to travel from town to town. Snow is the one character without a real-life counterpart. The third baseman has made repeated efforts to break into the Major League by pretending to be Cuban; he even slicks down his hair to give himself a Cuban look. Brashler said, "In *Bingo Long*, his part was originally very minor. But he was so phenomenal they kept giving him more camera time. God, he's funny."[3]

Barwood was asked how he and Robbins came to create the "Charlie Snow" character. He wrote:

> As we thought about the story, … we noticed the bittersweet undertone of frustration, hope, and expectation buried in the narrative prose. Someday—the big leagues! They were beckoning, they were out there, just out of reach. Well, there is no "narrative prose" in a drama, and we wondered how to convey the tone of the book to the screen. At first, it seemed almost impossible. Our solution was to embody all these unspoken yearnings into a hapless character of our own creation. So we added a new face, someone who would try anything, no matter how absurd, to reach the majors. But, paradoxically, we only did so in order to remain faithful to the Brashler book. When the movie project finally got underway, John Badham and Rob [Cohen] cast Richard Pryor in the role, to our surprise and delight.[4]

The team embarks on a barnstorming tour of the Midwest. Their first stop is a small, rustic town where they are being sponsored by Mr. Holland, the owner of a general store. He convinces the team to parade down Main Street to attract a crowd for the game. Tension develops when Leon makes it clear that he does not like this idea. He is, after all, a proud man who wants the team to earn respect and make an honest dollar.

A player on an opposing team, Esquire Joe Calloway, asks to join Bingo's team. At first, Bingo is not interested in him. He jokes that the big and brawny Esquire Joe should be a quarterback. But the player demonstrates such exceptional talent on the field that they quickly recruit him.

The poster for *The Bingo Long Traveling All-Stars & Motor Kings* (1976).

The All-Stars' growing popularity does not go unnoticed by the Negro League owners. Bertha, the owner of the Charcoal Kings, wants to bring Bingo Long's All-Stars team back to St. Louis for an exhibition game, which she is sure will attract a large crowd. But Sallie is determined to put the All-Stars out of business. He sends goons to pay off, or intimidate, the team's sponsors.

Without being able to work in the black community, the All-Stars play an exhibition game against a minor league white team, the Chiefs. At first, the white players and their fans taunt the black players. A couple of boys toss firecrackers into the All-Stars' dugout, which is a source of great amusement for the crowd. The situation gets even worse as the game continues. The first baseman of the Chiefs trips an All-Star player, Fat Sam, as he steals first base. Fat Sam lunges at the first baseman, but he's held back by a teammate. The altercation incites the crowd to stand and boo the visiting team. But, then, Charlie tears the seat of his pants sliding into a base, which causes the crowd to roar with laughter. The team charms the crowd with their clowning and wins their admiration with their playing. In the end, the All-Stars win the game.

The winning streak continues. Sallie sends his goons to beat up Rainbow and steal the team's emergency fund. Next, the goons attack Charlie while he's in bed with a prostitute and threaten him with a razor. Charlie leaps off the balcony to get away and falls into a passing car.

Charlie is attacked again by Sallie's goons at a ballfield. This time, they grab hold of the player and cut him with straight razors. He staggers onto the field, covered in blood.

The All-Stars use what money they have to get Charlie medical help. When the team is unable to pay their hotel bill, the sheriff confiscates their car and puts it up for auction. The team works on a potato farm to raise the money to bid on the car, but the local car dealer is easily able to outbid them. As revenge, Bingo sabotages the sheriff's car and steals a Packard from the dealer's lot. Leon disapproves of Bingo's actions and leaves the team.

Bingo keeps the team together despite their loss of Leon, but he relies more now on gimmicks. When we see the team again, the roster includes a dwarf catcher and a one-armed first baseman. Sallie sees that the popularity of Bingo's All-Stars is greater than ever; in fact, their success is drawing fans away from his own team. He finally agrees to let Bingo's All-Stars play against the League All-Stars. The stakes of the game are high. Bingo's team can join the League if they win, but they will have to rejoin their old teams at half their old salary if they lose.

Leon is willing to play again for the All-Stars to beat Sallie, but the team owner gets his goons to kidnap the power hitter. They take Leon to a back room in Sallie's funeral home, where they tie him up and shut him in a coffin. Leon breaks out of the coffin in full view of a gathering of mourners. He reaches the field with just enough time to hit a ball out of the park. Bingo's All-Stars win. Not only are they admitted into the League, Sallie's Ebony Aces are ousted from the League.

It is a happy ending in every way for Bingo's All-Stars. Charlie, who has fully recovered from his wounds, shows up at the locker room to congratulate his teammates. A pair of scouts invites Esquire Joe to join the Brooklyn Dodgers, which will break the National League's color barrier. Bingo realizes that this may mean the end of the Negro League, but he believes he can continue to attract fans with his wild promotional stunts.

The film was to be directed by Spielberg, but he ran into delays while finishing *Jaws*. He was replaced shortly before the cameras rolled by a young television director, John

Badham, who specialized in crime-dramas. He had recently received acclaim for the television film *The Gun* (1974), which shows the way that a Smith & Wesson revolver changes lives as it passes through a series of owners. Badham, who grew up in Alabama, was familiar with the Birmingham Black Barons and was eager to work on the film.

The film was shot in various Georgia locales—Macon, Monticello, Jeffersonville, and Savannah.

Pryor was combative when he arrived on set. He wrote in his autobiography, "I wasn't speaking to Billy Dee when we did *Bingo Long*."[5] He suggested that it was a personality conflict. But this hardly tells the full story. Pryor was upset with Williams because, he believed, the handsome leading man had stolen his last girlfriend, Patricia Heitman. Pryor refused to stay at the same hotel with Williams and made a point of renting his own home.

On his first day on the set, Pryor became hostile toward Badham. The problem was that the director admitted to him that he had little exposure to black people as a child and that he became afraid the first time he saw a black person. Pryor asked Cohen, "What kind of fucking cracker asshole did you hire to do this movie?"

Pryor later became upset when Badham set up the scene where Charlie jumps off the balcony. The director had a padded platform set up below the balcony, but Pryor still didn't feel safe enough to make the jump. He walked off the set, intending to fly back to Los Angeles. He told Cohen, "I hate that fucking cracker! He don't tell no nigger to jump and the nigger jump!" Cohen begged Pryor to finish the scene as it was crucial to Cohen's career as a producer to get the film completed. Pryor relented for Cohen's sake.

Pryor had a great fear of injury. Later, he refused to perform a scene in which a knife is thrown at his foot. A stand-in had to be brought in for the scene. Towards the end of production, the driver of a camera car nearly struck Jones, who was leading the ballplayers' motorcade on a motorcycle. Jones laughed off the incident, but Pryor threatened again to leave the film. But Pryor's hostility for Badham paled in comparison to his hostility for Williams. He became enraged when he saw Williams talking to his new girlfriend, who had flown in from Los Angeles for a visit. Pryor insisted that he was going to bring a gun to the set to shoot Williams. The actor took the threat seriously enough to demand that Cohen take action to get his co-star under control.

Brashler wrote: "Several members of the Indianapolis Clowns, a latter-day black barnstorming ball club, were signed to present authentic hijinks and infield stunts."[6] These scenes, as entertaining as they were, met with controversy. The author noted:

> Many of the former players were irked that the film concentrated primarily on barnstorming. Their organized leagues consisted of serious, high-level competition, they said, and the film did not emphasize that to their satisfaction. Others, such as Cool Papa Bell, pointed out that the movie showed players in brothels and bars, and Cool, the good married man and Baptist that he was, was bothered by that. Satchel Paige did not like the scene where the team drummed up interest in an upcoming game with a strutting, high-kicking parade down Main Street. "I never danced in no street," Paige said to me.[7]

The parade turns into a big dance number. A player juggles a baseball while another does cartwheels. It could not have pleased Paige that the parade scene was so well-received by audiences that it ended up being featured on posters for the film. But the entertainment value of the film cannot be discounted. The fact is that, despite the general inaccuracies alleged by Paige, Bell, and others, the film was highly effective in renewing interest in the Negro Leagues.

James Earl Jones wrote: "This upbeat movie captured a lot of fans. But the critics were hard on us because they expected a black cast to exude black rage. They wanted the tragedy of black baseball players in the black baseball leagues, not the comedy we gave them. They wanted political relevance and content and protest. They couldn't accept that this was not a black film, but simply a film about black people."[8]

Car Wash (1976)

Production and Distribution: Universal Pictures.
Producers: Art Linson and Gary Stromberg.
Director: Michael Schultz.
Screenplay: Joel Schumacher.
Photography: Frank Stanley.
Editor: Christopher Holmes.
Music: Norman Whitfield.
Release date: October 22, 1976.
Running time: 97 minutes.
Cast: Franklyn Ajaye (T. C.), Bill Duke (Duane), George Carlin (The Taxi Driver), Irwin Corey (The Mad Bomber), Ivan Dixon (Lonnie), Antonio Fargas (Lindy), Jack Kehoe (Scruggs), Clarence Muse (Snapper), Lorraine Gary (Hysterical Lady), The Pointer Sisters (The Wilson Sisters), Richard Pryor (Daddy Rich), Tracy Reed (Mona), Henry Kingi (Goody), Pepe Serna (Chuco), Ray Vitte (Geronimo), Garrett Morris (Slide), Leon Pinkney (Justin), Renn Woods (Loretta), Lauren Jones (Marleen), Leonard Jackson (Earl), Sully Boyar (Leon "Mr. B" Barrow), Melanie Mayron (Marsha), Darrow Igus (Floyd), Otis Day (Lloyd), James Spinks (Hippo).

This is a fast-paced comedy that showcases the misadventures at a Los Angeles car wash during a ten-hour work day. The cast of colorful employees includes Lonnie, an ex-con; Duane, a militant black activist; and Lindy, a brash homosexual.

Daddy Rich (Pryor), a televangelist who heads The Church of Divine Economic Spirituality, arrives to have a bird dropping removed from the hood of his shiny gold limousine. The preacher, who wears a diamond-encrusted crucifix around his neck, expounds on the value of money. He instructs the faithful to believe in the Lord, believe in yourself, and believe in the Federal green. "For a small fee," he says, "I'll set you free."

Schultz made a call to Pryor about making a cameo in *Car Wash*. He had worked with the comedian before on the aborted "Timmons from Chicago."

The Daddy Rich character was modeled after the Reverend Ike, a Los Angeles minister who promised followers prosperity on the condition they pay him for his personal blessing. He once said, "It is the lack of money that is the root of all evil. The best thing you could do for the poor is not to be one of them."[1]

Schultz said, "The base of it was written out, but Richard always added or made the material his own. He was so funny, so brilliant, that I would just let him do what he wanted to do because he was [the] comic genius, not me. I didn't know anything about comedy, but I knew when something was good. So he would throw little ad-libs and stuff but the main concept was written."[2]

Pryor wrote: "On the set of *Car Wash*, I was too coked out to know any better."[3] Yet, he got the job done.

Pryor as Daddy Rich in *Car Wash* (1976).

Schultz found Pryor to be "extremely sensitive"[4] to the way that people reacted to him. He studied their body language and mannerisms. Margot Kidder said, "He didn't miss an eyelash-flicker."[5] His third wife, Jennifer Lee, said, "Richard was a very hypersensitive human being. If he saw a look of judgment, or scorn, it could wound him as deeply as if someone had taken a knife to him."[6]

Roger Ebert endorsed the film. He wrote: "We meet the rest [of the characters] in a dizzying, nonstop kaleidoscope of cars, soul music, characters, crises, crazy kids on skateboards, hookers, television preachers, and lots of suds and hot wax—not to mention the Mad Pop Bottle Bomber, whose bottle turns out to be a cruel disappointment. The movie's put together with a manic energy, we never even quite get introduced to half the people in the cast, but by the movie's end we know them, and what they're up to, and we like them."[7]

Pryor did a variation of Daddy Rich a few months later on *The Richard Pryor Special?* (May 5, 1977). David and Joe Henry wrote: "Richard's Rev. White, a funkier, more media-savvy incarnation of his signature minister character, descends a grand spiral staircase in a gold-trimmed white jumpsuit and enormous afro as the choir sings 'For the Love of Money.'"[8]

Silver Streak (1976)

Production: Frank Yablans Presentations and Miller-Milkis Productions.
Distribution: Twentieth Century-Fox Film Corporation.
Producers: Edward K. Milkis and Thomas L. Miller.
Director: Arthur Hiller
Screenplay: Colin Higgins
Photography: David M. Walsh.
Editor: David Bretherton.
Music: Henry Mancini.
Release date: December 3, 1976.
Running time: 114 minutes.
Cast: Gene Wilder (George Caldwell), Jill Clayburgh (Hilly Burns), Richard Pryor (Grover Muldoon), Patrick McGoohan (Roger Devereau), Ned Beatty (Sweet), Clifton James (Sheriff Chauncey), Ray Walston (Mr. Whiney), Stefan Gierasch (Johnson), Len Birman (Chief),

Valerie Curtin (Plain Jane), Richard Kiel (Reace), Lucille Benson (Rita Babtree), Scatman Crothers (Ralston).

Colin Higgins, best known at the time for writing the screenplay of *Harold and Maude* (1971), was inspired to write the script for *Silver Streak* while watching Alfred Hitchcock's *North by Northwest*. The story is filled with elements from that 1959 comedy-thriller.

George Caldwell (Wilder), a mild-mannered book editor, is traveling to his sister's wedding on the Silver Streak train. George opens a door in his compartment without realizing it leads into an adjoining compartment. He is embarrassed to find a beautiful woman, Hilly Burns, dressed in lingerie. Hilly is amused to see this shy man become flustered and apologetic. Having taken a liking to George, she joins him for dinner in the dining car. It comes out in their conversation that Hilly works for Professor Schreiner, an art historian who is on a publicity tour for his new book about Rembrandt. She tells George that her boss is on the verge of exposing a gang of art forgers.

(The producers originally approached Jacqueline Bisset to play Hilly, which was a role specifically designed for an actress who could serve as eye candy. Jill Clayburgh was fresh from *Gable and Lombard* [1976], which had been her first starring role on the big screen. Not wanting to be a star along the lines of Marilyn Monroe, Clayburgh was determined to do more in her career than look good in lingerie. "Sure, Marilyn Monroe was great," she conceded, "but she had to play a one-sided character, a vulnerable sex object.

Pryor is amused by Patrick McGoohan's exquisite villainy in *Silver Streak* (1976).

It was a real fantasy."[1] She later got to do serious acting in *An Unmarried Woman* [1978], a film that established her as a principal actress of the era. Ronald Bergan of *The Guardian* wrote in 2010: "Clayburgh had the kind of warmth and witty sophistication barely seen in Hollywood since [Carole] Lombard and Jean Arthur."[2] He identified her greatest asset as "her ability to show both strength and vulnerability."[3] It was a loss for *Silver Streak* that the filmmakers made little room for Clayburgh's warmth and wit.)

After dinner, George and Hilly get cozy in her compartment. The couple is in bed kissing and getting undressed when George witnesses a dead body being tossed off the side of the train. "There was a man hanging outside the window!" he cries. "He was shot in the head!" Hilly is incredulous.

In the morning, George comes across a book in Hilly's possession. It is a volume on Rembrandt, written by her boss. George looks at the author photo on the back cover and knows immediately that it is Schreiner, the corpse thrown off the train. Caldwell embarks on an investigation of the incident. He visits Schreiner's compartment to check on the professor and stumbles upon a pair of unsavory men, Mr. Winey and Reace, rummaging through Schreiner's belongings. They get rid of him by throwing him off the train. Mr. Winey and Reace then take Hilly prisoner so she can't tip off the police.

(Richard Kiel, a brawny 7'2" actor, made Reace a formidable figure. Reace, described in the script as an "ugly pug with gold teeth," was a forerunner to Kiel's wordless, metal-mouthed assassin Jaws in *The Spy Who Loved Me* (1977). Mr. Winey was played by veteran character actor Ray Walston, best known for his role as Uncle Martin in the 1960s sitcom *My Favorite Martian*.)

A farmer, Rita Babtree, returns George to the train in her 1930s biplane. George is passing through the dining car when a gregarious vitamin salesman, Bob Sweet, asks him to lunch. George confides in Sweet about the dead body. Sweet reveals that he is an undercover FBI agent who has a passenger, Roger Devereau, under surveillance. Devereau is a phony art expert who has authenticated two Rembrandt forgeries. He had Schreiber killed because he uncovered letters written by Rembrandt that could prove his guilt.

(Bob Sweet was played by the acclaimed actor Ned Beatty. Patrick McGoohan, with his darkly menacing glare, made Devereau one of the vilest, and most effective, villains in film comedy history.)

George is escorting Sweet to his cabin when the lights go out and a shot is fired. When the lights come back on, George finds Sweet dying from a bullet wound. Sweet believes the shot was meant for George. A porter sees George standing over Sweet's dead body with the murder weapon. "Holy moly!" he shouts. "You shot him!" (The porter was played by the scene-stealing comic actor Scatman Crothers.)

Reace chases George through

Wilder and Pryor are an unbeatable team in *Silver Streak* (1976).

the corridor. George takes refuge in a baggage car, locking the door behind him. He knows he has little time to escape before this powerful giant breaks down the door. He uses every bit of his strength to pry open the side door, accidentally dropping the gun in the process. He comes across a spear gun, which he takes with him as he exits the car. Reace pursues him to the roof of the car. George fires a spear into Reace's chest, causing him to topple off the train. George is then knocked off the train by an overhead signal.

(Director Arthur Hiller had to mount cameras on top of the train and hang them off the side to get various action shots. He said, "I had this clever idea.... I'd like to see [Reace's] point-of-view while he was falling down to the ground. So I asked the cinematographer [David M. Walsh] if we could get a cheap camera, put it in a box, cut a hole for the lens and we'd just throw it off the top of the train. Hopefully it wouldn't break, and if it did break it was cheap so we wouldn't lose too much." The camera survived, which surprised Hiller and Walsh, but the shot failed to achieve the point-of-view effect that the director wanted. Hiller said: "The funny thing is that Gene Wilder couldn't stand the safety devices on his legs when he was on top of the train and we had to prepare it in such a way so that two stunt men could be lying down on top of the train and—obviously, safely—hiding and holding his legs while he was acting. He preferred that to [wearing the safety devices]."[4] Pryor and Wilder both display a fair amount of physical comedy in the film. At the time, Wilder was reading about Buster Keaton doing his own stunts and he believed that *he* should be doing his own as well.[5] Pryor said, "That was really [Gene] hanging out and me hanging onto his belt. And that was really a train going fifty

Pryor, Gene Wilder, Jill Clayburgh, Patrick McGoohan, and Ray Walston in *Silver Streak* (1976).

miles an hour. Of course, they had me wired to the train."[6] Hiller clarified in later interviews that the film's stunt coordinator, Mickey Gilbert, stood in for Wilder on the more dangerous stunts.)

George visits a sheriff's office for help, but the sheriff learns that he is being sought for murder and places him under arrest. George escapes by stealing the sheriff's car, unaware that a thief named Grover T. Muldoon (Pryor) is sitting, handcuffed, in the backseat. The men drive to a train station in Kansas City, where police have converged to apprehend George. Grover uses shoe polish to disguise George as a black man. The disguise allows them to get past the police and aboard the train.

(Wilder learned quickly how to respond to Pryor's improvisations. It was important that what he said in response to Pryor's improvisation made sense in relation to the plot, whether what he said was funny or not did not matter at all. Wilder said in a 2007 interview, "I had no idea where [some lines] came from. But I didn't question it; I just responded naturally. I didn't try to think of a clever line.... A great death trap for actors if you're improvising is you say, 'I'll think of one that's even funnier than that, or more clever than that.'"[7])

Once back on the train, George is captured by Devereau. Grover enters the cabin, disguised as a steward, and spills coffee in Devereau's lap to distract him. "You ignorant nigger," snarls Devereau. Grover pulls a gun from his jacket and threatens to "whup the white off [Devereau's] ass." When Devereau's men engage them in a shootout, George and Grover get themselves out of the line of fire by jumping off the train.

George and Grover are met by federal agents, who are aware of Devereau's criminal misdeeds and plan to stop the train and arrest him. Chief Donaldson (Birman) wants George to come with them. George says goodbye to Grover, but Grover becomes worried about him and joins the stakeout team.

(Hiller said, "Originally, Pryor did not return with Wilder to the train the second time. After they are rescued by the FBI, Grover said, 'I want to go home,' and did—and that was the end of him. But once Colin and I talked to Pryor, we got so enthused with *his* enthusiasm that we decided he had to come back. So Colin rewrote the script." But it was not possible to give Grover a meaningful role in the story. Rovin aptly noted, "The film is still fundamentally the romance between Caldwell and Hildegarde, wrapped up in the Devereau intrigue."[8])

Devereau shoots the engineer and places a tool box on the brake pedal to prevent the train from stopping. Devereau is shot by Donaldson, topples out of the engine cabin, and is decapitated by an oncoming freight train. In the meantime, George and Grover get back on the train and rescue Hilly. The trio remains on board as the runaway train crashes at full speed through Chicago's Union Station.

George and Hilly make plans for a romantic date at the park. Grover steals a sports car on display in the terminal.

Pryor later claimed that he never understood the plot of *Silver Streak*. The truth is that the complications surrounding the Rembrandt letters are not important. This plot device, as Alfred Hitchcock famously said, is known as the *MacGuffin*. The plot can be described in a single sentence: George stumbles onto a murder conspiracy and battles the bad guys to rescue a pretty girl.

Director Hiller's comedies invariably centered on a two individuals (e.g., Jack Lemmon and Sandy Dennis in 1970's *The Out-of-Towners*; Alan Arkin and Peter Falk in 1979's *The In-Laws*, 1979) caught up in extraordinary circumstances. He recalled:

On *Silver Streak*, it was Alan Ladd who came up with the idea of Gene Wilder, and when he said it, I thought, "Of course, that's perfect, I hadn't thought of Gene for that." And Richard Pryor was a thought of, I forgot, my producers Tom Miller and Eddie Milkis, one of them or both of them—they came up with that idea, and I thought, "Yes, I had seen Richard on stage," and I remember thinking, it was about three weeks after Betty Ford had her mastectomy, and he made a joke about it, and I thought, "Boy, if he can make a joke about that and I can laugh and still feel for her, that man's an actor." And so when they suggested it, I thought, "Great idea," and we brought Richard in. It was at the time he wasn't interested in particularly in acting in films…. But he came to see me because he had seen *[The] Man in the Glass Booth* [1975], fell in love with it, had seen it like fourteen times, and as we talked, he found out I also directed *[The] Hospital*, and he just signed. That was it. He loved both pictures."[9]

Wilder's casting was a surprise to Higgins, who imagined George Segal in the lead role. Wilder remembered his agent sending him the script (then called "Super Chief") in 1975. The actor said that he was the one who suggested Pryor for the role of Grover. At first, Miller and Eddie Milkis opposed casting Pryor because the actor had recently walked off *The Bingo Long Traveling All-Stars & Motor Kings*. But Hiller and Wilder changed their minds.

Hiller said, "When I got Richard Pryor to agree to be in the film, we got so excited." The producers discussed hiring another actor as back up if Pryor proved undependable. Hiller insisted that this was not necessary. He said, "I've heard things about Pryor misbehaving on other pictures, about arguments and fights, not showing up, and that sort of thing. But on this film we had no problems like that at all." Hiller maintained this sunny portrait of *Silver Streak*'s production in every interview. "All of us really enjoyed it," Hiller said, "and a lot of that is due to Gene Wilder. Gene is very giving, very easy to work with." Rovin wrote: "It was Wilder's patience, good humor and generosity as a performer that really won Pryor over."[10]

The filmmakers approached Amtrak about borrowing one of their trains for the production, but the company believed it would be bad publicity to show murderers running amok on their rail line. Fortunately, they found another railroad service that was willing to accommodate them. Hiller said, "Canadian Pacific Railroad agreed to let us paint up a train and to use it."[11] The use of a Canadian Pacific Railroad train required Hiller to move the production crew to Southern Alberta.

Pryor remained professional throughout the shoot. But he did get upset on at least two occasions. The comedian's mood on the set soured when Mel Brooks showed up to take Wilder to lunch. Brooks hugged Pryor and shouted to other cast members that Pryor was "wonderful and talented." Pryor was unmoved by Brooks's praise and good cheer. He still felt hurt that he didn't get the Black Bart role in *Blazing Saddles*. Rovin wrote that, once Brooks left, the actor "stalked off to his dressing room."[12]

The second time Pryor got upset had to do with the blackface scene. Wilder said that, during the read-through, Pryor became "more and more morose"[13] and finally had to speak up. He told Wilder: "You're in there in the bathroom, in the men's room, and you're putting shoe polish on your face, and a white man comes in and he doesn't think that it's anything unusual because that's how niggers behave, right?'" He insisted, "I'm going to hurt a lot of black people doing this scene." Wilder was very sensitive to what Pryor had to say. He believed that, in regards to race matters, he had to listen to Pryor because "he's the teacher here."[14] Wilder then asked Pryor how the scene should go. Pryor replied, "It should be a black man who comes in, who sees what you're doing, knows right away that you're white and doing this because you must be in some kind of trouble.

And he says, 'I don't know what your trouble is, mister, but you got to keep with the music.'"

Hiller welcomed Pryor's revision of the scene. Later, after the scene was shot, he showed Pryor the rushes to make sure he was satisfied. "He was happy with it," insisted Hiller. But the director regarded it as a pointless exercise in the end. "To be honest," said Hiller, "there was very little difference between the two versions that I was aware of."[15] Rovin wrote: "All Pryor had done was make Grover a little less tolerant of Caldwell in blackface, torn between necessity and the fact that that makeup traditionally has been used to degrade blacks. The change in his attitude signaled to the audience that Pryor and his character, Grover, had accepted the disguise only as a clumsy attempt to *be* black, not as a visual gag mocking blacks."[16]

Despite Hiller doing everything he could to accommodate him, Pryor later denounced the film for the blackface scene. He said, "They felt that having a real black actor in the movie would sort of make it all right."[17]

A last draft of the script was released on March 26, 1976, which was just sixteen days before shooting commenced. This is the script the cast would have for the read-through. Here is how the blackface scene is handled in the script:

> A little White Guy enters and stands at the urinal.... The White Guy can't help but keep looking over at George as he straightens up the flashy jacket, the shades [and] the crazy beanie. Finally Georgia is satisfied. He takes the radio and gives himself the once-over in the mirror.
>
> GEORGE: Looking good. Looking fine. Looking real fine! OK, just loosen up, sugar. Move those hips. All you whiteys have a tight ass. (*George turns and makes for the door. He sees the guy standing at the urinal, staring at him in open amazement.*)[18]

The Shoeshine Guy has a similar reaction when he sees George exiting the bathroom. The script reads, "The old man's jaw drops open in shock."[19]

The "little White Guy" was ultimately eliminated. The Shoeshine Guy enters the bathroom. At first, he is aghast to see George blackened with shoe polish and going crazy, rehearsing his new walk and his new dialect (Wilder went far off the page with this business). But, then, the man smiles. "Hey," he says, "you must be in pretty big trouble, fella! But, for God's sake, learn to keep time."

Grover returns with the train tickets. In the script, he says, "C'mon, Mister Bojangles. Let's get going." Pryor's line in the film is much funnier: "We'll make it past the cops. I just hope we don't meet no Muslims."

No one in the script believes that the white man with shoe polish on his face is a black man. They think he's crazy. Staring at a man "in open amazement" is not, as Pryor said, a man who "doesn't think it's anything unusual." Pryor was able to make the scene funnier, which is good, but he was wrong to assume Hiller, Higgins, Wilder, and everyone else working on the film was so insensitive that they failed to consider the feelings of black viewers.

Hiller, a true gentleman, never spoke badly of Pryor. He said, "We had, you know, people say, 'How, what's it like to work with a comedian?' And I said, 'No, I was working with an actor with a great comedy sense.'"[20]

Pryor didn't support the film when it was released. He said, "So I'm the token black, a modern Willie Best. It was a career move. And I'm sorry I did it. But I'll be glad when the movie is out and over with."[21] Pryor misjudged the film, which proved to be his first big success. *Silver Streak* was a film loved by comedy fans and disliked by critics. Vincent Canby of the *New York Times* wrote: "'Silver Streak' was directed by Arthur Hiller, a man whose work defies generalization. He's made good films (*The Hospital*), dreadful ones (*Plaza Suite*) and one gold mine (*Love Story*). *Silver Streak* is one he may want to forget as quickly as possible."[22]

After *Silver Streak*, Pryor became interested in starring in a black version of *Cyrano de Bergerac*, which would have had the actor fitted with a large prosthetic nose to play the famed poet-swordsman. But Pryor pulled out of the project on his agent's advice because the studio, Twentieth Century-Fox, put a novice director in charge.

Higgins went on to great success after his work on *Silver Streak*. He is best known today for directing *Foul Play* (1978) and *9 to 5* (1980).

When Wilder died in 2016, today's race-conscious journalists mostly remarked on the actor's politically incorrect blackface scene in *Silver Streak*. The scene received prominent attention in obituaries written by Elahe Izadi (*Washington Post*), Steven Zeitchik (*Los Angeles Times*), Robbie Collin (*The Telegraph*), and Stephen Dalton (*The Hollywood Reporter*).

Greased Lightning (1977)

Production: Third World Cinema and Warner Bros.
Distribution: Warner Bros.
Producer: Lester Berman and Hannah Weinstein
Director: Michael Schultz.
Screenplay: Lawrence DuKore, Kenneth Vose, Leon Capetanos, and Melvin Van Peebles.
Photography: George Bouillet.
Editors: Randy Roberts and Bob Wyman.
Music: Fred Karlin.
Release date: July 1, 1977.
Running time: 96 minutes.
Cast: Richard Pryor (Wendell Scott), Beau Bridges (Hutch), Pam Grier (Mary), Cleavon Little (Peewee), Vincent Gardenia (Sheriff Cotton), Richie Havens (Woodrow), Beau Welles (Earl Hindman), Noble Willingham (Billy Joe Byrnes)

Greased Lightning dramatizes the true-life experiences of stock car racing champion Wendell Scott. Scott learned to drive fast while transporting moonshine whiskey through the backwoods of Virginia. He attained legendary status in the field for being the first African-American to win a race in NASCAR's Grand National Series. Wikipedia reports, "Scott's career was repeatedly affected by racial prejudice and problems with top-level NASCAR officials. However, his determined struggle as an underdog won him thousands of white fans and many friends and admirers among his fellow racers."[1]

The original draft of the script was by Lawrence DuKore and Kenneth Vose. Vose wrote: "I've always been a racing fan. I used to listen to the Indy 500 on the radio when I was a kid in Brooklyn. The fascination with racing never left and to this day I seldom miss an Indycar or Formula One race…. As for myself, I got my competition license in 1974 and raced open-wheel cars in the SCCA until 1980."

Vose got the idea to write and direct a documentary on Scott. As he recalled:

> During a time when I was a writer/director at a small production company that made commercials and corporate films I discovered that one of the owners was a bit of a car guy. I pitched them on the

Pryor is locked up in jail for transporting moonshine whiskey in *Greased Lightning* (1977).

idea of a one-hour documentary about Wendell Scott to be called "Good 'ol Boy.".... and they went for it.

    I met Wendell for the first time at Texas World Speedway in 1974, pitched him the idea as he was eating old cold pizza while working on his racecar and he agreed. Somehow, after spending time with Wendell, it finally dawned on me that his story was too good for a standard TV doc. It had to be a feature film.²

DuKore wrote: "Ken and I were documentary film editors at CBS in the Walter Cronkite unit, which meant we were cutting room neighbors when I first began writing screenplays. Each time I finished a script, I gave [it] to Ken to read.... One day Ken told me that he had a story that would make a good movie. He told me about Wendell Scott."³

Vose recognized that DuKore's experience in writing screenplays would make him a useful collaborator on the project. The two traveled to Danville, Virginia, to get the full story from Scott. Their work on documentaries inspired them to gather as many facts as they could to tell Scott's story accurately. Vose wrote: "[W]e spent about a week listening to his incredible life story as he drove us around to visit the actual locations for many of the events that eventually showed up on screen."

It can be difficult to encapsulate a person's life within the usual restrictions of a biopic, but DuKore could not remember having problems when writing the script. "We didn't dwell on Wendell's relationship with his wife Mary because theirs appeared to be a good marriage. It was always about Wendell and his dream, to race stocks. And of course the dramatic event always centered on racism and Jim Crow in the late fifties, morphing to the nineteen seventies when Wendell's acceptance and victories (on the track) coincided with Supreme Court decisions (Brown v. Board of Education), Dr. King, Robert Kennedy and the history of the civil rights movement."⁴ DuKore continued, "I wrote the first draft and Ken improved upon it (thank God!) with his revised draft, after which I found out that a producer named Hannah Weinstein was looking for a project for

Cleavon Little and Pryor in *Greased Lightning* (1977).

Richard Pryor, who had just made *Silver Streak*.... I went up to her New York office and left a copy of the script (then called "Good Old Boy") on her desk. Two days later, she called. The following week, Ken and I had a contract."[5]

Weinstein founded the Third World Cinema Corporation to produce films with African-American artists. The company's one previous film was *Claudine* (1974), a comedy-drama that starred Diahann Carroll and James Earl Jones as a couple struggling with love, money, and children in Harlem. It was a policy of Third World Cinema that no film could be produced by the company unless an African-American director and writer were attached to the project. Vose suggested Melvin Van Peebles as a director. Van Peebles agreed to direct the film as well as contribute as a writer.

Vose and DuKore met with Van Peebles at his office in New York City. Vose was forever impressed by one aspect of the meeting: "[Van Peebles] pretty much told us that we sucked as screenwriters but that he could fix everything."[6]

DuKore doubts that the film would have been made if Weinstein hadn't been looking for a vehicle for Pryor. He wrote: "Making movies is ... mostly about timing."[7]

When we first meet him, Wendell Scott is struggling to provide for his wife and kids as a taxi driver. Wendell grows frustrated because he knows the money he earns will never allow him to fulfill his dream of opening a garage. He approaches a bootlegger, Slack, to get extra work transporting moonshine whiskey.

For five years, Sheriff Cotton and his men fail in their efforts to apprehend Wendell, who is simply too fast for them. Slack is arrested in a raid and asks Wendell to take over one of his runs. But it turns out that Slack set him up as part of a plea deal and the police have patrol cars situated to capture him.

Billy Joe Byrnes, who owns the local racetrack, sees that Wendell has the potential to be a champion stock car driver. He tells him that he will persuade the sheriff to drop the more serious charges and release him on probation if he can prove his skills on the racetrack. As the first black stock car driver, Wendell is greeted with hostility at the racetrack by other drivers, some of whom attempt to run him off the track during the race. He manages in the end to make it across the finish line, an accomplishment that fills him with great pride. He decides at that moment to pursue a career in racing.

A crucial scene takes place at a racetrack in Jacksonville, Florida. Sports journalist Tommy Tomlinson wrote: "[Scott] won only once, in Jacksonville in 1963.... But when the race ended, NASCAR officials said Buck Baker had won, and that's what the fans went home thinking. The officials went over to Scott later and said there had been a 'scoring error.' Scott got his winner's check. But he died in 1990 without ever getting the trophy."[8]

Scott did not believe there was a scoring error. The problem, he insisted, was that the sanctioning body did not want him in Victory Lane with the white trophy girl, whose primary duties were to hand the winner the trophy and congratulate him with a kiss.

Beau Bridges and Pryor in *Greased Lightning* (1977).

On screen, Wendell continues to show his racing skills over the next few years. He becomes a celebrity once he joins the Grand National circuit. But then, he crashes his car during a race and has to be hospitalized. Although Mary insists that he retire, he remains determined to return to racing. He surprises friends and family when he finally announces he's returning to the Grand National.

The Jacksonville was the only race that Scott won. But a NASCAR champ doesn't need to win races. NASCAR has a system that awards points and earnings to riders who finish a race in the top 10. Scott finished in the top 10 in 147 out of 495 races. It was on the basis of this achievement that, from 1966 to 1969, he was consistently ranked in the top 10 of racers. But the filmmakers had to build the climax around a race. A film audience did not care about a driver achieving championship status based on points; they wanted to see the driver being the first competitor roaring across the finish line in a major winner-take-all race. So, that's what the audience got with Wendell's Grand National comeback.

Wendell is so anxious during a pit stop that he drives away before his crew has finished attaching the lug nuts to a tire. He runs twenty more laps with his tire wobbling, but he passes his rival Beau Welles and reaches the finish line for another NASCAR victory. The film freezes on a final shot of Wendell waving the victory flag.

The role of Scott was originally offered to Cleavon Little, but the producers changed their minds suddenly. They told Little that, after reconsidering the matter, they thought he was not right for the role; he was better suited to play Scott's friend Peewee. Little was so disappointed that he turned down their offer. He had a film coming up with Robert Altman and didn't need to bother with *Greased Lightning*. But, according to Little, executives at Warner Bros. stepped into the negotiations. The studio, which was producing both *Greased Lightning* and the Altman film, informed the actor that he couldn't do one film unless he did the other. Little, though upset by the studio's tactics, acquiesced. He came to regret his decision after the Altman film was canceled.

Pryor wrote: "I was blown away when a movie that seemed to have substance came along and the producers wanted me to star. Was I ready to carry a film?"[9]

Greased Lightning was filmed in various towns in Georgia, including Winder, Athens, Madison, and Bryon. The car races were filmed at Athens Speedway and Middle Georgia Raceway.

As usual, studio executives were worried about Pryor. He recalled: "[T]he studio worried about my volatile reputation. I was more concerned about doing a good job, and to that end I vowed to stay clean throughout the entire movie. I rented a farmhouse on some of the prettiest property I've ever seen, and flew my grandmother out from Peoria to take care of things."[10]

For once, a film ran into personnel issues that had nothing to do with Pryor. "It got off to a rocky start when the original director, Melvin Van Peebles, tried stirring up shit about there not being enough jobs for blacks on the production," he explained. "His effort fizzled when I refused to support him."[11]

Vose wrote: "Reports coming out of Georgia during the first week or so were not promising. I received a call from Hannah concerning changes to the script and then one asking me to come to L.A. and look at the dailies with her. The upshot was that Melvin was taking a different approach to Wendell's story and was indeed changing the tone of the film. Pryor was also said to be unhappy. Hannah fired Melvin and got Warner Bros. to shut down the production for a couple of weeks until she could bring in a new director."[12]

Van Peebles exited the film a month into production. He told the *Los Angeles Times*, "My version was more stylized and [Warner Bros.] wanted it more naturalistic."[13]

Schultz said,

> I heard after the fact, "Oh, Richard's doing this movie called *Greased Lightning* with Melvin Van Peebles directing," and I said, "That dirty dog, he's supposed to wait for my movie [*Which Way Is Up?*]!" (laughter). So, evidently, Melvin and the producer had some severe creative differences about making the movie so either Melvin quit or they fired him and the movie came to a standstill. Well, Steve [Krantz] and I were going down to the set in Georgia to work on the script [for *Which Way Is Up?*] with Richard, ... And so I knew a little bit about what was going on but not that there was any conflict there. So, when Melvin left the scene, Richard called me up and said, "Would you come and take over this movie?" I thought to myself, "Oh, no, I do not want to...."[14]

But he did it anyway. Pryor said, "Michael Schultz came in and saved it."[15]

Van Peebles got a screenplay credit even though, according to DuKore, his only contribution to the script was the new title, "Greased Lightning." The inspiration for that was a hot rod named Greased Lightnin' that was featured in the stage musical *Grease*.

When he joined the project, Schultz brought in Leon Capetanos to handle revisions. Capetanos is best known today for his collaborations with director Paul Mazursky on the scripts for *Moscow on the Hudson* (1984), *Down and Out in Beverly Hills* (1986), and *Moon Over Parador* (1988). DuKore was satisfied with Capetanos's work: "[He] did a good job."[16]

Pryor was glad to have Scott as a consultant on the film. He said, "[Scott] is an amazing person, more amazing than in the film. And I'm glad the film is that way, too. He dismissed it like the game, whatever the game was supposed to be, when a nigger was supposed to be in his place. He didn't even fight, you know what I'm sayin'? But he still went on and he did his thing. He said: 'Oh, okay, s'cuse me, let me just go do what I want to do. That's what knocked me out about him, because he's got a lesson for everybody."[17]

Scott instructed Pryor on driving a stock car. As Pryor recalled:

> I went down with the intention not to drive because I'm afraid of cars and I said, "I'm not going to drive more than thirty-five miles an hour." But then you go around the track a couple of times ... you get to go faster and faster. Wendell showed me how. I drove once. I was going about ninety miles an hour on the track in a '71 model and the engine blew—that's because I didn't know how to drive, 'cause I didn't shift to third from second.... Then the brakes locked—you've got to see the footage of me sitting there with a little smile, because in my mind I said, "Well, God, you saved my goat. You didn't have to be in the car, I told you that."[18]

Scott said, "I had a very good relationship with Richard. I would tell him how to do things, and he was very cooperative. And he never did use one word of profanity the whole time we were making the movie. I'm a little old-fashioned, and so they warned me that the guy would be cursing. But I guess he respected my feelings."[19]

Despite his good relationship with Pryor, Scott was not happy as a consultant. He didn't like the fact that, except for Pryor, the people working on the film rarely took his suggestions. He also expressed concern about the way his pit crew was portrayed. Scott said, "Hutch was really a great big guy, not small like Beau [Bridges]—and I was *lucky* he was big because he and I had to fight our way out of the race track a lot of times." Scott's mechanic, Linwood Carter, was portrayed in the film as a mechanical genius. Scott said, "They should've used that character for comic relief. Linwood was perfect for that:

he was so stupid he could barely change a tire. But he was the best I could do for a pit crew, and you never got that from the movie."[20]

In the film, Wendell's fourth-place finish in his first Grand National race earns him a special prize—dinner for two at a steakhouse. Wendell doesn't bring his wife to the restaurant—he brings Hutch. A drunken racist approaches their table, insulting them. Hutch kicks the man to the floor and uses the restaurant's Confederate flag to hold other customers at bay while he and Wendell exit the restaurant with their steak dinners. Janet Maslin of the *New York Times* wrote: "[The white patrons] clearly find Mr. Bridges' character the more dangerous and unsavory of the two."[21]

The character of Hutch was based a man named Earl Brooks. Scott's biographer, Brian Donovan, wrote:

> Two of Scott's white friends, Buck Drummond and Lynchburg racer Earl Brooks, played a vital role for Scott in these early years of his driving career. Both were large, tough men who did not mind arguing or throwing a punch. Sometimes they served as Scott's bodyguards and advocates, protecting him from fights and taking his side in wrangles with officials. "I'd have had to fight my way out of some of the places where I raced because the drivers didn't accept me if it hadn't been for Earl Brooks.... He took care of a lot of business for me," said Scott.[22]

One time, a promoter tried to cheat Scott out of prize money. Donovan wrote:

> Drummond tore off his shirt and confronted the promoter. A brawny roofer and building contractor, Drummond stood over six feet tall and weighed more than two hundred pounds. He told the promoter, Scott said, that "Y'all going to pay this boy. This boy here's a nigger, and you think you ain't going to pay him, but I'll die for him right here." Man, he was ready to go to war. Quickly, the promoter paid Scott.... Later, Scott said, Drummond apologized to him for saying the word *nigger*. He said he just wanted to talk to the promoter in his own language. Scott told him not to worry. He never heard Drummond use the word again.[23]

Pryor said that Scott's approach toward race relations "was different from how I would do it as a black man today, because I would have taken a shotgun with me. And he don't have none of that feeling."[24] But that is not true. Scott asserted himself aggressively on the racetrack. Tomlinson wrote: "A driver named Jack Smith started giving Scott trouble in 1962. Scott had shattered Smith's track record in Savannah, so Smith set out to wreck Scott—and he finally did in Winston-Salem. The next race came around, and on the pace lap, Smith pulled up close and pointed his finger at Scott. Scott pulled out a gun and pointed it at Smith. That was pretty much the end of that feud."[25]

Scott made it clear to the filmmakers that he never shied away from a confrontation. But they did not want their sports hero to threaten his opponents with a gun. They preferred that Pryor portray Scott in a more docile manner. Rovin wrote: "[T]he producers felt it best to restrict the flare-ups to Beau Bridges' character so that their hero wouldn't be unlikable."[26] The one time in the film that Pryor is allowed to express rage occurs in the scene when he is denied his rightful trophy at Jacksonville.

Scott was eager to become involved in different areas of production. He took pride in building replicas of his old cars for the racing scenes. Donovan wrote: "A sizable share of Scott's profits [as a whiskey runner] went into building the highly modified cars that a whiskey runner needed to escape his pursuers. The cars Scott built look like drab, ordinary sedans, but with their souped-up engines and stiffened springs, they could outrun police cars even while hauling heavy loads."[27] But the veteran driver grew bitter after the filmmakers refused to let him double for Pryor in the racing scenes. It seemed unfair when he saw that the man hired to double for the film's fictional villain, Beau Welles, was, according to Scott, a man "who had really been one of my worst enemies on the racetrack."[28] It turned out that the man, Neil Castles, Sr., had established himself as a stunt man in previous films. But it worked out for Scott in the end. Schultz didn't think that the race footage that Van Peebles had shot was realistic and agreed to let Scott recreate his racing feats.

Greased Lightning benefits greatly from Schultz's natural, relaxed directorial style. It is a breezy, entertaining film that would do well on a double bill with *Bingo Long*. But the film comes across at times as an uneven blend of action, comedy, and biography. It was likely due to the recent success of *Smokey and the Bandit* (1977) that the film's comic car chases received the greatest prominence in the film's trailers. The sheriff crashes through a chicken house, which collapses in every direction. Audiences did not go to see this film expecting a profound historical drama about segregation. They went to see a cops-vs.-moonshine-runners carsploitation comedy, which was a familiar car chase genre that began with *The Road Hustlers* (1968). Later films in the increasingly successful genre included *White Lightning* (1973), *The Last American Hero* (1973), *It's Up to Us* (1973), *Big Bad Mama* (1974), *Moonrunners* (1975), *Moonshine County Express* (1977), and *Hooch* (1977). Schultz said, "Burt Reynolds had done a movie called *White Lightning* where he played an ex-con moonshiner, and so this was a complete non-comedic, straight dramatic role and Richard was intrigued by that."[29]

Andy Devine defined the genre's plump, clownish redneck sheriff in *The Road Hustlers*. *Greased Lightning* filled this stock role with Vincent Gardenia, who had already played an easily outwitted and frequently flustered sheriff in *The Front Page* (1974).

Jeff Bridges, Beau's younger brother, starred in *The Last American Hero*, a biopic about another moonshine-runner-turned-stock-car-champion, this one specifically dramatizing the career of NASCAR champ Junior Johnson. Runners like Johnson built their reputations on outdriving the law. In time, the runners competed against each other for bragging rights in informal races that were held along the winding mountain roads of the Appalachian region. In 1947, the racers organized NASCAR, which transformed the backwoods races into popular entertainment. Today, NASCAR is a multi-billion dollar industry.

Vose and DuKore wrote a novelization of *Greased Lightning* that varies in many ways from the finished film. Scott's story greatly benefits from the additional depth and detail that the authors were able to provide in the novel. Meanwhile, *Greased Lightning* the movie was disparaged by a number of critics for being a formula sports biopic. Marshall Fine of the *Clarion-Ledger* wrote: "How many times has the story been filmed? Young, underprivileged athlete battles his way to the top against incredible odds. At the peak, he has a crippling accident that takes him out of competition, possibly forever. The will to win is not dead, however; while his wife begs him to quit, the athlete gears up for one last try at the crown."[30] But formula sports films, fictional or nonfictional, have been vastly entertaining in their own narrow way for more than a hundred years.

Robert Boris, who would later give Pryor another dramatic turn in *Some Kind of Hero*, said, "[Richard] really loved *Greased Lightning*.... He loved that because it was based on a true story.... He talked about that film a lot with me during [the] two weeks I spent with him at his house in Hawaii."[31]

Scott was dissatisfied with the money he made from the film. He was paid $25,000 up front and promised a percentage of the profits. He expected to become rich once the film was released. But it never happened. Warner Bros. claimed that the film lost money.

It bothered Scott even more that Pryor didn't keep in contact with him. He expected the film star to help him to launch a new career as a stunt driver.

Pryor was at a crucial time in his career. He was about to move on to his second star vehicle.

Which Way Is Up? (1977)

Production and Distribution: Universal Pictures.
Producer: Steve Krantz.
Director: Michael Schultz.
Screenplay: Carl Gottlieb and Cecil Brown, adapted from "The Seduction of Mimi" by Lina Wertmüller.
Photography: John A. Alonzo.
Editor: Danford B. Greene.
Music: Paul Riser and Mark Davis.
Release date: November 4, 1977.
Running time: 94 minutes.
Cast: Richard Pryor (Leroy Jones), Lonette McKee (Vanetta), Margaret Avery (Annie Mae), Morgan Woodward (Mr. Mann), Marilyn Coleman (Sister Sarah), Bebe Drake-Hooks (Thelma), Gloria Edwards (Janelle), Ernesto Hernandez (Jose Reyes), Otis Day (Sugar), Morgan Roberts (Henry), Diane Rodriguez (Estrella Reyes), Dolph Sweet (The Boss), Timothy Thomerson (Tour Guide), Danny Valdez (Chuy Estrada), Luis Valdez (Ramon Juarez), Paul Mooney (Inspector Caine), Harry Northup (Chief Goon).

Pryor said of *Which Way Is Up?*, "It's about working people and success and failure."[1] He saw the lead character, Leroy, as a young man who had yet to find who he is and recognize his greatest strengths. He said, "[He] doesn't know he is bright yet."[2]

Leroy (Pryor) and his wife, Annie Mae (Avery), live with Leroy's father Rufus, Rufus's young wife Janelle (Edwards), and Janelle's two small children. Leroy is frustrated because Annie Mae keeps rejecting his sexual advances. It makes it worse that he can hear his father through the bedroom wall having passionate sex with Janelle.

Leroy works as a fruit picker. He is on a ladder, picking oranges, when

Luis Valdez hails Pryor for his brave support of the union in *Which Way Is Up?* (1977).

members of the Field Workers Union arrive at the orchard to protest. The orchard owner's goons and the police arrive to break up the protest. Leroy's ladder is accidentally tipped over by a forklift, which lands him in the middle of the protest. The union leader, Ramon Juarez, believes that Leroy has bravely come forward to support their cause. He is declared a hero. (This is similar to a scene in *Modern Times* [1936], in which Charlie Chaplin's Tramp character innocently picks up a red flag that dropped off the back of a truck and suddenly finds himself leading a throng of communist agitators through the street.) The orchard owner's goons show up at Leroy's home with carbines and shotguns. The chief goon hands the alleged agitator a bus ticket and instructs him to leave town.

Margaret Avery and Pryor in *Which Way Is Up?* (1977).

Harry Northup appears in the film as the chief goon. He had admired Pryor since he had seen him perform stand-up at the Improv in the 1960s. He was even more impressed by the comedian's work in multiple roles in *Which Way Is Up?*. He said, "I think that's his best work as an actor."[3] Northup worked on the film for a week. He socialized mostly with Luis Valdez, Danny Valdez, and Diane Rodriguez. Valdez, who came from a family of migrant farm workers, had founded the El Teatro Campesino, a theatre troupe that consisted exclusively of farm workers. He is best known today as the screenwriter of *La Bamba* (1987).

Northup said that he made a point to play his character as "a hard, nasty guy."[4] The fact that the fruit pickers were black and Mexican and the goons were white created a racial tension in those scenes. This is the way the first such scene was described in the script:

> ANGLE ON THE GOONS
> (They are big, ugly, strike-breaking, head-cracking, nigger-whipping Redneck Crackers, all Tee-shirts, beer bellies, baseball hats, boots and jeans.)
> CHIEF GOON: Let those men work, you commie faggot!
> SECOND GOON: Juarez, you stink, you smell!
> THIRD GOON: I can smell you from here, you rotten commie bum!
> (The other goons pick up on the insults and hoot and jeer, trying to drown out Juarez's clarion voice.)[5]

Northup knew that he had done a good job because, after he finished the scene, he was greeted grimly by a black sound man, Willie Burton. Northup wrote: "[Willie] was peeling a grapefruit. He said, 'If this was a bomb, I'd throw it right in your face.'"[6]

Pryor was not cordial towards the actor either. Northup wrote: "I remember walking around Richard as he sat in his director's chair, in between scenes, and he looked at me

Pryor takes his job seriously as a factory foreman in *Which Way Is Up?* (1977).

with a sense of wariness, as if I might hit him."[7] But Northup said, "I saw Richard at the wrap party in Westwood and he was friendly to me."[8]

As the film continues, Leroy ends up in Los Angeles, where he falls in love with a union organizer named Vanetta. She becomes interested in Leroy once she learns that he was a labor hero in his hometown. He moves in with her and, before long, the couple has a baby.

Leroy earns enough money as a hotel porter to support his family. The family is, by every indication, content. But, then, Leroy is carrying wine bottles through a corridor when he encounters a hitman preparing to assassinate Juarez, who is speaking at a conference. Leroy shouts in alarm, which causes the hitman to miss his target.

Leroy is interviewed about the incident by a police detective, Inspector Caine. He notices that the detective is wearing the same type of uniquely decorative gold ring worn by the orchard owner and the hitman. He refuses to identify the hitman for fear he will be killed. The owner of Agrico, who hired the hitman, is grateful that Leroy kept his mouth shut. He tells him that he wants him to be the manager of an orange juice canning factory that is located back in Leroy's hometown.

Leroy, who wants to maintain a respectable image as the factory manager, returns to his wife, Annie Mae, while he maintains a secret residence for Vanetta and his child on the other side of town. Vanetta accepts the arrangement on the condition that Leroy never has sex with his wife.

During his absence, Annie Mae has gotten a job and gotten to see more of the world. It is through her new worldliness that she has become sexually liberated. This is no longer the shy wife he knew before he left town. Annie Mae finds her newly successful husband attractive and is eager to have sex with him. But Leroy keeps telling her that he is too tired for sex. Annie Mae becomes desperate to excite Leroy. She figures that he might enjoy bondage and discipline play. He has just climbed into bed to fall asleep when she saunters into the room in scanty black lingerie. She quickly comes up behind him and handcuffs him to the bed. She snaps a whip. "Behold," she proclaims, "the Baroness Monique!" Annie Mae straddles Leroy's back and rides him like a horse. She is bouncing up and down so hard that she breaks the bed. Leroy's family arrives home just in time to see the couple in action. Rufus, appalled, shouts, "He turned into a freak like his mama!"

Annie Mae complains to her girlfriends that Leroy is uninterested in having sex with her. This causes rumors to spread that he is gay. The situation gets worse when he finds out that Annie Mae managed to become pregnant without him. Leroy is furious. He storms into his house and grabs Annie Mae by her throat. She reveals to him that the father of her child is her spiritual counselor, Reverend Lenox Thomas. She explains that she became desperate because Leroy wasn't having sex with her. Leroy demands to know why she never talked to him about the problem. She says that she assumed Leroy was either impotent or gay. Leroy is outraged. "I'll tell you what I am," he says, "I'm plenty of man, baby! When it comes to fucking, I am *numero uno*. Because I got an old lady across town, baby, and she loves it. You know what I mean? Not like you. She *loves* it!" He reveals to Annie Mae that he and Vanetta have a baby boy. He expects this to be the last word on the matter. But, as he turns to leave, a knife comes flying past his head and gets stuck in the door. Now, it's Annie Mae's turn to attack *him*. She charges after him with a meat cleaver.

Leroy's vanity demands that he take revenge against the reverend, regardless of the consequences. He goes to the church to assault the man in front of his congregation. But he is moved by the reverend's sermon, which is inspired by the Gospel of Matthew: "Do unto others as you would have them do unto you." In his vindictive state of mind, Leroy takes this to mean that he should do to the reverend what *he* has done to *him*. (Pryor described Reverend Thomas as "flashy, conducts services as if they're rock concerts."[9]) He decides then and there to seduce the reverend's wife, Sarah, the church pianist. This, he is sure, will hurt the man far more than a beating. Leroy approaches Sarah for piano lessons and makes with the sweet talk. Sarah resists him at first, but she eventually succumbs to Leroy's charm. After the two have sex, Leroy admits to Sarah the reason that he seduced her. She is infuriated to learn that her husband got Annie Mae pregnant, but she is even more infuriated to learn that Leroy made a fool of her. She attacks him as violently as Annie Mae attacked him earlier. She insists that he has not fully punished her husband for his infidelity: Leroy must get her pregnant. Sarah becomes very aggressive, exhausting Leroy with her sexual demands. He no longer has the stamina to have sex with Vanetta, which creates a divide between the couple.

Leroy has become a no-nonsense manager at the plant, which has made him unpopular with his old friends. It has turned out that, due to his recent decisions, he has lost the love and respect of his friends and family.

Once Sarah is pregnant, Leroy confronts the reverend during a church service to deliver the news. Other women in the church rise from their seats to denounce the reverend for seducing them as well. The reverend is chased into the street by his congregation and is fatally struck by a tour bus.

Leroy approaches Sarah at her husband's funeral to express his condolences, but she glares at him and tells him to "get lost." Annie Mae returns her wedding ring to him. Vanetta leaves town with their son. Leroy now has no one. He is so distraught that he quits his job. The final scene shows Leroy walking, alone, down an empty road.

On April 8, 1975, *The Hollywood Reporter* announced that producer Steve Krantz had contracted Pryor to star in an American remake of Lina Wertmüller's Italian comedy *The Seduction of Mimi*. Pryor brought in a friend, Cecil Brown, to write the script. Schultz said: "[W]e were so disappointed in what he had delivered that even Richard, who recommended him, said, 'Oh, man, I'm sorry. This is not working.' So, we hired Carl Gottlieb, somebody that we would never think of to write this material, because he had the comic sensibility that we were looking for in making this Italian piece a real American piece."[10]

Gottlieb had written sketches for Pryor to perform on Flip Wilson's variety show. As he recalled, "[The sketches] played very, very well."[11] So, he seemed like a good choice for the project. He also said:

> The producer suggested we work together and I listened to what Richard wanted to do. He and I went to Barbados. I went with my wife and Richard went with Pam Grier, who he was dating at the time. He rented a villa for two weeks and we spent the time there writing ... talking about the characters. He thought he could have fun playing several different characters instead of just the lead role. Richard said, "I can do Mudbone.... I can do the preacher" and Michael Schultz thought that was a great idea. So I re-wrote the script to accommodate those characters.[12]

Gottlieb ran a tape recorder while he and Richard threw out ideas. "It was a very healthy collaboration because [Richard] was very intent on making the movie work," Gottlieb said.[13]

Wertmüller made a point in *Mimi*, as she had with her other films, to create characters that were vulgar and grotesque. This was well suited to Pryor's earthy style of comedy. Gottlieb also thought that the political elements of *Mimi* suited Pryor. He said:

> [The film is] about farm labor and agribusiness and the exploitation of workers, which came directly out of Lina Wertmüller's particular brand of Italian socialism.... I was happy to write it because I came from political theater. I was very happy to get as much politics as I could into the movie, especially with a spokesman like Richard, who really spoke across class lines but whose experience was with the underclass ... black or white, it didn't matter. Real blue collar. Still, he was very funny. All I had to do was listen to the cadences of his speech and reproduce it as a screenwriter. The same with the other actors. I knew several of the Hispanic actors from the L.A. comedy scene.... [I]t all worked out fine.[14]

Saul wrote: "The farmworkers' union now gave the movie its moral thrust; it was the larger solution to a world where blacks and Latinos worked for poverty wages in the fields while company bosses snaked around in limos, surrounded themselves with goons, and ordered hits on union leaders. The union's adversary in the film is Agrico Industries, a hydra-headed conglomerate whose motto is 'We Grow on You' and whose top executive has the all-white suit and decadent manners of a southern plantation owner."[15]

Production was delayed because the change of directors on *Greased Lightning* put Schultz and Pryor behind schedule in Georgia. Shooting commenced in Los Angeles on January 6, 1977. Schultz said, "That script was a completely fluid animal up until the day we started shooting. It was an idea that we were constantly molding and mashing around to try to make it real for America."[16]

Schultz said of Pryor, "He was a joy to work with. Very creative. Very funny."[17] He found him to be less predictable than other actors with whom he had worked. He said, "Richard would never say the same line twice…. It was great fun but it was something you really couldn't plan on."[18] Schultz had to manage his star's unpredictability as well as his anxiety. He said, "Richard's a worrier. Everything's been going so smoothly, he think something's going to go wrong. He asked, 'How's it going? Does it *look* all right?' I said, '*Perfect!*' Richard finally smiled and said, 'Jus don' fuck with it, huh? It just feels so natural it *can't* be right."[19]

Pryor gave Schultz credit for helping him create his characters: "He helps me find them and listens, weighs what I say and lets me flow."[20]

Avery later said that Pryor was her favorite leading man. She described him as "a very shy man, a very talented man."[21] She was charmed, as many women were, by his vulnerability.

The filming was completed, on schedule, in fifty-six days.

Wertmüller described *The Seduction of Mimi* as the "simple story of a man in relation to his society or in conflict with it, a man who arrives unprepared, naïve, and is confronted with the machinery of a certain society which he is forced to make peace with."[22] Grace Russo Bullaro, author of *Man in Disorder: The Cinema of Lina Wertmüller in the 1970s*, identified the writer's protagonists as "[underdogs] confronted by powerful institutions."[23] She wrote: "Mimi has been manipulated by outside forces that he does not understand and that he foolishly and blindly believes to be in his control."[24]

Mimi doesn't like being forced to vote for the Mafia's candidate, Carmine Cannamozza, in a forthcoming political election. Mafia goons say, "Anyone lacking respect for Mr. Carmine Cannamozza shows a lack of respect for Don Calogero." Mimi votes for the Communist candidate who opposes Cannamozza in a secret ballot that's not really secret.

Mimi has to leave town to avoid being killed for his defiance. He moves to Turin, where he gets a job with a construction company. When a co-worker suffers a fatal fall from a scaffold, Mafia men figure that the man was an undocumented worker and they can avoid trouble by dumping his body someplace where no one will find it. They throw the corpse into the back of a truck. Mimi also gets into the back of the truck, assuming the men are taking his friend to the hospital. When the mobsters find Mimi there, they plan to kill him and make it look like a traffic accident. But Mimi, thinking quickly, convinces them that his wife is a godchild of Don Calogero. So, instead of being killed, he is given a soft, high-paying job.

The film manages, in broad and vigorous strokes, to combine the elements of a sex comedy with the elements of a social satire. For Mimi, power struggles are deeply ingrained in labor and sexual relations. The film involves his seduction of a different woman in each act of the story, but even more, it involves his own seduction by money and power.

Mimi feels compelled to assure his own personal advancement but he also feels relentless pressure from his friends to achieve solidarity with his fellow workers. His co-workers, who are calling for better conditions and wages, criticize Mimi for failing to attend their meetings. Mimi's excuse is that he has to do better for his son. One of them replies, "We all have children, dammit. Some of us give a shit. Some of us don't. That's all." Wilkins wrote: "[T]he party members function like a Greek chorus, the voice of Mimi's conscience, reminding him at every step that he has a choice."[25] It is a conflict that he is unable to resolve.

Wertmüller makes the mistake of suggesting that a man must choose between security and dignity. Life, for the most part, is not as simple or rigid as that. Bullaro wrote: "When these false dichotomies are created, the director shirks the more difficult responsibility of finding a middle ground."[26]

Gottlieb was mistaken in his interpretation of *Mimi*'s politics. Wertmüller expressed cynicism in regards to the political elements of the story. Mimi shows that he is giving up on communism when he has his mistress, Fiore, remove the portrait of Lenin over their bed. Wertmüller was more interested in the sexual politics. The film's labor politics must, in Wertmüller's view, eventually be overshadowed by this. But Gottlieb, in contrast, saw unquestionable moral value in laborers fighting for rights.

Wertmüller is willing to mock the opposing ideologies of communism and capitalism because she mistrusts ideology in general. She said, "Ideology is dangerous. Man must try to keep a clear head and try to think for himself about how to confront problems, where we are, where we come from—to all the big questions of life."[27] It could be confusing for some that the director refuses to pick a side in this war of political philosophies. John Simon of *New York Magazine* wrote: "[A]mbivalence is what makes [Wertmüller's] films so rich: the realization that nothing is black or white; this or that."[28]

Don Vito tells Mimi that capitalists are orderly and efficient and that communist principles lead to unproductivity. He tells Mimi, "Communist dreams aren't for you. We need bosses here. There's things to organize." He wants Mimi to, in the words of Wilkins, "side with 'the bosses' (whether capitalist or Mafioso) against the workers, who, like Mimi, are seen as feckless dreamers who need a strong hand to guide them."

Mimi comes to echo Don Vito's vision in the end. He says, "We need order around here. There has to be profits or the plant won't function…. Progress has confused everyone. It's a swindle."

Wertmüller was denigrated by a number of critics for her crude depiction of Marxism. Bullaro does not see the director's portrayal of Marxism as relevant because Mimi never truly commits to the ideology and, in the end, it has no real effect on the story.

Mimí falls in love with a communist activist, Fiore (Mariangela Melato). Stuart Galbraith IV of DVD Talk wrote: "[H]e wins her over with persistent teary-eyed declarations of love."[29] Bud Wilkins of *Slant Magazine* wrote: "Mimi's conquest of Fiore allows him to adopt a new identity. He stands in front of a mirror, his once unruly locks restrained by a hair net, trimming his mustache. Each persona requires its corresponding mask."[30]

Generoso Fierro of Forces of Geek recognized the challenge that Schultz had to "[convert] the eternal schlubby Mimi of Wertmüller's film into Leroy, a California grape picker who accidentally becomes a union leader."[31] Gottlieb told *Mother Jones* magazine: "We didn't want to use the Mafia as the heavies, so we made it Agribusiness—conglomerates who just happened to grow food as their product. Our story is about a guy who would always make the expeditious choice, the most convenient, the most attractive, the most comfortable, and that just about ruins him—until the end of the picture. Then he finds his strength: he sees that every time he's made the expeditious choice it puts him in deeper shit."[32]

Saul wrote: "Wertmüller's *The Seduction of Mimi* was a ripe Italian parable about the idiocy of machismo: its title character was a bumbler in politics and love, confused enough to become, in turn, a Communist and a tool of the Mafia, and foolish enough to think that he can enter the bedrooms of three different women without paying a price for his conniving...."[33]

Leroy is foolishly carried along by his emotions—fear, lust, love, and revenge. He is obsessed with his own masculine vanity and strength, but it is the women in his life who demonstrate greater vanity and strength.

Leroy is making his way awkwardly through life, struggling to find out who he is and what his place is in the world. Pryor is uninhibited in the film. He is wild and vulgar. He engages in pure slapstick, which is not present in the original version. At one point, Pryor looks to start a conversation with Vanetta by joining her on a jogging trail. He struggles to keep up with this fit young woman who has obviously traveled this trail on many occasions. Finally, he becomes so exhausted that he collapses and flops to the ground. The scene is something out of an early Woody Allen film; it works well for Pryor as well.

Which Way Is Up? is, without a doubt, a funny film. Gottlieb was a clever writer who understood Pryor's strengths as a performer. Leroy, a character plagued by fear, anger, and frustration, is well-suited to him. Gottlieb has modestly stated, "All I had to do was listen to the cadences of [Richard's] speech and reproduce it as a screenwriter."[34] But he did more than that. The film only fails in comparison with its superior predecessor, *The Seduction of Mimi*. Giancarlo Giannini is masterful in the title role. Mimi's arrogance and vanity are not conveyed by the actor in a way that deters the viewer from liking him. These are just flaws that make Mimi human and, in the end, expose him as a tragic figure. Galbraith wrote: "[Giannini is] spectacularly foolish on camera, alternately oafish, cowardly, and full of Sicilian bravado, childish, joyful, terrified, heartsick, and disingenuous."[35] It is, from beginning to end, a rich and endearing performance.

Then, we come to climax of the story. Mimi's rival is shot by a Mafia gunman. Mimi, who is unjustly blamed for the murder, is sent to prison.

Biskind wrote:

> [A]t the moment of his release, he is set upon by mobs of children from the various families for which he is now responsible: Fiore and her child, Rosalia and her child, and Amalia and her six children. In order to support them, he is forced into the employ of the Mafia. The penultimate shot reveals the scene [as] the reverse of the opening one: Mimi is distributing leaflets to the workers of the rock quarry from the same sound truck we saw at the beginning. He has come full circle. Fiore, coming upon him in the humiliating scene, repudiates him. She drives off with a little red truck marked with a hammer and sickle, leaving Mimi a broken, isolated figure, alone in a featureless landscape.

The landscape is important to the story. The stark and barren sulphur quarry has a much greater impact than the lush citrus groves of sunny California. But *Which Way Is Up?* is designed, in every way, to avoid the grimness of *Mimi*. Unlike Mimi, Leroy shakes off his reversals like a bad hangover and moves on. This is the way the final shot of *Which Way Is Up?* is described in the script: "And he proudly turns his back and walks away, leaving Agrico forever. He turns a corner, and almost bursts into a headlong run, but retains control, and walks away (fast) from his troubles, gaining strength as he goes." One source described Leroy's walk as "jaunty."[36] He is obviously happy to be free of everyone. It is suggested by this happy ending that he is too shallow to suffer for his mistakes. He knows that he screwed up, but, in the end, it worked out to his benefit, so it's not something he needs to worry about.

Mimi's cocky attitude is deeply ingrained. The bravado that Leroy often exhibits is a pretense, more a defense mechanism than an actual feeling or outlook. The arrogance and vanity that is so pivotal to Mimi's downfall are clearly not the emotions that govern Leroy. As portrayed by Pryor, Leroy is helpless, vulnerable, exasperated, and desperate. Mimi and Leroy are alike in that they both operate on an emotional level. Their emotions are more important to them than morals or reason. Either man does whatever he believes he has to do for the moment to carry on. But Leroy is different from Mimi in that he is motivated more by fear than vanity.

Saul wrote:

> Richard's Leroy Jones is a man at the mercy of his impulses, a chameleon whose foolishness takes on the color of each world he passes through. With his wife, Annie Mae, at the beginning of the film, he's a fool for sex.... With his lover Vanetta, the liberated woman who supports the farm workers and subsists on a diet of carrot juice and organic food, Leroy is a fool for romance. He tries to jog alongside her until he plotzes headfirst into the ground; he dresses in flowing caftans that match hers; he promises his undying fidelity to her. And with "Sister Sarah," the wife of the preacher who has given Annie Mae a child, he's a fool for revenge—the fool of fools. He breaks his promise to Vanetta by courting Sister Sarah extravagantly, and the full weight of his confused life crashes down upon him.... We laugh not at the mayhem that Leroy causes—and that the film does not minimize—but at the all-too-human confusions within his character. Leroy wants to be both sensitive and macho, a man of the people and his own boss; he pulls on every string and watches his life unravel from all sides.[37]

It's difficult to believe that Leroy, as we have come to know him, would react with violent and unhinged outrage over his wife's affair. He has shown himself to be timid and humble. He is, by no stretch of the imagination, a volatile narcissist. Besides, he is no longer emotionally engaged in his marriage, which he has seen fit to turn into a shabby charade. Vincent Canby of the *New York Times* wrote: "Miss Wertmüller's original story keeps intruding on 'Which Way Is Up?' at inopportune moments that force its characters to behave in arbitrary, out-of-character ways. It's as if Michael Schultz, the director, and the writers every now and then remembered they'd bought the rights to a very funny Italian film and thought they'd better get something for their money."[38]

Leroy is introduced in the film begging his frigid wife, Annie Mae, for sex. The character is more aggressive in the script. He is demanding rather than begging. The following is noted by Gottlieb:

> LEROY: (he grabs her by the throat and whispers hoarsely) Bitch, you better open your legs, or I'll kick your ass.[39]

In the film, Leroy's temper flares only briefly when he delivers part of the scripted line: "Open your legs, bitch!"

This scene is played differently in *Mimi*. Mimi is able to have sex with his wife, but he finds the sex unpleasant because his wife will not participate. She lies stiffly, stares at him, and sobs. "That same scared expression," he says in disgust. "Like a lamb to the slaughter." Mimi doesn't beg or demand. He has been through this too often. He is content to complain to his wife and malign her character as he proceeds with the sex act. He has a wry way of expressing his frustration, which brings humor to this otherwise disagreeable scene.

Rufus, who is gruff, disapproving, and demeaning in his treatment of his son, was modeled after Pryor's own father, Buck. Buck will return in a more realistic interpretation in *Jo Jo Dancer*. In Gottlieb's script, Leroy becomes annoyed with Buck and openly says to him, "Fuck you." In the film, he doesn't dare confront his father and mutters the invective under his breath. His father says, "I heard that! Fuck you, too, boy!"

Pryor's biggest challenge in the script had to be Leroy's attack on Annie Mae. He had a long history of treating his own wives violently. It was a side of him that he didn't want the public to know about. Now, he had to strangle a make-believe wife for the cameras, and he had to make it funny. Nothing about the scene—not the adultery, not the domestic violence, not the illegitimate pregnancy—should be funny. But, nonetheless, it turns out funny. The turnabout in which Annie Mae becomes the attacker and Leroy becomes the terrified victim is a great comic reversal. Pryor manages in the scene to find humor in livid anger, maddening frustration, and, finally, unmitigated fright. The way Annie's Mae's kitchen knife comes flying across the room and the *thwang* it makes as it becomes embedded in the door turns the scene into a veritable Bugs Bunny cartoon.

The original scene in *Mimi* is far more complex. Mimi is confused by the situation. He wants to emancipate himself from his backward Sicilian ways. He wants to see himself as an intelligent and rational modern man. But old-fashioned cultural patterns of behavior are too deeply ingrained. He feels jealous and possessive. He believes that he needs to exact revenge to defend his honor when another man impregnates his wife. His friend Pippino tries to change his mind by saying, "You're intelligent, a metal worker, communist. So forget the vengeance stuff. Show everyone how to be civilized, with no fuss." Mimi responds by furiously picking up a wrench. He exclaims, "Destroy the honor of my family, whore!" But then he has second thoughts and agrees with Pippino. Mimi, himself, acknowledges that the urge for violent retribution is part of an outmoded code of conduct. "A communist would never do this," he tells himself.

After he enters his home, Mimi marches slowly towards his wife, Rosalia (Agostina Belli), who is at the kitchen table, sobbing. Their eyes meet. He breaks down crying, too. "But why?" he asks. The camera is focused tightly on his face. Wertmüller, who appreciated the expressiveness of Giannini's eyes, often featured the actor in tight close-ups. Mimi speaks to his wife movingly of his humiliation and his concern for the honor of his family. Giannini's performance verges on tragedy, but the actor knows to keep his expressions just broad enough so that the scene cannot be taken too seriously. Then, he leaps on Rosalia in a wildly comic fashion. Joseph Jon Lanthier of *Slant Magazine* wrote: "He goes momentarily berserk on his fallen bride, with his limbs and hair locks erupting spasmodically and his eyes bulging with slighted perniciousness."[40] There is no mistake at this point that the scene is meant to be absurd and we are allowed to laugh.

"The insult must be wiped out!" he shouts as he tightens his hands around her throat. But then he remembers her wedding ring and he removes his hands from her throat to remove the ring from her finger. He must disown Rosalia as his wife to restore his honor. His emotions are pulling him in every direction.

Mimi kicks Rosalia as she is down on her knees. He stands over her and demands that she confess. The camera points upwards at him. He suddenly resembles a righteous priest ordering a sinner to repent. Biskind wrote: "Mimi … reveals his adherence to the old double standard: sexual freedom for himself and sexual fidelity for his wife."[41]

Rosalia begins her tale of adultery. "I went for a license," she says.

"Whore's license?" he asks.

She explains that she met a sergeant and he kept offering her honey bonbons.

"A few bonbons and you lift your skirt?" he grumbles.

He becomes even more insulted when he learns Rosalia had sex with the sergeant in the cabin of a crane.

"He was guarding a site," she explains. "It was raining."

He is incredulous. "My missus got herself knocked up on a *crane*?"

But, then, Mimi admits to having a mistress who bore him a beautiful son. The film switches to Mimi's point of view just in time to show Rosalia charging at him with a meat cleaver, a monstrous glare in her eyes. The film speed is accelerated slightly to make the enraged wife look like a supernatural force. The image is surreal, frightening, and funny—all at once. It resembles a shot out of an *Evil Dead* film. Wilkins wrote: "Mimi's sense of triumphant indignation turns to terror."[42]

Gottlieb pared down the scene, leaving out much of the couple's discourse. This, unfortunately, left out significant notions about their relationship.

Then, Mimi sets out to seduce the sergeant's wife. Fiore has already warned him in no uncertain terms, "If you so much as touch another woman, even your wife, you'll never see me again. Because while love lasts, I want it to be perfect." But Mimi sees adultery as a male prerogative.

Mimi's revenge plan, though it avoids violence, is vulgar and uncivil. Wilkins wrote: "As Mimi forges ahead with a plan that is clearly disgusting to him, the woman grows larger and more powerful, and he grow smaller and more helpless."[43] Wilkins noted, "Techniques used in the (seemingly sincere) seduction of his mistress Fiore become exaggerated and ridiculous—are treated as parody—in his ... seduction of Amalia, the wife of the man who cuckolded him."[44]

A great controversy was generated by *The Seduction of Mimi* for the moment in which Amalia disrobes and exposes her unsightly posterior. Wertmüller maintained that Amalia's bare buttocks are crucial to the film. It is through the jarring spectacle of this deformed monstrosity of an ass that Wertmüller exposes the folly of Mimi's revenge. It assures that the viewer feels repulsed by the situation into which Mimi has put himself. Wertmüller said, "[The spectator] no longer identifies himself with Mimi, but sees Mimi as an idiot." This is no way for him to restore his honor. It was due to the importance of the scene that the director applied painstaking efforts to cast a body double with just the appropriate derrière. She was appalled when the Cannes Festival asked her to cut the scene. "I told them: 'Sorry, but that scene is THE catharsis and I won't touch it.' And in fact I am intensely proud of it."[45]

R. C. Dale of *Movietone News* recognized the power of the scene. He wrote: "Mimi has been watching with growing amazement and horror as the woman disrobes. As the fatal moment approaches, he cowers defenselessly in the sheets.... [T]he woman's flab-cheeked ass, distorted by [an extreme wide-angle] lens into a mammoth, genuinely obscene mountain of undesirable flesh, heaves itself onto the bed and hippoes its way inexorably towards the consummation of Mimi's revenge—and of a magnificently conceived bit of artistic comic distortion."[46]

Biskind was equally struck by the scene:

> The ironic turning point, where Mimi-the-victimizer is disclosed as Mimi-the-victim, trapped by his own designs, is a grotesque sequence in which the overweight Amalia, whom he is about to seduce, casts coquettish glances over her shoulder while undraping her obese and doughy body. This is a puzzling sequence, one for which Wertmüller has been and should be criticized. She plays it for laughs, cutting back and forth between Amalia's body and Mimi's face, even intervening to exaggerate his impotent terror with wide-angled distortions that transform Amalia into an animate

mountain of flesh, heaving and undulating into the foreground while Mimi huddles at the other end of the bed.[47]

But Schultz did not share Wertmüller's viewpoint. He was unwilling to take an unadorned ass without pleasing proportions and grossly distort it with a wide-angle lens to manifest the disorder and ugliness of the circumstances. He was making a vastly different film.

Gottlieb suggests in his script that Sister Sarah is a large, powerful woman, but he never explicitly describes her proportions and he never has the character bare her buttocks. Why am I led to believe Sister Sarah is large and powerful? Sister Sarah is introduced playing the piano at church. She is described as "dwarfing the small spinet she's playing."[48] Gottlieb notes that, when Sister Sarah finally submits to Leroy's seduction, she "descends on him in an avalanche of desire."[49] An avalanche typically describes the powerful descent of a large mass of snow, ice, and rocks. Here is the post-coital action described by Gottlieb: "Leroy is lying sleepily in Sarah's big arms. He starts to move, only to find himself trapped.... [H]e starts to edge out from her powerful grip."[50] But it is never implied that Sister Sarah is unattractive in any way. This is the way that Gottlieb describes the scene in which Sister Sarah undresses to have sex with Leroy.

LEROY'S POINT OF VIEW: Sister Sarah disrobing. An awesome sight.[51]

The fact that Sister Sarah looks awesome as she bares her body would likely inspire the spectator to greatly admire Leroy for achieving this sexual conquest. It defeats the purpose of the scene as defined by Wertmüller.

Leroy's folly is instead conveyed by slapstick. Sister Sarah pushes Leroy away, sending him crashing into a grand piano. The piano slides to one end of the trailer, tipping the trailer off its foundation.

The casting of Sister Sarah moved the character further away from her *Mimi* counterpart. The filmmakers were not about to give the role to an overweight actress like Mabel King, who played team owner Bertha Dewitt in *Bingo Long*. The actress they selected instead was Marilyn Coleman, a woman who was neither fat nor unattractive.

Max Julien had thought it was insulting to black people for Michael Campus, the director of *The Mack*, to focus a derisive sex scene on a big black woman. It may have been the same type of thinking that caused Schultz to avoid depicting Sister Sarah as an overweight black woman. This could have, in his mind, recalled the unflattering big-bottomed mammy caricatures that had been perpetuated by Hollywood films.

Modern film critics are trying desperately to redefine our ideas of beauty. In recent days, Joseph Jon Lanthier of *Slant Magazine* hailed Fiore's ass. He wrote: "Wertmüller empowers this husky woman with off-kilter sensuality; her engorged bottom becomes a proud and surrealistic distortion of normalcy we take for granted, a Dali clock of an ass melting itself out of sex objectification."[52]

Physical imperfection is a motif of *Mimi*. The gangsters who control the town are part of a single powerful clan. Mimi repeatedly comes across various brothers, uncles, and cousins in the clan and he is able to instantly identify a family member's bloodline connection through a common feature: a circular pattern of unsightly facial moles. Wertmüller emphasizes the obvious by zooming in her camera on this imperfection. In *Which Way Is Up?*, the Agrico villains are free of moles. Instead, the filmmakers identify their connection to the criminal fellowship by having each of them wear the same style of bloodstone ring. The rings are so big and shiny that they are as prominent in scenes as the facial moles.

An analysis of *Which Way Is Up?* would not be complete without an acknowledgment of Margaret Avery's important contribution to the film. Avery, funny and sexy as Annie Mae, stands out in two of the film's key scenes—the dominatrix scene and the pregnancy scene. It is a shame that she never again worked with Pryor.

Pryor was so happy with *Which Way Is Up?* that he wanted to remake another Wertmüller film, *Swept Away* (1974). That film involves an arrogant rich woman who becomes shipwrecked on an island with a deckhand from her yacht. The deckhand takes control and degrades the woman, which leads her to fall in love with him. The sexual cruelty of the character appealed to Pryor. He envisioned Cybill Shepherd as his island lover.

Pryor was briefly attached to a sequel to *The Sting* (1973). When Paul Newman and Robert Redford declined to reprise their roles, Universal Pictures considered Peter Boyle and Walter Matthau as replacements. As of May 9, 1977, the studio had cast Pryor and Jackie Gleason in the lead roles. At the time, a script by David Ward was to be rewritten by Carl Gottlieb. The studio later announced that Lily Tomlin and Richard Burton had joined the cast. According to news reports, the film was to be titled "The Next Sting." But the project was suspended for five years. The film finally went into production with the original script by Ward. Gleason was still on board, but Pryor, Tomlin, and Burton were replaced by Mac Davis, Teri Garr, and Oliver Reed.

During this period, Pryor was supposed to star in a film adaptation of George Orwell's *Animal Farm*. He said to Lee Grant of the *Los Angeles Times*, "It's a unique story, tender and filled with magic. Sad and funny."[53] The film was never produced.

Blue Collar (1978)

Production: TAT Communications Company.
Distribution: Universal Pictures.
Producer: Ron Guest.
Director: Paul Schrader
Screenplay: Paul Schrader and Leonard Schrader, suggested by source material by Sydney A. Glass.
Photography: Bobby Byrne.
Editor: Tom Rolf
Music: Jack Nitzsche.
Release date: February 10, 1978.
Running time: 114 minutes.
Cast: Richard Pryor (Zeke), Harvey Keitel (Jerry), Yaphet Kotto (Smokey), Ed Begley Jr. (Bobby Joe), Harry Bellaver (Eddie Johnson), George Memmoli (Jenkens), Lucy Saroyan (Arlene Bartowski), Lane Smith (Clarence Hill), Cliff De Young (John Burrows), Borah Silver (Dogshit Miller), Chip Fields (Caroline Brown), Harry Northup (Hank), Leonard Gaines (IRS Man), Milton Selzer ("Sumabitch"), Sammy Warren (Barney), Charlie T. Hernandez (Jimmy Martinez), Jerry Dahlmann (Superintendent), Denny Arnold (Unshaven thug), Rock Riddle (Blond thug).

Pryor spoke to the *Los Angeles Times* about *Blue Collar* as he prepared to go on location. He said, "[*Blue Collar* is] about factory workers in Detroit and unions, management versus employees."[1] He added, "The project is a very serious one, the humor coming only from the humanness."[2]

Pryor argues with the factory foreman (Borah Silver) in *Blue Collar* (1978).

Three friends, Jerry Bartowski (Keitel), Smokey James (Kotto), and Zeke Brown (Pryor), work together on an assembly line at the Checker Motor Company in Detroit, Michigan. The men have formed a special bond, often sharing their grievances about their jobs. They feel trapped, believing there's more to them than the work they do on the assembly line.

Ben Sachs of the *Chicago Reader* wrote: "The scenes in the auto plant feature compelling shots of machines and men hard at work that recall both the *verité* documentaries of Frederick Wiseman."[3] Frederic and Mary Ann Brussat of *Spirituality and Practice* wrote: "Men, black and white, working on an automobile assembly line. The sound of equipment screeching and the sight of sparks flying. In the opening scenes of this compelling film, the camera prowls up and down the working area of the plant while a gut churning rock 'n' roll soundtrack hammers into our consciousness the repetitiveness and monotony of such labor. This raw energy in the beginning of *Blue Collar* continues to tick away like a time bomb...."[4]

Zeke is the angriest and most dissatisfied member of his group. He and Jerry are both supporting families, which makes them closer than self-indulgent bachelor Smokey. They are always broke and they feel humiliated to be unable to adequately provide for their families. Jerry says, "Sometimes I get so depressed, I start thinking about the shit I promised Carolyn, shit I ain't never gonna be able to do." Zeke responds, "I know, a man's supposed to be able to take care of his family. I never was good with money. I'm just fuckin' always broke, man."

Zeke talks Smokey and Jerry into helping him rob the union office. The trio only get away with six hundred dollars, but the union claims a loss of ten thousand dollars to their insurance company. During the robbery, the friends had obtained a ledger that shows the union is using money from the pension fund for illegal loans. Zeke says, "They weren't regular loans, man. They were, like, shark loans. You know what I mean? They all had high rates of interest. *High*." Zeke photocopies a page from the ledger and sends it to the union boss, Eddie Johnson, with an anonymous note that demands money for the ledger's return.

Pryor as a disgruntled factory worker in *Blue Collar* (1978).

Smokey doesn't have the money to pay the thousand dollars he owes his bookie, Charlie T. Hernandez, but he assures him that he has money coming his way. He then confides in him about the blackmail scheme. Hernandez is arrested by the police for storing a massive inventory of stolen merchandise in a rented garage. The inventory includes a gun used in a police shooting, which could allow the police to charge the bookie as an accomplice in the shooting. Hernandez knows that the police are only trying to pressure him for information on his contacts. He agrees to reveal what he knows about the union robbery if the police cut him a deal. One of the union's connections in the police department passes this information to Johnson.

At Little Joe's bar, Smokey overhears two men planning to attack Jerry at his home. Smokey phones Jerry's home and talks to his wife, Arlene. She tells him that Jerry is working his second job at a nearby gas station and that the children are at their grandparents' home. This means that Arlene will be home alone when the goons get there. Smokey needs to get her out of the house without panicking her or telling her what's going on. He tells her that Jerry split his pants and he needs her to bring him another pair. Later, when the men arrive at Jerry's home, Smokey is waiting for them with a baseball bat. He is enraged and demands to know who sent them. He shoves one man down the porch steps and beats the other with the bat.

Johnson can see that Zeke is ambitious and he is sure that he will break ranks with his friends in exchange for a job as shop steward. He is not worried about Jerry, who will no doubt "buckle under a little pressure." But he sees Smokey as someone he can't control. "Now, this bastard," he says "he's a two-time loser. He'll make us pay through the ass forever, then fuck us for the fun of it." So, he decides to get rid of Smokey and make it look like an accident. The next day, Miller summons Smokey to the paint room. Smokey is prepared to use a handheld paint sprayer to do detailed paint work on a car. But the automatic paint sprayers turn on suddenly. Smokey presses the "off" switch, but the sprayers keep going. He tries to open the door, but it has been blocked by a forklift. His lungs fill up with paint as he struggles to force open the door. He is finally able to smash open a window with his fists, but the damage has already been done. His head and face are covered in blue paint, the same blue paint that has presumably gone down his throat and inside his lungs. He slumps forward through the window frame. In the end, his death is ruled an accident and Miller is fired for negligence.

Realizing that Smokey was murdered, Jerry tells Zeke he wants to go to the FBI. Zeke is adamantly against this. "I'm *black*, Jerry," he says. "The police aren't going to protect *me*." Zeke accepts the job of shop steward. Jerry turns himself over to the FBI as a witness in the government's ongoing case against union corruption.

In the final scene, FBI agents accompany Jerry to the factory to clean out his locker. Zeke confronts him, calling him a "scumbag." Jerry snidely replies, "I see they finally fixed your locker, Zeke." He replies, "Hey, scumbag, I'd sure hate to be living in those pretty little white shoes." The two men accuse each other of being sellouts. Their exchange quickly degenerates into racial slurs. Zeke arms himself with a pipe wrench. Jerry grabs a hammer. The two men, ready for battle, lunge toward each other. The film freezes on

The climactic battle between Pryor and Keitel in *Blue Collar* (1978).

this image. Something that Smokey told them is replayed in voiceover: "They pit the lifers against the new boy and the young against the old. The black against the white. Everything they do is to keep us in our place."

Sydney Glass, an aspiring screenwriter, attended a Writers Guild seminar at which Paul Schrader spoke. He told Schrader he wanted to write a script about his father's experiences working in an auto plant. The script, as he envisioned it, had to be dark to realistically capture his father's pain and struggle: he committed suicide the day before he was scheduled to retire. Schrader went off with his brother, Leonard, to write a dark script about workers in an auto plant. Glass sued Schrader for stealing his idea. It made the situation worse that Glass was black. The black caucus of the Writers Guild got behind him, ensuring that he received screen credit.

Blue Collar turned out to be Schrader's directorial debut. He described the project as "a film about auto workers, three best friends who get involved in a robbery. It begins as a comedy ... like most things in life."[5] Schrader said in another interview,

> I wanted to write a movie about some guys who rip off their union because it seemed like such a self-hating act ... [to] attack the organization that's supposed to help them.... In their minds, and in the minds of a lot of people in this country, the union, the company, and the government are synonymous ... [but with] different logos.... Everyone's trying to outmaneuver his fellow worker, and the easiest way to create tension in the work force is through race, because everyone has this big button called racism mounted on their chest, so ... you just reach over and push [that] button, and people start fighting amongst themselves.[6]

Zeke is described in the script as follows: "A wiry, urban-bred black with an oversized wife and five kids. His wit and temper have labeled him a malcontent by both the union and the company." Lucy Saroyan, who was dating Pryor at the time, introduced the actor to Schrader. Convincing Pryor to play Zeke enabled the director to obtain financing.

The "oversized wife," described elsewhere in the script as "Jemima-like," was discarded prior to casting. Zeke's wife was played by a cute and slender actress named Chip Fields. It was the same type of situation that arose when Schultz had to cast the role of Sister Sarah for *Which Way Is Up?* A fat black woman was deemed an offensive stereotype.

The studio wanted Schrader to cast a white actor opposite Pryor and Keitel. Schrader likely would have complied if he had not seen Yaphet Kotto in *Across 110th Street* (1972) and thought that he would be perfect for the film.

Shooting started on May 9, 1977. The production company was not given permission to film in any of the major auto plants in Detroit. They ended up filming in the Checker auto plant in Kalamazoo and Chrysler's Jefferson Avenue Assembly Plant, a historical plant that was built by the Hudson Motor Car Company in 1910. Schrader shot in Kalamazoo for two weeks, in Detroit for two weeks, and in Los Angeles for two weeks.

Schrader said, "As a first time-time director, I knew I wasn't going to teach anybody how to act, and I knew I wasn't going to get a big star. So I went to three actors, each of whom was pushing for his career, and each of whom was not independently bankable. Then I took all three of these bantam roosters, dropped them into the same pit, and made sure that nobody got out first."[7]

Pryor improvised a lot. Schrader talked about him "moving around the script."[8] A favorite scene in the film shows Zeke watching *The Jeffersons* on television. Here is the way the scene is described on page 17 of the shooting script:

ZEKE: Goddamn Oreo motherfucker. Where the dumb nigger like that get so much money? Sold his ass, I'll tell you that. All his goddamn honky friends....
(*Carolyn, Zeke's wife, sits Jemima-like in her chair, trying to hear the TV over Zeke's incessant bitching.*)
CAROLYN: If you hate it so much, why don't you just turn it off?
ZEKE: I work three years for that sucker, and I'm damn sure going to watch it. Only thing that works in the house anyway.

Here is the dialogue as delivered by Pryor and Chip Fields in the film. (Note that the spelling of the wife's name had changed):

ZEKE: Now that shit is pitiful. I don't know how in the fuck a nigga like that gets some money anyway. This is the dumbest shit—look at this motherfucker. Look like a motherfuckin' ostrich. Look at that shit....
CAROLINE: If you hate it so much, why don't you just turn it off?
ZEKE: Turn it off? Are you kiddin,' baby? Took me three years to pay for that motherfucker. We gonna watch everything they show on it. All the shit they show. And even the snow when the motherfucker go off, I'm gonna sit here and watch that. It's the only thing that works in the house anyway.

Harry Northup, who plays Hank, worked on *Blue Collar* for two weeks in Kalamazoo, and two weeks in Detroit. He said, "When I came on the set of *Blue Collar*..., Pryor remembered me from *Which Way Is Up?* He made his hand into a fist, raised it to me in a greeting."

Northup was a longtime friend of Keitel, whom he met while studying Method acting with Frank Corsaro. Pryor, though not a trained actor, intentionally or unintentionally used elements of the Method in his portrayal of Zeke; his improvisations brought much of his personal experience into a scene. Northup fondly remembers improvising with Pryor during a bar scene. He believes that, of all the actors that he has ever worked with, Pryor was one of the fastest and most imaginative at improvisation. "[O]nly Robert De Niro was better," he said.

Zeke was supposed to be annoyed with the music that Hank was playing on the jukebox. Part of their improvisation involved playfully trading racial barbs. Zeke asked Hank to play a particular song he liked. Hank replies, "Go get a quarter from your welfare mama and play your own. You don't want to listen to nothing but your own noise."

"I never did like that son of a bitch," Zeke grumbles.

Northup wrote: "After lunch that day, as we began to work on the set, Pryor said to the cast and crew, 'I hate everyone here. I'm going back to my hotel and when you're ready to work, call me,' and walked off the set. Everyone was stunned."[9]

Schrader tried to read Pryor's lines to the actors off camera, but it became difficult to carry on. Northup said, "I think the day's work was pretty much ended."[10]

Keitel told Northup that his improvisations may have hurt Pryor's feelings. Northup was surprised to hear this because he saw Pryor as, in his words, "a tough cookie."[11] Northup wrote: "When I got back to my hotel room, I called Richard. I told him that if I had hurt him with my improv, I apologize. He sounded medicated. 'No, it was not you. It was Yaphet. He wasn't matching shots.'"[12] Another cast member told Northup he noticed Kotto drinking a lot of cognac that day, which may have adversely affected his performance.

Rushes for the day showed that Pryor and Northup had done well at refining their dialogue during their improvisation: it turned out to be an amusing exchange. Zeke shouts to Northup, "Say, Hank, my man, give me a little break on the hillbilly music, partner?"

Hank responds, "It's *my* money and I'll play what *I* want." He smiles wryly before adding, "That's what I like about the South."

Zeke looks pained as he holds his hand to his heart. "Hank...," he says. "I thought he loved me." He then grumbles under his breath, "I can't stand that motherfucker."

The dialogue is similar to the script, but Pryor and Northup tempered the anger of their scripted words with humorous asides. In the script, Zeke flat-out demands that Hank "don't play any more of those goddamn cowboy songs." Hank responds, "Fuck that, Zeke." He insists that he worked hard for the coins he is putting in the jukebox and he has a right to play the music he wants to hear. Zeke grumbles, "Mutha-fucking cowboy." Hanks never smiles or wisecracks. Zeke never feigns heartbreak. The enmity that the two characters have for one another is pure and ugly. In the film, racial hostility bubbles beneath the surface with code words like "hillbilly," "cowboy," and "partner." Hank refers to "The South" as a declaration of white power. The only honest statement in the conversation—"I can't stand that motherfucker"—is said in a low voice so that the other person can't hear it.

Northup was impressed by Pryor, Keitel, and Kotto; they formed, he said, a "marvelous partnership."[13] But, in his view, Pryor clearly stood out from his co-stars. He said, "Even though Harvey Keitel, a friend, gave a strong, deep, poignant performance, and Yaphet Kotto, a magnificent actor, was great, I give the edge to Pryor—for being lean, cogent and tough."[14] He admired the fact that Pryor was able to "use his body to transform his character"[15] and managed in his performance to reveal "an inner consciousness alive in Zeke."[16]

As usual, Pryor's drug use made him unstable, unreliable, and violent on set. This became a problem when he had to work with Keitel, who needed eight or nine takes to warm up. He found that, by going through the material again and again, he was able to better explore his character and refine his performance. But Pryor became bored if he had to do more than three takes. Schrader said, "By the fourth or the fifth take, he would already be downhill because he'd be running out of gas. So, you had to grab him very, very early."[17] Pryor decided that he would do no more than three takes. As far as he was concerned, they were going to do it his way or no way at all. He made his position clear by pulling out a pistol and pointing it at Schrader's head. After that, Schrader had Keitel warm up before Pryor arrived on the set.

Sergio of Indiewire wrote: "Things got so tense that once Pryor and Keitel got into a fist fight."[18]

George Memmoli, a short, rotund comic actor who played one of the factory workers, also had a run-in with Pryor on set. Rovin wrote: "Pryor took offense at something Memmoli said and slugged the actor. When Richard grabbed a chair and hit him over the head, Memmoli ended up with a fractured skull, Pryor with a one-million-dollar lawsuit."[19]

The lawsuit was reported in newspapers across the country; what was left out of the story was exactly what Memmoli had said to rile Pryor. Northup, a witness to the incident, knew exactly what was said. Pryor was sitting in a chair in between scenes when Memmoli walked up to him and said, "Suck my cock." Northup wrote: "I got the feeling that George was trying to be funny."[20]

But Pryor was not having it. He told Memmoli, "I'll whip your ass."

"Okay," said Memmoli, "whip my ass and then suck my cock."

Northup wrote: "Pryor got off his chair, grabbed the chair and hit Memmoli [with it]."[21]

Memmoli's remark no doubt provoked Pryor due to an incident of sexual abuse that he suffered as a child. Pryor wrote candidly about this in his autobiography. Hoss, an older boy in his late teens, strode up to Pryor in an alleyway...

> Right away, I knew he was trouble.... I should've run.... It was as if the terror I felt paralyzed me. Glued me in place and made me easy prey. Hoss threw me against the wall in a darkened corner shielded from the view of anyone passing by. Then he unzipped his pants and put his dick into my mouth.
> "Suck it," he ordered.[22]

Pryor did as he was told. He wrote: "Hoss walked off happy and left me trembling in the chilly darkness. I cried in shock and tried to make sense of what had happened. I knew something horrible had happened to me. I felt violated, humiliated, dirty, fearful, and, most of all, ashamed."[23]

It is unwise to make incautious comments to a man haunted by demons. But Pryor still had no right to become violent. This is especially true if we take into consideration Memmoli's own backstory. Little more than a year earlier, the actor had been severely injured in a car stunt staged for *The Farmer* (1977). He was unable to work for months, which meant giving up a prominent role in *Taxi Driver* (1976). So severe were his injuries that they led to his death in 1985. Considering Memmoli's frail physical condition, it was especially brutal that Pryor fractured his skull.

Pryor had grown up around violence. While living in the bordello, he often saw his beloved grandmother ruthlessly beat a disobedient hooker with a cudgel. Saul described Marie employing various methods of violence.

> To enforce the law of the house, Marie had her straight razor. Prostitutes would meet the razor if they tried to cheat her of her customary 50 percent share of the take; johns would be sliced on the face if they tried to leave without paying. (One childhood friend of Richard Pryor's recalled "a lot of men" walking around Peoria "with nasty scars around their face.") In later years, Marie upgraded to a pistol, which she carried strapped to her leg. Most of the time, she didn't need to draw her weapon or even use her fists. She simply said, referring to her size-twelve shoes, "I'll put my twelves up in your ass," and the trouble went away.... One of Richard's neighbors recalled being devastated, as a young girl, by what she saw on the sidewalk of North Washington Street, right in front of Marie's brothel. Marie was whaling with her fists on the body of a black woman, most likely one of her prostitutes.... The woman would struggle to get up; Marie would knock her back down, hard enough to draw blood.[24]

This sort of violence was, as he saw it, just something his grandmother had to do. Even worse, he had to regularly watch his father beat his mother. His father and his grandmother were the biggest influences in his life when he was growing up; why shouldn't he be violent, too?

He had a long history of violence by the time he went to work on *Blue Collar*. He had been expelled from high school for throwing a punch at a teacher. He had beaten up a landlord. He stabbed a heckler with a fork. He lunged at a hotel manager with a knife (*New Yorker* journalist Joan Acocella claims he stabbed the man in the eye). He stabbed a man in a movie theatre for laughing. He pulled a gun on his manager, Bobby Roberts. It was just something he did. It was a normal event to him. Pryor's friend Cecil Brown said, "Richard didn't see taking a chair to somebody's head as such a horrible thing."[25] In his later years, Pryor admitted to having been "a violent man." Violence had an undeniable appeal to him. It was, he found, an effective way to "bulldoze people all over."[26]

Months after production ended, Schrader felt comfortable enough to talk about the battles to Sue Reilly of *People* magazine. "We fought sometimes like crazy," he said, "but I feel quite strongly that Richard will be the biggest black actor ever."[27]

In recent years, Schrader has talked at great length about Pryor. At one point, he said, "He really was one of the unhappiest people I ever met."[28] It was a stressful experience for the director to engage with someone as troubled as Pryor for the six weeks the film was in production. "I barely survived it," said Schrader. He explained, "When you are working with someone who lives in a world of crisis and unpredictability, you're never really relaxed. You never know from one moment to the next. You're working with Richard Pryor and everybody is smiling. Then, half an hour later, he is angry and he walks out. You never know if he is going to come back. You're living that way all the time."[29]

Schrader stressed that Pryor was the worst actor he ever dealt with, mostly because of the racial politics. He said, "You could deal with bad behavior and irresponsible behavior and drunken behavior, but race behavior is another thing. [It's hopeless] when an actor says to you—like Richie said to me—'The first white man I ever met came to my mama's door to *fuck* her. And you're just like him.'"[30]

Schrader remembered, "He had wide polar swings of mood. He had what I used to call back then The Big and Black Problem, which was that he both wanted to be big and black. By big, I mean hugely popular across the board. By black, I mean in terms of black politics."[31] Pryor came to admire activists like Malcolm X, Angela Davis, and Ishmael Reed, who were, he said, "uncompromisingly black."[32] While in Berkeley, he befriended two activists, Cecil Brown and Claude Brown, who spoke to him often about black causes. He came to believe that, first and foremost, he had to stand as an activist for the black community.[33]

Schrader elaborated on Pryor's unpredictability. He saw that, when he was in a good mood, he was able to charm everyone on the set. But the charming Richard Pryor didn't last. He wasn't comfortable having everyone love him. Schrader said, "[H]e'd go home that night and stew. And he'd say, 'What kind of Tom am I? I'm everybody's black pal.' And the next day he would be *mean*."[34]

It was something that Schrader saw throughout the shoot. He said, "[H]e was like a pendulum swing. He would turn on people. He would instigate racial situations and get angry. Everyone hated him. And then he would use that to let the pendulum fly back the other way, and spend the next day ingratiating himself enormously until he had everybody eating out of his hand. So, you could be pretty sure on one given day [that], if he was extremely nice, the next day he was going to walk in and kick somebody's ass."[35] Pryor, according to Schrader, had to do "something very pathological and very dramatic" to let everyone know that he was "black enough."[36] To put it in another way, he didn't want to be big if it meant not being black and he didn't want to be black if it meant not being big.

It remained a stressful set from the first day to the last. Anger is an infection that can spread quickly. Working with an angry co-star made Keitel and Kotto angry, too. Schrader said, "[Directing] was an extremely painful experience with these guys. After about a week, the hatred really came out. And after two or three weeks, they weren't speaking to each other at all. It was just trench warfare."[37]

Schrader said, "[I]f this is what movie-making was like, I didn't want to do it anymore. I quickly learned to confine myself to talent management—not a day went by without some sort of confrontation. Right after you said, 'Cut,' a fight would start."[38] The director had to concentrate on getting the master shot because he didn't know when one of the actors would walk off after a couple of takes and refuse to come back to the set.

In 1998, Schrader talked further about the situation on the UK television series *Scene by Scene*. He didn't think he would finish the film when Pryor stopped working and made arrangements to drive out to the airport. Schrader said, "It was my first film and, if I didn't finish it, I would never direct again. My aspirations to be a film director were over. And I was just sort of overwhelmed by this emotion and I started crying. And Richie Pryor ... took one look at me and said, 'Well, you gonna be a man or you gonna be a pussy?' And I said, 'Richard, let's go back to work.'"[39]

Schrader admitted, "It was partly my fault. I had invited three bulls into a china shop and told each one they were the alpha bull ... and then stood back."[40] By the end, the three leads were no longer talking to one another and refused to rehearse with one another. Pryor was doing cocaine. Kotto was drinking.

Schultz didn't see it as Pryor's fault at all. He believed that Schrader made *Blue Collar* a "terrible experience"[41] for him by pitting the actors against each other for dramatic effect. "I think that going from the great fun experience of *Which Way Is Up?* to just hating the experience that he was having in *Blue Collar*.... I think that's when he started up again doing drugs, but I don't know. I wasn't there. I just heard from him about how much he hated doing what he was doing."[42]

Pryor said, "It's an emotionally violent movie and I felt pain when I made the film. The energy of the work brought me down."[43] Northup believed that Pryor had gone deep into Zeke's state of mind, becoming as disgruntled and defensive as the downtrodden auto worker.

At the time of the film's release, journalists remained interested in the reported fighting on the set. Roger Ebert of the *Chicago Sun-Times* discussed the matter with Kotto, who said:

> I don't pay any attention to that stuff. Far as I was concerned, we had an exceptional group of people doing an exceptional job. As to whether everybody got along with everybody else at every moment, what difference does it make, as long as we got a great movie?
>
> If I had a problem, maybe it was that I would know my lines, and then Pryor would come in with brand new lines out of his own head, man, and what are the rest of us supposed to do? I had to figure out my relationship with him in terms of the fact that the movie is about two black guys and one white guy. Pryor was playing an ethnic character—he was the black in the movie. I figured, we can't have two black ethnic portrayals in this movie, that'll get repetitive.
>
> So you know what I did? I played an Italian. Right! An Italian in a black skin—I modeled my character after this kid I grew up with. You won't find one so-called black mannerism or colloquialism in my entire performance. It was weird, man. I had to stretch myself to play that role. I had to find new places to be coming from. And this movie is so good. I did, I actually went to see it.[44]

Keitel didn't want to end up as a comedian's straight man; Pryor didn't want to end up as Keitel's black sidekick. But Pryor resented Kotto far more than Keitel. As he saw it, Kotto was playing his role as if he was Jim Brown and he was expecting Pryor to be "the dumb nigger."[45] Vincent Canby of the *New York Times* later complimented Kotto for his "cool, self-assured performance."[46] So, while they were filming the orgy scene, Pryor became enraged. He called Kotto a "big greasy nigger."[47] But Kotto didn't react. He was too drunk to mind Pryor's insults. So, Pryor had to take further action to get his point across—he whacked Kotto over the head with a folding chair.

Brown wrote: "For actors like Billy Dee Williams and Yaphet Kotto it was the same. They were trained actors who had gone the traditional way for success in Hollywood. Yet, here was somebody who was raised in a whorehouse and who had been kicked out of grade school after smacking his teacher, who was the real star."[48]

Kotto said, "Richard is a very sensitive man. How do you describe a genius? People misunderstand Richard, as they misunderstand Lenny Bruce, Van Gough, guys like that, who have their art. How does Richard Pryor do what he does, exposing himself, his mind, sharing his soul? That's very painful."[49]

Kotto did not see Schrader as a genius, however, at least not when he spoke about him in 1980. "He's not a director," he said. "He may be a writer, but he's not a director. Everything in that part, including the bandanna I wore around my head, I brought to the movie myself. I knew exactly where I was coming from. He didn't give any help to the actors."[50] Schrader is unlikely to argue this point. He has admitted that he didn't figure out how to be a director until he made *American Gigolo* (1980). He said that he mostly spent the production of *Blue Collar* herding his actors from one shot to the next.

Kotto, much like Pryor, was not an easygoing actor. Director Guy Hamilton admitted to having trouble with him during the making of *Live and Let Die* (1973). The trouble, Hamilton said, began the first time he met the actor in Jamaica. "He starts off thinking he should be playing Bond—seriously. He was very badly behaved, he would try and make life difficult."[51] Kotto complained that the dialogue of the black characters was inauthentic: "There were too many [lines like] 'Hey, baby!' We don't talk like that, man, we really don't."[52]

Kotto elaborated on the subject to journalist James M. Tate:

> No, there were so many problems with that script.... I was too afraid of coming off like Mantan Moreland.... I had to dig deep in my soul and brain and come up with a level of reality that would offset the sea of stereotype crap that Tom Mankiewicz wrote that had nothing to do with the black experience or culture. The way Kananga dies was a joke ... and ... well ... the entire experience was not as rewarding as I wanted it to be. There were a lot of pitfalls that I had to avoid, and I did.... Jeez, it was the first black Bond villain.... I wanted to be original ... but there was nothing I could draw on from Tom's script. It was a trap. If I had played it the way it was written, every black organization in the world would have been on my case.[53]

Kotto had issues that extended beyond casting and script. He pressured producer Harry Saltzman to hire black stunt coordinators. He acted as if he didn't like other cast members. Roger Moore, the actor who was actually cast as Bond, said in interviews that Kotto was cold and distant. Moore was disturbed that, when the production moved to New Orleans, Kotto responded to the crowds of black locals with the Black Power salute. Kotto said, "I stayed away from everybody. It may have appeared I had a chip on my shoulder because I was quiet. I am not there to socialize. I think Method actors are misunderstood. Maybe [Moore] wasn't used to Method actors."[54]

Kotto spoke further about his scenes in *Blue Collar*. By the time the orgy scene was shot, they had "gone so far off the script."[55] He said, "I'm told Paul Schrader was annoyed, at least that's what I'm told. The whole thing had become one improvisation after another, but if my memory serves me correct, he told me and Harvey and Richard to improvise. He said we were 'director proof' actors and to 'improvise when you feel it's necessary.'

Then when we did as directed, I'm told he was annoyed. Well I don't really know if he was or not. But he was lucky to have had us. The movie is a classic."[56]

Northup acknowledged that it was a difficult shoot. While in Detroit, the actor saw the following pronouncement written on a wall: "We came to Detroit looking pretty & left looking raggity." That became the line that Northup has invariably used to describe his experience working in Detroit on *Blue Collar*.

Keitel, meanwhile, will not discuss *Blue Collar*. He talks about his work in other films, including *Mean Streets* (1973), *Taxi Driver* (1976), *Fingers* (1978), *Reservoir Dogs* (1992), *Bad Lieutenant* (1992), *The Piano* (1993), and *Pulp Fiction* (1994). *Blue Collar*, apparently, is a film he would like to forget.

Brown wrote:

> Harvey's bitterness lingered longer than Richard's. When I lived in Berlin in the 1980s, I would attend the Berlinalle Film Festival, where I once ran into Harvey. I told him that I was a friend of Richard, who often spoke of him.
> "Yeah? What did he say? How's that white honkie?"[57]

The Playlist Staff noted:

> *Blue Collar* borders on being a naturalistic masterpiece, full of small moments that, had any other filmmaker been in charge, would have been the first to hit the cutting room floor. In fact, much of the movie consists of the three actors standing around and shooting the breeze on the assembly line or in the local bar, mostly about how strapped for cash they are (Keitel's daughter needs braces, Pryor has been lying on his income tax, and Kotto is in deep with some loan sharks). Once they make the heist, the movie shifts gears and becomes a darker beast altogether.[58]

At one point in the film, Zeke is visited by an IRS agent, who has figured out that Zeke has claimed false dependents on his returns. The agent lets Zeke know that he owes the government $2,460.75 in back taxes. Pryor no doubt identified with Zeke. Penelope Spheeris was working at his house in 1969 when an IRS agent arrived to talk about Pryor's failure to pay taxes for three years. He had his lawyers wrangle with the IRS over the issue, but it was impossible for him to win the case. He hadn't bothered to pay taxes during a period in which he earned $250,000. In 1974, a judge found Pryor guilty of willful failure to pay his income taxes.

Schrader described the film as being about "the politics of resentment and claustrophobia, the feeling of being manipulated and not in control of your life."[59]

The script opens as follows:

> AUTO WORKERS. In the 1920s they came to Detroit like pretty girls to Hollywood. In the 1970s they are bored, brutalized, exhausted, angry. Most hate their jobs. Many hate their lives.

The tracking shot of the assembly line is described:

> The goddamn line. Fifty-five cars in an hour, 4,400 cars a week, 220,000 cars a year. Two shifts a day, eight hours a shift, plus 90 minutes for lunch, 46 minutes to drink a Coke or take a piss.
> All along the line, men work silently and monotonously. Hard young black faces. Sweating old white faces. Men with Afros and crewcuts, plain-faced women with outdated hairdos. Bodies hustling everywhere, arms moving, legs moving. Take home pay $150 a week, with overtime, $9,000 a year. Moving, moving.
> Overhead "mules" lower car frames onto the line. The staccato sound of power wrenches and power-drills attached to long electric cords. Metal parts pushed into place—panels, fenders, roofs, hoods, floor pans.
> Machinery moving, forklift unloading, welding iron sparkling. And the brilliant colors: sunflower yellow, glacial blue, cranberry red, sandalwood, pewter, lime, gold.

> A man pounds at the soft drink machine, curses and runs back to the line. And the noise. Always the relentless pounding of heavy machinery.

Schrader wanted to show the plant as a hellish world. But, in the finished film, we see no hard or sweating faces. We see no one pounding on a soft drink machine. We see a group of people working hard to assemble cars. We see people doing their jobs, which is something to be admired.

Blue Collar is engrossing as a crime-drama and a relationship-drama. It fails as a social issue drama. The men believe their bosses are exploiting them with low wages and poor working conditions and their union is doing nothing to protect their interests. Our evidence of management's exploitation comes in three parts. First, a worker is frustrated that he is repeatedly losing money to a vending machine. He takes out his frustration by crashing a forklift into it and then attacking it with a wrench. Second, Zeke complains at a union meeting that he can't get anyone to fix his broken locker. He explains that he has to use a ballpoint pen to force open his locker. He says, "I'm sticking 'em in there and they keep breaking off. I done blew twenty dollars on ballpoint pens." He doesn't appreciate the rep's effort to placate him. "Man," he cries, "flick my Bic!" That last line, which was Pryor's one ad-lib in the scene, is the line that makes people laugh and the line that most often gets quoted.

The broken locker and the broken vending machine are hardly proof that the plant employees are suffering grave indignities at the hands of management. But Schrader has something else to stir up your emotions. We learn that Jerry has been unable to afford braces for his daughter, Debby. Debby is so desperate to straighten her teeth that she has rigged up a pair of braces out of a coat hanger. The makeshift braces have cut into her gums and made her mouth bloody. Do you care about the auto workers now? Do you see now how they're being exploited?

Brian Rothenberg, a spokesman for the United Auto Workers, informed the author that the dental benefits negotiated in 1973 contracts would have covered 50 percent of the cost for braces. At the time, this was a unique benefit for auto workers. It is true that braces were as expensive in 1978 as they are today. Jerry's out-of-pocket cost for his daughter's braces could have been as high as a thousand dollars, which would have certainly cut into the family's budget. But it was still affordable. In any case, it isn't a reason to rob the union that provides your dental benefits.

Detroit auto workers were well paid in the 1970s. They earned significantly more than Schrader claimed. According to UAW data, workers at the General Motors plant earned an hourly wage that would in today's dollars be $24.75 per hour.[60]

John Barnard, author of *American Vanguard: The United Auto Workers During the Reuther Years*, wrote: "The auto workers, whose weekly wages in stable dollars rose from $56.51 to $249.53 between 1947 and 1975, were the best paid blue-collar workforce in the world, solidly middle class in economic standing, able to support middle-class levels and habits of consumption."[61]

Zeke tells the IRS agent that he is taking home $210 per week. That would make his annual take-home pay, when adjusted for inflation, $42,723. At the time, Detroit auto workers often received substantial bonus payments besides their hourly and overtime pay. Think about this when Jerry tells his famished young son that he cannot afford for him to eat more than one serving of Hamburger Helper. The scene strains credibility.

In movies, the only cure for the overworked-and-underpaid blues is to find a way to stick it to the man. *Blue Collar* is *9 to 5* without the catchy Dolly Parton song and an acetylene torch in place of a Xerox machine. But it doesn't work. Vincent Canby of the *New York Times* praised the film for its depiction of the autoworkers' day-to-day lives, but he believed the film went "awry ... in its melodramatic plotting."[62]

Julius Kassendorf of *The Solute* readily accepted that the workers were being exploited. He wrote: "Schrader's film is a dehumanizingly real depiction of life on the line. As you're working as hard as you can go, some jackoff foreman denigrates you and prods you into moving faster."[63]

The fact that a man walks around the factory floor to supervise their work does not represent brutalization. The Brussats wrote: "All three feel the grinding, oppressive, and entrapping quality of their work."[64] We must grind to eat. It bothers the Brussats that it doesn't make the men feel "a sense of pride and solidarity"[65] to be members of a union. "[I]nstead...," said the Brussats, "the union treats them the same way their bosses do—as children."[66] But we see how the men behave without supervision in their personal lives. The story, in all its twists and turns, grows out of the inexhaustible foolishness of the men. Jesse Hassenger of *A.V. Club* wrote: "Their complaints are sometimes disorganized or petty, and they indulge some pretty awful behavior in the name of blowing off steam, particularly in a sequence that offers the bizarre sight of Harvey Keitel and Richard Pryor attending a coke-fueled sex party together."[67]

Their bad behavior has been justified by critics who can only see them as symbols of the working man. Jamie Kitman of Trunkworthy wrote: "Lost in their own lives, minds dulled by hard repetitive labor, disgruntled by heartless, polluting employers and a corrupt union deeply in bed with management, they party 1970s Detroit-style, knowing no one has their interest at heart, mindless but not unaware."[68] The idea is that only a person without sympathy for the downtrodden working man can condemn Zeke, Jerry, or Smokey.

A sense of hopelessness pervades the film. This is a world where everyone is corrupt, which means that no one can be trusted to do the right thing. Film critic Peter Biskind wrote: "Schrader is a bit confused, so he's telling us a little of everything. He doesn't like the unions, but he doesn't think they can be changed, especially by the rank-and-file who were so dumb they rob their own local safe and then botch the job. But somehow, the film has eluded Schrader's own political limitations. It is an Aesopian fable, a case study in carrot-and-stick political pacification. Pryor, Keitel and Kotto are pawns of the system, which divides and conquers. The irreconcilable elements (Kotto) are destroyed, while the 'reasonable' elements (Pryor) are bought off and the weak ones (Keitel) are fatally compromised."[69]

Schrader wants us to believe that the factory management is corrupt, the union is corrupt, and the government is corrupt. He makes a particular effort to expose the corruption of the union officials, whom he depicts as thieves, liars, and murderers. Stanley Rogouski of the blog "Writers Without Money" wrote: "[T]here's barely a capitalist villain in sight. The United Auto Workers Union, on the other hand, might just as well be the mob. In fact, it is the mob."[70]

Unfortunately, the workers are corrupt, too. The three men are willing to go as far as using physical violence against any poor soul who gets in their way. This is learned the hard way by an elderly security guard at the union office. Here is the way the scene as described in the script:

> The Guard looks up. *This is what he sees: three men, two black, one white, walking toward him*: One, a huge black man, has whirligig glasses and carries a power drill. Another, also black, has huge buck teeth and wears a propeller beanie. The third, white, has an arrow through his head.
> Smokey coldcocks the Guard on the side of the head. He slumps to the floor.

The whirligig glasses may have been designed by Schrader to make the men look less menacing, but, in fact, it makes them appear more demented, more frightening. It is reminiscent of the scene in *A Clockwork Orange* (1971) in which a juvenile gang brutally attacks a couple in their home while wearing clownish masquerade masks.

Zeke claims that he engages in robbery, then assault, then blackmail and, finally, betrayal—all because he wants to take care of his family. It is fair to assume that Johnson wants to take care of his family, too. Does that make his actions acceptable? We can see that Johnson can be personable. At home, he's probably the sort of man who cheerfully bounces a grandson on his knee. But Zeke's home life is not as joyful. It is hard to believe that he is motivated by his family's best interests when he is mostly hostile to his wife and children. His never-ending anger and duplicity in his home cannot be overlooked or excused. He has to lie to his wife so he can go out and meet up with his friends for an orgy with hookers. He tells his wife that he is going to help a friend move. She can see that he is dressed too well to be moving furniture. But he is willing to pour out his lies, whether convincing or not, to get of the house. Pryor is able to draw an extraordinary amount of humor from this scene without deviating from the script. His wife knows that he's lying, but he remains determined to stick to his lies and look as innocent as possible while doing it.

Brown said that it worried Pryor to play a black man who turns out to be a snitch. "I can't see playing a Tom like that," he told Brown.[71] Zeke's unheroic actions made the film demeaning to black people, he thought, and Schrader needed to find a way to redeem him.

Schrader added an extra scene in which Johnson calls Zeke into his office to offer him the shop steward job. Zeke expresses anguish and uncertainty as he ponders the offer. He is not about to take his decision lightly and think only of himself. He leans forward in his chair, tensely and grimly. He says that he will accept the job if he has Johnson's assurance that Smokey and Jerry will not be harmed and he will have the authority as shop steward to make positive changes for the workers. Johnson agrees. Regardless of the thoughtfulness that he expresses in the scene, Zeke is never truly redeemed. He has made a deal with the devil.

We see the foreman be more abusive in the third act. He becomes frustrated trying to squeeze past an overweight worker. He grouses, "Come on, fat ass, you take up more room than an elephant." He asks a black man, "Hey, boy, you pick cotton this slow?" These lines do not exist in the shooting script. Obviously, Schrader decided during shooting to put a sharper point on the antagonistic relationship between the workers and the foreman. A lawsuit was once filed against General Motors because a manager regularly mocked a worker's stutter. The judge did not see that this behavior rose to a level of workplace harassment that would make General Motors liable to pay damages.

It is best to forget about the social issues and just take this as a straightforward drama. Zeke is a fascinating character, and Pryor's performance in the role is outstanding. Bailey was impressed by the scene in which Pryor laments his inability to handle his money and take care of his family. "Pryor doesn't reach for sympathy," he wrote. He also conveys subtlety in the post-orgy scene. Bailey added, "He and his friends sit on that couch in a daze, their sweet escape now little more than a blistering hangover. And a big Pontiac billboard peeks in through the window behind them, mocking them, a reminder that they still belong to their employer—that, as [Zeke] says earlier, 'Everybody knows what the plant is. The plant is just short for plantation.'"

Schrader held himself up as an advocate of the poor and downtrodden. He said, "Even though [I'd been] a middle-class kid, the fact that [we'd] lived in a poor part of town gave me the sense that rich people aren't going to give you anything, you're going to have to take it."[72] But Schrader isn't likely to have spent much time in his life with his script's "men with Afros or crewcuts" or "plain-faced women with outdated hairdos." He has observed these people from afar and has looked down on them. Biskind believes that Schrader saw the characters as "jerks" and that it took the actors to make the characters more than that. He wrote: "*Blue Collar*'s losers aren't victims because they're smart, tough, resilient and, above all, truthful."[73]

The profound drama of the film doesn't come from the protagonists' relationship with the auto plant, their relationship with their union, or their relationship with the FBI. It comes from the relationship of the three friends. The disintegration of that relationship is the core of the film. It is their falling-out that makes it a tragedy.

The film does make room for outright comedy, however. This is certainly the case when the worker drives a forklift into a vending machine. Humor is also prevalent when the men make their final preparations for the heist. Smokey tries to synchronize watches, only to find that neither Zeke nor Jerry have a watch. Zeke is suddenly a sheepish little boy when he says, "I ain't got no watch, Smokey." The comedian goes straight for the laugh in his delivery of the line. Humor comes from the funny Halloween disguises (Pryor wears plastic fangs and a propeller hat, Keitel wears X-ray specs and an arrow through his head) and the scene in which the men throw fingers to resolve a dispute. Humor comes from a headline in which the union office robbers are dubbed "The Oreo Gang."

The final scene is slightly different in the script. The workers are openly hostile as Jerry passes them. One calls him an "asshole scab." Another calls him a "stoolie." Jerry is not looking for trouble. He says nothing to the workers. He ignores Zeke as he tries to stare him down.

Jerry, as portrayed by Keitel, is not so passive: he is fully committed to cooperating with the FBI. He strides through the factory with fearlessness and indignation. Northup improvised the line "That ain't nothing special to look at."

Keitel creates sympathy and admiration for his character that is not entirely written into the script. He stands out in the scenes with his family and brings a great deal of raw emotion to his final scene in the plant. Northup said, "Harvey is a strong, emotional, daring actor, with a great sense of humor and explosiveness."[74]

Admittedly, this final scene is contrived in the context of the plot. It is hard to believe that Jerry had anything so important in his locker that he had to personally visit the factory to retrieve it. But any sort of contrivance can be overlooked as a final confrontation between Jerry and Zeke is needed to conclude the story.

In the script, Zeke says, "I'd hate to live in your shoes, you scum fink." The line in the film becomes "Hey, scumbag, I'd sure hate to be living in those pretty little white shoes." Jerry's shoes are actually white, but Pryor emphasizes the word *white* as if he is making a reference to something else entirely. The argument builds to the racial slurs in the script, but the racial conflict explodes on screen once the scene gets underway. Zeke doesn't call Jerry "hillbilly," "cowboy" or "partner," as he called Hank in the bar scene at the start of the film. He now calls Jerry "white boy" and "jive honky." Jerry calls Zeke "nigger" three separate times. Their racial animosity is no longer an underlying element of their words.

In the script, Zeke calling Jerry a "scum fink" is followed by the following stage direction:

> Jerry stops and turns.... Jerry and Zeke step closer to each other, each boiling over with hatred.

In the film, Jerry doesn't stop and turn. He doesn't waver at all in his actions, advancing on Zeke in a patently aggressive manner. The FBI agents hold him back at first, but he is too angry to be restrained and quickly pulls away from them.

A fight is described in the script. Jerry knees Zeke in the groin. Zeke punches Jerry in the face, which causes his nose to bleed. Jerry picks up a wrench, but Zeke punches him before he can use it. Jerry's face is streaming with blood, but he is not deterred. The script reads, "Jerry swings the wrench full force at Zeke's skull." The action was to freeze at this point.

The film differs in that it leaves the entire fight to the audience's imagination. That final image says everything that needs to be said without blows being exchanged or blood being spilled.

Critics regard Pryor's performance in *Blue Collar* as the best dramatic performance of his career. Vincent Canby of the *New York Times* wrote: "Richard Pryor has a role that makes use of the wit and fury that distinguish his straight comedy routines."[75]

After *Blue Collar* wrapped, Pryor set to work on a variety show for NBC. He argued vehemently and incessantly with the network, which resulted in the show being canceled after only four episodes were completed. The network was shocked by Pryor's material, including a skit in which he uses a machine gun to shoot down a bunch of white people.

Dave Zurawik of the *Detroit Free Press* interviewed Pryor during his publicity tour for *Which Way Is Up?* He wrote: "Richard Pryor sounds like a pretty angry guy." He then suggested that this is the reason that people don't like him. A publicist told the reporter, "You're interviewing Richard one on one. Good luck. Where should we send the flowers?"[76]

Zurawik asked Pryor directly: "What are you so mad about? Is it racism? Do you hate whites?"

> Pryor doesn't flinch. His voice becomes quiet.... He insisted that he only became angry because television executives had censored his sketches. "And, no, I don't hate whites. I have been married to two white women and I've had children by them. And I love them very much. There are a lot of whites in my organization that I keep in the job. I think that racism, black racism, is a charge they want to put on me. They want to make me a radical or raving lunatic because I won't play the game because I don't need them. But I'm not that way. I found the kind of happiness on my own."[77]

The series' cancellation cleared Pryor's schedule, allowing him to enter into negotiations with Universal to star in a remake of *Arsenic and Old Lace*. But, in the end, he chose instead to take off two months to work on a new stand-up act. The material later formed the basis of Pryor's second concert feature, *Richard Pryor: Live in Concert* (1979).

The Wiz (1978)

Production: Universal Pictures and Motown Productions.
Distribution: Universal Pictures.
Producer: Rob Cohen.
Director: Sidney Lumet.
Screenplay: Joel Schumacher, from the book *The Wonderful Wizard of Oz* by L. Frank Baum, and the stage musical *The Wiz* by William F. Brown.
Photography: Oswald Morris.
Editor: Dede Allen.
Music: Charlie Smalls.
Release date: October 24, 1978.
Running time: 134 minutes.
Cast: Diana Ross (Dorothy), Michael Jackson (Scarecrow), Nipsey Russell (Tinman), Ted Ross (Lion), Mabel King (Evillene), Theresa Merritt (Aunt Em), Thelma Carpenter (Miss One), Lena Horne (Glinda the Good), Richard Pryor (The Wiz).

Motown Productions, which had produced *Lady Sings the Blue* and *The Bingo Long Traveling All-Stars & Motor Kings*, set up a deal to produce a big-budget film version of the Broadway hit *The Wiz*. One of the first actors they approached to be in the film was Bill Cosby, who was offered the role of the Tin Man. But the casting process took a number of twists and turns and Cosby never ended up in the final cast.

The director, Sidney Lumet, had made a career out of making social dramas, including *12 Angry Men* (1957), *The Pawnbroker* (1964), *Fail-Safe* (1964), *Serpico* (1973), and *Dog Day Afternoon* (1975). But *The Wiz* was to be no drama, no *12 Angry Munchkins*. Lumet was determined for this film to be "an absolutely unique experience that nobody has ever witnessed before."[1] He didn't want it to be anything like MGM's 1939 classic *The Wizard of Oz*. He assured an interviewer that he "didn't use anything from it."[2] He added, "[W]e wanted to make sure that we never overlapped in any area."[3]

Pryor went from his subtle and controlled performance in *Blue Collar* to a loud and manic performance in *The Wiz*. His cowardly wizard is nothing like the bold wizard that André De Shields originated on stage. De Shields played the part like he was James Brown, who wore a dazzling white jumpsuit and cape and seductively swiveled his hips while he sang. He was funky, sexy, flashy, and regal. Pryor is none of that. He is introduced cowering beneath a blanket. He wears a rumpled (though stylish) bathrobe. In his brief appearance, he whimpers, stutters, and wheezes. He is too nervous to ever stand still—pacing, jumping, and falling to his knees. He hyperventilates at one point. Being loud and manic is, by itself, not funny. Pryor was much funnier when he wasn't trying so hard.

The Wiz proved to be a critical and commercial failure. Critics had all types of terrible things to say about the film. Forty years later, film historians still have nothing nice to say, calling it "expensive crud"[4] (Tom Shone), "cockamamie"[5] (Tom Hischak), and "one of the decade's biggest failures"[6] (Charles Henry Harpole).

Pryor started work on *The Wiz* on December 10, 1977. Within the past month, he had been hospitalized twice due to chest pains. He claimed that he was suffering from stress and exhaustion. He denied his grandmother's claim to a reporter that he had suffered a heart attack. He had signed on for a week's work on *The Wiz*, but he needed to stay on the film longer while Diane Ross recovered from eye problems caused by the bright lights used to illuminate the immense sets. Pryor sat in a dark corner of the set

The Wiz (1978)

Pryor in *The Wiz* (1978).

between scenes. When a production photographer approached him to take a photo, he flung his arm over his face and had him escorted off the set.

During production, Pryor was arrested for firing a gun at his wife, Deborah McQuire, and her two friends, Beverly Clayborn and Edna Solomon. An anonymous friend told *People* magazine, "He shot out the tires, windshield and basically killed the car."[7] But Hollywood executives were no longer bothered by Pryor's blowups. He sold tickets. As of May 1978, Pryor had a development deal with Universal and a multi-picture deal with Warner Bros. Sue Reilly noted in *People*: "Universal [has] ... set Pryor up with a multi-picture deal and a handsome brown-and-gold office bungalow on the lot

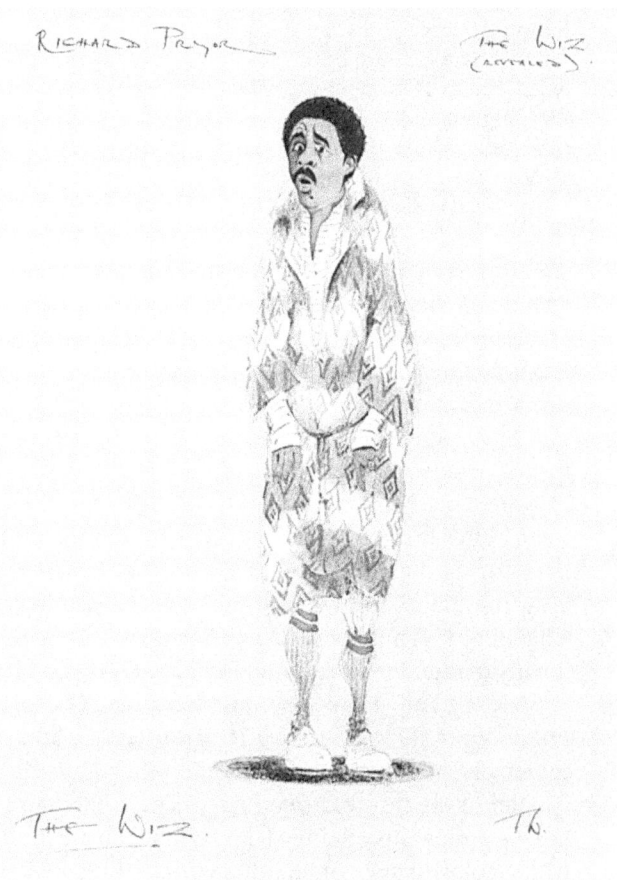

The costume design for Pryor's robe in *The Wiz* (1978).

next door to Telly Savalas. The price was $2 million plus, but that doesn't buy exclusive rights to Richard Pryor. He has an even sweeter four-to-six-movie commitment with Warner Bros. and properties in the works with Paramount and Columbia. It must also tickle his irony that his divorce from NBC was the cushiest of his career—he collects $2 million not to appear on any other network for five years."[8]

Pryor needed vast sums of money to support his drug habit. So, he was willing to sign multi-picture deals with Universal, Columbia, Warner Bros., and Paramount, even though it was not possible for him to make all of the films for which he was contracted. He certainly could not be a prolific movie star when he was locked inside his mansion, working himself into a continual stupor.

California Suite (1978)

Production: Columbia Pictures and Rastar Films.
Distribution: Columbia Pictures.
Producer: Ray Stark.
Director: Herbert Ross.
Screenplay: Neil Simon.
Photography: David M. Walsh.
Editor: Michael A. Stevenson.
Music: Claude Bolling.
Release date: December 22, 1978.
Running time: 103 minutes.
Cast: Jane Fonda (Hannah Warren), Alan Alda (Bill Warren), Maggie Smith (Diana Barrie), Michael Caine (Sidney Cochran), Walter Matthau (Marvin Michaels), Elaine May (Millie Michaels), Richard Pryor (Dr. Chauncey Gump), Bill Cosby (Dr. Willis Panama).

Ray Stark, the head of Raystar Films, made a deal with Columbia to produce a film version of Neil Simon's 1976 Broadway play *California Suite*. The play presents four separate stories set at The Beverly Hills Hotel. The style of the segments varied to make each one a counterpoint to the others. Two of the segments are broad and farcical; the other two are subtle and poignant.

Stark convinced Pryor to handle the broad comedy of a segment called "The Visitors from Chicago." Pryor's character was Dr. Chauncey Gump, a physician on vacation with his wife, Lola, brother-in-law Dr. Willis Panama, and his wife, Bettina. The vacation goes wrong after the couples engage in a contentious mixed doubles tennis match. Bettina is hurt during the match and Willis accuses Chauncey of having caused her injury by lobbing the ball. The two men get into an argument, which escalates into a fist fight. Chauncey is sympathetic in contrast to Willis, who is insufferably selfish, pompous, and inconsiderate. Pryor recommended to Stark that he get Bill Cosby to play Willis.

Cosby had starred in a number of successful feature films, including *Uptown Saturday Night* (1974), *Let's Do It Again* (1975), and *Mother, Jugs & Speed* (1976), but his career on the big screen had come to a standstill. He could not get funding for a film version of the novel *Sitting Pretty*. The comedian thought he could do well playing the novel's protagonist, Sidney J. Prettymon, an alcoholic janitor who lives in a low-rent hotel with a colorful assortment of down-on-their-luck people. Cosby complained that finan-

The poster for *California Suite* (1978).

ciers failed to see the potential in the property. He said, "They tell me it's not funny enough, it has no violence and only one minor sex scene. I think it's funny, and it would get funnier in the making."[1]

Cosby was glad to accept the role from Stark. He said, "On the stage, these roles were played by white actors [George Grizzard and Jack Weston], but in the movie you've got these upper-middle-class characters being played by black actors. I think that's good."[2]

Pryor and Cosby were faithful to the script. Cosby said, "When you're shooting a Neil Simon script, yes, you stick to the words. Otherwise, I don't like a tight script. I'd like to be able to improvise with the comedy on the set. That's the way that Sidney [Poitier] and I work together."

Pryor argued with his director, but at least the argument didn't get physical. Cecil Brown wrote: "One [black] actress complained to Richard that [the] director [Herbert Ross] was not respectful, and that he was not as open to them as he was to the white actors."[3] Pryor took up the issue with Ross, who became upset and called Stark to the set. Stark was furious about the situation, but he spoke to Pryor in private and the two men were able to work out their differences.

The different comedy styles do not mix well. *Variety* decried the film for "veering from poignant emotionalism to broad slapstick in sudden shifts."[4] Dave Kehr of *Chicago Reader* found that the film compared unfavorably to the recent Robert Altman film *The Wedding* (1978), which relied on a similar "multicharacter structure."[5] Kehr noted that, unlike Altman, Ross "failed to achieve relative fluidity" in bringing together the segments. The tragicomedy segments, "Visitors from New York" and "Visitors from London," earned critical acclaim for their empathetic characters and deeply emotional situations. The segments garnered awards for Maggie Smith (Academy Award) and Jane Fonda (Los Angeles Film Critics Association Award). The slapstick wrestling match between Cosby and Pryor, however, received nothing but derision.

The doctors bicker from the moment they are introduced. We don't get to know the characters first. We don't have the situation develop in an orderly and understandable way. We just get two men who want to tear each other apart.

The slapstick is laid on thick throughout the segment. Sheila Frazier, as Cosby's wife, takes a wild swing at the ball and hits Cosby squarely on the head. Pryor tries to jump over the tennis net, but he trips on the net and falls flat on his face. Cosby slams Pryor into a garden trestle. Pauline Kael of *The New Yorker* wrote: "[It] is a disaster, and not only because it has no comic rhythm. When the black doctors stumble around a flooded hotel room, crash into each other, and step on broken glass, and Cosby bites Pryor's nose, the sequences have horrific racist overtones. (Inadvertently, the movie seems to be saying that while these black men may be educated, they're still savages.)"[6]

Cosby was infuriated by the reviews. He took out a full page ad in *Variety* to blast critics for accusing him and Pryor of acting like "clownish savages." The Chicago visitors were not doctors in the play. It could be that the filmmakers elevated the characters' social status to avoid criticism that they were making blacks look like dumb savages. It didn't work.

Cosby was still fuming about the matter two years later. He said in a 1980 interview, "Some critics ... accused producer Ray Stark of racism because Richard Pryor and I tore up the hotel in *California Suite*. They didn't stop to realize that nobody was having fun in the picture. Maybe it was not too clearly defined that these two fellows were just tired of each other."[7]

California Suite (1978) 107

Cosby (in white) and Pryor were accused by critics of being "savage clowns" in *California Suite* (1978).

While promoting *California Suite*, Cosby told reporters that he and Pryor were talking about working on another film together. He said, "We agreed that whatever we do must have two elements: one, it's got to be funny; two, it must have some sociological meaning."[8]

On March 6, 1979, Marilyn Beck reported in her column that Simon was writing a vehicle for Pryor and Cosby called "The Oddest Couple." This was but one of many vehicles being fashioned for Pryor at the time. David Felton of *Rolling Stone* wrote:

> In May, he starts working with Cicely Tyson on a movie called "Family Dreams" for Universal. After that, there's a spy spoof for Paramount; "The Charlie Parker Story" for Warner Bros.; and a project he's particularly excited about, a World War II movie he's planning with Giancarlo Giannini. And Neil Simon, after seeing *Richard Pryor Live in Concert*, immediately began writing a script for Pryor and Marsha Mason, Simon's wife. It's tentatively titled "Macho Man."
>
> "The thing that's good about it for me is people get to see what I do," Pryor said of the concert film [*Richard Pryor Live in Concert*]. "'Cause Ray Stark, who produced *California Suite*, had never seen me work, right? And when he saw the movie, him and Neil, they got real excited about what they saw that I could do. They said they had no idea, or they would have had me do something different in their movie." Simon talked to him about two potential projects.[9]

"The Oddest Couple" was not a project that got far. There was still talk of Pryor starring in "Macho Man" in August 1979, however. The *Pittsburgh Press* reported, "Pryor will get

[one] million plus gross points."[10] It is interesting that he planned to work with Giannini; he had already remade one of his films, *The Seduction of Mimi*, and had talked about remaking another, *Swept Away*. The untitled World War II vehicle had been on Pryor's schedule for at least a year before this *Rolling Stone* article appeared.

Pryor's career came to a sudden standstill when his grandmother died in December 1978. He wrote: "[A]fter Mama died, nothing struck me as funny.... [The film offers] seemed too much to handle. Instead of taking advantage of being a hot commodity, I was awash in a depression that crashed over me following Mama's death. I truly felt as if I was flailing underwater, stuck in a surreal nightmare."[11]

The Muppet Movie (1979)

Production: Henson Associates and ITC Films.
Distribution: Associated Film Distribution.
Producer: Jim Henson.
Director: James Frawley.
Screenplay: Jerry Juhl and Jack Burns.
Photography: Isidore Mankofsky.
Editor: Chris Greenbury.
Music: Paul Williams and Kenny Ascher.
Release date: June 22, 1979.
Running time: 97 minutes.
Cast: Jim Henson (Kermit the Frog, Rowlf, Dr. Teeth, and Waldorf), Frank Oz (Miss Piggy, Fozzie Bear, Animal, and Sam the Eagle), Jerry Nelson (Floyd Pepper, Crazy Harry, Robin the Frog, and Lew Zealand), Richard Hunt Scooter, Statler, Janice, Sweetums, and Beaker), Dave Goelz (The Great Gonzo, Zoot, and Dr. Bunsen Honeydew), Charles Durning (Doc Hopper), Austin Pendleton (Max), Scott Walker (Frog Killer), Lawrence Gabriel Jr. (Sailor), Ira F. Grubman (Bartender), H. B. Haggerty (Lumberjack), Bruce Kirby (Gate Guard), Tommy Madden (One-Eyed Midget), James Frawley (Waiter), Arnold Roberts (Cowboy), Carroll Spinney (Big Bird). Other Muppet performers were Steve Whitmire, Kathryn Mullen, Bob Payne, Eren Ozker, Caroly Wilcox, Olga Felgemacher, Bruce Schwartz, Michael Davis, Buz Suraci, Tony Basillcato, and Adam Hunt. Guest stars were Edgar Bergen, Milton Berle, Mel Brooks, James Coburn, Dom DeLuise, Elliott Gould, Bob Hope, Madeline Kahn, Carol Kane, Cloris Leachman, Steve Martin, Richard Pryor, Telly Savalas, Orson Welles, and Paul Williams.

Pryor's cameo appearance in *The Muppet Movie* is neither funny nor remarkable. Gonzo approaches Pryor, a balloon vendor, to buy a balloon for his love, Camilla the Chicken. But Pryor is a slick salesman. While Gonzo ponders whether to get a red or green balloon, the vendor tells him, "A beautiful chicken like that deserves two balloons." When he sees he has Gonzo on the hook, he presses forward to make an even bigger sale. "I have guys come in all the time," he says, "sometimes they buy a bunch of balloons for the girls. They go gaga for them." Gonzo eagerly buys a bunch of balloons, which have sufficient buoyancy to lift him off his feet and send him floating across the sky.

Austin Pendleton recalled that the film was shot on "a very unhappy set."[1] He explained, "Jim [Frawley] was very unhappy directing that movie. And I noticed that was the only time the Muppet people used an outside person to direct a Muppet movie.

They never did that again. After that, it was either Jim Henson or Frank Oz. And I would have liked to have been in one of those, because those sets were very harmonious. But this was not."

For once, Pryor was not involved in the unhappiness. He did not whack Fozzie Bear over the head with a chair. He did not make Kermit cry. He did not try to beat Swedish Chef with a sock filled with coins. He did not urinate on Miss Piggy.

Pryor hadn't been in front of film cameras much during 1978 and 1979. Brashler, the author of the *Bingo Long* novel, was hired to interview Pryor at the time. As he recalled, "I was warned not to stay at his house after midnight, that the drugs and the guns got strange. When I'd interviewed him, he said that that was all behind him. He's probably the most racist man I know in entertainment. I don't say that in any derogatory way; it's that his material depends so much on race. Pryor said that if it wasn't for race, he'd be the biggest comedian in America. Some say that without race, he wouldn't be a comedian."[2]

Pryor as a balloon vendor in *The Muppet Movie* (1979).

Wholly Moses! (1980)

Production and Distribution: Columbia Pictures.
Producer: Freddie Fields.
Director: Gary Weis.
Screenplay: Guy Thomas.
Photography: Frank Stanley.
Editor: Sidney Levin.
Music: Patrick Williams.
Release date: June 13, 1980.
Running time: 103 minutes.
Cast: Dudley Moore (Harvey Orchid/Herschel), Laraine Newman (Zoey/Zerelda), James Coco (Hyssop), Tanya Boyd (Princess), Madeline Kahn (The Witch), Richard B. Shull (Jethro), Sam Weisman (Talent Coordinator), John Ritter (Satan), Paul Sand (God's Angel), Jack Gilford (Tailor), Richard Pryor (Pharaoh), David Lander (The Beggar), John Houseman (The Archangel), Dom DeLuise (Shadrach).

Wholly Moses! borrows key plot elements from *Monty Python's Life of Brian* (1979). A couple of tourists, Harvey and Zoey, meet on a Holy Land bus tour and discover a lost

Pryor plays an angry pharaoh in *Wholly Moses!* (1980).

Dead Sea scroll called the Book of Herschel. Hershel's life parallels that of Moses. He, too, is placed in a tiny ark and sent floating down the Nile the day the Pharaoh decrees the death of all male Israelite children. He, too, finds himself on Mount Sinai the day God delivers the Ten Commandments. Hershel ends up doing more than Moses to fulfill God's will, but Moses takes all of the credit.

Wikipedia reports, "On the final day of shooting, Richard Pryor, who was signed to do a one-day shoot as the Pharaoh, didn't show up. With production at a complete standstill, frantic calls were made. There was even some talk of replacing him with Cleavon Little. Several hours later that afternoon, Pryor finally appeared but then refused to play the scene as written with a trained lion by his throne."[1]

Critics complained that the film was tame and predicable. But Pryor is not tame in his four-minute cameo. He portrays the Pharaoh as a man with uncontrollable rage. It is not a nuanced performance on the comedian's part. The shouting and exaggerated facial expressions that he conveys are not funny. Pryor was prominently featured in the marketing, which led people to believe that he had a more extensive role in the film than he did.

Dudley Moore was paid an extraordinary salary to star in the film. He later admitted in a letter to a friend that the film was "very drab."[2] He added, "The material was very bad in that film…. [I]t is piece of crap, but I thought mistakenly that it would have been fun to do."[3]

In God We Tru$t (or Gimme That Prime Time Religion) (1980)

Production and Distribution: Universal Pictures.
Producer: Howard West and George Shapiro.
Director: Marty Feldman.
Screenplay: Marty Feldman and Chris Allen.
Photography: Charles Correll.
Editor: David Blewitt.
Music: John Morris.
Release date: September 26, 1980.
Running time: 97 minutes.
Cast: Marty Feldman (Brother Ambrose), Peter Boyle (Dr. Melmoth), Louise Lasser (Mary), Richard Pryor (God), Andy Kaufman (Armageddon T. Thunderbird), Wilfrid Hyde-White (Abbot Thelonious), Severn Darden (Priest), Eddie Parkes (Tap-Dancing Man), Stephanie Ross (Female Newsreader).

Alan Spencer, a close friend of Marty Feldman, said, "Marty was very, very critical of America, which is not the best thing to do for an outsider sometimes."[1] Feldman was upset to see politicians in America exploiting religion for their own personal gain. He thought he could effectively oppose this trend by producing a sharp-edged religious satire. Spencer said that Universal executives were uncomfortable with the film, especially after Feldman told them he had gotten Richard Pryor to play God.

The story begins at a monastery. A monk, Brother Ambrose, leaves the monastery on orders from the abbot to find the five thousand dollars needed to pay their mortgage. The abbot believes that Armageddon T. Thunderbird, a television evangelist, is a great philanthropist who can be persuaded to save the monastery. "State your case and you will get the money," he says. (Thunderbird is played exuberantly by Andy Kaufman.)

The monk has never seen the outside world. He is terrified just to see sunlight for the first time. After he becomes accustomed to his new surroundings, he naïvely befriends a fake faith healer, Dr. Sebastian Melmoth (Peter Boyle), who travels the country in a broken-down bus that serves as a mobile church (it even has a steeple on the roof).

Thunderbird, who is in fact ruthless and greedy, sees profit potential in Dr. Melmoth's Traveling Church. He envisions riches to be gained from a fleet of "prayer mobiles" that can cover the whole country. Thunderbird relies on the advice of a supercomputer, G.O.D. (General Organizational Directivator). G.O.D. advises that he use the monk, whom he is confident will make a devout and pure disciple, to lead the crusade. Thunderbird has his goons kidnap Ambrose and bring him to his office. The evangelist agrees to give Brother Ambrose the money to save his monastery from bankruptcy if he will act as the front man to his fleet of mobile churches.

Dr. Melmoth and Mary convince Brother Ambrose that Thunderbird is a hustler. Brother Ambrose returns to Thunderbird's office, where he reads the Bible to G.O.D. The computer is inspired by the Bible to engage in a charitable act. It arranges for guards to remove $5 million from Thunderbird's vault and dump it off the roof to the bystanders below. Ambrose flees Thunderbird's office with the paid certificate for the monastery mortgage. Thunderbird's goons chase him through the city. He is rescued by crane by the actual God.

Pryor in *In God We Tru$t* (1980).

In the end, Ambrose gives up the monk order to marry Mary.

Marty Feldman played memorable supporting roles in a number of popular movie spoofs, including *Young Frankenstein* (1974), *The Adventure of Sherlock Holmes' Smarter Brother* (1975), and *Silent Movie* (1976). Jerry Henshaw, an executive at Universal, thought that Feldman was a genius, a potential star who could play leading roles. Henshaw signed the comedian to a five-year contract. Feldman's first film, *The Last Remake of Beau Geste* (1977), was a spoof of P. C. Wren's classic 1924 Foreign Legion adventure novel *Beau Geste*, which had been adapted for the stage (in 1929) and screen (in 1926, 1939, 1966). Feldman's take on the story did not live up to its title: it was remade yet again in 1982.

Feldman kept an editor with him on location in Madrid so that footage could be assembled during production. But Feldman did not like how scenes were turning out, causing him to panic and fire his editor. He called Jim Clark, a director and editor with whom he had worked on *Every Home Should Have One* (1970) and *The Adventure of Sherlock Holmes' Smarter Brother*, and begged him to fly to Madrid to assess the situation. Clark looked at the scenes that Feldman had shot. He later wrote: "Marty's direction wasn't good at all."[2] He told Feldman, "The script is good, but what I'm seeing on the screen isn't funny."

Clark brought in another editor, Artie Schmidt, to help him salvage the footage. Schmidt said, "I spent twelve hours looking at all the dailies that had been cut. They weren't very good. The screening gave me a huge headache and I wondered if I had made the right decision."[3] He told Clark, "This is terrible! Why do you want to get involved?' Clark felt obligated to Feldman, who was a friend. But the situation did not get better. Clark said, "[E]very day we saw the rushes and every day there were no laughs."[4] Feldman didn't take any of Clark's advice to improve on his direction. Clark said: "I used to call him and rage and scream and say, 'But this isn't funny.' 'Don't matter, love. Don't matter, love. It's all right. It's all right. Don't worry,' he would say. He eventually finished shooting and we still had this two-hour sprawl of unfunny film which he'd completely fucked up."[5]

Ned Tanen, the president of Universal's feature production, also hated Feldman's film. He showed it to his vice president, Verna Fields, a former editor who had cut *American Graffiti* (1973) and *Jaws* (1975). She hated it, too. Feldman pleaded with the executives for a chance to reshoot scenes. They agreed, but it didn't help. Clark wrote: "Marty flew to London to do some additional dialogue with English actors and while he was away, Verna Fields coerced me to re-cut certain scenes."[6] Schmidt was involved in the new cut. He remembered Fields directing him and Clark to make extensive changes. Spencer said, "When Marty returned, he saw a completely different version of this film … [it] had been recut from head to toe."[7] The studio's complaint, according to Spencer, was that the film was "non-linear"[8] and "surreal."[9] Clark said, "[Marty] was very angry about it. He now felt that I was siding with the studio against him, so our relationship went sour at that point and it never recovered."[10]

To preserve his vision, Feldman was willing to fight harder against Universal than the Foreign Legion had fought against the Tuareg. The studio previewed the cut by Fields, Clark, and Schmidt and previewed an entirely new cut that Feldman had assembled with another editor. Two separate scores had to be written. Clark wrote: "[Both versions] got identically bad marks, which was interesting because the two versions were radically different, though they contained identical material."[11]

The final decision came to Tanen. According to Clark, Tanen decided to stick with the linear construction of the studio version but use the scenes as assembled by Feldman. It was, to the surprise of many at the studio, that this patchwork cut was profitable at the box office.

Gary Arnold of the *Washington Post* announced, "The inexplicable success of 'The Last Remake of Beau Geste' has encouraged the studio to humor Marty Feldman again."[12] Universal allowed him to proceed with his next project, *In God We Tru$t*.

Clark concluded from the experience, "Marty was not an easy man to deal with."[13] He was not the only one to hold this opinion. Feldman continued to be a pain to the Universal executives, which called into question the studio's decision to keep him around.

Arnold hadn't liked *The Last Remake of Beau Geste* and his opinion of *In God We Tru$t* was even worse. He wrote: "'In God We Tru$t,' an imbecilic satire of crooked evangelism, proves that Feldman still doesn't know what he's doing behind the camera. His sense of humor is once again exposed as outmoded and mawkish, his technique as shabbily amateurish…. 'In God We Tru$t' is an unmitigated disgrace."[14] Amid his brutal attack on the film, Arnold did make a point to commend Kaufman for his "robust caricature of outrageous hypocrisy."[15]

Universal terminated Feldman's contract only days after the film was released.

Two separate plagiarism lawsuits were filed against *In God We Tru$t*, the first by bestselling novelist Donald Westlake, who claimed that the film took its plot from his novel *Brothers Keepers*. Certainly, the set-up for the novel is similar to that used by Feldman. A monastery is going to be torn down to make room for an office building. The monks hold a lease for the property, but that was issued during the 1700s and was never registered with the city. Brother Benedict leaves the monastery to take whatever action he can to stop the developers from tearing down the monks' home. He encounters a variety of eccentric characters in the big city. He even develops a romantic interest in the daughter of a wealthy building contractor.

The second lawsuit was filed by two reputable television writers, Mort Lachman and Ed Simmons, who alleged that *In God We Tru$t* was based on their 1971 screenplay

"Albert." The problem with the lawsuit was that a German company, CBM Productions, had bought the screenplay and only the production company had the standing to sue for copyright infringement. CBM Productions had no interest in initiating a lawsuit.

Pryor, ebullient and childlike as the G.O.D. computer, is entertaining in his brief role. The actor was made to look like the fatherly God of Renaissance art—long white hair, beard, and mustache. Of course, his dark skin color was designed as a twist on the old image. At least the role shows Pryor in a better light than the angry pharaoh role in *Wholly Moses!*

Stir Crazy (1980)

Production and Distribution: Columbia Pictures.
Producer: Hannah Weinstein.
Director: Sidney Poitier.
Screenplay: Bruce Jay Friedman.
Photography: Fred Schuler.
Editor: Harry Keller.
Music: Tom Scott.
Release date: December 12, 1980.
Running time: 111 minutes.
Cast: Gene Wilder (Skip Donahue), Richard Pryor (Harry Monroe), Georg Stanford Brown (Rory Schultebrand), JoBeth Williams (Meredith), Miguel Ángel Suárez (Jesus Ramirez), Craig T. Nelson (Deputy Ward Wilson), Barry Corbin (Warden Walter Beatty), Nicolas Coster (Warden Henry Sampson), Joel Brooks (Len Garber), Jonathan Banks (Jack Graham), Erland Van Lidth (Grossberger), Franklyn Ajaye (Young Man in Hospital), Cedrick Hardman (Big Mean), Luis Ávalos (Chico), Grand L. Bush (Slowpoke) Herbert Hirschman (Man at Dinner Party), Mickey Jones (Guard # 8), Billy Beck (Flycatching Prisoner), Lee Purcell (Susan).

Scriptwriter Bruce Jay Friedman said, "The idea [for *Stir Crazy*] wasn't mine—it was a producer's named Hannah Weinstein, who told me about this phenomena in Texas where prisoners staged a rodeo. That's all I was given. I wrote the screenplay, and Hannah was able to cast Richard Pryor and Gene Wilder."[1]

The story quickly establishes the relationship of its two lead characters. Skip Donahue (Wilder), an aspiring playwright, and Harry Monroe (Pryor), an out-of-work actor, are having trouble holding down jobs in New York City. Skip comes up with the idea of the two of them driving cross-country and getting a fresh start in Los Angeles. The run-down van that is supposed to get them there breaks down in Arizona. They don't have the money to get it repaired, so they need to find temporary jobs. Skip learns that a bank is running a promotion for a new checking account. He convinces the manager that he and Harry can bring the bank more customers by performing a song-and-dance act in their lobby. The next we see of Skip and Harry, they are singing and dancing at the bank in woodpecker costumes.

While Skip and Harry are at lunch, two criminals use the woodpecker costumes as disguises and rob the bank. Skip and Harry are arrested for the robbery. Skip is optimistic that the real robbers will be caught and is determined to use his experience in jail as research for a script. But, due to their incompetent court-appointed attorney, Skip and

Pryor and Wilder behind bars in *Stir Crazy* (1980).

Harry are sentenced to 125 years in state prison. The men become hysterical. Guards hustle them outside the courtroom to a bus, ready to transport convicts to prison.

At the Glenboro State Prison, Warden Walter Beatty makes as much as $100,000 every year enrolling his inmates in a prison rodeo. The warden makes a point to test new inmates' rodeo skills by getting them to ride a mechanical bull in his office. Skip proves to have exceptional ability, managing to remain in the saddle even after the controls are turned up to top speed. A fellow prisoner, Jesus Ramirez, tells Skip that they may be able to escape during the rodeo. Skip acts quickly to get his friends, Harry, Jesus, and Rory, assigned to his crew.

A defense attorney, Meredith, is convinced that Skip is innocent. A six-year-old girl who witnessed the robbery noticed that one of the robbers had the tattoo on his hand—the image of a hand squeezing a heart. Neither Skip nor Harry have such a tattoo, which means they have to be innocent. But the police refuse to give any credence to the little girl's testimony. Meredith is determined to investigate further and prove Skip and Harry's innocence. She visits numerous tattoo parlors in the area to identify the man who was given this particular tattoo. She learns the name of the man and is told that he frequents the Rough Riders strip club. She goes undercover as a stripper at the club to find him.

Skip, Harry, Jesus, and Rory successfully follow their escape plan, which mostly involves the convicts crawling beneath rodeo bleachers. Meredith and Len see Skip and Harry escaping in an SUV and follow them to an abandoned airplane hangar. Meredith tells Skip that she helped the police locate the real bank robbers. Skip and Meredith happily embrace before driving off with Harry.

Wilder wrote: "A famous producer by the name of Hannah Weinstein read an article

Poitier (top) and Pryor enjoy a laugh between scenes in *Stir Crazy* (1980).

in the newspaper about a rodeo that was held in prison. She took the writer, Bruce Jay Friedman, for a visit to the prison. When they got back to New York, Bruce wrote the first draft of "Prison Rodeo." Months later, the title was changed to *Stir Crazy*."[2]

Friedman met Wilder for dinner and was taken aback by his demeanor: "He seemed very distraught, to the point of losing consciousness."[3] Wilder confessed that he couldn't figure out how to play his character. Friedman calmed the actor down with a single word: *Candide*. A French satire first published by Voltaire in 1759, *Candide* involves a naïve optimist who is abruptly introduced to the hardships of the world.

Poitier briefly brought in Charles Blackwell, who had worked with him on *A Piece of the Action* (1977), to punch up Pryor's dialogue, but Blackwell's contribution to the script was not significant enough for him to receive screen credit.

Pryor was difficult during production. Stan Shaw, who acted in *Bingo Long* and *Harlem Nights*, was one of his close friends. He said, "Success doesn't change you. It just magnifies who you are."[4] Pryor's friend David Banks, who was a writer on *The Richard Pryor Show*, said, "Richard had thirteen personalities. Nine of them you could deal with. But them other four could be a motherfucker."[5] Franklyn Ajaye, who played a convict in *Stir Crazy*, acknowledged that Pryor was talented. He said, "Every comedian looked at him with awe for the brilliance he was bringing out." But he didn't like what he saw when he looked past that talent. David and Joe Henry wrote:

> Ajaye said he never felt any personal warmth for Richard as a person, ever since their first meeting in 1969 when Ajaye reported for work on *Uncle Tom's Fairy Tales* and found him screaming abuse at Shelley [Pryor's second wife]. "There was absolutely zero he could teach me about living," Ajaye says.

"I could learn from him how he did his comedy, but I didn't see anything about how he lived his life that I wanted to emulate. Zero. He was very tempestuous. I didn't even like to be around him. I don't like being around volatile people. I have no interest in being around geniuses. Those tempestuous volatile geniuses the media likes to hold up. But I had the deepest admiration for his artistry. As a stand-up, not as an actor. He was just a troubled man. He was heavy into the drugs, heavy into alcohol.... Who's sane doing that? *Nobody*. Just look what happened to [John] Belushi. Freddie Prinze.... Robin Williams survived it, but he was headed down the same road."[6]

Poitier and Wilder stayed at a hotel, but Pryor demanded that the production company rent him a house, a responsibility that fell to Jack Young. Young said, "I rented the same house for [Pryor] that I had gotten for James Arness; however, he destroyed the place and it cost the company a lot of money to put it back in good condition."[7] Then, Pryor got mad because it was a two-hour commute from the house to the set. He demanded that he be transported back and forth by helicopter.

Pryor runs from an angry bull in *Stir Crazy* (1980).

Pryor tried to make friends with the prisoners by sneaking drugs to them. It is questionable if this tactic worked well. Young, who was also in charge of casting extras, said that Pryor was not well liked at the prison. He noted, "I guess he had done something or said something about the inmates. When time came to shoot those scenes, Pryor refused to show up for fear of his life. We had to put their real guards, with real guns and bullets, in the scene before he would come to work. All the time we were shooting, he was constantly looking over his shoulder and was scared to death. Not a nice guy."[8]

Pryor was asked what his thoughts were about the prison. He said, "Stay out of the laundry. That's where Jimmy Cagney got it in *Each Dawn I Die*. In the laundry. Trust me. I know. They always do it to you in the laundry."[9]

Greg Ferrara, a film critic with the TCM website, wrote: "[Pryor's] bodyguard later admitted to Pryor's agent, David Franklin, that Pryor was freebasing cocaine every night during the shoot. This made the star's behavior erratic and paranoid." Jennifer Lee, who was dating Pryor at the time, said, "He was based out of his fuckin' head."[10] Pryor acknowledged in his autobiography that he was struggling terribly with drugs while shooting *Stir Crazy*. He said, "I was just about gone. Wow! I was destroying myself. I was self-destructing."[11]

Pryor had reason to be distressed that his illegal drug use might get him locked up in prison with the inmates. He wrote: "I started buying coke through a connection with some motorcycle gangbangers. Unbeknownst to me, they were being monitored by state police and federal agents, including a visit to and from my trailer and my hillside home."[12]

He became so paranoid, in fact, that he believed members of the crew were trying to kill him. At one point, he claimed that crew members were driving out to his house and firing shots into the building.

David Henry said, "Charles Weldon, who acted in the film, told me he didn't know how a person who consumed so much drugs could continue to work. According to Charles, there was one scene they shot after being up for at least five nights partying with women and freebasing. Charles said he didn't even remember doing that scene."[13]

Pryor was obviously coked up when he was interviewed on the set by a Mormon high school public access cable television show. He said, "What do you wanna know about this movie? It sucks!" At one point, he abruptly asked the interviewer, "Can I play with your dick?" Bailey examined the interview extensively in *Richard Pryor: American Id*. He wrote: "[Pryor] wipes sweat from his face, rubs his nose, and smokes nervously."[14]

Pryor was not in the least bit cooperative. He even refused to wear the woodpecker costume for the bank scenes. He later agreed to do so for publicity shots.

Rovin wrote: "Poitier minimizes the difficulties he had with Pryor, stating only that he 'loved' working with him. However, in conversations with crew members, words like *depressed* and *erratic* surfaced frequently in connection with Pryor. He would make statements like, 'I'm sick of the film business,' and walk off the set...."[15]

Elahe Izadi of the *Washington Post* wrote: "Wilder reportedly has said they weren't good friends, and that Pryor wasn't pleasant to be around when he had drug problems."[16] And, indeed, Wilder was angry about Pryor's behavior during the shoot. He wrote: "It's difficult to continue loving someone who shits on you—but I did, because of the moments of magic that we had shared together."[17]

In a 2013 interview, Wilder was upbeat when talking about *Silver Streak*. "The first one was really good," he said. "We got along really swell."[18] But he was less happy talking about *Stir Crazy*. "Sidney was going nuts," he said.[19] He remarked about Pryor, "It wasn't easy when he was on something."[20] He described Pryor as being "sullen"[21] during the production. He said. "He would come to the set fifteen minutes, forty-five minutes, an hour, an hour and a half late and it would bug all of us."[22] Bailey wrote: "He showed up hours late for work—when he showed up at all."[23] Wilder kept quiet for fear his co-star would storm off the set. He elaborated on the situation in his autobiography:

> When Richard would finally arrive on the set, he was all smiles, happy-go-lucky: "How are you doing?" So Sidney and I put on a happy face is, and the work began.
>
> One day during our lunch hour in the last week of filming, the Craft Service man handed out slices of watermelon to each of us. Richard and the whole camera crew and I sat together in a big sound studio, talking and joking. Some members of the crew used a piece of watermelon as a Frisbee, and tossed it back and forth to each other. One piece of watermelon landed at Richard's feet. He got up and went home. Filming stopped. The next day, Richard called and asked for Sidney and the whole

camera crew, and me, to assemble in the studio. When we were all sitting there—like children in the kindergarten class—Richard walked in, introduced us to his aunt or grandmother—I'm not sure which—and then announced that he knew very well what the significance of the watermelon was and why that piece of watermelon was specifically thrown at him. He said that he was quitting show business and would not return to this film. He got up and walked out, leaving us stunned. There was no filming the next day.[24]

The crew member who threw the watermelon was fired.

Ferrara wrote: "[A]ccording to Pryor's manager [David] Franklin, he and Pryor used the incident to get another half million out of the studio for Pryor to complete the film. Franklin knew if Pryor left the shoot and didn't return it could destroy his career so he negotiated the deal for Pryor but remarked later that the relationship was strained from that point on."[25]

Franklin said Pryor didn't believe that he deserved to be talented and successful. He said, "I mean, Richard is the greatest comedian in this country, in terms of modern comedians, black or white, name 'em all. They know it and he knows it. And yet—it's a guilt thing. He does not believe that he should have so much, and so he will try to give it away, to reject it. He will constantly try to prove to people who he should cut loose from—the vultures, the hangers-on—that he's one of them. And he's not. And the only thing they can do is bring him down."[26]

Wilder was willing to tolerate Pryor's bad behavior to finish the film. Many people cared about getting the film finished, even if Pryor didn't. Wilder wrote: "If Columbia Pictures had not succumbed to Richard's demands, and if I were a cocky, son-of-a-bitch movie star, and if Sidney Poitier had not held in his rage, there would have been no *Stir Crazy*. For the sake of my psychological health, I should have let out my anger at the time that I was angry. From the point of view of getting the picture made—I'm glad I didn't. The picture was a great success."[27]

Still, Wilder could never forgive Pryor. He wrote: "The whole country found out a short while later that he freebased cocaine and set himself on fire. That doesn't endear him to me, but at least it helps explain why some of his behavior was not malicious—just crazy."[28]

Pryor and Wilder made a perfect odd couple on screen. Pryor, the perennial pessimist, comically contrasted with Wilder, the perennial optimist. Pessimist vs. optimist. Realist vs. idealist. Sullen fool vs. ebullient fool. The reason for their success, according to the film's promotional literature, was that Wilder's "trusting innocence [was] the comedic opposite of Pryor's born-wise penchant for expecting the worst."[29] Rovin wrote: "[T]here's no question that Pryor, the frightened kid putting up a tough-guy facade, and Wilder, the shrieking lunatic hiding behind the veneer of continental sophistication, had a seesaw effect on each other. One served as ballast while the other was in the air."[30]

Here is the way the film's popular holding tank scene is described in the script:

> (*As they approach the large Holding Tank Cell, Harry starts hunching his shoulders, moving his head, swinging one arm ... walking differently, walking hard, walking cool, walking "bad"*)
> SKIP: (*half whisper*) What are you doing?
> HARRY: Gettin' "bad." That's how it goes down in places like this. If they think you bad, they won't fuck with you—if they think you weak, that's your ass. You got to go in bad.
> SKIP: (*starts making "bad" faces, "bad" moves—very badly*) Yeah, I gotcha.

Skip and Harry enter the cell. Harry says, "What? What did you say? I don't wanta hear no shit...! Sheee-it...."[31]

Pryor embellished the dialogue during production. In the film, Harry says, "I'm getting bad. You'd better get bad, Jack. 'Cause if you ain't bad, you gonna get *fucked*. You bad, they don't mess with you." He gives the black power sign to a black man in a cell. "Hey, Holmes, get down!" He turns to Skip, who is badly mimicking his swagger, and says, "You're a little *too* bad, ain't you?" Harry and Skip enter the cell. Harry looks around, glaring at the men. He says, "That's right, that's right, we bad. That's right. We don't want no shit either. We don't want no *sheee-it*." It's this type of embellishment before the cameras that makes great comedy. David Denby of *New York Magazine* wrote: "Indeed, the funniest thing in *Stir Crazy* ... was Pryor's gotta-get-bad strut down the prison corridor."32

Wilder was no slacker when it came to improvisation. Friedman said, "What's interesting is that Richard treated every word you wrote as if it were scripture. Gene was looser. For Gene, the dialogue was just a starting point."33 As he explained:

> There's a moment in the film when [Wilder's] supposed to act crazy in the prison to get relieved from some duties, and he felt he needed my help, which was preposterous because he woke up in the morning crazy. I did what I could and, later on, I made a visit to the set and saw him beside the mechanical bull that was used to practice for the real bull he'd be riding in the rodeo. He was petting the mechanical bull and saying, "Nice horsey." I didn't write "nice horsey," I would never *write* "nice horsey," my characters don't *say* "nice horsey." *Bedwetters* say "nice horsey." So I was a bit irritated and left the set. Richard Pryor caught up with me and turned the situation around, saying, "I never met a writer like you. Take the money, don't take any shit, and you're out of here. I have fifty dollars in cash, I believe I'll do the same."34

The courtroom scene is a classic. Richard Rushfield of Uproxx wrote: "When they learn they are heading to jail for 125 years, their dual meltdown is pure, unfiltered, comedy perfection." The script simply reads: "Skip and Harry jump up and react to the sentence." It was left to Pryor and Wilder to create their reaction. It is comparable to the dual meltdown perfected years earlier by Laurel and Hardy. Laurel erupts in a fit of sobbing, punctuated by high-pitched shrieks. Hardy, addled by fear, bugs out his eyes and howls epically.

Within the next few years, Pryor was put into similar courtroom scenes in *Bustin' Loose*, *Brewster's Millions*, and *Critical Condition*. It was always the same basic idea. A bad-tempered judge is unwilling to heed Pryor's plea for leniency and sentences him to extensive prison time, which causes the man to crumble to pieces. But those other courtroom scenes pale in comparison to the one in *Stir Crazy*.

It is a common complaint that the second half of the film is not as good as the first. Rushfield wrote: "The escape plan unfolds, it seems, in slow motion, over the course of an hour laying out the scheme to basically, take a piece of wood off the rodeo bleachers and crawl out."35 Pryor doesn't get to display his unique humor as he is rolling through a trapdoor, unscrewing a vent, or climbing out of a ceiling. The escape is not interesting and, more important, it is not funny.

A more serious mistake was made in separating Wilder and Pryor during the escape plan. Once Wilder and Pryor are apart, the film is bound to lose its energy.

Friedman said that he was disappointed with Vincent Canby's review of *Stir Crazy*. Canby wrote: "What appears on the screen ... appears to have been improvised, badly, more often than written."36 This was not something that Friedman expected because Canby had always been complimentary of his work. He decided to find a theatre that was showing *Stir Crazy* and see how audiences were responding to the film. He went to one near his home in Manhattan only to learn that tickets for the film had been sold out for the next two showings. He traveled to a multiplex theatre on 86th Street and met with a long line that extended up the block. The line, he was pleased to learn, was for *Stir Crazy*.

Canby was one of many critics who expressed disapproval of the film. A few thought it compared unfavorably with *Seems Like Old Times*, a comedy competing for the same box-office take. *Seems Like Old Times* was written by Neil Simon, whose script adaptation of Friedman's short story "A Change of Plan" became *The Heartbreak Kid* (1972). Simon created his own story of rough bank robbers who frame an innocent for their crime. It includes fewer four-letter words, less shouting, and less impolite behavior, but it also made far less money than *Stir Crazy*. Regardless of the bad reviews, *Stir Crazy* turned out to be Columbia's highest-grossing comedy. The public loved it.

Friedman said, "I like that movie very much; I just like the way it worked out. I could recognize my voice every once in a while watching that movie." But he added, "My one regret with *Stir Crazy* is that I didn't do more with Richard's character. I should have fleshed his character out more, and I didn't. I feel bad about that."[37]

"Now that *Stir Crazy* is completed," said Pryor, "we're on the look-out for another property to do together. When we find it, we'll know it. Meanwhile, will keep doing our own thing."[38] Pryor and Wilder even talked about remaking a Laurel and Hardy film.

Within two months after the release of *Stir Crazy*, Wilder asked Poitier to read a script called "Traces," which was written by David Taylor and Henry Rosenbaum. Taylor said that the script was a serious action-thriller, inspired by *North by Northwest*. The lead part was written for a Cary Grant–type, which meant that the star of the film needed to have charm, good looks, and elegance. But Wilder believed that the role, like his role in *Silver Streak*, could be taken in another direction. He and Poitier gained the interest of Columbia's top brass, who immediately saw an opportunity to reunite Wilder and Poitier with their *Stir Crazy* cohort Pryor.

Taylor and Rosenbaum went to Columbia to talk about the script with producer Martin Ransohoff. The project moved forward quickly. The writers had a meeting in Poitier's living room. Poitier wanted them to leave the story as it was but to tailor the protagonist to Wilder. "He wanted the character to be wacky,"[39] said Taylor. They went through three or four drafts before they had a shooting script.

The film was to be a comedy-thriller similar to *Silver Streak*. Again, Wilder was to get caught up in a web of intrigue. It was Alfred Hitchcock's familiar but irresistible "wrong man" plot, which invariably presents an innocent man on the run for a murder that the audience knows was committed by someone else. Again, Pryor was to come along to lend support. It was announced, in May 1981, that he had agreed to take part in the film, which was reported to be a direct sequel to *Silver Streak*.

It has been widely reported that Pryor abandoned the project and his part was rewritten for Gilda Radner. But that's not true. Taylor said that Pryor's name was mentioned in passing once or twice, but he never understood that Ransohoff was making a serious effort to get him for the film. Taylor told the author that Gilda's character, Kate Hellman, was always part of the film and the idea was to introduce an entirely new character into the story for Pryor. But Taylor was not optimistic. He couldn't see how they could fit in a new role that would be big enough to attract him. In the end, he never had to write the new role because Pryor never took a real interest in the project.

The film went into production under a new name, *Hanky Panky* ("a meaningless title,"[40] complained Gene Siskel). The film turned out to be an action piece that focused more on the chase than the characters. Aram Goudsouzian, author of *Sidney Poitier: Man, Actor, Icon*, wrote that Radner "plays it straight" while Wilder "flails about in a comic vacuum."[41]

The film is devoid of jokes, which is its greatest problem. Laughs are sought by simply having Wilder act hysterical or scamper away whenever he is at risk of being arrested by police or murdered by spies. It is Radner's role to look empathetic and do her best to soothe her agitated companion. As it turned out, the film's hectic pace and Wilder's hysterics failed to distract audiences from the fact that the jokes just weren't there.

Taylor didn't like the finished film. He agreed with a critic of the *Washington Post* who said that *Hanky Panky* was a "Murky Turkey." Taylor accepted part of the blame. He admitted that he and Rosenbaum were unable to successfully tailor the lead role to Wilder. He thought that the film would have worked better if they could have built up Radner's part more and let Wilder play off her. "Wilder was best when he was able to play off another actor,"[42] said Taylor.

For months, various news items indicated that Bruce Jay Friedman had been commissioned by Hannah Weinstein to write a sequel to *Stir Crazy*. Dick Lochte of the *Los Angeles Times* wrote: "Bruce Jay Friedman, whose screen writing finally clicked with 'Stir Crazy,' is at work on 'Deep Trouble' for the same stars, Gene Wilder and Richard Pryor."[43] The *Cincinnati Enquirer* reported under the headline: "'Deep Trouble' Is Next": "'Stir Crazy' producer Hannah Weinstein is plunging into 'Deep Trouble,' the first of her new multipicture pact with Columbia Pictures. 'Trouble' will reteam Gene Wilder, Richard Pryor and 'Stir Crazy' writer Bruce Jay Friedman."[44] Columnist Marilyn Beck wrote: "[Wilder's] supposed to reteam with Richard Pryor in Columbia's 'Deep Trouble,' but says he won't make a definite decision until he sees the final script. 'Neither Richard nor I have any interest in doing another *Stir Crazy*. We want something that's different, fresh and a stretch.'"[45] The *Ithaca Journal* reported:

> Gene Wilder and Richard Pryor are supposed to do "Deep Trouble" together but are waiting to see a script, and both claim it won't be another "Stir Crazy."
>
> "We are not interested in smooth sailing," says Wilder. "We are interested in climbing, taking a chance."[46]

In a recent interview, Friedman told the author that Weinstein never talked to him about writing a sequel to *Stir Crazy*. He added that he never, at any time, wrote a script called "Deep Trouble." He knew that Weinstein wanted to make another film with Pryor and Wilder, but she never came to him about it. The fact that Wilder and Pryor had done so well with Friedman's material should have put the writer at the top of the list to craft another film for the actors. Yet, it never happened. Friedman said, "They never go back to the man who invented the wheel."[47]

United Artists proposed that Pryor star in a remake of *The Man Who Came to Dinner* (1942). *The Man Who Came to Dinner*, which originated as a Broadway play in 1939, involves a cranky and overbearing houseguest who must extend his stay after slipping on a patch of ice and breaking his hip. The houseguest was a theatre critic in previous incarnations, but United Artists planned to change that for their update. According to Rovin, the idea was for Pryor to play "an African president stranded in Georgia."[48] The title was to be "Southern Comfort." It sounds like the studio wanted to turn a classic comedy about an obnoxious houseguest into a comedy about racism. The same narrow and misguided thinking would later create problems for Pryor's remake of *The Toy*. Studio executives could not see Pryor as a comedian. They saw him as a *black* comedian, and insisted that his race play a major role in his vehicles.

Bustin' Loose (1981)

Production and Distribution: Universal Pictures.
Producers: Richard Pryor and Michael S. Glick.
Directors: Oz Scott and Michael Schultz.
Screenplay: Roger L. Simon and Lonne Elder III; story by Richard Pryor.
Photography: Dennis Dalzell.
Editor: David Holden.
Music: Mark Davis.
Release date: May 22, 1981.
Running time: 94 minutes.
Cast: Richard Pryor (Joe Braxton), Cicely Tyson (Vivian Perry), Robert Christian (Donald Kinsey), George Coe (Dr. Wilson T. Renfrew), Earl Billings (Man at Parole Office), Bill Quinn (Judge Antonio Runzuli), Fred Carney (Alfred Schuyler), Peggy McCay (Gloria Schuyler), Roy Jenson (Klan Leader), Alphonso Alexander (Martin), Kia Cooper (Samantha), Edwin de Leon (Ernesto), Jimmy Hughes (Harold), Edwin Kinter (Anthony), Tami Luchow (Linda), Angel Ramirez (Julio), Janet Wong (Annie), Nick Dimitri (Frank Munjak), Morgan Roberts (Uncle Humphrey), Inez Pedroza (Herself), Gary Goetzman (Store Manager), Paul Mooney (Marvin), Paul Gardner (Anchorman), Ben Gerard (Man), Vern Taylor (Highway Patrolman #1).

It was noted in the film's promotional literature that Pryor had come up with the story and that the finished script was developed by Lonne Elder III, best known for his Oscar-nominated script for *Sounder* (1972). But it is more likely that the project began when producer Ray Stark brought Pryor a ten-page treatment by Elder titled "Family Dreams."

Pryor liked that the "Family Dreams" story was largely serious. He felt ready to make another drama. As producer, he had the authority to select a writer to work on the finished script. He selected Roger L. Simon. Simon wrote:

> I reread the ten-page treatment for "Family Dreams." What I really feared was that the film would not be much more than the story I was given, the sentimental tale of an ex-con (Pryor) whose parole officer forces him to drive a group of orphan children across the country on a bus. Along the way, the ex-con,

Pryor plays a surly parolee in *Bustin' Loose* (1981).

of course, is humanized by the kids and wins the heart of the children's tart schoolteacher who, also predictably, had been disdainful of the ex-con at the outset. Verna Fields—the former editor of *American Graffitti* and *Jaws* and the studio executive in charge of the project ...—summed up the premise as "*African Queen* on a bus." Only I was afraid this version of *African Queen* would be trite and simplistic.[1]

Let us examine the plot in more detail.

A parolee, Joe Braxton (Pryor), expects to go back to prison for attempting to rob televisions from a warehouse. But his parole officer, Donald (Christian), offers him a deal. Donald's girlfriend, Vivian Perry (Tyson), is a teacher at a school for children with special needs. The city has had to close the school due to budget cuts, and Perry has been tasked with getting the students relocated. She has been unable to find a place for eight of the most troubled students and has come up with the idea to take them to her aunt's farm outside of Seattle, Washington. The only way she can take the trip is if Donald finds a mechanic who can fix a broken-down old bus that belongs to the school. Donald is against Vivian making the trip; he needs Joe to look at the bus and tell Vivian that it cannot be repaired. But she becomes angry with Joe's unfavorable assessment. She insists that nothing will stop her and the children from driving to Washington as planned. She expects Donald's "expert" to find a way to get the bus running. Joe, who wants no part of this, exposes Donald's ploy to her. Donald now tells Joe that he will send him to jail unless he gets Vivian and the children to Washington safely.

A deleted scene featured Vincent Price as an alcoholic mechanic who gets the bus running again. Marilyn Beck wrote: "Pryor holds the veteran actor in such high regard that he paid for a party in his honor when Price arrived on the Seattle film location. Just about everyone turned out—except Pryor, who remained at his rented home."[2]

Oz Scott, the director, got along well with Price. Scott said that Price had a good work ethic. "I always appreciated that," he said. He fondly recalled talking with Price about his old horror movies and Price telling him "some great stories." Price did not get along too well with Pryor, however. The comedian's wild improvisations made the dialogue in the script irrelevant. The veteran actor found himself waiting patiently for a cue that never came. Scott said, "Vincent sat there and nothing happened."[3] Price told Scott, "Oz, you know, I'm old. I memorize lines, I'm sorry. If he could just give me a cue line I'll be okay." Scott discussed the problem with Pryor, who was agreeable. "I got it," he said, "I got it, Oz, I got it." But the next take was no better. Scott said: "[Richard's] going on and on. And Vincent realizes he's not going to get a cue line. So Vincent takes all his lines and turns them into a soliloquy. So he's just going on, Richard's going on, and ... it doesn't make any sense. It never made the movie, but it's hysterical to see these two guys off on their own tangents."[4] Price told Scott that he had made 110 films and never had this sort of problem before.

A fabulous chemistry emerged from uniting Humphrey Bogart and Katharine Hepburn in *The African Queen* (1951). The chemistry between Pryor and Tyson is not fabulous. Their time on screen together is, frankly, woeful. Simon remembered Tyson being mad that her character wasn't given any funny lines. But, from the writer's perspective, the straight-laced actress couldn't be funny no matter what lines he wrote for her.

The couple's offscreen time together was no better. Pryor wrote: "Erratic and ornery from dope, I must've worn out Cicely to the point where she spoke to her husband, who called me one afternoon in my trailer and in his own way asked me to shape up."[5]

Joe does not start out as an appropriate caretaker—he intimidates the children by telling them he was in prison for murder; in another scene, he teaches them strip poker.

Troubled children win Pryor's heart in *Bustin' Loose* (1981). His co-star is Cicely Tyson.

But he eventually develops a close relationship with the children and works hard on their behalf. He does everything from taking them fishing to listening to their troubles.

The children are, indeed, a troubled group. Harold, a blind boy, is obsessed with proving he can drive. Anthony is a pyromaniac who accidentally burned down his house and killed his parents. Samantha, an overweight girl, is desperately attached to a large teddy bear named Dakota. Annie, a Vietnamese immigrant, was forced to work as a prostitute before she came to the United States. Joe takes his role as caretaker seriously once he stops Anthony from setting a fire and sees Anthony suffer a painful fit afterwards.

Joe goes looking for help when the bus gets stuck in mud. He is not immediately aware that a group of Klansmen have come along and are creeping up behind him. Joe tells the head Klansman that the children are blind and he needs to take them to a hospital for a groundbreaking new surgery. The Klansmen are sympathetic and push the bus out of the mud.

On set, Scott became worried that the Klan scene wasn't working. He said, "[We] were, like, all trying to figure out, 'How do we make the Klan funny?' And it just wasn't there on paper." Joe looks to dupe the Klansmen by suddenly screaming: "They're all blind! It's a hospital bus! They're on their way to get an operation…." Scott didn't think this would get a laugh. He asked Pryor to improvise something funny. Pryor looked at him. It was like Fred Williamson putting him in front of the camera and just expecting the jokes to roll out. Pryor said, "But you're the director. You're supposed to tell me how to be funny." In the next take, Pryor suddenly came up with the line: "We're on our way to the Ray Charles Institute for the Blind to get that miracle operation, the one they show on *The Oral Roberts Show*." The Klansman immediately softens and offers to push the bus out of the mud. Pryor says, "You're a great American and a great human being." The crew laughed hysterically. Pryor believed he had gotten the laugh that Scott wanted. But, then, Scott asked him to do the scene again. Scott said:

> Richard gets quiet. "Oh, oh, oh, yes. That's right. Mr. Director. You're Mr. Director. Mr. Director wants me to do it again. I'll do it because Mr. Director wants me to do it again. You know everybody else liked it, but Mr. Director." So he gets on there, does the exact same line. The guy says, "Get on the bus. We'll give you a push." He says, "You're a great American. A great human being." He takes the Klansman's face. It was an old stunt guy. Takes his face and kisses him on the lips. It went from laughter to stunned silence, because it had gone from extremely funny to brilliant....

Donald learns that Vivian has falsified records to take the children to Washington. He tracks the group to a motel. Vivian agrees to return the children to Philadelphia the following morning. While Donald is asleep, Vivian and Joe gather up the children and drive off into the night. Donald phones the police to report Joe as a fugitive. He speeds after them in his car and gets them to pull over to the side of the road, but they refuse to be deterred in their mission. Donald later has to show police officers his identification, but he doesn't realize Joe switched wallets with him and he now has Joe's identification. The police promptly arrest him as a fugitive.

Anthony tries to start another fire, but Joe gets to him in time. Anthony breaks down and cries about his dead parents. He explains that he was playing with a lighter near some curtains and they caught fire. Joe assures him that his parents' death was an accident.

Annie shows Joe a picture of the bus that she drew. She asks if he wants to take her back to his room to have sex. Joe becomes angry. He tells her that she doesn't need to sleep with men to get them to like her. He lets her know that she is a talented artist and she is more likely to have a good life if she focuses her attention on that. Vivian, who overheard the conversation, thanks Joe for helping the troubled girl.

The bus arrives at the farm, but it is revealed that Vivian's aunt will lose the farm unless she can pay the bank fifteen thousand dollars. Vivian is discouraged when she is turned down for a loan.

Joe becomes enraged when Vivian tells him that, without the money, they have no choice but to take the children back to Philadelphia. His eyes bulge. His voice cracks. His arms flail in every direction. He looks scary. He insists that only losers give up, and he is *not* a loser.

Ernesto, who overheard this conversation, tells the other children that Vivian is breaking her promise to them and is taking them back to Philadelphia. Joe, still angry, comes along in time to hear this. He shouts at Ernesto to shut up. Ernesto tells him, "Go take a hike!" Joe becomes even angrier now. "Shut up!" he shouts again, slapping Ernesto hard enough to knock him to the ground. He shows no remorse for hitting a child. He feels justified to get tough with the children, who have so little self-confidence that they can easily give up their dreams. "You guys are somebody, man," he says. "Stop this shit! The woman put her ass on the line for you. And you don't think nothing about yourselves. WE'RE NOT LOSERS!!!!" His voice softens. "Hey ... we're not losers." He drops his voice to a whisper when he says for a third and final time: "We're not losers."

Pryor's rage is so real and so sudden that the scene is uncomfortable to watch. An actor showing realistic rage in a film can be something that makes a film more powerful, but it has to make sense in the context of the story. The story never built to this scene, which makes Pryor's rage abrupt and misplaced. It doesn't work for an actor to suddenly set aside silly slapstick business to stage a revival of *East of Eden*.

Actor K. C. Wright wrote that Uta Hagen, who trained actors to emphasize realism in their performances, "encourages actors to substitute their own experiences and emotional recollections for the given circumstances of a scene."[6] Pryor was an angry man: he ferociously battled personal demons that drove him to self-hate. He no doubt brought his own experiences and emotional recollections to the scene, but neither apply to the scene. An actor can, by bringing too much of himself to the fore, get in the way of the scene and distance himself from the character he is playing. That seems to be happening here.

In the script, the scene in which Joe rallies the group plays out much differently. He breaks up a fight between Ernesto and Martin. Samantha tells Joe that Martin got upset because Ernesto told him that Miss Perry was going to take them back to Philadelphia. Joe says, "All y'all are wrong. Miss Perry put her ass on the line to try and give you something: a home. And you know what? They'd put her in jail for that. And now you all are going to fight when she's feeling miserable…. Yeah, we might have to go back to Philly. But Vivian's down there feeling bad that we can't keep going."

Joe considers robbing a bank, but then he sees a "DARE TO BE RICH!" ad for a pyramid scheme and gets an idea to scam money from the organizers. He dresses up as a cowboy, pretending to be a rube with lots of money to invest. At the first opportunity, he snatches up money that the con artists have collected from the group. Vivian, who comes into town to find Joe, happens upon the meeting just as he is getting ready to leave. The two rush out the door together, closely pursued by the con artist's goons. They chase them into a warehouse, where a slapstick battle ensues. The warehouse provides a variety of props, from a samurai sword to an inflatable raft. Vivian sets the money on fire to create a distraction. Joe switches on an air boat propeller to blow the goons off their feet while he and Vivian escape.

The banker and his wife are moved by the children's plight and assure Vivian that they will give her the money she needs to keep the farm. Donald arrives at the farm during the banker's visit. Joe explains to the children that he must go back to Philadelphia with him. The children are heartbroken. He explains that he must accept the consequences for his wrongdoing. The children present him with a document they prepared for him. It is their personal pardon for his crimes. He is close to tears. He hugs the children goodbye. Donald is so moved by the love the children express for Joe that he decides to let him go.

Simon wrote about the writing process in his memoir, *Turning Right at Hollywood and Vine: The Perils of Coming Out Conservative in Tinseltown*. He noted, "I would write twenty or so pages of the script, send them to him via a studio courier …, and then drive out to his place a few days later to discuss them. Pryor was always highly supportive of what I was doing, amazingly so for a movie star."[7] According to Simon, Pryor did an immense amount of cocaine during their meetings.

The two men visited an orphanage in Sunland for inspiration. Simon wrote: "Pryor was remarkably kind and gentle with the kids who gathered idolatrously around him. He seemed to empathize with them in a deep way."[8]

Pryor wanted Simon to direct the film, but the NAACP was putting pressure on

Slapstick silliness dominates the final act of *Bustin' Loose* (1981).

Universal to use more black directors. The studio selected Oz Scott, who had directed a popular Broadway play, *For Colored Girls Who Have Considered Suicide / When the Rainbow Is Enuf.*

Scott recalled that the story had special significance to Pryor.

> [Richard] said, "I've got two big problems: kids and women, and I want to investigate this. And if you make me look bad, I'm gonna kill you." Those were his words, and I'm not paraphrasing. So *Bustin' Loose* was very much a drama. It was very much about a guy who, you know, was looking for a home, a family. And remember the name of *Bustin' Loose* was "Family Dreams." That was the original title…. And, you know, Richard really reached out to those kids, and really had some great moments with those kids, that he really took responsibility for those kids. You know, if you really look at *Bustin' Loose*, there is a lot of heart there. It's not just balls-out comedy.[9]

Scott's first decision was to fire Simon and bring in a black writer to draft a new script. When the new script failed to satisfy the studio, Scott was instructed to return to the original one. "At this juncture," wrote Simon, "my friend Richard was nowhere to be seen. Poor Oz Scott, way out of his depth, was soldiering on by himself."[10]

Scott admitted that he had a rough time working with Pryor. At one point, the comedian became angry with him and asked him to "step outside."

> I said, "Richard, if I step outside we ain't gonna fight, 'cause I'm gonna get in a car, and then I'm gonna get on a plane and get the hell out of here." You know what they say about, you know, burning behind your ears. I never knew what that was about until I was with Richard Pryor, and I literally

started burning behind the ears.... He got me so mad. And I remember the president of Universal looking at me, said, "Oz, you gonna be okay?" [I said,] "I'm gonna be okay. I'm gonna be okay." You know again, I'm going to put one foot in front of the other. He's not gonna, he's not gonna take me down, you know, which sometimes that happens. But I try to be, like Lloyd [theatre director Lloyd Richards] says, "Oz, just ... you know, don't get angry, you know, just do your job."[11]

Simon remembered: "Verna Fields had been informing me of the progress of the editing process, and it wasn't good. The movie wasn't cutting together. Evidently, Oz Scott didn't have a sense of film continuity. The studio had a lot of money invested in Pryor, but they had a useless film."[12]

Universal was willing to let it sit on the shelf until *Stir Crazy* became a big hit. Now, they wanted to find a way to fix it. Simon recalled: "They were considering doing the unthinkable—starting over, almost from scratch. Oz was fired and Michael Schultz—the director of *Car Wash* and the Negro Ensemble Company—took over."[13]

Schultz came to the rescue just like he had on *Greased Lightning*. Said Simon: "Verna showed Schultz my original screenplay. He was stunned that they hadn't used that in the first place.... Michael Schultz and I took what amounted to a few minutes of Oz Scott's existing footage, fashioned a brand new script (using some of my old pages) for the rest, and shot [for] another seven weeks."[14]

Joe gets the money in a different way in the shooting script. He is confident that he can make the fifteen thousand by joining a craps game at the Blue Corral Lounge. The problem is, he needs a five hundred dollar stake to be let into the game. He sells the bus, which nets him $250. Then, he spends three days doing logging work. Vivian finds Joe shooting craps at the Blue Corral Lounge. He gets his bankroll up to fifteen thousand and wants to risk it for the chance to win fifty thousand, but Vivian stops him and convinces him to leave with her. The dealer advises them to leave out of a back door, but the exit leads them out into an alleyway where a couple of sore losers are waiting. Vivian runs away while Joe fights off the men. He is losing the fight and is about to be badly beaten. But, then, the script reads: "*A truck comes blazing down the alley, bearing down on the hoods. It is Vivian.*"[15] The hoods jump out of the way. Joe jumps into the truck. The hoods get into a pickup truck and pursue Joe and Vivian. The trucks are side by side as the hoods try to slam Vivian off the road. One of the men leans out of the window with a shotgun and takes aim at Vivian. She quickly grabs the money and throws it out of the window.

The script reads: "*Joe is doing all he can to keep Vivian from throwing the money away. Vivian manages to start throwing the money out the window. Joe is reaching over Vivian, desperately trying to keep the money from flying away. CUT TO INTERIOR OF HOODS' PICKUP. Both hoods are so excited about seeing all the money flying around that the Hood who's driving loses control of the pickup. CUT TO EXTERIOR OF THE ROAD. The Hoods' pickup goes sailing high in the air, landing in a creek.*"

The scene cuts back to Vivian and Joe. It is noted, "*Vivian is ecstatic. Joe is glum.*" This material was replaced when Schultz came on board.

Pryor was still in the hospital being treated for his burns when Universal made arrangements for scenes to be reshot. During his time in the hospital, the actor's weight dropped from 150 pounds to 130. His overall condition was not good. One of his doctors, Dr. Richard Grossman, said: "If you saw our patient without his dressings you would faint. Most people would. There is virtually no skin on his torso. You can see the raw muscle tissue, fat tissue and the cartilage on both ears."[16] As it turned out, some trickery was needed to make shots match. His costumes were padded to hide much of the weight loss. He also had to wear a kerchief around his neck to cover scars. But nothing could be done about his face, which was noticeably thinner in the new scenes.

Tyson saw a big change in her co-star's personality. He was quiet now and he would retreat to his dressing room whenever he wasn't needed on set.

Schultz was with Pryor when he looped the earlier scenes. He said, "Up on the screen was a Richard Pryor that was heavily overweight and puffed from excessive alcohol. Richard looked at himself … and tears came to his eyes."[17]

The end results did not turn out well. The extensive reshoots explain the inconsistency in tone and performance that is evident throughout the film. The new scenes featured more slapstick. Take, for instance, the scene in which Joe rushes to stop the blind boy from driving away with the bus. This is the way the scene is described in the script: "*Joe slips and falls while chasing after the bus. The bus disappears through a mass of trees and comes to a complete stop when it runs into a tree.*"[18] In the film, Joe ends up hanging off the side of the speeding bus and screaming for his life.

The effort to convert the film from drama to comedy is also evident in a scene in which Joe struggles to put out one of Anthony's blazes. Anthony is in a trance as he ignites a piece of newspaper and tosses it at a haystack. The script reads, "*At the last possible second, Joe rushes forward and grabs it in his hands, pushing the fiery newspaper to the ground and stamping it out.*" Joe turns angrily on the child. "What the hell you think you're doing?" he shouts. The script continues with Anthony's reaction:

> Suddenly, Anthony starts to shout, then scream. Then, in a bewildered mix of groans, cries and tears, Anthony throws himself to the ground and starts kicking and screaming, completely out of control.
> Joe, unable to cope with this, stands there and stares at Anthony, whose kicks and screams grow to [an] unbelievable level. His cry of need is desperate.

The decision was made during shooting to add funny business to the scene. Joe drops to his knees and slaps at the flames with his cap. A farmer shows up with a shotgun, presuming that vandals are destroying his property. Joe is so preoccupied having a gun pointed at him that he puts his cap back on his head without realizing it's on fire.

Seeing the top of Pryor's head in flames would undoubtedly remind viewers of the comedian's recent plight, running through a suburban neighborhood ablaze. It would be interesting to see how the scene scored on preview cards. The heartwarming misadventures of a parolee helping a group of disadvantaged children get to a new home is suddenly interrupted by a glaring reminder of the star's horrific near-death experience. It is bound to be a distraction and it is likely, for most people, to be discomforting. But it could be that this is a naïve assumption. The truth is that many people came to see the film because they were curious to see how Pryor was holding up after his recovery. Maybe, viewers took the scene as a playful wink by the comedian.

It is more important to consider that Anthony's pyromania plays a pivotal role in Joe's character arc. When he sees Anthony setting the fire, Joe shouts angrily at the boy and shoves him out of the way. He feels guilty afterwards because he realizes Anthony would not have become distraught if he had treated him more compassionately. Later in the film, when Anthony sets another fire, he approaches the child in a tender manner. He hugs him and comforts him, which has a more positive effect. The film needed this subplot regardless of what associations the scenes might have.

The studio kept Simon hidden for fear the NAACP would become angry to learn that the film was written by a white man. Simon was so embarrassed by *Bustin' Loose* that he didn't mind being kept hidden. He believed that it would have been a much better film if the filmmakers had stuck to his original draft.

The movie opened number one at the box office. It ranked number 20 on the top box-office hits of 1981. *Bustin' Loose* and *The Four Seasons* (1981) kept Universal out of the red that year. But Simon was angry for years that the film's producer, Pryor, cheated him out of substantial royalties.

The movie received mixed reviews. A particularly stinging assessment came from *New York Times*' Vincent Canby.

> Only the incomparable Richard Pryor could make a comedy as determinedly, aggressively sentimental as "Bustin' Loose," which is about eight needy orphans and a $15,000 mortgage that's due, and still get an R-rating.... [O]ne longs for his every assault on genteelism in "Bustin' Loose," a film that would otherwise be painful.... [It] is Mr. Pryor's somewhat obsequious attempt to capture the family audience.... This movie is a cheerfully hackneyed, B-picture vehicle.... "Bustin' Loose" is not unbearable, though a soft-hearted Richard Pryor is not a terribly funny Richard Pryor.... Most of the time, Mr. Pryor gives the impression of holding himself in, of being on his best behavior but itching to do something in epic bad taste.[19]

Bailey wrote: "In the closing shot of *Bustin' Loose*, as he's embraced by the quirky kids he's mentored and a children's choir sings about how love is everywhere and he reaches out to his lady love, you can all but see the defanging process begin. Defanging might be too soft a word; as critic Julian Upton writes, 'Pryor had to be castrated before the studios gave him a real shot.'"[20] David Handelman of *Premiere* magazine observed that, during this period, Pryor went from "trailblazer to relic."[21] Hassenger was dismayed to see the actor making lightweight studio comedies. He wrote: "[H]e was more of an assembly-line worker, like the put-upon employee he plays in Paul Schrader's *Blue Collar*."[22]

Pryor said he had been humbled by his near-death experience and that he was grateful to be alive. He remarked that, at the time of his suicide attempt, his head was "lost in a haze of vodka, coke, and anger."[23] People who attempt suicide later report having felt intense anger and aggression directly prior to the act (Apter, Bleich, Plutchik, Mendelsohn & Tyano, 1988; Garfinkel, Froese & Hood, 1982; Myers, McCauley, Calderon & Treder, 1991).

Pryor was a self-destructive man who had a tendency to sabotage his own success. But something else may have been going on with him. Susanne Babbel wrote in *Psychology Today*, "People who have experienced trauma may associate the excitement of success with the same physiological reactions as trauma."[24]

Pryor never denied that he was less funny after his near-death experience. He spoke to Gene Siskel on this subject in a 1983 interview. "I don't think I'm as funny as I used to be," he said. "I'm finding it hard imitating Richard Pryor."[25] Bailey believed that the problem was that the comedian no longer felt anger and it was anger that had always "serv[ed] as his beacon."[26] "I ain't angry, man," he told an audience in 1981. "I try to be angry, but I don't know what to be mad about!"[27] He was, in many ways, a changed man. He told Barbara Walters in 1980, "The part of me that wanted to die, did."[28]

Pryor's fans, who had seen the comedian express raw anger, raw fear, and raw pain on stage, demanded that the comedian act the same way in his films. They didn't want to see him play an innocuous fool. They wanted him to be ferocious and dangerous.

It was debated throughout Pryor's career if the comedian was at his funniest when he was angry. Colin Beckett of the *Brooklyn Rail* observed: "Pryor was frequently criticized … for playing weak, buffoonish characters."[29] Beckett noted that the fear and cowardice that Pryor exposed in his stage act was balanced out with a "furious pride" and "righteous anger."[30] But, said Beckett, "his screen appearances could sometimes resemble the Stepin Fetchit stereotypes that his comedy had exploded."[31] Beckett insisted, "Only in *Blue Collar* (1978), as an auto worker backed into selling out his union buddies, did he manage to summon all of the contradictions he embodied onstage."[32]

But what did a comedy designed to spotlight a ferocious and dangerous Pryor look like exactly? What type of narrative could support a funny man with a talent for expressing raw anger, raw fear, and raw pain? What would the character arc be in a comedy that presented anger, fear, and pain as its protagonist's defining features? We saw these emotions bursting free in *Bustin' Loose*, but it didn't benefit either character or story development.

Pryor was comparable to W. C. Fields in the way that he was able to depict resentment, mistrust, and frustration. David Denby of *New York Magazine* described Pryor in the same way one could describe Fields: "a tempest of bluster relieved by vicious muttered asides."[33] But, at other times, Pryor resembled Bob Hope, a perpetual coward who worked his hardest to convince people he was a great hero and a great lover. Even when he was choking Margaret Avery in *Which Way Is Up?*, Pryor was a coward who was trying to convince others of his masculinity. He quivers uneasily as he tells Avery, "I'm plenty of man, baby! I am *numero uno*."

Pryor's anger defined him to most people onstage and off. Early in his career, he was told by an emcee in a St. Louis club, "You've got to talk to the people. You always look like you want to kill them."[34]

Craig Kellem, Pryor's agent at G.A.C., said, "There was always a danger, a subtext. Is he gonna get mad? Is he gonna show up on time? The big question was, who was going to get Richard Pryor out of bed to go to dress rehearsal? Usually, you'd try to get the most naïve guy in the office to do it. Nobody else wanted to face his wrath."[35]

Jonathan Lyons, animator and author, believes that anger can be funny; that, in the right hands, it can even be raised to an art form. As Lyons points out, we can see that anger can be sublimely funny by viewing the hot-headed antics of Moe Howard, the eternally exasperated leader of The Three Stooges.[36]

Comic anger is best in larger-than-life depictions, which is the reason it is reserved for such cartoon characters as Donald Duck and Yosemite Sam. No one can throw a temper tantrum like Donald Duck. He jumps up and down, swings his fists in every direction, and quacks out unintelligible swear words with an explosive fury. Yosemite Sam acts in much the same way except, instead of swinging around his fists, he blasts a pair of six-shooters into the air.

Anger comes in different forms. An angry outburst can be an expression of pain or frustration. It can also be a frightening display of outward aggression. Dramatic actors, like George C. Scott and Jack Nicholson, made it their special talent to convulse audiences with their onscreen anger. Nicholson, more than any other actor, has brought volatility to a wide variety of roles. Evan Puschak of Nerdwriter wrote: "No two expressions of anger are the same—not in real life and not in Nicholson's work. Sometimes his anger is comedic, sometimes it's cartoonish, sometimes it's quiet, sometimes it's misplaced, and sometimes it's deeply, deeply wounded." He noted that Nicholson's could be "focused, pointed anger; or generally frustrated anger; or petulant, childlike anger." It could be an expression of desperation, an expression of vulnerability, or an expression of paranoia. Kerry Levielle of Indiewire concurred. She said of Nicholson: "Each scream and each gesticulation is calculated and reflective of the personality of the character.... [I]t's not just red-faced flailing. It's a truly revealing element of a character that Nicholson has a natural mastery for."[37] But an actor incorporating anger into a dramatic performance is different from an actor incorporating anger into a comic performance.

In many of his films, Pryor is as cantankerous and impotent as Fields in *It's a Gift* (1934) or *The Bank Dick* (1940). But Pryor is rarely as nuanced or complex as Fields. Fields offered a finely developed characterization that could sustain a feature film. Moe Howard never had to sustain a feature film. Neither did Donald Duck. Neither did Yosemite Sam. A comedian could not hold an audience's interest having a temper tantrum for ninety minutes.

Ted Knight expresses anger in a beautifully funny way in *Caddyshack* (1980). But that is an ensemble comedy that does not rely on Knight to promote story or character development. His character arc carries him from seething anger at the start of the film to explosive anger at the climax. It is by no means an expansive arc, nor does it need to be.

In *The Big Lebowski* (1998), John Goodman portrays a man who is easily frustrated and quick to anger. Goodman's character, Walter Sobchak, manages in his habitual outbursts to expose his childish nature. But, like Knight's character, Sobchak is not central to the plot.

Adam Sandler started out in his early films portraying an angry man-child. But take a look at Sandler's performances in *Billy Madison* (1995), *Happy Gilmore* (1996), and *Big Daddy* (1999). The comedian's flare-ups have no real substance. It is mock, tongue-in-cheek anger. It is goofy, cartoonish shtick. Donald Duck looks like Brando compared to Sandler. Sandler's is not the type of raw anger that Pryor produced on stage. Besides, Sandler had to eventually move away from this sometimes off-putting persona to broaden his appeal.

Anger plays a pivotal role in two types of character arcs. Either an angry man becomes calm or a calm man becomes angry.

Let us start with the latter. Here we have the angry man who discovers joy and satisfaction and is able to finally let go of his anger. This is the premise we just explored in *Bustin' Loose*. Pryor's Joe Braxton is a stock character—the crusty but benign protagonist. He is trapped in a difficult situation by his parole officer. His frustration at having the children thrust upon him sets him on edge and causes him to occasionally lose his temper. But it is obvious from the start that his bark is worse than his bite.

Bustin' Loose, which veers wildly between comedy and drama, compares poorly to the most memorable films in this genre. It is awkward, uneven, and ineffective compared to *The Bad News Bears* (1976), which also involves a down-and-outer who bonds with a group of children. Walter Matthau, a beer-guzzling ex-ballplayer who cleans pools for a living, is hired to coach a rag-tag bunch of misfit Little League players rejected by other teams. Matthau is gruff with the children at first, but he eventually comes to care about them. The curmudgeon is, as usual, cured of his anger by love. *The Bad News Bears* is the best W. C. Fields film that Fields didn't make. (It's not hard to imagine Fields sneaking a drink from a flask in the dugout.)

Elements of comedy and drama blend subtly, smoothly, and imperceptibly in *The Bad News Bears*. Elements of comedy and drama remain loose and jangly as they float around and collide into one another through major portions of *Bustin' Loose*. Pryor abruptly transitions from an intensely dramatic scene in which he slaps a small boy to a broad comedy scene in which he wears a flashy cowboy outfit and speaks in a Texas dialect so overblown that it would make Yosemite Sam cringe. How does that match up?

Even Sandler, with his goofy shtick, did well with the curmudgeon-finds-love-with-a-child premise in *Big Daddy*. But Pryor couldn't figure out how to make the premise work for him.

No comedian could ever express anger more effectively than Albert Brooks. The highlights of Brooks's riches-to-rags comedy *Lost in America* (1985) include Brooks fuming at his boss for cheating him out of a promotion (which causes him to lose his high-paying job); Brooks shrieking at his stressed-out wife for gambling away their life savings (which causes her to walk out on him); and Brooks losing his cool at being taunted by children during his first day as a minimum-wage crossing guard (which makes him look like an utter fool). This is hurt anger. This is desperate anger. But Brooks comes to realize that his petulance has only made matters worse. He realizes that a man cannot survive in the world unless he calmly accepts the occasional incident of humiliation, victimization, or bullying. He realizes that sometimes a person has to, in his own words, "eat shit."

Friendship resolves anger in *Planes, Trains and Automobiles* (1987), *Due Date* (2010), and most Francis Veber comedies. The best double act comedies are friendship comedies. The films that Pryor made with Wilder fall into this genre. In his vehicles with Wilder, Pryor is free to express desperate anger, hurt anger, and frustrated anger as he had the gentle and uplifting Wilder to provide ballast. It is the reason their partnership worked so well. Speaking of Veber, Wilder and Pryor could have made a great vehicle out of Veber's *Les fugitifs* (1986).

Then, we have the calm man who finds his inner fury. A beleaguered man will, if under too much pressure, explode in anger. Shakespeare wrote: "The smallest worm will turn being trodden on." One of the best comedies in this genre was *National Lampoon's Vacation* (1983), in which meek family man Clark Griswold (Chevy Chase) goes berserk during an ill-fated cross-country trip. Many other comedies feature oppressed workers who suddenly wage a revolt against an abusive boss. Among the most well-known entries in this genre are *9 to 5* (1980), *Office Space* (1999), *Swimming with Sharks* (1994), and *Horrible Bosses* (2011). Of course, a mean old boss is not the only type of oppressor. Fields epitomized the henpecked husband who occasionally finds the courage to stand up to his shrewish wife.

Pryor turns on his bosses in a dramatic way in *Blue Collar*. But this film does not fit within the worm-turns mold. Anger keeps Pryor's character, Zeke, trapped in a rut from start to finish. His character arc takes him from explosive anger (at the union meeting) to restrained anger (at Smokey's death) and then back again to explosive anger (at the climax). Zeke has gone nowhere on his anger treadmill.

It is hard to imagine Pryor starting out timid and compliant for the purposes of a slow-burn comedy. A film that introduces the fiery comedian as a gentle fellow would likely be seen as an outrageous betrayal by fans. A film of that type would be a disaster, right? Let us save this discussion for Pryor's lamb-to-lion comedy *Moving* (1988).

In *Network* (1976), Paddy Chayefsky mocked the crusty but benign protagonist that was prevalent on television in the 1970s. In the same film, Faye Dunaway says, "We want a prophet, not a curmudgeon." Pryor's most ardent fans wanted the comedian to be a prophet, not a curmudgeon. But a fire-and-brimstone prophet makes a bad comic protagonist.

Bustin' Loose's similarities to *The African Queen* are not as pronounced as the film's similarities to *Father Goose* (1964), in which an uncongenial beach bum (Cary Grant) becomes the reluctant caretaker to a schoolmistress (Leslie Caron) and her seven young refugee students after the group's plane crash-lands on an isolated South Seas island. *Father Goose* is beloved by many classic film fans. Grant smoothly blends the serious and funny qualities of his character, creating a reprobate that is gruff but endearing. Grant and Caron are charming together, whether engaged in a battle of wills or finally letting down their defenses long enough to fall in love. Of course, it is never possible for *everyone* to love a film. A critic at Time Out Film Guide describes *Father Goose* as "a sludge of turgid drama and pallid comedy."[38] But the premise of *Father Goose* generated a far greater amount of sludge when it was revived for *Bustin' Loose*. Pryor fails to show the finesse of Grant or Bogart or Matthau in crafting his reprobate role. But, as suggested before, the actor is hindered by the disjointed script. It is jarring when a funny scene in which Pryor is hanging off the side of a speeding bus is followed by a grave scene in which Pryor comforts a troubled young boy whose arson habits caused his parents to perish in a house fire.

The scene in which Annie approaches Joe for sex is similar to one in *Father Goose*. One of the students, Elizabeth (Stephanie Berrington), develops a crush on Grant's beach bum character, Walter Eckland. She approaches him when they are alone. "Mr. Eckland," she says, "you may kiss me." Eckland suppresses a smile. "I may?" he responds. With mock passion, he sweeps her up into his arms. "Oh, my darling. I have thought of nothing else since that moment we met. This first burning kiss is but the beginning. Tonight you will leave those children and come live with me on my boat." As intended, Eckland's overblown seduction technique scares the girl, causing her to run away from him. It's a funny little scene. In contrast, the *Bustin' Loose* scene is dark, angry, and disturbing. It belongs in an entirely different film.

In 1987, *Bustin' Loose* was adapted in a television series starring Jimmie Walker and Vonetta McGee.

Pryor was scheduled to play Josephus, a slave in ancient Rome, in *History of the World: Part I* (1981). But it was a month before shooting was to begin that Pryor set himself on fire. The role was recast with Gregory Hines.

At the time, preparations were also underway for *Trading Places* (1983). Director John Landis said, "The script was developed for Gene Wilder and Richard Pryor. And when I was sent the script, Richard Pryor, unfortunately, had his accident where he burnt himself rather badly."[39]

Herschel Weingrod, who co-authored the script with Timothy Harris, agreed with Landis's version of events. He said, "Originally we wanted Richard Pryor and Gene Wilder for the movie. The studio asked us if we had a second choice if they couldn't get Richard and I said I'd seen a guy on *Saturday Night Live* who would be good. I never thought he'd be a movie star, though."[40]

Of course, the *Saturday Night Live* guy who became a movie star was Eddie Murphy, who co-starred in *Trading Places* with Dan Aykroyd. *Trading Places* received enthusiastic reviews and went on to become the fourth highest-grossing film of 1983.

When director Walter Hill and producer Larry Gordon originally talked to Paramount about casting *48 Hrs.* (1982), the consensus among the studio executives was that the cop should be played by Clint Eastwood. But Eastwood was quick to reject the role. He said, "It was a time when I just wasn't in the mood to do a detective thing."[41]

Hill mostly supported Eastwood's account except that the veteran actor failed to mention that he asked Hill and Gordon for the convict role. Hill said,

> Larry and I flew up to Carmel to see [Eastwood] and he liked the project, but felt he'd already done that kind of cop character enough, so he wanted to play the criminal. I began tailoring it to that end when Eastwood decided to do Don Siegel's *Escape From Alcatraz* (1979), and since he played a prisoner in that one, that was really the end of his interest in our project. At which point I suggested we try to get Richard Pryor to play the criminal.... But Paramount did not see the wisdom of that, so I went off and did *The Long Riders* and *Southern Comfort*, and then I got a call saying Nick Nolte wanted to do *48 Hrs.*, and was I interested in doing it with him and a black actor? I said, "Absolutely." [W]e couldn't get Richard Pryor, who was a huge star by then, so we decided to go for Gregory Hines, but he wasn't available either. Eddie Murphy's agent had sent me a lot of tapes of him, and Paramount approved him, so we went with him.[42]

At the start of 1982, director Harold Ramis was in pre-production on an adaptation of the novel *A Confederacy of Dunces*, which was to star John Belushi as eccentric misfit Ignatius J. Reilly and Pryor as Reilly's wily janitor acquaintance Burma Jones. Belushi's death on March 5, 1982, put an end to the project.

Some Kind of Hero (1982)

Production and Distribution: Paramount Pictures.
Producer: Howard W. Koch.
Director: Michael Pressman.
Screenplay: James Kirkwood and Robert Boris, based on the book *Some Hero* by James Kirkwood.
Photography: King Baggot.
Editor: Christopher Greenbury.
Music: Patrick Williams.
Release date: April 2, 1982.
Running time: 97 minutes.
Cast: Richard Pryor (Eddie Keller), Margot Kidder (Toni Donovan), Ray Sharkey (Vinnie DiAngelo), Ronny Cox (Colonel Powers), Lynne Moody (Lisa), Olivia Cole (Jesse), Paul Benjamin (Leon), David Adams (Kid), Martin Azarow (Tank), Shelly Batt (Olivia), Susan Berlin (Jeanette), Mary Betten (Female Teller), Herb Braha (Honcho No. 2), Anthony R. Charnota (Base Commander), Matt Clark (Mickey), Judy Farese (Bandit No. 1).

Robert Boris, who revised James Kirkwood's original script, said:

> I know [Richard] cared more about *Some Kind of Hero* than most of his other films. I've always considered myself incredibly lucky to have had the opportunity to spend two weeks with Richard at his house in Maui with Michael Pressman and Howard Koch. I went out to his house every day for those two weeks, mostly to talk alone with Richard about the movie, because he really cared about that one, and he had real input into what he wanted the *Some Kind of Hero* script to be. That character was a dream for him, but the movie didn't give his audience what they wanted. It was too dramatic and there wasn't enough of Richard Pryor doing that wild and crazy stuff that they wanted him to give them.[1]

Boris stressed Pryor's contribution to the script: "I can tell you that Richard's input on that movie was to be massive and significant.... [W]e would spend as much as eight hours a day talking about the movie."[2]

Pryor and Ray Sharkey struggle to survive in a POW camp in *Some Kind of Hero* (1982).

Pryor's character, Eddie Keller, serves as a U.S. Army private during the Vietnam War. He is captured by the Viet Cong in February 1968, during the Tet Offensive. At the time of his capture, he has his pants down around his ankles so that he can defecate in the bushes. He spends the next six years in a POW camp.

Eddie challenges a captain to a basketball match as a way to get his friend Vinnie (Sharkey) released from solitary confinement in a sweatbox. But the match turns into a fight once the captain, who is losing, elbows Eddie hard in the stomach.

Boris said:

> The thing I remember with the most affection about the shooting of *Some Kind of Hero* is the stuff with Richard in the POW camp at the beginning of the film. We shot so much stuff there that didn't make the finished movie. There were some wonderful things that Richard created there. Like when it begins to rain and Richard jumps up on his bunk and begins to dance around in it like he's Gene Kelly in *Singin' in the Rain* [1952]. He did stuff that you do when you're trying to survive in impossible conditions. It was all very inventive, fresh, and it all came from his heart. I love all that stuff. Also, his relationship with actor Ray Sharkey—who passed away later on from a drug overdose—was unique and intense. Richard really tried to help him through that—he was very loving and he cared a great deal about Ray. Some of those scenes between Richard and Ray—they just came up with those together. That stuff was beautiful and magical. In the end, Michael Pressman, the director, just realized that we couldn't spend that much time in the POW camp.[3]

Drug problems prevented Sharkey from finishing his work on *Some Kind of Hero*. Pryor and his wife, Jennifer Lee, provided the actor with help. Pryor told Sharkey that he would like to find another vehicle in which they could co-star.[4]

Other historical events play into the plot. The Viet Cong respond to Richard Nixon's election by initiating a propaganda campaign against the United States. They claim that the United States is committing war crimes and they pledge to furnish confessions from POWs to support their allegations. POWs are tortured by the Viet Cong in an effort to make them sign confessions. Eddie finally relents to sign a confession to get medical help for his dying friend. He is released in January 1973, as part of Operation Homecoming, which is an outcome of the Paris Peace Accords.

Eddie has trouble readjusting to civilian life once he gets back home. His wife, Lisa, has fallen in love with another man. But it gets worse. The man convinced her to expand their bookstore to include a card shop. She tells Eddie, "We flopped. Bankrupt. All your money, too, and the store, all gone. I'm sorry." He is laughing and crying as she says this. His laughter rises to its peak when she asks him if he wants a divorce. He replies sarcastically, "I need a couple of hours to think about it."

Boris said, "Richard and Lynne rehearsed that sequence many times and he would keep adding new stuff for both of them. That's a magical moment in the film."[5]

Pryor in *Some Kind of Hero* (1982).

As if this isn't bad enough, Eddie's mother has suffered a stroke and has been placed in a convalescent home. She cannot continue to receive care unless Eddie comes up with the money to pay her bills. Eddie becomes depressed and drowns his sorrows at a bar, where he is comforted by a kindly prostitute named Toni (Kidder).

Toni had a much smaller role in the original screenplay, but it was expanded when Kidder agreed to do the film. Still, Kidder is not introduced until two-thirds of the way into the story. To better understand her role, Kidder hung out with prostitutes in San Francisco. Peter Lester of *People* wrote: "[Kidder] once nearly hustled for real during her research but then backed off."[6] But Kidder did well in the role without the extra homework. Boris said, "[Richard and Margot] had a great chemistry together. Intense, personal, and very caring."[7]

The Army has information from several officers that some POWs had conspired to aid the enemy. This has spurred an investigation. Because he had signed a statement that accused the United States of war crimes, military officials have to consider his case as part of their investigation, during which they will withhold his back pay. He is assured by Colonel Powers that it is a temporary situation and that he will ultimately receive the allotted amount. He receives convalescent pay to help him get by, but he cannot wait for the rest of the money that he is owed.

Eddie buys a water gun that looks like the real thing. He tries using the gun to rob a bank, but the water gun leaks in his pocket and the teller is appalled, thinking he has wet his pants. Embarrassed, Eddie quickly exits the bank. Later, Eddie tries to hold up a clothing store, but the little old lady who runs it beats him with an umbrella.

Eddie watches a pair of businessmen make a large withdrawal at the bank and follows them into a public bathroom. He uses his toy gun to rob them. He has the men get undressed so he doesn't have to worry that they will follow him. He learns once he opens the briefcase that he has made off with $100,000 in treasury certificates. Toni is angry that Eddie has become a thief. She leaves him.

Eddie arranges to sell the treasury certificates to a gangster, Tommy Morella. He meets Morella's men, Sal and Paulo, in a hotel room. The men attack him to steal the

Pryor and Lynne Moody in *Some Kind of Hero* (1982).

treasury notes, but Eddie beats the men unconscious and takes their money. Eddie makes an anonymous call to the police about a bogus emergency before changing into his uniform and walking out of the hotel, unnoticed. Toni, who has evidently forgiven Eddie, is waiting in the parking lot to pick him up.

Eddie is now able to get his life back in order. He uses Morella's money to pay his debts, sends the treasury notes back to the bank, and sends his uniform back to Colonel Powers.

Pryor said of *Some Kind of Hero*, "I get the opportunity to do some work that doesn't depend on my being zany. I'm a character and not a caricature. That other stuff wears out. The serious roles mean longevity. I can do other things."[8] Pryor gave credit to director Michael Pressman "for stopping and helping me the many times I thought I couldn't do it. With him, I was able to go inside and find new places.... What's important here is the humanness of the experience. I'm interested in the universal feelings of desperate people. This is everyman kind of stuff."[9]

Ronny Cox, who played Colonel Powers, said at the time, "I think [*Hero*] is going to establish Richard Pryor as one of the great actors in this town. He's always been known as a fine comedian, of course, but this is a serious film and he's excellent. The thing about Richard is he's so honest—he's so hard on himself. He's one of those few guys who can make you laugh and cry at the same time."[10]

Lois Armstrong, a reporter for *People*, wrote: "In one scene that called for Kidder to screech up in a car to rescue Pryor from a seedy downtown hotel, Richard cracked up everyone by leaping out of the shadows in an inflated Superman suit."[11] A publicity still for the film features him wearing the suit.

Kidder told Armstrong, "I find it wonderful working with [Richard]. He is an extraordinarily serious and dramatic actor and a warm and special person. I love him very much."[12] The actress's feelings for Pryor had not diminished when she spoke about her experiences on the film in 2009. She said:

> I fell in love with [Richard] in two seconds flat.... I defy any woman in those days.... He was smart and funny and sexy, and you wanted to take care of him. He was wonderful.... He was just—Richard was irresistible.... I remember when we were doing the love scene in *Some Kind Of Hero*, we got in bed nervously. Then he looked up, and it was very genuine, and he went, "[Gasps] Richard Pryor's in bed with Lois Lane!" And it was so cute! [Laughs.] He was really adorable. He was a wonderful, wonderful, wonderful man. Much underrated as a human being. I mean, he was really generous and kind and thoughtful, and I think the best actor I'd worked with, in the sense of when you were in a scene with him, it was like doing a dance. He didn't miss an eyelash-flicker. He was so in the present. And I remember saying to him, "God, you're really a good actor. Why does everybody insist you be funny all the time?" And he said, "Yeah, I know my craft." I mean, he was really a good actor, but everybody wanted him to be funny, and that didn't work. Halfway through, the powers that be at Paramount decided he had to make [*Some Kind of Hero*] funnier. And he was heartbroken about it.[13]

The press got word that Pryor and Kidder were filming a graphic sex scene together. Heavy makeup had to be used to cover the burn scars on his arms and torso. Lester wrote: "[T]heir graphic sex scenes—in bed and bathtub—are said to be steamy enough to snag an X rating."[14] Kidder, herself, said of the scenes, "They're not pornographic but very, very hot."[15] The actress saw the scenes as an important part of the story. She explained that, in the bedroom scene, Pryor's character breaks through her defenses and brings her to orgasm.

Lester asked Kidder if, as the tabloids suggested, the chemistry that she and Pryor demonstrated on screen was also something that developed off screen. Kidder denied it. She replied, "I adore Richard but we weren't having an affair. He's cute, but he's got a girlfriend."[16] Lester also wanted to know if the actress saw "evidence of the drug-addicted wild man of yore."[17] Kidder said, "He's so full of power and wisdom. I kept waiting for him to turn into 'the lunatic.' But he never did. I was devastated when the work was over."[18]

The couple was, in fact, dating. But their relationship didn't last long. Pryor wrote: "My six-month relationship affair with *Hero* co-star Margot Kidder ended just before the movie did, when she discovered that I was cheating on her. She didn't get mad—much. But she got even by coming over to the hotel where I'd taken up permanent residence and scissoring my Armani wardrobe hanging in the closet."[19]

New York Magazine reported that Paramount heavily edited the film's interracial sex scenes. The bedroom scene was pared down significantly and the more explicit bathtub scene was, according to the magazine, "virtually eliminated."[20] Pressman made it clear to the magazine that he disagreed with the studio's action. The scenes had no sooner been shot than every major newspaper across the country granted them prominent coverage. The newspapers cited "sources who've seen the rushes." It is conceivable that the studio never intended to allow the sex scenes to appear in theatres in unexpurgated form. The scenes, which Kidder described as "very, very hot"[21] and *People* noted were "steamy enough to snag an X rating,"[22] were likely designed to stir up controversy and generate publicity.

The film is, in at least one way, similar to *Blue Collar*. Again, the men in charge aren't treating the protagonist fairly and the protagonist turns to thievery as a remedy to the situation. The film was meant as a straight drama, but the studio couldn't see having Pryor in a film and not having him be funny. A number of comic scenes were added to the script. Their insertion creates abrupt shifts in tone throughout the film, with the comedy undercutting the drama. The quality of Pryor's performance varies as well. He is subtle in the serious scenes, exaggerated in the comedy scenes. He performs his medical examination scene for straight laughs. He acts even sillier later at a dentist office.

Surprisingly, the comedy business persists as the crucial tensions of the story are brought together in the third act. It is something out of a Jerry Lewis movie when a teenage boy squirts Pryor in the face with a water gun. Pryor, impressed by the realistic design of the water gun, purchases it to use in the bank robbery. In the next scene, he practices with the gun in front of a mirror, a parody of the classic scene from *Taxi Driver* (1976). Pryor is ready to draw the water gun at the bank, but the gun leaks in his pocket and makes it look as if he wet his pants. He is so embarrassed that he runs off before completing the robbery. He next tries to rob a clothing store, but the old woman who runs the store beats him over the head with an umbrella and chases him out. The broadly choreographed hotel room fight that climaxes the film borders on slapstick. Eddie quickly gains the advantage by squeezing Paulo's balls. He follows this neat move by giving him a kick in the groin. Once Sal drops to the floor, Eddie knees him in the face. Each blow is punctuated by an exaggerated sound effect. This cannot have been part of the combat training that the war veteran received at boot camp. Yet, Eddie manages with his crude fighting technique to beat both men unconscious.

The expulsion of waste matter is a theme of the film. The film opens with Eddie being surrounded by Viet Cong as he defecates. In the novel, the soldier is taken captive while urinating. He writes, "I was with my limp dribbling dick in my hand. Great!" The pivotal moment when Eddie robs the treasury notes from a businessman occurs while the man is defecating in a bathroom stall.

In the novel, Eddie uses an actual gun in the bathroom robbery. A toy gun was likely substituted to make Eddie more sympathetic in the film. The novel differs in other significant ways. Eddie completes his transaction with Sal and then sees a suspicious van parked outside the hotel. He keeps his eyes on the van and sees Sal interact with the men inside. It is obvious that he is about to be ambushed. Eddie enacts a quick escape plan, which simply entails making an anonymous call to the police and changing into his uniform, without a physical altercation ever occurring. But this sort of quiet climax is not what audiences were expecting.

The experiences of American POWs in Vietnam was less funny than a leaky squirt gun. Maureen Callahan of the *New York Post* wrote:

> They beat George McKnight for thirty-six hours straight; they beat and tortured Denton so brutally his arms turned black; Jim Mulligan was strung up and beaten for six days, Nels Tanner for seventeen. Sam Johnson was so brutalized that when he finally submitted, he literally could not write the apology demanded by the Vietnamese. He was able only to sign it, and when he was thrown back in his cell, he heard Jerry Denton whispering to him from next door.
> "Sam, Sam, it's OK, buddy."
> "I made them write it, Jerry," he replied. "But I had to sign it."
> "It's OK, Sam," Jerry said. "You're okay. Hang on, you did good."
> Each of the men would break, and each of the men understood. In fact, they all worried about Ron Storz, who had been in solitary for four years and had tried to commit suicide with a razor. Jerry Denton urged Storz to say whatever he had to so he could get out: His life was in danger, and it wasn't a violation of the military's Code of Conduct.[23]

The Vietnamese's most famous prisoner, John McCain, was another American soldier who signed a false confession. He wrote: "They took me up into one of the interrogation rooms, and for the next twelve hours we wrote and rewrote. The North Vietnamese interrogator, who was pretty stupid, wrote the final confession, and I signed it. It was in their language, and spoke about black crimes, and other generalities. It was unacceptable to them. But I felt just terrible about it. I kept saying to myself, 'Oh, God, I really didn't have any choice.' I had learned what we all learned over there: Every man has his breaking point. I had reached mine."[24]

After *Some Kind of Hero* wrapped production in July 1981, Pryor had many film projects presented to him, yet he made no commitments for nearly a year. Finally, he decided to star in a film for Universal called "Color Man." The film, which was to feature Pryor as a newscaster, was set to start shooting under the direction of Michael Apted in June 1982. But the film never happened. Pryor chose to make another film instead.

The Toy (1982)

Production: Columbia Pictures Corporation and Rastar Pictures.
Distribution: Columbia Pictures.
Producer: Phil Feldman.
Director: Richard Donner.
Screenplay: Carol Sobieski, based on the film *Le jouet* by Francis Veber.
Photography: Laszlo Kovacs.
Editors: Richard Harris and Michael A. Stevenson.
Music: Patrick Williams.
Release date: December 10, 1982.
Running time: 110 minutes.
Cast: Richard Pryor (Jack Brown), Jackie Gleason (U.S. Bates), Ned Beatty (Mr. Morehouse), Scott Schwartz (Eric Bates), Teresa Ganzel (Fancy Bates), Wilfrid Hyde-White (Barkley), Annazette Chase (Angela), Tony King (Clifford), Don Hood (O'Brien), Karen Leslie-Lyttle (Fraulein), Virginia Capers (Ruby Simpson), B. J. Hopper (Geffran), Linda McCann (Honey Russell), Ray Spruell (Senator Newcomb).

Pryor was interviewed by the *Los Angeles Times* on April 1, 1982. In the past, the comedian had come across to interviewers as aggressive, threatening. Today, he was soft-spoken. He said that he was preparing to shoot a film in Baton Rouge, Louisiana.[1] The film was *The Toy*, a remake of a popular French comedy called *Le jouet* (1976). Bailey wrote: "Rastar pushed [Pryor] to do *The Toy*, wanting the sure-fire comedy first, so 'The Charlie Parker Story' was rescheduled for 1984."[2]

Pryor's character in the film is Jack Brown, an unemployed journalist who is about to lose his home if he can't show the bank he has a steady job. He applies for work at the employment office of Bates Enterprises. Sydney Morehouse, the vice president of personnel, politely informs Jack that their only job opening is for a part-time maid. Jack, undeterred, expresses interest in the position. Morehouse is stunned. "You're obviously a journalist," he says. "You should go see the people at Mr. Bates's newspaper." Jack lets him know that the paper, *The Bugle*, isn't hiring blacks. He insists that, if Morehouse doesn't consider him for the maid position, he will have to sue the company for sexual discrimination. Jack is given the maid job and directed to the home of U.S. Bates (Gleason). He is so desperate to earn a paycheck that he doesn't hesitate to put on a maid outfit. The head maid sends Jack out to serve food to Bates and his elite dinner guests, but his strange appearance and clumsy serving skills infuriate the host. This is undoubtedly the worst scene in the film and it just may be the worst scene in Pryor's entire film career. Why does Jack dress as a maid? The scene makes no sense, has nothing to do with the plot, and shows Pryor being embarrassingly unfunny.

Pryor is shipped in a crate to a rich brat in *The Toy* (1982).

Gleason is a bland straight man to Pryor, mostly acting unmoved by his co-star's noisy and overbearing antics. Vincent Canby of the *New York Times* wrote: "Everyone is wasted, including Mr. Gleason, who always looks as if he's just come from the barber."[3]

Morehouse gives Jack a job as a janitor at Bates department store. Bates's son, Eric, is being escorted through the store to pick out a gift. He is intrigued when he sees Jack knocking over mannequins and playing with toys. "I know what I want," he tells Morehouse. "I want the black man." Morehouse is unable to change his mind, but he has a much easier time acquiring Jack's cooperation. He keeps laying fifty-dollar bills into Jack's hand until his resolve dissipates and he agrees to play along.

Jack is delivered to the Bates mansion in a wooden crate. Mr. Bates is outraged to learn that his son has purchased a store employee. He tells Jack that he will pay him an additional $2,500 to entertain his son for a few days. The boy, who sees his father using his great wealth to control those around him, decides to emulate him, thereby showing him the error of his ways. But, as much as he wants to teach his father a lesson, he is also a lonely child who enjoys having a new friend. He quickly becomes attached to his entertaining playmate.

Jack suggests another way the boy can shame his father. The two will create a newspaper to expose his father's mistreatment of workers. They conduct interviews with several of Bates's employees, who are relieved to express their many grievances. As expected, the exposé that Jack and Eric finally publish enrages Bates. He organizes a lavish garden party to honor Senator Newcomb, but Jack and Eric realize that the party's true purpose is to raise funds for the Ku Klux Klan. To ruin the guests' merriment, Jack and Eric ride go-carts through the house. As they tear down tents and knock over tables, the guests flee in terror. Bates chases after them in a golf cart, but he ends up driving into a swimming pool. Jack dives into the pool to rescue him.

Bates is grateful to Jack for saving his life and asks to join him in a drink. He opens up to Jack about his feelings for his son. He would do anything to have his son love him like he loves Jack. Jack tells him that he just needs to show his son fatherly affection.

Pryor and Jackie Gleason in *The Toy* (1982).

The film may have been worth watching if we believed the characters and cared about them, but the sentimentality never comes across as genuine. It is impossible to ever imagine Jack warming up to either the child or the father. The film wants us to accept in the end that, regardless of his bad behavior throughout the film, Bates is really a good guy at heart as well as a sensitive father who desperately needs his son's affection. Odie Henderson of Big Media Vandalism wrote: "Gleason's newspaper magnate is a horrible sadist one minute, a concerned dad who wishes his son would connect with him the next. Gleason comes prepared to play a complete asshole—his scene with Ned Beatty, an employee his ruthlessness has driven to alcoholism, is truly unnerving—but *The Toy* demands that we root for his happily ever after with his kid."[4]

Bates decides to take his son to Europe for a vacation. By now, Eric doubts that he can ever get his father to recognize his own flaws and become a better person. This makes him reluctant to stay with his father. At the airport, he jumps into a taxi and flees. Eric wants to live with Jack, but Jack insists that he give his father a chance. Bates arrives in his limousine. Father and son embrace while expressing their love for each other. Bates offers Jack a job at *The Bugle*.

After Bates and Eric drive away, one of their wealthy friends drives up in a limo. She asks Jack if he would take care of her bratty son. The bratty son shoots a toy gun at Jack, hitting him square in the forehead with a suction cup dart. Jack runs off in a mad frenzy.

Donner didn't bother to direct Pryor—he said that directing Pryor "was like playing four-walled handball when you're blindfolded."[5] Margot Kidder said,

The Toy (1982)

> [M]ost directors didn't direct him, they just let him go, thinking suddenly he could turn in a brilliant performance just by—I don't know what they thought. They were a little intimidated by him. I remember visiting him on *The Toy*, and my dear Donner was directing it, and Richard was really frustrated, because Donner wasn't directing him. Donner had directed me so meticulously [in *Superman*], I don't think I could have failed with Donner. But I think he, too, was a little flummoxed as to how to approach Richard. So they didn't get along, which broke my heart.[6]

Pryor's lack of direction was obvious to critics. Mike Hughes of Gannett News Service wrote: "Pryor is a brilliant actor, but he needs to be told 'no'–sometimes rather firmly. There's no evidence of Pryor restraint. The actor whines and whimpers so freely that the humor disappears." Ed Blank of the *Pittsburgh Press* identified his "lack of proportion" in "the eyes widening, the arms flailing, the Cinemascope reacting."[7] David and Joe Henry wrote: "One such scene early on in *The Toy* has Pryor caterwauling in bulging-eyed fright as he goes rolling head over heels down the department store toy aisle in an inflatable Wonder Wheel."[8]

David Henry said, "I never thought Richard was very good when he was trying to be funny. His brilliant characterizations happen when he's embodying these characters on the stage, and he's true to them. Richard doesn't make fun of them. *The Toy* begins with him doing this bug-eyed stuff. To me, that's not Richard Pryor, so I've never watched the whole thing."[9]

Rumors circulated that Pryor and Gleason weren't getting along. the *Journal News* noted, "Reportedly, the stars didn't warm to each other."[10]

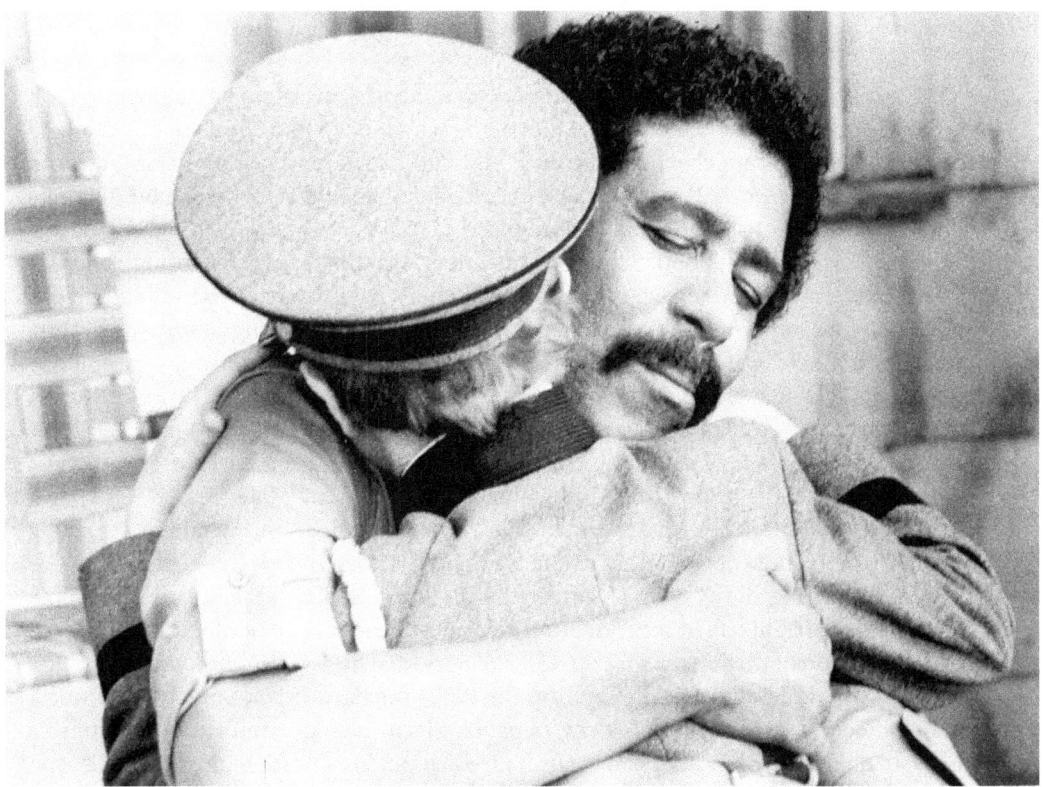

Pryor learns to love a rich brat (Scott Schwartz) in *The Toy* (1982).

Was this true?

Gleason was asked about Pryor in a 1980 interview with *People* magazine. He said, "I'd like to see him do an act without the blue stuff. You come out and say, 'Somebody's going to kick my black ass,' you're going to get a laugh. But I'd like to see him say something without that. I think he can do it."[11] The statement was not a ringing endorsement of Pryor, but it does suggest that Gleason had respect for him.

Pryor went into the project with great enthusiasm. As he said, "I've loved Jackie Gleason for years."[12] His affection for the comic icon only grew during production. He wrote in his autobiography: "Jackie and I hit it off famously, like kindred souls. The shit Jackie talked between set-ups was funnier than anything we got in the movie. He knew about gangsters, gamblers, comics, vaudeville, strippers, and sharks. He'd start talking about something that happened in the 1970s and then suddenly he'd be swirling around the 1920s and '30s, describing people and joints so good I could smell them. One day he asked me to get him some grass. I found some and gave it to him on the bench where we used to sit and talk."[13]

Pryor admitted that he and Gleason had different styles of working: "Gleason don't waste no moves. When they say 'action,' he knows exactly where he's going to turn his head. But I don't like being tied down to stone. I feel different at different times; I'd like to go with what I feel rather than what I'm saying."[14] Gleason didn't mind playing straight for Pryor, whose uninhibited performance became frenzied at times. He explained his approach to working with Pryor as follows: "You figure how's he's going to perform and you adjust."[15] But Pryor still enjoyed performing with one of his comedy idols. He said, "Gleason's a great man who knows it frontwards and backwards, who is a professional *on the dime*. I learned a lot from him."[16]

Pryor also got along well with his other co-star, Scott Schwartz. The casting director, Pennie du Pont, originally intended to find a boy who looked like Gleason, but changed her mind once she met Schwartz. Ms. du Pont, who had recently cast Aileen Quinn in the title role of *Annie* (1982), had a knack for recognizing child actors who could handle the responsibilities of starring in a feature film.

At the start of production, Schwartz was interviewed by a reporter from his hometown of Bridgewater, New Jersey. The reporter thought that Schwartz's friends and neighbors in Bridgewater would be interested in hearing how the young actor was getting along with Pryor. Schwartz said, "[H]e's a very quiet man, a very nice person, very polite."[17] Schwartz quickly adapted to Pryor's style of working. He said in 2013, "I was on the set with Richard two weeks and I was ad-libbing with him. He used to say, 'Who gives a shit about the script? Just say something close. It don't matter.'"[18] He described Pryor as the "greatest human being to ever walk the planet."[19]

Ned Beatty noticed Pryor's mood swings. He said, "[He's] on the edge ... sending us signals from somewhere slightly where we're not."[20]

Pryor wrote: "I didn't care much for the picture. Like the others, I did it for the monies."[21] He outright called the film a "piece of shit."[22] He was not alone in his opinion. George Anderson of the *Pittsburgh Post-Gazette* wrote: "'The Toy' reminds you of nothing so much as an old Jerry Lewis movie from the 1950s. Richard Pryor, one of the funniest men on screen, is turned into a gawky slapstick klutz, having oatmeal dumped on his head by an obnoxious little boy. Call it *The Babysitter*, put Fred Clark in the Jackie Gleason role, and you have a perfect Jerry Lewis movie for the late show. Best of all, you can tune it out."[23] Gary Minich of *Herald and Review* wrote: "[*The Toy*] has a busted mainspring."

Minich mostly blamed the editing: "The film moves jerkily from one sequence to the next, the camera angles are often wrong for the action and detract from it, actors step on one another's lines, the storyline is poorly laid and meanders back and forth.... [T]he choices glued together here seem mostly wrong, amateurish.... *The Toy* is like a child's playroom—strewn with baubles, but messy and disorganized."[24] Blank wrote: "[T]hey've gone for broad, easy, repetitive laughs: pie-throwing, gooey substances dumped on heads, wildly impertinent sex questions by a nine-year-old."[25]

Betsa Marsh of the *Cincinnati Enquirer* couldn't figure out if the film was meant to be a slapstick comedy, a weepy-eyed melodrama, or a social satire.[26] The strongest review came from Gene Siskel, a prominent critic with the *Chicago Tribune*:

> Richard Pryor is a saint of sorts, a goody-goody elder statesman in Richard Donner's "The Toy," a comedy about a spoiled white brat who asks his extremely wealthy father (Jackie Gleason) to "buy" him a black man for a present.... At regular intervals in the film, St. Richard delivers sermons, accompanied by heart-tugging music, to a little boy on how to be and have a real friend and to Jackie Gleason on how to be a real father. This new Pryor image as the conscience of the white man is a continuation of the sweet, post-accident Pryor we first met in *Bustin' Loose* and later saw in his more raucous concert film, *Live on the Sunset Strip*, which was highlighted by St. Richard's anti-drug message.[27]

Siskel didn't like sermons, saints, sentimental music, or anti-drug messages. This makes the late critic seem crabby, but this film has had a way of making people crabby. The idea of a rich white man buying a poor black man brought the film an overwhelming amount of flak.

It is useless to argue with detractors that Jack is not a slave in the film. He is paid a substantial amount of money to act as a boy's playmate for a week. Slaves were not paid. Slaves were not free to leave once the terms of employment were fulfilled. Jack was a live-in babysitter. The most slavish character in the film is Bates's assistant Sydney Morehouse (Beatty), who is white. Morehouse is treated so inhumanely by Bates that he has taken to drowning his sorrows in liquor.

Controversy began with the movie poster. Featured prominently was the following text:

> When Jackie Gleason told his son he could have any present he wanted, he picked the most outrageous gift of all.... Richard Pryor.

It wasn't only that a bratty rich kid asked his father to buy him a black man. It was made worse that Gleason's estate resembled a plantation. The film managed, in the view of detractors, to reconstitute slavery. It is similar to the response that HBO recently received for announcing the upcoming series *Confederate*, an alternate history saga that imagines what America would be like today if the South had won the Civil War. One critic suggested that a better title for *The Toy* would be "The Lighter Side of Slavery."

Siskel wrote a special feature article to vent all of the vitriol he felt towards *The Toy*. During this period, he had become a one-man Greek chorus when it came to Pryor's career. He now wrote: "Seeing this 'new' Richard Pryor again in 'The Toy,' one can't help feeling nostalgic and wanting to see the old, more angry Pryor. And—good news—one can see the old Richard Pryor in Eddie Murphy's role in '48 Hrs.', a powerhouse, crime-busting action picture directed by Walter Hill."[28] He continued: "Murphy is at his best in an explosively funny scene when he tries to impress Nolte by walking into a redneck bar, impersonating a detective and demanding information about one of the killers. Among

Murphy's more gentle lines: 'I hate you, white people.' It's a role that just three years ago would have gone to only one man—Richard Pryor."[29] Siskel complained that "[b]lack anger" had been "held in check in the movies since its heyday a decade ago with such pictures as *Sweet Sweetback's Baadasssss Song* and *Super Fly*."[30] A black man's fury on screen is not meant to be a character trait that advances a story. It is meant to be a social statement.

Siskel thought it was "explosively funny" for a black man to express hatred of white people. The man need not express his feelings in a pun, or a quip, or a double entendre. He just needed to say, "I hate you, white people." No critic ever demanded that Jonathan Winters or Jerry Lewis express unmitigated hatred of another race and no critic ever expressed disappointment if racial hatred was absent from a comedy performance. But this was something unique that many put upon Pryor. It was more important that he express black rage and black defiance than express black funny. Could Pryor be his own man or was it his burden to represent the black community? People who wanted to laugh didn't care about his race. They just wanted him to be funny. Studio executives didn't care about his race. They just wanted him to make money. But the critics mostly cared about his race. Some critics cared *only* about his race.

Jack's dignity was important in the context of the story, but critics also saw his dignity as important in the context of Jack's race. Bill Nichols of the *Clarion-Ledger* was upset that Pryor failed to "maintain the dignity of both his race and heritage."[31]

Pryor argued with Paul Schrader during the making of *Blue Collar* that the director needed to change the script so that Zeke didn't become a sellout. He was afraid of the reaction of his black fans if they saw him play a black man who willingly gave up his dignity. Jack was arguably an even worse sellout than Zeke. He barely resisted when Bates, the arrogant magnate, proposed that he surrender his dignity for a quick payout. Pryor had changed in the four years since he made *Blue Collar*. Now, he didn't bother to complain about the script or demand that Jack be redeemed in any way.

Bailey wrote: "Full of jiggle jokes, crotch-punches, pie fights, cartoon sound effects, sped-up action, and unearned pathos, *The Toy* is probably the worst Pryor vehicle of them all, topping even those with fewer laughs or lower production values by the sheer odiousness of its Southern-plutocrat-buys-a-black-man premise. ('I can't be bought. This got settled in the Civil War,' Pryor insists—as, shockingly, a Confederate flag hangs on the department store wall behind him, unnoticed.)"[32] The film was designed to appeal to the political left and ended up offending them instead. The filmmakers were aware of the slavery analogy and made a point on a number of occasions to address it. Pryor was specifically cast in the film to allow the filmmakers to make a comment on slavery. M. Enois Durate of High-Def Digest wrote: "Richard Donner's *The Toy* aspires to be a socially conscious comedy exploring such topical concerns as racism, the desperation of the working class, and the uncompassionate nature of the wealthy."[33]

The racism is far more explicit in the script. In the department store scene, O'Brien escorts Jack to Eric. He says, "His name is Jack Brown. Jack, this is Master Bates."

Eric replies, "I'll call him 'nigger.'"

"I'll call you 'prick,'" he snaps. He tells O'Brien that the boy needs a good whipping.

Perhaps they would have done better to cast a sweet and vulnerable Teddy bear like John Candy in the lead role. Blank had an interesting idea regarding casting. He wrote: "Buster Keaton would've been the perfect American toy."[34] As it turned out, Pryor's dark skin made this film about something it should never have been about.

Julian Upton of *Bright Lights Film Journal* wrote: "[*The Toy* is] a witless and degrading farrago that casts Pryor as an expensive plaything for a spoiled little white boy. *The Toy* could have had allegorical potential, not just regarding Pryor's career but for all those ethnic actors in Hollywood, but it fell far short of any such insight, and existed solely to show Pryor freaking out and looking scared."[35]

Saul Austerlitz wrote in *Another Fine Mess: A History of American Film Comedy*, "The film gestures at social awareness but for all its halfhearted attempts at racial sensitivity, and references to the legacy of slavery, *The Toy* is nothing short of appalling—a reminder of how Hollywood, with the best of intentions, could pervert Pryor's legacy. This mixed-up farce and social treatise accidentally pegged Pryor's problem; he was being boxed and sold in the market, his own voice stifled in the rush to lucre."[36]

Gary Arnold of the *Washington Post* wrote: "Pryor is probably as much to blame for the miscalculations as producer Ray Stark and his principal slapdash haberdashers, director Richard Donner and screenwriter Carol Sobieski. "The Toy" merely widens the gulf that has been evolving between Pryor's performing techniques in his concert films, which reveal a brilliantly inventive and touchingly personal approach to the audience, and the broader, sentimentalized methods he evidently considers appropriate for general-audience comedies."[37]

Bailey pointed out that, in the fall of 1981, the comedian told an audience at the Comedy Store, "I just don't give a fuck! You just reach a point in your life, you say, 'So what? So fuckin' what?'"[38]

Henderson wrote:

> In the right hands, Gleason's bulk and bluster, and Pryor's desperate ingenuity, could have made *The Toy* work.... Instead, Carol Sobieski's screenplay adaptation dumbs Veber's idea down in some rather offensive ways. She can't make up her mind about anything tonally, and some of her more intriguing ideas are either forgotten or neutered at the last minute.... Not once does Sobieski's script let Pryor lose control, except to do things like climb up a door in fast motion as if he were Willie Best reincarnated as Sylvester the Cat.[39]

Speeding up footage to show an actor running fast is never funny—and this happens *three* times in the film. Jack becomes so frightened when the boy lobs a firecracker at his feet that he scrambles up the side of the door. Jack runs rapidly across a lake stocked with piranha. His fantastic speed allows him to skirt along the top of the water as the fish nip at him, leaving his clothing in shreds. The last we see of Jack, he is running in fast motion up a street.

In Sobieski's defense, the fishing scene in her script has no piranha. Instead, Jack and Eric tell each other jokes, including one about Dolly Parton's breasts. Jack gets his fishing line tangled in tree branches, which is supposed to get a few laughs. Eric is able to eventually reel in a small fish, but the fish never tries to bite him. It is a quiet scene designed to build the relationship between Jack and Eric. Also not in the script is Jack climbing the door, Jack riding the Wonder Wheel across the store, and Jack running up a street like The Flash. It is by no means a good script, but it isn't as cartoony as the film turned out to be.

Jack has inexhaustible patience, which is out of character for Pryor. In an effort to humiliate her husband, Fancy Bates brings Jack before their dinner party guests. She exclaims, "We're selling them in our toy stores now!" Jack stands helplessly and shamefully at her side. Through much of the film, Pryor is quiet and weary between outbursts of mugging.

The film compares unfavorably with *Le jouet*, which is more underplayed and often ominous. François Perrin (Pierre Richards) tries to win his freedom in a table hockey game. He agrees to stay an extra year for every goal that Eric (Fabrice Greco) scores. Alternately, Eric has to let François leave if he is able to score more goals than him. François starts out badly, but then gets into a rhythm and pulls ahead. The boy abandons the game when it becomes obvious that he is going to lose. François is stunned. "Then I won," he says. "Why can't I go, then?" The boy looks at him with a blank stare. "Don't get fooled," he says, "you're well-off here. Dad will give you a big heap of cash." François looks hopeless. The scene is played for drama and suspense. It has no music, only the sound of the players jerking the control rods and the balls banging around the table top. The shots are kept tight to emphasize the players' fierce focus.

There is no bulging-eyed fright or Wonder Wheel in the original film. Richards is simply standing next to a collection of life-sized dolls when the boy singles him out for purchase. The boy sees him as being as much an empty object as the dolls.

Jack's antics in the department store serve as the perfect audition for a man who aspires to be a boy's playmate. He's being paid to clean the store, but that's not what Eric sees when he encounters him. He is running around with a football and throwing a pass at a mannequin modeling a football jersey. It doesn't concern Jack when his football pass topples a couple of mannequins. How is it possible to have fun without making a mess? Jack further defers his cleaning duties to climb onto the giant inflatable wheel for a wild ride across the retail floor. This destroys the premise established in the original film. François is a serious journalist who has a vested interest in maintaining his dignity. Jack is a ready-made playmate. Playing with toys is more gratifying to him than his dignity.

Pryor is constantly playing with toys in the film. The filmmakers believed that it would entertain audiences to have Pryor do funny things with the endless toys in Eric's playroom. But this turned Pryor into a prop comic, which he never was. This would have been a more appropriate job for Robin Williams, who could be hysterically funny with props.

François will lose his job as a journalist with the father's magazine if he doesn't play along with the child. *Le jouet* is, in the end, a story of the way an employee can become completely dominated by a powerful, cold-hearted employer. But Jack is not employed by Bates. He just needs money to ward off foreclosure and he is willing to indulge the crazy whims of a child for a quick payday. Jack has less at stake than François, who is truly trapped in his situation.

François is resentful. He tells the newspaper's editor-in-chief, Mr. de Blénac (Jacques François), "My place is in the editorial office, not in his son's playroom." The film becomes surreal as this proud man finds himself lost among endless toys. He tries to escape, but he realizes that this manipulative little boy has him trapped. It is difficult to believe that François could ever develop affection for a brat as terrible as Eric. This is a flaw of the film that carries over to the remake. The remake is even worse in that it also wants the audience to have sympathy for Eric's father.

In the original film, the boy does not reconcile with his father. The father, Rambal-Cochet, is a soulless, tyrannical industrialist. Nothing will make him change his ways. Eric refuses to leave in his father's limo, jumping instead into François's arms, clinging to him as tightly as he can. François looks dumfounded. The film freezes on this desperate image as the credits roll. This was such a defining image for the film that it later appeared on the poster. The message, evidently, is that despotic parents are destined to lose their children.

The script for the American version of *The Toy* has an entirely different ending.

Bates explains to his son that he shares in his power. Eric asks his father if this means he can "make anyone around here do anything I want?"

"Absolutely," his father says.

Eric tests his father by asking him to drop his pants. The script reads, "*Bates, profoundly embarrassed, but refusing to look the liar in front of his kid, unbuckles his pants and drops them. He wears boxers shorts, printed with the Lacoste alligator.*"

Jack drops his pants, too. Eric, inspired by his father and Jack, drops his own pants. The script reads, "*The three of them, arms around each other's waists, head for the limo, taking mincing little steps, their pants around their ankles, laughing.*" The trio is now one happy family. Jack, who started out the film in a maid's dress, undoubtedly serves in this strange new family as the mother.

In 1983, writers and directors still saw Pryor and Wilder as a viable team. Norman Panama, Barry Levinson, and Vicangelo Bulluck collaborated on a thirteen-page treatment for a Pryor/Wilder project called "All The King's Horses." Nothing else is known about the treatment, which was never expanded into a script.

In May 1983, Columbia Pictures gave Pryor $40 million to produce four films within the next five years. Pryor hired Jim Brown, former NFL running back, to head his new production company, which he named Indigo. He announced that the principal objective of Indigo was to provide opportunities for black filmmakers. Brown worked closely with the NAACP to achieve this objective.

Superman III (1983)

Production: Dovemead Films and Cantharus Productions.
Distribution: Warner Bros.
Producers: Pierre Spengler, Ilya Salkind, and Alexander Salkind.
Director: Richard Lester.
Screenplay: David and Leslie Newman.
Photography: Robert Paynter.
Editor: John Victor Smith.
Music: Ken Thorne.
Release date: June 17, 1983.
Running time: 124 minutes.
Cast: Christopher Reeve (Superman/Clark Kent), Richard Pryor (Gus Gorman), Jackie Cooper (Perry White), Marc McClure (Jimmy Olsen), Annette O'Toole (Lana Lang), Annie Ross (Vera Webster), Pamela Stephenson (Lorelei Ambrosia), Robert Vaughn (Ross Webster), Margot Kidder (Lois Lane).

The title sequence of *Superman III* expands on the title sequence of Frank Tashlin's 1956 classic *The Girl Can't Help It*. Again, a shapely blonde manages with her distracting, hip-wiggling walk to wreak havoc on the cityscape. In the earlier film, Jayne Mansfield's overpowering sexuality causes blocks of ice to melt, milk bottles to boil over, and eyeglasses to shatter. Now, Pamela Stephenson causes a hot dog vendor to crash his cart into telephone booths, which topple like dominoes, and a motorist to crash his car into a fire hydrant, which swiftly disperses enough water to leave the motorist floating around inside his vehicle.

Lester replaces Tashlin's playful visual metaphors with crude mayhem.

Pryor's character, Gus Gorman, is introduced playing with a yo-yo while he waits in line at the Metropolis unemployment office. We are meant to know with this scene that Gus is an innocent, hapless man-child. David Newman and Leslie Newman inserted a great deal of black slang like "jive" and "sucker" into Gus's dialogue, which can be awkward at times.

Gus is informed by a clerk he has been collecting unemployment benefits for thirty-six weeks and that they are about to expire. Gus sees a matchbook advertisement for a training course in computer programming. He takes the course, amazing his instructor with his talent for manipulating computer code.

Gus gets a job as a computer programmer at Webscoe Industries, but is dissatisfied with his pay and looks to find a way to profit from his newfound hacking skills. He works out a scam known as "penny shaving," which involves transferring the percentages of cents rounded up or down in Webscoe's prolific financial transactions to his own personal account. The money accumulated from these transfers proves to be substantial.

Gus is not inconspicuous about his new wealth. He turns up at work one day in a flashy new sports car, which draws the attention of Webscoe CEO Ross Webster. Webster figures out that Gus has been stealing money from him, but he admires the man's ingenuity and thinks he can employ him in his plans for world domination. He threatens to file a criminal complaint against Gus unless he will use his programming skills to control a weather satellite and get it to create a tornado that destroys Colombia's coffee crop. This way, he will be able to monopolize the coffee market. Gus is worried that, if he accesses the weather satellite through his own computer, it would be easy for legal authorities to trace the tampering back to him. Webster suggests that he use a computer at one of his company's small subsidiaries, Wheat King, which is located in Smallville.

Gus arrives at Wheat King in the middle of the night. He convinces Brad, the night watchman, that he has traveled from the Cleveland headquarters to check on an order that came up short. It isn't enough that Brad believes his story. He needs to ensure that he can work in privacy and that Brad cannot get in his way. So, he brings out a portable bar and invites Brad to have a drink with him. He keeps pouring drinks for Brad until the man passes out. The scene has an unfunny subtext. It was established in an earlier scene that Brad, an old classmate of Clark Kent, became an alcoholic after his days as a champion quarterback at Smallville High School.

(In the middle of the scene, Gus suddenly turns up in a big, funny hat, much like the big, funny hat he wore in *Bustin' Loose*. No filmmaker with respect for Pryor's talents would think he needs a big, funny hat to get laughs.)

Gus now tries to activate the computer, but he runs into a security problem. The computer cannot be activated unless two officials stand at different computer stations and insert the appropriate keys at the exact same moment.

The double key launch routine provides good old-fashioned physical comedy. Gus figures that, even though Brad is unconscious, he still might be able to help with the second key. He sits Brad in front of the computer station and wraps his fingers securely around the key, but, unexpectedly, Brad slumps forward and collapses to the floor. Gus remains undeterred. He ties the string from his yo-yo around Brad to hold him in place. Then, as he inserts the first key into the proper slot, he jerks the yo-yo string so that the man falls forward, and perfectly inserts the second key into the second slot.

After a bit of finagling, Gus is able to take control of the weather satellite and com-

Pryor wears a big funny hat in *Superman III* (1983).

mand it to emit laser beams at a cloud mass above Columbia. The heat of the laser beams increases the air pressure, causing the clouds to transform into a severe tornado.

Webster is caught by surprise when Superman arrives to prevent the tornado from destroying the crop. (In the script, Superman is described using his heat vision to dry the flooded fields in Colombia. The scene was replaced in the film with one in which Gus acts out Superman's amazing deeds to Webster. This bit of business was added during production because, up to this point, Pryor had little opportunity to be funny.)

A big gag in the film involves a ski slope that Webster has built on the roof of his skyscraper. Gus, determined to test his skiing skills, wraps a pink tablecloth around his shoulders and climbs to the top of the slope. It is just when he goes speeding down the slope that he realizes he doesn't know how to stop. He screams in terror as he goes sailing off the roof. The script reads: "*At the end of his trajectory, gravity takes over. He falls straight down (camera pans down to watch) ten stories and lands on an awning above the doorway of the apartment building. This, in turn, functions as a mini-slope, and he skis right off it and lands in the middle of the street.*"[1] The script has Gus dropping ten stories, but Lester shows the man dropping at least fifty—and he lives! Newton's law of gravity exerts no control in the film's gag-dominated world. Mike Ryan of the *Huffington Post* wrote: "Gus Gorman survived his fall…. Sure. Why not?"[2] Christopher Reeve complained about the ski slope scene in his autobiography, *Still Me*, citing it as an example of Lester's fondness for over-the-top gags.

The evil industrialist now realizes that he needs to get rid of Superman to continue with his world-domination plans. Gus gets the weather satellite to locate and analyze fragments of Krypton that are floating around in outer space. He then goes about creating

Pryor dressed in the infamous pink tablecloth for the infamous skiing-off-a-skyscraper scene in *Superman III* (1983).

a synthetic version of Kryptonite. He randomly adds tar to the mixture as a substitute for an element the satellite is unable to identify.

The residents of Smallville gather for a ceremony to honor Superman. Gus arrives, disguised as a U.S. Army general. He thanks Superman for "saving our bacon" and presents him with a gift—his synthetic Kryptonite. (Pryor could have made the general as much a comic blowhard as *Car Wash*'s Daddy Rich, but he barks out dialogue about molded plastic that makes no sense and isn't funny.)

The fake Kryptonite doesn't kill Superman on the spot as normal Kryptonite would. Instead, it draws out a malevolent side of his personality. The new version of Superman finds himself corrupted by heightened dark emotions, including anger and depression. He takes out his frustration by embarking on a spree of large-scale vandalism, including blowing out the Olympic Flame and straightening the Leaning Tower of Pisa.

The morally upright Superman eventually reemerges and splits apart from the corrupt Superman. The two versions of Superman battle amid the wreckage of an auto junkyard. The good Superman is strangling the bad Superman when the bad Superman fades and disappears.

Superman pursues Webster to the villain's new desert fortress. Gus's supercomputer attacks him with missiles, a ploy that fails. Next, the computer bombards him with a ray of artificial Kryptonite. Gus is horrified to see Superman succumbing to this. He attacks the computer with an axe, which gives Superman the opportunity to flee. The computer, realizing it needs to defend itself from further attack, converts Webster's sister and accomplice, Vera, into its own cyborg guard. The Vera cyborg attacks Gus, Ross, and his girlfriend Lorelei, firing blue energy blasts from its eyes. Superman arrives with a canister of acid, with which he is able to destroy the machine.

Superman is grateful to Gus for saving his life and does not turn him over to the authorities. Instead, he flies him to a West Virginia coal mine and advises the boss to give him a job.

Ryan wrote: "So, let's add up all of the things that Gus Gorman did wrong in this movie. He embezzled money, hacked a weather satellite, used that satellite to almost destroy Colombia, poisoned Superman with sorta Kryptonite, endangered the world's oil supply and built an ultimate computer that almost killed Superman. What is Gus' punishment for all of this? His punishment is a job recommendation from Superman."[3]

Pryor had talked enthusiastically with Johnny Carson about the Superman films on *The Tonight Show*. This gave producers Ilya Salkind and Alexander Salkind the idea to cast Pryor in *Superman III*. While on location in London, Pryor used an enormous amount of drugs. That is all he had to say about his experience in making the film.

Bailey wrote: "[T]he movie was a mess, and by its conclusion [Pryor's] a bit player, farting around in cutaways and doing halfhearted slapstick. It's sort of insane how much the movie just plain forgets about Pryor, especially considering how much they were paying him."[4]

Ryan wrote: "Time has not been kind to *Superman III*." He added, "The first film was epic. The second was fun. The third is neither."[5] Roger Ebert of the *Chicago Sun-Times* wrote: "*Superman III* is the kind of movie I feared the original *Superman* would be. It's a cinematic comic book, shallow, silly, filled with stunts and action, without much human interest."[6] Pauline Kael of *The New Yorker* wrote: "What's strange about the movie is that the best things in it aren't developed, and what Superman and the other characters do doesn't seem to have any weight."[7] Eleanor Mannikka of AllMovie wrote: "[T]his mix of vile deeds and fantasy heroics drops the 'S' out of cosmic and goes for comic instead."[8]

For the rest of his life, Pryor was embarrassed when anyone mentioned *Superman III* to him. In a 1995 interview, he said, "[*Superman III*] wasn't my fault. They did give me $4 million, so I did what the director said. But I didn't get to do shit in it."[9]

Pryor was scheduled to follow *Superman III* with a Charlie Parker biopic. Joel Oliansky, who wrote the script, said, "I know he wants to do it, that he's very anxious to have this chance to stretch himself professionally."[10] Oliansky was surprised when Pryor backed out of the project. Bailey wrote:

> And then ["The Charlie Parker Story"] disappeared.... As he drifted further from the stage, and further from the street characters that populated his act, [Pryor] seemed irrevocably removed from the twentieth-century reality he'd once so vividly dramatized. Pryor was a superstar now, wealthy and peaceful and, well, distant. In 1988, he appeared on the NBC special *The Comedy Store's 15th Year Class Reunion*, and spent most of his set talking about his recent experience buying and driving a Ferrari Testarossa. (Who the fuck can relate to that?)[11]

Bradford Evans of SplitSider reasonably questioned if Pryor, who was not a trained dramatic actor, could have played the serious roles that were being offered to him. Pryor must have doubted his acting abilities, himself, because he dropped out of the Charlie Parker project and later dropped out of a biopic for Malcolm X. Evans wrote: "Pryor was a wildly talented comedian but playing such a controversial and dramatic role [as Malcolm X] would have been a bit of a stretch."[12]

In 1987, Pryor talked about his acting abilities with Larry King. He said, "I don't think that I can act at all, to be honest. I just can be who I am.... I don't call it acting.... I've seen actors, great actors. I go to the movies and wish I could do what they do—De Niro, he just gives me chills, and if you see a great film, you see actors in it do great performances, you could tell that I'm not one of them."[13]

A comedian who was able to demonstrate acrobatic grace and shape-shifting ability on stage should have been well-suited to motion pictures. But Pryor rarely was at his best in his narrative films. Als wrote: "Generally, ... Pryor had a *laissez-faire* attitude toward acting.... Perhaps no character was as interesting to Richard Pryor as Richard Pryor. He certainly didn't work hard to make us believe that he was anyone other than himself as he walked through shameful duds like *Adiós Amigo!*"[14]

Pryor admitted in late 1982 that he had lost interest in making films. He said, "I want to take some time for Richard and just enjoy myself a little bit."[15]

Meanwhile, Gene Wilder still looked forward to reteaming with Pryor. He said in June 1982, "Ever since *Stir Crazy*, there have been lots of scripts for Richard and me."[16] But, insisted Wilder, he had to be picky because he didn't want to do *Stir Crazy II* or *Stir Crazy III*. "Good material is very hard to find," he

Pryor poses as a three-star general in *Superman III* (1983).

said, "and I don't want to be repetitious. After all, the script is 70 percent of the whole thing, and writing still is the most important part of making movies."[17]

Wilder was confident that he and Pryor would do well with the right script. He said: "With Richard, something magical happens. We're totally non-competitive, but very supportive and freewheeling. We talk, we work, we flip out together. It's rare because we're both funny and will use one another. It's not like a comic-straight man relationship like Abbott and Costello or Martin and Lewis. It's more like the relationship between Stan Laurel and Oliver Hardy, whom Pryor really loves and admires."[18] Wilder's interest in Laurel and Hardy brought him back to his *Hanky Panky* writers, David Taylor and Henry Rosenbaum. Taylor said that he and Rosenbaum were on the MGM lot to rewrite a script. They were on their way to lunch when they encountered Sidney Poitier, who told them to talk to Melville Tucker about working on a story idea. Tucker, who had turned out dozens of westerns in the 1940s and 1950s, led the production team on six of Poitier's films since 1969. Taylor called him "an old warhorse."[19] Poitier told the writers that Pryor was "kinda involved."

He asked, "Could you write for a black man?"

"What's the difference?" responded Taylor.

Poitier laughed.

The first draft of the script was submitted under the title "All Day Suckers." Today, Taylor has only a vague memory of it. The story, as he recalls, is set in New York City in the 1930s. Pryor and Wilder are servants to the world's greatest detective. They are fearful of their employer, whom Taylor described as "a mean son-of-a-bitch."[20] While he is away, the clumsy servants do a great deal of damage to his house. A woman shows up and mistakes Wilder for the detective; he goes along with this so that he and his buddy can vacate their jobs before the real detective returns. The project eventually adopted the title of a 1929 Laurel and Hardy comedy, *Double Whoopee*, but plot elements came from another (and better) Laurel and Hardy short called *Another Fine Mess* (1930). Laurel and Hardy create mayhem in a mansion while the owner, a hot-tempered big game hunter named Colonel Buckshot, is on an expedition in Africa. Hardy covers up his identity to visitors by pretending to be Colonel Buckshot. Laurel plays along, pretending to be Buckshot's maid Agnes.

There was a lot of enthusiasm for Wilder's project at first—Taylor called this the "honeymoon period"—but then the project started to fall apart.

Wilder brought in a new writing team, Peter Seaman and Jeffrey Price, to revise the script. Seaman and Price had recently earned their first big screen credit with *Trenchcoat* (1983), a comedy-thriller involving an aspiring mystery writer (Margot Kidder) who is drawn into an international conspiracy to smuggle stolen plutonium out of Malta.

When asked about the "Double Whoopee" project, Seaman went digging through his files and found a draft he and Price had written in 1983. He wrote:

> Jeff Price and I did a rewrite (or two) for Gene Wilder on a script he was hoping to do with Richard Pryor. We never worked with Richard, only Gene. It was an Abbott and Costello slapstick piece set in the 1920s. Gene and Richard play servants to a "master detective" named Jack Peabody. Gene ends up impersonating Peabody—with Richard as his servant—on a cruise ship to Cuba. There's a rich dowager with a precocious niece he's hired to protect, a bad guy with three fingers, etc. Hijinx ensue. Not sure why it never happened.

The project remained viable for years. A final draft was completed by Wilder on December 7, 1987. A copy of that script is available in the Gene Wilder Papers at the University of Iowa. It allows us to imagine a Pryor and Wilder collaboration that might have been.

The scene that was to introduce Wilder as Peabody's butler Homer and Pryor as Peabody's valet Binky was undoubtedly inspired by Laurel and Hardy.

Homer and Binky camp out in Peabody's bedroom while the detective is in India tracking down an assassin. Peabody, who captured the assassin sooner than expected, arrives back in town. He summons a cab to take him home. The driver recognizes him from a newspaper photo and starts a conversation with him.

The driver asks, "Somebody up this early?"

He says, "The two nitwits who work for me oughta be up by now. If they're not, God help 'em."[21]

Cut to a shot of Homer and Binky sleeping together in the master's bed. The script reads, "[They're] wearing long flannel nightshirt and stocking caps. They look like two babes in the woods as they lie there ... sound asleep. All around the bed are the remnants of a pig-out feast from the night before."[22]

Homer wakes up thirsty. He is reaching for a pitcher of water on the nightstand when Binky is unsettled in his sleep by a nightmare. Binky rolls over and gets his arms entwined with Homer's. Homer struggles to pour water into his glass despite having Binky's arms in his way. As he pours the water, he fails to notice that he is missing the glass and spilling it on the bed. Binky awakens and feels the wet sheets. Worried that he has wet the bed, he "gives a slow look at the movie audience."[23] The two men argue. Binky throws talcum powder into Homer's face, and Homer hurls the pitcher of water into Binky's face. Then, the two men get into a pillow fight, which causes a pillow to split open and spew its goose feather stuffing into the air.

Homer and Binky panic when they hear Peabody arrive home. Peabody calls out to them, but they ignore him and scurry off to hide. The detective hears scuffling noises coming from his bedroom and assumes that prowlers are present. The script reads, "*Peabody walks to a gun case and pulls out TWO IVORY-HANDLED REVOLVERS. A sadistic gleam appears in his eye.*"[24] He finds Homer with his face covered in talcum powder and Binky soaking wet with goose feathers stuck to his hair. Homer pretends he is sleepwalking, but Peabody knows he's lying. He grabs him by the neck and shakes him. Peabody is on the verge of seriously injuring Homer when a wine bucket falls off a closet shelf and knocks the great detective unconscious.

Homer and Binky decide to flee before Peabody wakes up. They are on their way out the door when Grace Powell arrives. Grace needs Peabody to escort her niece Lula to Cuba to meet with her dying father, who intends to turn over his fortune to his daughter. An escort is necessary, she explains, because she has reason to believe an assassin is out to murder her niece. This is when Homer pretends to be Peabody and agrees to accompany Grace and Lula on their ocean voyage.

Binky is clearly meant to be the Hardy character. Homer frequently looks to him for guidance. Binky is hesitant to go on the ocean cruise as Homer's servant.

> HOMER: But what am I going to do without you? I won't know what to say. I'm not as smart as you are. It'll be just like it was at school ... when all the kids made fun of me when I didn't know the right answers to the questions (he starts to cry). And then the teacher made me stand in the corner, with a dunce cap on my head, and they all—"
> BINKY: ALRIGHT, ALRIGHT ... that's enough.[25]

As Homer and Binky walk up the gangway to the steamship, Homer begins to have doubts that he will be able to keep up the pretense. He insists that the high society passengers can already tell he's a fraud and that's why they're staring at him.

BINKY: What are you talking about?
HOMER: Everybody's staring at me. Look at them.
(*OTHER PASSENGERS are staring at Homer.*)
BINKY: Hmm. They *are* staring at you. That's funny. I wonder what—
(*Binky looks down and sees, for the first time, that Homer is holding Binky's hand.*)[26]

In their sumptuous cabin, Binky eats caviar while taking a bubble bath. The camera pulls back to reveal Homer scrubbing Binky's back with a long-handled brush. The script describes a number of homosexual images—the duo sleeping in bed together, walking hand in hand, and bathing each other.

Homer and Binky's dialogue could have easily been written for Laurel and Hardy.

HOMER: I have to hand it to you, Binky. I thought that this was going to be another one of your bad ideas. But it's turning out just swell.
BINKY: Well, I hope from now on you'll have a little more faith in me.
HOMER: You bet I will.[27]

Later, Homer and Binky attend a masquerade ball dressed as ballerinas. But their fun for the evening is disrupted by the Three-Fingered Man, who follows them onto the deck and attempts to shoot them. Homer, Binky, and Lula take cover in a lifeboat. The Three-Fingered Man uses an axe to cut the ropes securing the boat, causing it to drop into the ocean.

Homer, Binky, and Lula are adrift at sea. They do their best to plug up leaks created by bullet holes in the hull of the lifeboat. It turns out that Lula was the captain of a sailing team in college. The script reads: "*Homer and Binky watch as Lula takes command and starts to convert the crippled lifeboat into a sailboat.*"[28] Lula is able to sail the boat directly to Cuba, where her father, Ed Powell, is dying. It turns out that Dr. Hawthorne, who is attending to the terminally ill patient, is actually the Three-Fingered Man. This villain has installed a fake niece as the sole heir to Powell's fortune and has been slowly killing Powell with snake venom. Peabody arrives in time to expose the bogus doctor's scheme. The Three-Fingered Man pulls a gun out of his medical bag and is about to shoot Peabody when Homer and Binky burst into the room dressed as flamenco guitarists. Binky grabs the hypodermic needle with the snake venom and jabs it into the Three-Fingered Man's buttocks. This brings about his rapid demise.

In the end, Homer and Binky are paid five thousand dollars for their services. They use the money to buy a banana plantation in Cuba.

Seaman enjoyed revisiting the script for the purposes of this book. "[I]t was pretty damn funny!" he wrote. Price and Seaman went on to great success with *Who Framed Roger Rabbit?* (1988), *Doc Hollywood* (1991), *How the Grinch Stole Christmas* (2000), and *Shrek the Third* (2007).

In 1983, Pryor was also in talks to star in a comedy/drama with Richard Dreyfuss called *Ain't No Hero*. *Jet* magazine described the plot as follows: "Pryor would play a World War II G.I., Dreyfuss, an Italian soldier—both of whom are trying to desert."[29] It sounds like a remake of the Lina Wertmüller film *Seven Beauties* (1975). It may also have been the World War II film that Pryor had once talked about making with Giancarlo Giannini.

On September 26, 1983, *Variety* reported that Pryor and Burt Reynolds were set to team up for a Blake Edwards comedy inspired by another Laurel and Hardy film, *The Music Box* (1932). Within months, both Pryor and Reynolds had left the project. Joe Baltake of the *Philadelphia Daily News* wrote: "Edwards' initial impulse, a good one, was to sign Burt Reynolds as Ollie and Richard Pryor as Stan. But Pryor, with a series of lackluster films to his credit and worried about another, backed out. Then Reynolds and Edwards had a violent falling out early in the production of Warners' 'City Heat.' Edwards left the project, left Warners and took 'The Music Box' with him to Columbia."[30] By the time shooting began in March 1985, the "Stan" and "Ollie" roles had been recast with Howie Mandel and Ted Danson. The film was released as *A Fine Mess* in 1986.

Edwards's film was not the only attempt to team Pryor and Reynolds, who had been interested in working together for a while. Producer Lawrence Gordon proposed teaming the actors for *48 Hrs.* (1982). Friedman, who wrote *Stir Crazy*, remembers being contacted to work on a film with Pryor and Burt Reynolds. He believes it started out as a vehicle for Pryor and Wilder, but Wilder had to back out due to a scheduling conflict. Friedman had to refuse the offer because he wasn't on good terms with Reynolds, who had never forgiven the author for writing an unflattering article about him for *Playboy*. Reynolds was likely offended as soon as he saw the article's sly title—"Burt Reynolds Puts His Pants On."

Friedman remembered nothing else about the project. For various reasons, it is unlikely it was *48 Hrs.* or the Edwards film. But it is known that Pryor and Reynolds became involved in a third project. The only information available on this comes from Masco Young's column in the *Philadelphia Daily News*: "Hot box office superstars Burt Reynolds and Richard Pryor will team up in a film now being written for Columbia Pix by Michael Kane—all about the exploits of mercenaries in South America."[31] Around the same time, Pryor was offered the role of Sandman Williams in *The Cotton Club* (1984), but he asked for more money than the production company could afford. The role was given instead to Gregory Hines.

Pryor's production company, Indigo, had yet to make a film. As he wrote in his autobiography: "Indigo was a fiasco, something much bigger than I could handle. I didn't know how to run a company, and, come to think of it, I didn't even want a company, you know? Jim Brown did, though. I made my friend Jim president…. Jim, a complex man, liked running that company more than I liked having it. He hired lots of people. He made lots of noise. He commissioned numerous scripts. Started up all sorts of projects."[32] But he didn't like the scripts that Brown had developed. "He fucked around and turned down Prince's *Purple Rain*. That movie would have been great for us, but Jim thought it didn't have enough black people among the production assistants or whatever. I said, '*So?*' 'No, see, you got to have black people. This is a black thing.' I said, 'What we gonna do, Jim?' I felt like I was mad. I was insane. I told Jim Brown over lunch that I didn't want this company, and Jim cried. *Jim Brown*, you dig? I didn't care because I was tired of this shit."[33] Pryor fired Brown and replaced him with Charles Smiley, a lawyer who had worked as vice president of ABC Sports in the 1970s. More recently, he had served as a manager for the Commodores and Natalie Cole.

Brewster's Millions (1985)

Production: Universal Pictures, Davis Entertainment, Lawrence Gordon Productions, and Silver Pictures.
Distribution: Universal Pictures.

Brewster's Millions (1985)

Producers: Lawrence Gordon and Joel Silver.
Director: Walter Hill.
Screenplay: Herschel Weingrod and Timothy Harris, based on the novel *Brewster's Millions* by George Barr McCutcheon.
Photography: Ric Waite.
Editors: Freeman Davies and Michael Ripps.
Music: Ry Cooder.
Release date: May 22, 1985.
Running time: 97 minutes.
Cast: Richard Pryor (Montgomery Brewster), John Candy (Spike Nolan), Lonette McKee (Angela Drake), Stephen Collins (Warren Cox), Jerry Orbach (Charley Pegler), Pat Hingle (Edward Roundfield), Tovah Feldshuh (Marilyn), Hume Cronyn (Rupert Horn), Joe Grifasi (J.B. Donaldo), Peter Jason (Chuck Fleming), David White (George Granville), Yakov Smirnoff (Vladimir), Rick Moranis (Morty King), Milt Kogan (Heller), Carmine Caridi (Salvino).

Herschel Weingrod and Timothy Harris set out to update the classic *Brewster's Millions* story for Bill Murray. The writers envisioned Murray as an unemployed astronaut selling knock-off jeans on the streets of Manhattan. This idea was dropped when Walter Hill was hired as director. Hill, a big baseball fan, asked the writers to change the character to a baseball player. Hill was respectful of the time-tested story and did not want the writers to, in any way, vulgarize it.

Hill got Pryor involved in the project. Weingrod said, "When Richard Pryor decided that he wanted to do this, the first thing that he said to all of us was, 'I don't want race to play a part in any of this. In other words, the fact that I am a black man should never

Pryor and John Candy are best friends in *Brewster's Millions* (1985).

actually come up. I don't want to play this like I've played other roles, where I am a street character or I am clearly African American. I don't want it to be like my live performances. I don't want it to be like any of that stuff. I just want to play it like a character."[1] Pryor read the script and told Weingrod that he enjoyed it. He liked that it was a sweet story.

Candy agreed to take the part once he heard that Pryor was starring and Walter Hill was directing. Hill told Candy, "I'd love to have you in the picture. I'm afraid the way the script stands there isn't much for you to do. But I'll do my best to expand the part for you."

Let us delve into the film's intricate, twisty plot.

Monty Brewster (Pryor) is a Minor League Baseball pitcher with the Hackensack Bulls. He loves being a pitcher, which makes it hard when he is thrown off the team for being arrested in a bar brawl. Present at his hearing is J.B. Donaldo (Joe Grifasi), whom Monty saw taking photographs of him at his last game. Monty is sure that Donaldo is a scout. Donaldo asks for permission to speak to the judge. He informs him that he represents anonymous parties who have instructed him to post Monty's bail.

Donaldo escorts Monty and his friend Spike Nolan (Candy) to the law offices of Granville & Baxter. Monty is sure he is about to be offered a job by a major league team. He is introduced to Edward Roundfield, who tells Monty that he is a representative of Rupert Horn. Monty doesn't recognize the name. He says, "I bet he's someone high up in the Yankee organization, right?" Roundfield responds that Horn was Monty's great-uncle, leaving Monty dumfounded. Roundfield explains that Horn was estranged from his family for fifty years and everyone assumed he was dead. The point of the meeting is that the man recently passed away and Monty, his sole living heir, is the beneficiary of his sizable estate.

The will drafted by Horn is no ordinary document. It imposes a number of strange conditions that the heir must follow in order to collect his inheritance. Roundfield explains that Monty has two choices. First, he can take $1 million immediately and leave. Or, second, he can inherit $300 million on the condition that he spends $30 million in thirty days. He can hire staff but he must get value for the services that the staff provides. He can donate only 5 percent to charity and lose 5 percent by gambling. He may not waste the money by purchasing and destroying valuable items. The most important condition is that he can have no assets at the end of the thirty days—otherwise, he forfeits any remaining assets and does not inherit the $30 million. Brewster is confident that he can spend the money and earn the full inheritance. But there is one final condition that he finds to be the most difficult—he cannot tell anyone about the arrangement.

It is a vital condition of the will that the law firm assigns an employee to keep track of Monty's spending. This job is given to a paralegal, Angela Drake. Granville and Baxter secretly assign a second employee to the case. Warren Cox, a junior lawyer with the firm, is tasked with sabotaging Monty's efforts so the law firm's scheming partners can take over as the executor of the estate and earn a sizable fee.

At first, Brewster rents an expensive hotel suite, hires a sizable entourage, and buys his old team, The Bulls. Meanwhile, Spike makes investments that earn Brewster a substantial amount of money. Monty is visibly distressed by the success of Spike's investments, which confuses his friend.

One member of Monty's entourage is Morty King, a bearded little man in a blue tuxedo, ruffled shirt, and bow tie.

"Who the hell are *you*?" a suspicious Spike asks.

Pryor becomes involved in politics in *Brewster's Millions* (1985).

"I'm Morty King, king of mimics, that's who! Anything you say I guarantee it'll be repeated."

(Amber Petty of IFC wrote: "[Rick] Moranis plays this confident weirdo with delightful skill…. [T]he idea of anyone crowning himself 'King of the Mimics' for doing a trick that little brothers use to annoy everyone is a pretty insane thought.")[2]

Monty hopes to get rid of a lot of money by running a political campaign. He realizes that the voters of New York are unhappy with the candidates running for mayor. He makes it the focus of his campaign to promote the ballot option "None of the Above." He makes campaign speeches accusing his two rivals, Heller and Salvino, of being thieves. Heller and Salvino join forces to sue Monty for slander. The lawsuit is a boon to Monty, who is able to end the matter with an out-of-court settlement of seven million dollars.

Monty hires the New York Yankees to play a three-inning exhibition game against the Bulls. The Bulls play admirably, but the Yankees are too good for them to beat. Monty is disappointed that his pitching skills weren't enough to withstand the might of the Yankee sluggers. But Roundfield comes to visit him in the locker room and tells him that his uncle would have been proud.

Monty panics when he learns he is leading in the election polls. If he wins, his annual salary as mayor will be treated as an asset under the terms of the will. This forces him to immediately withdraw from the campaign. He reiterates to the voters that, if they are dissatisfied with the candidates, they need to vote for "None of the Above."

Marilyn, an interior decorator hired by Monty, returns unneeded furniture to a retailer, which results in the refund of a twenty thousand dollar deposit. Warren deviously withholds the receipt for the refund.

Monty spends his last $38,000 on a post-game party. At the party, he doesn't feel as happy as he believes he should. He is disheartened that his extravagant spending has alienated Spike and Angela.

Minutes before the deadline, Warren reveals that Monty is not broke. He produces an envelope that contains twenty thousand dollars in cash—the furniture deposit. Monty is upset by this. Warren suggests that Angela might have been aware of the refund if she and Monty hadn't been carrying on "like a couple of rabbits." Monty punches Warren, knocking him to the floor. Warren threatens to sue Monty, who quickly hires Angela as a lawyer and hands her the twenty thousand dollars as a retainer for her services. Monty, left with no money, has met the terms of the will and inherits the $300 million.

Brewster's Millions presents a protagonist that indulges in conspicuous consumption. It was, to many critics, a perfect vehicle for the materialistic 1980s. But the story can be traced back much further. The extraordinary tale of Monty Brewster was introduced in 1902 as a novel by George Barr McCutcheon. It was later adapted into a stage play, a stage musical, and seven English-language films.

Dover Publications, who released a 2016 reprint of *Brewster's Millions*, summarized the book as follows:

> With the passing of his beloved grandfather, Monty Brewster inherits a long-anticipated million dollars. But he suddenly discovers that he can inherit seven times as much from his eccentric uncle if he spends every cent of his grandfather's money within a year. The carefree prospect of running through a fortune in order to receive an even greater windfall turns into a comic burden because of his uncle's stipulations: Monty must spend responsibly, showing good business sense, limiting his charitable contributions, and maintaining utter secrecy about the second inheritance.[3]

Pryor and John Candy strategize on the ballfield in *Brewster's Millions* (1985).

The motives of the eccentric uncle, James Sedgwick, are laid down explicitly by the executor, Mr. Grant. Sedgwick hated Monty's grandfather, Edwin Peter Brewster, for his bitter opposition to his son, Robert, marrying Sedgwick's sister Louise. Mr. Grant says, "[Edwin Brewster] refused to recognize [Louise] as his daughter, practically disowned the son, and heaped the harshest kind of calumny upon the Sedgwicks."

Brewster's grandfather was later remorseful that he treated Louise badly and sought to make amends by leaving a million dollars to her son Monty. It turns out that Sedgwick, who became a mining magnate, also named Monty as an heir, leaving his nephew $7 million in his will. But unusual conditions were written into the will by Sedgwick. He demanded that Brewster spend every last cent his grandfather willed him at once. The book reads: "It was to preclude any possible chance of the mingling of his fortune with the smallest portion of Edwin P. Brewster's that James Sedgwick, on his deathbed, put his hand to this astonishing instrument."[4]

What man would turn down the chance to exchange a million dollars for seven million? But other conditions are imposed on Monty. The *New York Times* noted (in regards to Winchell Smith and Byron Ongley's faithful stage play): "[Brewster] must tell no one what he is doing, but must dispose of the money logically [and] without unnecessary waste. Giving it away to libraries, or building churches, or anything of that sort is barred."[5] It was also stipulated in the will that, while he could not be indiscriminate in his dissipations, he could not be stingy either. "I hate a saint," the uncle noted. He specified, "[L]et him spend his money freely, but get his money's worth."

In the book, Monty throws a lavish ball. He charters a cruise that last months as he and his guests make various stops in Europe and Egypt. He loses more than fifty-six thousand dollars financing a concert tour of a Viennese orchestra. The problem is that most efforts that Monty makes to lose money only earn him more. He buys falling stock in lumber and fuel, but the stock turns around and earns him fifty-eight thousand dollars. He wins money gambling at a prize fight, a racetrack, and a Monte Carlo casino.

Monty is sworn to secrecy. This creates a conflict between he and his friends, who care a great deal about his welfare and want to do everything they can to limit his losses. The *New York Times* reported: "[H]is enforced secrecy makes many a laughable situation."[6] Dover noted, "His friends are aghast at his madcap extravagance—the gambling, the risky investments, the lavish parties—and Monty's romance with a banker's daughter is imperiled by his seemingly reckless spending."[7]

"Nonetheless," reports Wikipedia, "Monty repeatedly demonstrates a strong moral character. At one point, he uses his funds to bail out a bank to save his landlady's account, despite risking his eligibility for the will. At another, he jumps overboard to save a drowning sailor from his cruise ship even as his rich friends choose not to."[8]

Monty's girlfriend, Barbara Drew, rejects his marriage proposal because Brewster has shown himself to be fiscally irresponsible and has become inattentive in their relationship. A childhood friend, Peggy Gray, maintains faith in Monty and never wavers in her support of him. The book inevitably ends with Monty and Peggy becoming engaged.

Pryor said that *Brewster's Millions* was the first film on which he ever worked that he was completely sober. Hill found that working with the sober Pryor was a mixed experience:

> I had tremendous respect and admiration ... for Richard.... [But he] was in a fragile state of mind. I think that was pretty much a constant with him. He was usually either very defensive or very agitated.... Richard felt that, if he didn't take drugs, he probably wasn't funny. And he also felt that, if he

took drugs, he'd die.... The problem was compounded by the persona of John Candy.... Wonderful guy, wonderful guy. John was one of these guys [who], as soon as he walked through the stage door, he was on and he was funny. And he loved being funny to the crew and he knew everybody's name.... And he was just loved and funny and a great guy.... Richard was not an outgoing person. Richard was very much a performer when he performed. He was not a very funny guy off [camera].... He spent most of his time in his trailer. [On set,], he would be hunched over, watching Candy getting laughs. And, every once in a while, he kinda tried to turn something on with the crew. It was just awkward. People would try to laugh, but Richard would realize that they weren't really laughing.... It was so sad.[9]

McKee, Pryor's leading lady in *Which Way Is Up?*, played the role of Angela Drake. McKee noticed a significant change in the comedian. "I must say," she remarked, "that Richard's demeanor changed a bit after the accident. He seemed more introspective and a little less fun-loving, as is understandable after almost dying in an accident."[10] McKee said that Candy was "wonderful."[11]

Hill said, "I think I've only done one movie that is perceived to be a flat-out comedy and that was *Brewster's Millions* with Pryor. Whatever its deficiencies, I think the wistful quality was there. I was happy about that. The picture did well and made money."[12] According to Hill, it also became enormously popular with children in its television airings.

Many critics, however, denounced Universal Pictures for wasting Pryor's skills in what they perceived as a light, old-fashioned comedy. Janet Maslin of the *New York Times* called the film "a screwball comedy minus the screws"[13] that "does nothing to accommodate Mr. Pryor's singular comic talents."[14] Director Walter Hill, she said, did not understand "the advantages of screwball timing."[15] She held that the film's slow pace and lack of style gives it "a fatuous artificiality."[16]

Gene Siskel of the *Chicago Tribune* wrote: "[I]n the hands of the new Pryor—the post-fire Pryor, the nice and kind and gentle and sweet Pryor—*Brewster's Millions* comes across more as a TV variety show sketch then an exciting film adventure. Once again—and it's starting to sound like a broken record—Hollywood has failed to come up with a character equal to the cunning or range of emotion that Pryor has demonstrated in his stand-up comedy films."[17]

The onslaught of bad reviews persisted. Vincent Canby of the *New York Times* wrote: "Watching Richard Pryor as he forces himself to cavort with simulated abandon in *Brewster's Millions* is like watching the extremely busy shadow of someone who has disappeared. The contours of the shadow are familiar but the substance is elsewhere. *Brewster's Millions* is another in the series of earnest attempts to tame—to make genteel—one of the most original, most provocative, most unpredictably comic personalities to come on the American scene in the last twenty years."[18] Bob Thomas of the Associated Press wrote: "[T]he film plods to the expectable, heartwarming climax."[19] Ron Cowan of the *Statesman-Journal* wrote: "Pryor has lost his comic edge. There is little manic energy or edgy imagination here, just the nice-guy actor being nice."[20] Ken Tucker of the *Philadelphia Inquirer* pointed out that, as in *The Toy* and *Bustin' Loose*, Pryor "acts dumb and feigns wide-eyed innocence." He added: "[I]n recent years, Pryor has become obsessed with proving he can act like a nice guy, a normal person. What's disturbing is that Pryor's nice guy characters are invariably jerks and suckers, and bores to boot."[21]

The film is better than the critics claimed. The premise, which allows the protagonist to remain sympathetic while he acts the fool, is so appealing that it is hard to go wrong.

And, indeed, the film had one important fan. Hill said, "Richard liked the movie.

He told me several times, as the years went by, that the film was his favorite.... The film took him on as an actor. He played a comedic lead as an acting role. And he liked that. He didn't have to be a low comedian.... So he had this enormously warm spot in his heart for the movie."[22]

The story has certainly proven to be malleable in its long life.

The uncle and grandfather were converted into brothers for a 1921 film version starring Roscoe Arbuckle. The brothers are alive and well and the money they offer Monty is a gift rather than an inheritance. These brothers are much like the wickedly conniving brothers of *Trading Places* or, even more, the rich and eccentric brothers of Mark Twain's "The Million Dollar Bank Note." The film stresses Monty's frustration in spending money without acquiring assets. The *Arkansas Democrat* reported, "If he buys wildcat mining stock, they find a paying vein of ore; if he bets at long odds on the consistent loser at the racetrack, the other horses fall down and the old plug wins, netting our hero many times as much money as he bet. And so it goes until he despairs of getting rid of his million."[23] The film was so popular that Warner Bros. was negotiating with Arbuckle to make a sound version of the film at the time of the comedian's death in 1933.

The story received renewed success with a film adaptation produced in 1945. The script, written by Sig Herzig, Charles Rogers, and Wilkie Mahoney, added interesting twists to Monty's travails. The film was directed by the acclaimed Allan Dwan. Kent Jones, author of *Physical Evidence: Selected Film Criticism*, noted that, in his direction of this film, Dwan achieved "pure, unimpeded action, with a rhythm that's both exhilarating and a little bit nerve-wracking, like a merry-go-round that feels like it might go off-kilter."[24] This rhythm suits the story perfectly. Monty is on board a runaway train. He needs to constantly move forward in his spending. The *New York Times* summed up the plot succinctly: "The watchword is 'spend.'"[25] Spend. Spend. Spend. He has no time for romance or self-reflection.

Hill doesn't provide pure, unimpeded action. This is evident in the post-game scene. Monty feels bad that he has been overcome by the Yankees' power hitters. He is alone in a dark locker room, moping, until Roundfield comes along to give him a pep talk. This scene does not belong in *this* movie. Sentimental moments interrupt the flow. The flow is everything for this type of rollicking farce.

In Dwan's film, Monty has a fiancée he loves dearly. It is an established relationship that he prays will stay together through his whirlwind of mad spending. Monty remains possessed by a nervous energy through most of the story. This presents a problem in Hill's version. He wants us to believe that Monty can find love while frantically managing the mind-boggling terms of his uncle's multimillion-dollar will. Monty's frenzied spending hardly allows an opportunity for the light romance that Hill wants so desperately to introduce. It's like expecting an Olympic runner to woo a random spectator in the stands during a quarter-mile sprint. The story has no use for a love interest, which is the reason the only thing McKee gets to do in the film is stand off to the side and frown disapprovingly.

Universal Pictures had originally hired Peter Bogdanovich to direct *Brewster's Millions*. Bogdanovich intended to disregard the novel and play as source material in favor of making a direct remake of the 1945 film. He envisioned John Ritter as Monty Brewster.

A London-based company, Caralan Productions, called upon Herzig to rework his 1945 script for the British public in the early 1960s. Herzig was able, in many ways, to improve upon his earlier script. The result was *Three on the Spree* (1961), which was directed by Sidney Furie (*Lady Sings the Blues*). Monty figures to lose a substantial amount of money by producing an expensive stage show that is guaranteed to fail. Instead, the audience bursts into laughter seeing the ineptitude of the production. Monty abruptly closes the show despite the abundance of advance ticket sales, which prompts the show's leading lady, Trixie, to sue him. He gets Trixie to meet with him to discuss a settlement. But it takes an unexpected turn when Monty proposes marriage and then, in the same breath, breaks off the engagement. His fickle behavior has the desired effect of getting Trixie to sue him for breach of promise. The court case is the basis of the film's climax. Monty hires an expensive legal team, but he continually thwarts their efforts to defend him. He loses the case, but is disappointed by the low figure granted by the judge. So, he incurs contempt fines by arguing this point.

Pryor's version of the story has its own unique gags and situations. Tucker wrote: "Hill slowly moves the camera out into the outfield, where suddenly and impossibly a freight train comes chugging on tracks that cut across the open grass, moving steadily from left field to right field. The Bulls are so poor, apparently, that they have to practice in a ball park that doubles as a train route. It's a lovely, funny sight, a gag far more subtle than anything else in *Brewster's Millions*."[26] The gag came from a news story about a train that traveled through a minor league field in Mexico.

Bailey wrote of the film: "It's less a remake of those movies than of 1982's *Trading Places*, another story of a black man's sudden wealth, from the same screenwriters (complete with another nefarious pair of old-rich-white-guy villains)."[27]

Jo Jo Dancer, Your Life Is Calling (1986)

Production: Columbia Pictures and Delphi V Productions.
Distribution: Columbia Pictures.
Producer: Richard Pryor.
Director: Richard Pryor.
Screenplay: Rocco Urbisci, Paul Mooney and Richard Pryor.
Photography: John Alonzo.
Editor: Donn Cambern.
Music: Herbie Hancock.
Release date: May 2, 1986.
Running time: 97 minutes.
Cast: Richard Pryor (Jo Jo Dancer/Alter Ego), Debbie Allen (Michelle), Art Evans (Arturo), Fay Hauser (Grace), Barbara Williams (Dawn), Carmen McRae (Grandmother), Paula Kelly (Satin Doll), Diahnne Abbott (Mother), Scoey Mitchell (Father), Billy Eckstine (Johnny Barnett), Tanya Boyd (Alicia), E'Lon Cox (Little Jo Jo), Michael Ironside (Detective Lawrence), Ken Foree (Big Jake).

Pryor said that *Jo Jo* came out of personal reflection ("taking inventory"): "When you mess up … and remember, you're talking to an expert … the only way to put that stuff behind you and get on with your life is to be brutally honest. Self-deception is one of the worst drugs there is."

The original idea was for Pryor to write an autobiography, titled "Up from the Ashes."

Pryor and Paula Kelly in *Jo Jo Dancer, Your Life Is Calling* (1986).

He noted, "Following my accident, I had tried to write my autobiography but never quite got a grip on the three-hundred-pound alligator that was my life. Still too close to the fire. Didn't have perspective. I kept at it, though. Thinking about shit. Writing down bits and pieces, thoughts and shit. Finally, I asked Mooney and Rocco Urbisci, writer friend, to help me stitch it all together, and the result was *Jo Jo Dancer, Your Life Is Calling*."[1]

The tone of the film was something Pryor found difficult to establish. "Originally, I intended it to be a straight-out comedy, but I couldn't keep the sadness and emotion from spilling onto the page," he said. "It was beyond me, you know? Like therapy. I went with it."[2] He said in an interview, "This is a movie I had to do. I felt that once I got it past me, it would free me to do other work."[3]

Pryor made it clear that the film was not autobiographical. He said, "I gave Jo Jo some of the emotional content of my life. Maybe more than I meant to. But an autobiography is a factual account with real people, places, names, events. This isn't. Jo Jo goes through what I went through, yet it happens differently to him. Characters are combined from many people ... many feelings."[4]

Pryor was not sure himself where to draw the line between his life and Jo Jo's. He said, "Throughout the picture, I felt I was walking a narrow edge between my own reality and Jo Jo's fantasy. Which is which? I'm still not sure."[5]

For years, he accused *Blue Collar* director Paul Schrader of being a racist and said that the man got him back on cocaine. Yet, he approached Schrader to direct *Jo Jo Dancer*.

His agent told the director, "Richard believes you are the only one who understood him."[6] Schrader declined the offer.

Pryor returned to Peoria to film Jo Jo's childhood scenes. Being back in his home town only added to the emotion of making the film.

Many people waited with great anticipation to see it. Jay Boyar of the *Orlando Sentinel* found it to be enthralling. It was, to him, the equivalent of seeing *Lenny* directed by Lenny Bruce, or *Wired* directed by John Belushi. But most people, critics and the public alike, did not regard it as a good film.

The last half hour of *Richard Pryor Live On The Sunset Strip* features the comedian talking about his near-death experience. Roger Ebert wrote: "Watching 'Richard Pryor Live On The Sunset Strip,' a breathtaking performance by a man who came within a hair of killing himself with drugs, was like a gift, as if Pryor had come back from the dead to perform in his own one-man memory of himself."[7] Ebert said that it was Pryor's gift to be funny while being "painfully self-analytical."[8] He described this portion of *Live On the Sunset Strip* as "one of the most remarkable marriages of comedy and truth I have ever seen."[9] Audiences expected *Jo Jo Dancer* to build on *Live on Sunset Strip*. In their minds, it should have been an agonizingly soul-baring autobiography by a man who had come back from the dead. But *Jo Jo Dancer* is feeble and misguided. The risen comedian had failed as a director to trade his weak and corrupted flesh for spiritual power and glory.

The film lacks an organizing theme, which leaves it rough and disjointed. It is a loose, non-linear assembly of various episodes from Jo Jo's past. Flashbacks and fragments

Pryor makes his directorial debut with *Jo Jo Dancer, Your Life Is Calling* (1986).

that illuminate Jo Jo's life are intentionally arranged out of sequence. Pryor explained: "Memory doesn't work in nice, neat, chronological patterns that make things convenient for screenwriters. Jo Jo's mind skips around. So does the story."[10]

Pryor declared the film a failure even before it reached theatres. "I don't know what happened," he said. "I like the script and I'd do it again today. To see what I did with it makes me somewhat sad. I asked myself a thousand times, 'How could I have fucked it up?'"[11] He continued, "They want laughs—lots of laughs, which it hasn't got. It could be moving and good, but people may say, 'Why are you telling us this? We don't want to know this.'"[12]

Pauline Kael of *The New Yorker* wrote: "Pryor doesn't have the skills to tell his story in this form. As a stand-up entertainer, he sees the crazy side of his sorrows; he transforms pain and chaos into comedy. As a movie maker, he's a novice presenting us with clumps of unformed experience. It isn't even raw; the juice has been drained away. He was himself—demons, genius and all—in *Richard Pryor Live in Concert* and, though to a lesser extent, in *Richard Pryor Live on the Sunset Strip*. Here, trying to be sincere, he's less than himself."[13] "Perhaps the worst thing about *Jo Jo Dancer*," Julian Upton wrote in *Bright Lights Film Journal*, "is Pryor himself."[14] He continued,

> In what should've been a primal scream of a performance, a fusion of the electrifying power of his best stand-up with the howling demons that dogged him offscreen and offstage, the actor instead gives an awkward, largely poker-faced turn, occasionally hitting the high notes but generally looking lost in his own movie.... The disturbing truth of *Jo Jo Dancer* is that it confirms that Pryor's excitable greatness had vanished. All we see is the laundered Pryor of 1986 trying to imitate the wild, wired and reckless Pryor of a decade earlier—and as in *Here and Now*, it's an act he could no longer pull off.[15]

Pryor resurrects old stand-up routines that made him famous, but he is missing the old spark. David and Joe Henry wrote:

> It's all perfunctory, performed by rote in front of an accepting audience. Inevitably, it falls flat, merely set down for the record as it might be performed by a Richard Pryor impersonator. Jo Jo's renditions are stillborn, like museum pieces, empty of the struggle, the chaos, the sloppiness of discovery at the moment of conception in an uncertain encounter with a live audience. Richard knew what he was talking about when he told Mooney that no one could steal his material. As the sequence makes excruciatingly clear, no one but Richard Pryor knew what to do with it. Not even Jo Jo Dancer.[16]

By now, Pryor was deeply embarrassed about his drug addiction. The following was noted in the *St. Louis Post-Dispatch*:

> The dark side of Jo Jo (Richard Pryor)'s growing acclaim in the film's storyline is a reliance first on booze, then drugs. It is an aspect of the film which, Pryor admits, was painful to evoke as a writer, director and actor. Pryor said: "I look at the movie now and ask myself, 'Why did you show people that?' But I had no choice. It was something I had to do. I won't cop out, trying to explain why Jo Jo ... or I ... did drugs. I know why. I understand it even better after making the picture. But it's all there on film for people to take as they see fit. I'm one of the lucky ones. I was gone, crazy, out of my mind. But I'm alive."[17]

Vincent Canby of the *New York Times* wrote: "Though his early life was certainly enough to keep anyone in analysis for several lifetimes, the film sees it all in rosy terms that effectively deny the horror ... 'Jo Jo Dancer' reports incredibly harrowing details in schmaltzy terms that have little to do with what's being reported.... It's all sort of soft, self-congratulatory and, ultimately, more upbeat than the facts would seem to support."[18]

Pryor reenacts old standup routines in *Jo Jo Dancer, Your Life Is Calling* (1986).

Jennifer Lee, one of Pryor's ex-wives, wrote a review of the film for *People*: "Well, Richard, you blew it. I went to see *Jo Jo Dancer*…. I went looking for the truth, the real skinny. Well, guess what? It wasn't there…. How sad. After all, it was you who was obsessed by the truth, be it on stage or in your private life…. You had no sacred cows. That's why I fell in love with you, why I hung in through the wonder and the madness…. Listen to your white honky bitch, Richard: Ya gotta walk it like you talk it or you'll lose that beat."[19]

Upton wrote: "*Jo Jo Dancer, Your Life Is Calling* failed critically and commercially upon release. All that can be said about it now is that it does give us one last glimpse of a Richard Pryor who in some way resembled—physically at least—his old self. But all this would change in the months that followed."[20]

After *Jo Jo Dancer*, Pryor entered into negotiations with Columbia to star in a remake of the dark fairy tale *The Man Who Could Work Miracles*. The director was to be the highly acclaimed Norman Jewison (*The Cincinnati Kid*; 1965; *In the Heat of the Night*, 1967; *The Thomas Crown Affair*, 1968; *Fiddler on the Roof*, 1971; and *A Soldier's Story*, 1984). The project never came to fruition.

Critical Condition (1987)

Production and Distribution: Paramount Pictures.
Producers: Ted Field and Robert Cort.
Director: Michael Apted.
Screenplay: Denis Hamill and John Hamill (story by Denis Hamill, John Hamill, and Alan Swyer).
Photography: Ralf D. Bode.
Editor: Robert Lambert.
Music: Alan Silvestri.
Release date: January 16, 1987.
Running time: 97 minutes.
Cast: Richard Pryor (Kevin Linehan), Rachel Picotin (Rachel Atwood), Rubén Blades (Louis), Joe Mantegna (Arthur Chambers), Bob Dishy (Dr. Foster), Sylvia Miles (Nurse Maggie Lesser), Joe Dallesandro (Stucky), Randall "Tex" Cobb (Box), Joseph Ragno (Palazzi), Cigdem Onat (Dr. Alice Hoffman), Garrett Morris (Helicopter junkie).

Denis Hamill wrote: "This project had started when the producer Ted Field, founder of Interscope Pictures, asked if we could spin a tale from a news brief about an ordinary citizen who helped save a hospital during a blackout. John and I went back to Brooklyn and wrote a spooky little thriller about a pedophile serial killer who escapes from the psycho ward during the blackout and is heading for the pediatric ward. Only our Brooklyn working-class hero, Kevin Lenihan, can stop him. Paramount Pictures bought the script."[1]

Hamill's brother, Brian, worked as a still photographer on Michael Apted's *First Born*. He gave the script to Apted, who liked it. Apted and Field approached Paramount with the final draft.

At this point, the project took a big twist. Hamill wrote: "Dawn Steele, who was a dear friend of mine from before she became Paramount president, bought the package from Ted Field of Interscope. She sent the script to Richard. He wanted to do it. But Dawn called me and said, "We have good news and bad news. The good news is that Richard Pryor wants to do *Critical Condition*.""[2]

This *was* great news to Hamill. He wrote: "I worked real hard on acting casual because inside, I was gushing like a stage door fan. Pryor was then the funniest man on the planet and the top box office draw in Hollywood."[3] The rest of the conversation as Hamill recalls went as follows:

HAMILL: Holy shit! What the hell could be the bad news?
STEELE: Well now it's a comedy.

Pryor and Garrett Morris in *Critical Condition* (1987).

HAMILL: Dawn, there's nothing funny about a hospital during a blackout. People fucking die.
STEELE: With Richard Pryor they gotta die funny.[4]

"Oh well," wrote Hamill, "you'd turn *The Exorcist* into a gagfest if you had Pryor attached. So off my brother and I went on a rewrite assignment to our little storefront office on 11th Ave. in Windsor Terrace, where we did major surgery on the script, trying to locate the funny bone in a story about a hospital without power."[5]

The rewrite proved to be difficult. Hamill wrote: "[A]fter we did two drafts, Dawn called me to say they were hiring the very talented comedy team of Babaloo Mandell and Lowell Ganz to yuk the script up. We were kinda relieved. We'd pushed it as far as we could into comedy. They paid them more for a polish than we made on six drafts."[6] Production moved ahead once Mandell and Ganz turned in their work.

The plot begins with Kevin Linehan (Pryor) visiting a crime boss, Palazzi, to borrow money for a business venture. An undercover cop disguised as a blind man plants a wire on Kevin before he enters Palazzi's office. Palazzi agrees to give Kevin a loan if he delivers a briefcase of stolen diamonds for him. Kevin is getting nervous and looks to smoke to calm his nerves. When he reaches into his pocket for a cigarette, the wire drops out of his pocket and falls onto Palazzi's desk. The police burst in to arrest Palazzi. The fact that Kevin is holding a briefcase filled with stolen diamonds gets him arrested as well. Palazzi, who believes that Kevin set him up, vows to murder him in prison.

The opening scene is set up much differently in a draft of the script dated September 27, 1985. Kevin told Palazzi that he has found a buyer for his stolen mink coats. He has him set up the deal, expecting to receive a finder's fee. But the buyer is late for the meeting. Palazzi doesn't like to be kept waiting. Palazzi's goons, Waldo and Laslo, eye Kevin as if they're ready to give him a beating.

LENAHAN: Mr. Palazzi, it's only been ten minutes! (stalling) You know what it is? We're cranky because it's so cold in here.
PALAZZI: He's right. Don't break his arms. Set him on fire.
(*WALDO picks up a can of gasoline. LASLO tosses a lighter to PALAZZI, who flicks a flame.*)

Again, as in *Bustin' Loose*, Pryor is at risk of being set on fire.

The buyer arrives just in time to prevent Kevin from being set ablaze, but he turns out to be an undercover cop. Palazzi assumes that Kevin is part of the set-up and vows to murder him.

Kevin was transformed in the rewrite from a fence to a man in desperate need of a loan. It is a script change undoubtedly designed to make the character more sympathetic.

We arrive at the same point in either case. Kevin is willing to do anything to avoid being thrown in prison with Palazzi. During his trial, he acts deranged to get the judge to commit him to a psychiatric facility. He attacks his lawyer, he jumps up on a table, and he pretends to have a seizure. The judge refers him to Dr. Alice Hoffman for psychiatric observation. Kevin pretends to have demented reactions to the ink blots that Dr. Hoffman shows him. He acts aroused by a vulva-shaped inkblot, which he proceeds to lick. But he is diagnosed as sane and scheduled to be transferred to prison.

The hospital administrator, Arthur Chambers, is getting ready to leave for the day. He tells his administrative assistant, Rachel Atwood, that the usual emergency room doctor is unavailable and that he has called in an old friend, Dr. Edward Slattery, to serve as a fill-in.

Chambers visits the psychiatric ward when he learns that the patients are creating a commotion. He instructs the guards to lock up Kevin, who is the one who stirred up the other patients. Just when the situation seems hopeless for Kevin, hurricane winds knock out a power grid and create a city-wide blackout. A psychiatric patient who goes by the name Box takes this opportunity to launch a revolt. He gets the other patients to lock up the guards and tie Chambers to a chair. Now is Kevin's chance to escape.

Kevin puts on a white coat to look like a doctor. He breaks into Chambers's office to destroy his hospital records. Just then, Rachel enters and mistakes him for Dr. Slattery. Kevin has no problem pretending to be him, at least until he gets a chance to exit the hospital.

Stucky, a serial killer, is brought to the hospital in handcuffs by a police officer. The officer explains to the triage nurse that Stucky suffered injuries in a fight with another prisoner. Stucky, like Kevin, uses the chaos of the blackout to escape. The officer chases Stucky through a back door. Stucky, who is lying in wait, ambushes the officer and strangles him.

Kevin drives off in an ambulance, but the flood waters block his way. When he steps out of the vehicle to assess the situation, the flood waters wash it away. He has no choice now but to go back into the hospital.

Dr. Foster, a surgeon, is worried about admitting patients during a blackout. He tells Rachel, "Miss Atwood, you are standing on a malpractice time bomb." He insists that the best thing he can do is go home and wait for the electricity to return. But Rachel is heartened by Kevin's determination and boldness. He is able to pass himself off as a doctor simply by trusting the recommendations of the ER staff, which is not something the staff usually experiences. Kevin's trust encourages the staff, motivating them to find innovative ways to function without electricity. The best example of this occurs when Dr. Joffe gets the back-up generator to work temporarily by connecting it to ambulance batteries.

(The entire first act of the film is a set-up for a simple but clever premise, which Michael Wilmington of the *Los Angeles Times* perfectly summed up in a single sentence: "[A con man is] forced to step into the crisis-ridden mess, and improvise madly until the lights come on."[7] Phil Silvers used the same general premise to create one of the greatest sitcoms of all time. His classic quick-witted con man, Sgt. Ernie Bilko, often got himself into a big mess and then had to improvise madly to stave off a court-martial.)

The orderlies are hindered in their efforts to repair the main generator when the basement room where the generator is located becomes flooded. Kevin comes up with the idea to bring a generator from the helicopter landing pad into the hospital. When he cannot find enough people to carry it, he tells the patients in the detoxification unit that he will withhold their methadone pills unless they help. He leads the addicts forward with the generator while singing (to the tune of "A-Hunting We Will Go"), "The junkies on the go! The junkies on the go!" Dr. Foster is astounded. He denounces Kevin as a "gypsy doctor."

When the air conditioning stops working in the upper floors of the hospital, Kevin gets the idea to move the helicopter into the building and use the rotor blades to circulate air into the elevator shaft. The junkies attach ropes to the helicopter and try to drag it into the building, but the tonnage is too much for them to handle. The only way to move the helicopter is to get a pilot to fly it. A junkie tells Kevin that he learned everything about the repair and operation of helicopters in the military, but he has a fear of heights that prevents him from piloting a helicopter. However, he assures Kevin that he can instruct an untrained pilot on safely operating the flight controls. Kevin takes flight in

Pryor and Rachel Ticotin in *Critical Condition* (1987).

the helicopter as the junkie shouts out instructions into a walkie-talkie. The helicopter is harder to maneuver than Kevin expected, and the confusing instructions from the junkie provide little help. Kevin is in a full-blown panic as he struggles to land the vehicle. Once he astonishingly parks it next to the elevator shaft, he springs out of the cockpit and throttles the junkie.

Dr. Foster is reluctant to perform surgery on a worker who fell off a roof. Kevin is told by Joffe that, if the surgery is not performed immediately, the worker will likely be crippled for life. Kevin feels great compassion for him and presses hard to persuade Dr. Foster to perform the surgery. Kevin's inability to assist during the surgery exposes him to the surgeon as a fraud. But the surgery is successful and Dr. Foster is grateful to Kevin for encouraging him to do it. Box allows Chambers to contact Rachel by walkie-talkie to issue the patients' demands, the most important of which is that Kevin not be sent to prison. It is during a conversation with Box that Rachel comes to realize that his friend Kevin is the one she has mistaken for Dr. Slattery.

Rachel confronts Kevin about his deception, but he stands his ground and refuses to help get Chambers released if it means he has to go to prison. Kevin doesn't sputter excuses or hang his head sheepishly. He doesn't act in any way timid or embarrassed. He feels justified for defending his own life and he recognizes that he did a lot to help the patients and the hospital staff. He reacts to Rachel's rebuke with defiance and indignation. It is a restrained performance by Pryor that gets the character's attitude across effectively. At the end of the scene, Rachel offers to give him the keys to a speedboat at the dock in exchange for getting Box to free Chambers.

Once free, Chambers surveys the disorderly state of the emergency room. He is furious with Rachel and fires her on the spot. Meanwhile, Stucky sets a fire in the laundry room to create a distraction. Kevin, who has sped off in the boat, sees the smoke. He rushes back to the hospital to help by getting the hospital evacuated and putting out the fire. He tells Chambers it was his inadequate maintenance that created problems for the hospital during the blackout.

Stucky kidnaps Rachel and drags her to the furnace room. Kevin brawls with him and, in the end, knocks him out.

In the closing scene, Rachel joins Kevin on the speedboat and the couple speeds off to the city.

Hamill wrote:

> [I]n the spring of 1986, exterior shooting began on Governors Island. We arrived on the set wary after hearing all kinds of stories about Pryor being difficult, egomaniacal, aloof. Apted introduced us to Pryor. My first impression was that this larger-than-life legend was so slight. It was like shaking hands with a lightweight champion—huge and small at the same time. My second and lasting impression was that Richard Pryor was a gentleman—shy, humble, gracious. "Thanks for the script, fellas," he said. "I really like this character. I hope I bring him to life the way you intended."[8]

Hamill was permitted to watch the cast act out scenes. He wrote: "Richard cheered, laughed and applauded [Bob] Saget. He was kind and supportive to this upcoming comic, just a wonderful man. Never a prima donna or a Hollywood asshole. Total sweetheart. He once asked me if I minded if he ad-libbed some lines. I said, 'You're Richard Pryor, man. Ad-lib 'em all if you want. *Please!*' I wish he had. Instead when I was around he

Pryor and Rubén Blades in *Critical Condition* (1987).

always came to set sober, prepared, knew his lines, and was a total pro."[9] Hamill continued, "We stayed another week on the set, often shooting the breeze with Pryor between takes.... No one knew he was in the early stages of multiple sclerosis. We parted with a handshake and best wishes. We did not become friends or pen pals. I never met him again."[10]

Apted had done well helping Belushi to tone down his act in *Continental Divide* (1981); he did as well with Pryor in *Critical Condition*. It was a shame that the director didn't get to go through with earlier plans to direct Pryor in *Color Man*. Commenting on *Critical Condition*, Wilmington wrote: "[Michael Apted] logistically can bring it off, mix[ing] social realism and comedy."[11]

Pryor fell ill during production. Upton wrote: "In 1986, on the set *Critical Condition*, Pryor tried to respond to a call from director Michael Apted but found himself unable to get out of his chair. He couldn't get his legs to move. The director asked him to stop kidding around, but Pryor was frantic. He tried whacking his thighs, shaking his legs, but they remained inert. Some moments later, they came back to life, and Pryor got on with the scene he needed to shoot."[12] Pryor would learn from doctors that he had contracted multiple sclerosis, which disrupts the operation of the nervous system. Multiple sclerosis can cause many symptoms, including blurred vision, loss of balance, poor coordination, difficulty walking, slurred speech, tremors, numbness, extreme fatigue, muscle rigidity, problems with memory and concentration, paralysis, and blindness. Upton wrote of Pryor's appearance in *Critical Condition*:

> Pryor certainly looks out of sorts here—thin, spindly, and frail. But the most telling signs are in his face. With hindsight, one can see that the actor's curiously immobile expression and staring, glazed-over eyes are key indicators of the facial paralysis brought on by MS. Watching the film at the time, however, suggested simply, if disturbingly, that his comic essence must have somehow evaporated. And although Pryor is agile enough for the low-rent hysterics of the plot, he does display some awkwardness with the physical gags, which also jars, given his usual reliance on his body as a hopping, gyrating tool of comedy. For his keenest fans then, *Critical Condition* must have made for pretty disturbing viewing. On the precious few occasions it is funny, it's *despite* Richard Pryor.[13]

Pryor could have certainly done better with the role when he was in his prime. The script gives him a fair amount of funny material and allows him to express a wide range of emotions. Hamill knew that the comedian could get the most laughs whenever he acted agitated. He knew that he had made films funny with "eyes popping, crooked grin, neck veins pulsing."[14] So, he wrote scenes in which Pryor could get agitated. Pryor gets upset during a run-in with Fido, a patient who runs around the psychiatric ward, behaving like a dog. He can barely restrain himself as Fido refuses to get off his bed and then tries to take a bite out of him. Later, he chokes a conniving junkie who nearly got him killed by convincing him to pilot a helicopter. In these scenes, he manages to reveal sparks of his old self. But his condition wavered during production and this is reflected in his mostly restrained performance. In the next few years, the severity of Pryor's decline would be extraordinary, which his wife, Jennifer Lee, attributed to his years of drug abuse.

Pryor's diminished capacity is most apparent in his courtroom freak-out, which compares unfavorably with his courtroom freak-out in *Stir Crazy*. He just wasn't as dynamic as he was in his prime. But, while he has trouble using his body as a "hopping, gyrating tool of comedy," Pryor does well using his eyes to suggest his character's panic and desperation. Wilmington wrote:

> When Richard Pryor ... is on a roll, his eyes take on a strange, fiendish-little-boy mixture of desperation and glee, fear and crazy desire. It's an odd, intense expression. Bulging eyes, neck veins popping, mouth crooked over clenched teeth, he looks like a man holding a snake in one hand and something delicious in the other. That blend of weird terror and absurd joy permeates much of his best on-the-edge material.... Pryor seems thinner and less devilish since his accident, but his timing and camera sense remain supreme.[15]

This is not a slapstick comedy, which reduces the relevance of Pryor's physical limitations. It is comedy driven by the characters, their relationships, and their situations. Pryor is surrounded by an exceptional supporting cast. It is because the film is not raucous or rowdy that a finely subtle actor, Bob Dishy, is able command scenes as a high-strung doctor obsessed with the potential of lawsuits.

The film stands up well thirty years later. It has a good story, sympathetic characters, and funny situations. It's unfortunate that it has been largely overlooked.

In 1987, the critics were unfairly dismissive of the film. Wilmington wrote: "*Critical Condition* needs either more Chayefsky *Hospital*–like bile or more comic set-pieces for Pryor."[16] Desmond Taylor of the *Philadelphia Inquirer* wrote: "[I]t has all the vitality of a hospital waiting room at 2 a.m."[17]

While *Critical Condition* was in production, Pryor spoke to the *Los Angeles Times* about his work prospects. "In the past, Pryor said, deciding which films to star in has been left to his lawyer; now, he says, he is reading more scripts himself and wants to get even more involved in the selection process. 'I'm not getting a lot of scripts, though. Maybe they think I'm an old man now. But I wish they'd send me more scripts.'"[18]

In 1987, Chris Hodenfield of the *Los Angeles Times* compared Pryor with Danny Kaye. He wrote: "Certain comedians can make you cry. There's a great crop of comedians out there—sharp, fast, jagged, ready to offer you a modern education. Who among them would want to make an audience cry? A very few, such as Richard Pryor, have any access to genuine pathos."[19] He was, as Saul said, "a bundle of need."[20] He could convey the most jarring pathos. He could make despair funny.

Moving (1988)

Production and Distribution: Warner Bros.
Producer: Stuart Cornfeld.
Director: Alan Metter.
Screenplay: Andy Breckman.
Photography: Donald McAlpine.
Editor: Alan Balsam.
Music: Howard Shore.
Release date: March 4, 1988.
Running time: 89 minutes.
Cast: Richard Pryor (Arlo Pear), Beverly Todd (Monica Pear), Stacey Dash (Casey Pear), Raphael Harris (Marshall Pear), Ishmael Harris (Randy Pear), Randy Quaid (Frank/Cornall Crawford), Dana Carvey (Brad Williams).

In February 1987, Warner Bros. announced that Pryor was about to start production on *Moving*, a film in which the comedian was to "face the perils of residential relocation."

Moving (1988)

Andy Breckman wrote:

> [B]efore they started filming, we had a read-through of the script. I flew out to L.A. The whole cast sat around a big conference table. At some point in the script there was a scene where one of the characters—a senile old lady—takes a crap in the backyard. Shamelessly, in broad daylight. Like a dog.... But Mr. Pryor felt that scene didn't work. I respectfully disagreed. We went back and forth. He wanted it out. I thought it should stay. Finally, the director turned to Pryor and said, "Richard, is this something you feel strongly about?" And this is what Pryor did: he reached into his jacket and pulled out a gun! A real gun. A derringer—with two short barrels. I'd never seen one before but I could tell it was definitely real. I was so scared I almost blacked out. Pryor put the derringer on the table—*thunk*—and stared at me, sort of defiantly. It was like a saloon scene in a bad western. Everyone gasped and laughed nervously. Nobody said anything for about five seconds. Then I playfully ripped the page out of the script, indicating "Heh, heh, okay Richard, you win!" Everyone tittered nervously some more. Finally, Mr. Pryor put the gun away and the read-through continued.
>
> We never saw the gun again. Now here comes what I think is the really weird part: nobody ever mentioned it. Not then. Not for the rest of the meeting. Although, as I recall, everyone laughed at Mr. Pryor's lines a little louder from that point on.
>
> Here's what I was thinking: "What sort of pathetic, self-hating, paranoid junkie would bring a gun to a script read-through? I'm glad I don't have to direct him—I'd be afraid to ask for a second take!"[1]

Many more pages should have been ripped out of the script. *Moving* is too bland to make anyone laugh. Desmond Ryan of the *Philadelphia Inquirer* appropriately called the film "a mobile version of *The Money Pit*."[2] He summarized the film perfectly as follows: "[*Moving* is] an aimless comedy about the travails of a family transferring its worldly possessions across the country."[3]

The sole idea of the script is for a meek protagonist to be victimized at every turn and become angrier with each incident. The anger builds until the climax, at which time the protagonist strikes back with an insane fury. But Pryor's furious days were now behind him. Instead, a stunt man stood in for Pryor through most of his berserk spree.

Pryor could not be more timid when the film begins. Michael Healy of the *Los Angeles Daily News* wrote:

> Arlo Pear is such a meek man that when he gets angry, his nose bleeds even before it has been punched. And he is so inept at expressing his anger that, when his boss fires him after fifteen years on the job, Arlo can't remember which finger to flip at him. Now, who is the very last person someone sensible would choose to play a simpering role like this? How about the angriest comedian of the century, Richard Pryor.... What is wrong with Pryor? Why does he do these awful, bland, ineptly made movies and play these nicey-nice, bloodless characters? Why does he choose the turn himself into just another mediocre comic actor...?[4]

Every secondary character in the script is like the senile old lady. They dementedly enter Pryor's life long enough to, metaphorically speaking, crap in his backyard. These characters come in all sizes. At one point, Pryor has a confrontation with a brutish moving man played by professional wrestler King Kong Bundy.

Dan Craft of *The Pantagraph* wrote:

> [Pryor] wears one expression on his face throughout [*Moving*]—wide-eyed, this-can't-be-happening-to-me despair—and we do not believe it for a minute.... [He] was never meant to play the passive observer of disaster: If anything, he was put on this planet to foment it. To see ... [his] confrontations with crazed neighbors, crazed movers and a crazed young man ... hired to drive his expensive Saab from Jersey to Boise, is to see Richard Pryor ... conceptually castrated before our very eyes. He, not the others, should be playing ... the crazed neighbor, the crazed mover or the crazed driver. Instead, one of our most astute lampooners of the inequities of American society is turned into an impotent straight man, a patsy for the slapstick antics of a mugging supporting cast.... Even in his tailored

suits and newly-sprung beard (apparently an attempt to further "dignify" the character), Pryor looks supremely uncomfortable, as if he is fully cognizant of the fact that he has sold himself short by pretending to be something he isn't, wasn't, never-will-be.[5]

Janet Maslin of the *New York Times* wrote: "Nominally a comedy, this is in fact a horror story chronicling the hellish things that befall the Pear family's possessions en route, and documenting the general trauma of being uprooted."[6] She wasn't amused by the taming of the film's star. She wrote: "Richard Pryor has been given the full Bill Cosby treatment for his role in *Moving*, complete with charming family, fancy sweaters and brand-new Saab.... Mr. Pryor presides over all this with a Cosbyesque geniality that, coming from him, never stops seeming bizarre.... The whole film unfolds in an atmosphere of perfect blue skies, brand-new everything and complete racial harmony."[7] She also commented on Pryor's physical condition: "Sounding quiet, looking extremely thin and sporting a beard that changes shape from scene to scene, Mr. Pryor appears to be working at something less than full throttle, but every now and then some welcome hint of fury shows through."[8]

David Edelstein could have been thinking specifically of this film when he wrote: "Pryor muffled his blowtorch rage and impersonated shaky, pushed-around little guys who'd manage to stand up for themselves after much humiliation."[9]

Some comedians, like Bob Newhart, are great at playing meek, long-suffering characters. But Pryor was not Bob Newhart. This is not to say that Newhart could have made much of this dull script. Think of *your* last move. Remember your efforts packing boxes, getting estimates from movers, and showing your home to prospective buyers. It was probably more entertaining than this film.

Harlem Nights (1989)

Production: Eddie Murphy Productions and Paramount Pictures.
Distribution: Paramount Pictures.
Producers: Robert D. Wachs and Mark Lipsky.
Director: Eddie Murphy.
Screenplay: Eddie Murphy.
Photography: Woody Omens.
Editor: George Bowers.
Music: Herbie Hancock.
Release date: November 17, 1989.
Running time: 115 minutes.
Cast: Eddie Murphy (Quick), Richard Pryor (Sugar Ray), Redd Foxx (Bennie Wilson), Danny Aiello (Phil Cantone), Michael Lerner (Bugsy Calhoune), Della Reese (Vera), Lela Rochon (Sunshine), Arsenio Hall (Crying Man), Berlinda Tolbert (Annie), Stan Shaw (Jack Jenkins), Jasmine Guy (Dominique La Rue), Vic Polizos (Richie Vento), Gene Hartline (Michael Kirkpatrick).

Harlem Nights involves a nightclub owner who has to contend with threats from gangsters and corrupt police officials.

The film opens in Harlem, New York, in 1918. Sugar Ray (Pryor) is running a craps game when a customer becomes angry. The customer is getting ready to kill Ray when

Eddie Murphy (right) directs Pryor in *Harlem Nights* (1989).

a seven-year-old errand boy, Quick, pulls out a gun and shoots the man. When Ray learns that Quick is an orphan, he decides to raise the child.

Twenty years later, Ray and Quick (Murphy) are running an illegal casino called Club Sugar Ray. Ray is the staid elder who does his best to reign in his hot-headed protégé. A gangster, Bugsy Calhoun, is upset that Ray's club is taking away business from his own establishment, the Pitty Pat Club. He demands a cut of Club Sugar Ray's income to compensate for his losses. Calhoun has bribed a police detective, Sgt. Phil Cantone, to shut down Club Sugar Ray if Ray fails to comply.

Ray decides to scam Calhoun and leave New York. His scam centers on an upcoming boxing match that sets a mediocre boxer, Michael Kirkpatrick, against a popular champion, Jack Jenkins. Ray puts big money down on long-shot Kirkpatrick. Calhoun is aware that Jenkins frequents Club Sugar Ray and maintains a friendly relationship with the owner. He is certain that Ray has made a deal with Jenkins to throw the fight.

In fact, Ray doesn't care if Jenkins wins the fight or not because he plans to make his money robbing Calhoune's booking house. He arranges for a call girl, Sunshine, to seduce his bag man, Richie Vento. Sunshine rides with Vento when he makes his pickup at the booking house. Ray's croupier, Bennie, and his madam, Vera, drive their car into Vento's. Ray and Quick, dressed as police officers, approach the car and identify Sunshine as a heroin dealer. They explain that they have to remove Sunshine's bag from the car as it contains heroin. As it turns out, they actually remove Vento's bag of cash.

Not everything goes as Ray and Quick planned. Before the boxing match gets underway, Calhoune has his men burn down Club Sugar Ray. Ray is determined to fight back. First, he has his men blow up the nightclub. Then, he and Quick lure Cantone to a deserted bank building after hours and leave the corrupt cop tied up in a bank vault to suffocate. Calhoune and his men arrive at Ray's home to bring this conflict to a bloody end, but the place is empty. In searching the house, one of Calhoune's men opens a door that's rigged to a tripwire. A massive explosion obliterates the premises and its occupants.

With their enemies dead, Quick and Ray are able to leave town safely with the money from the booking house.

Pryor wrote: "It was Eddie's movie—that's what it was. I just wish that I'd been in peak form. For obvious reasons, I never felt obliged to inform anyone about the disease, but the fact was, the MS shit gave me a difficult time. It was my secret, and it put me in a dark place moodwise through most of the movie. I finished thinking that Eddie didn't like me."[1]

The public saw Murphy as a less angry version of Pryor, but Pryor saw Murphy as an angrier version of himself. "I never connected with Eddie," he said. "People talked about how my work has influenced Eddie, and perhaps it did. But I always thought Eddie's comedy was mean. I used to say, 'Eddie, be a little nice,' and that would piss him off. But Eddie can act. I don't care what people say, the motherfucker is a great actor."[2]

Upton wrote: "On the set, [Pryor] didn't warm to Murphy (several people have testified to his jealousy of the younger star), and he brought little of value to an already misjudged and badly misfiring film. Indeed, Pryor in *Harlem Nights* is a void—stiff, hollow, and unsmiling, a frozen image of a man hobbled by some morose lethargy. As thirties club-owner Sugar Ray, he is not meant to be the comic center of the film, but the Pryor of a decade earlier could at least have breathed some life into the proceedings. Here, the whole thing dies in the water."[3]

In 1990, Murphy discussed his experience working with Pryor in an interview with Spike Lee for *Spin Magazine*.

Pryor as a stylish nightclub owner in *Harlem Nights* (1989).

It was just written fucked up, and that's because I threw it together real quick. And then it was disappointing because Richard wasn't the way I thought Richard was gonna be. I thought it would be like a collaborative thing where I would get to work with my idol and then it would be like, "This is great." But Richard would come to the set, say his lines and leave. It wasn't like a collaborative thing.... Richard doesn't like me. That was what the whole thing was about.... [T]he only reason he did the movie was he got a big payday out of it, and trust me, the brother does not like me. And I used to have more Richard Pryor pictures up than Elvis Presley. And after I work with the brother and I found out shit, and you would meet people that are around him, know him, and the two camps meet and people start talking it's like, "Oh, shit." And it's really weird to find out your idol hates you and shit.[4]

Lee asked, "Do you really think he hates you?"[5]

Murphy replied, "I don't think he

Harlem Nights (1989) 185

Pryor plans with Redd Foxx and Eddie Murphy to outwit a mob boss in *Harlem Nights* (1989).

hates me; I just think he thinks I'm the reason why his shit ain't the way it used to be. And I ain't, 'cause I idolize the guy."[6]

Jennifer Pryor said, "Eddie was right behind Richard, right? And Eddie, of course, stole a lot of Richard's stuff. Let's be honest, he did. Including the red leather fucking *suit*, by the way. He admired Richard, this was the cat he was chasing, this was the guy, the man, the Mack. But, y'know, at the end of the day, he's gotta fuckin' hate him on some level, because he's never gonna be Pryor, is he? He's never gonna be Pryor. We love Eddie! Props to Eddie, Eddie's good at what he does. I'm not sure what that is anymore, but...."[7]

Murphy was right that *Harlem Nights* was "written fucked up." Roger Ebert observed: "This sort of sting operation could have been made amusing in a movie with more wit and style, but Murphy, the director and writer, moves the plot so laboriously that even the actors seem to be waiting around for something to happen."[8] No effort is made in the script to make Murphy's or Pryor's characters funny. Humorous business is instead put in the hands of Redd Foxx, Arsenio Hall, and Della Reese. It makes no sense to unite two of the era's biggest comedy powerhouses and then give them no opportunity to be funny.

An even greater flaw is the pointlessness of the sting operation, which is supposed to be the centerpiece of the film. The audience is made to follow the heroes as they carefully construct an elaborate scam to outdo their rivals. But then we get to the climax and the scam becomes irrelevant. The heroes defeat their rivals with sheer brute force, using bombs to decimate them in the most violent way possible. Ray and Quick have a vicious streak that make the characters off-putting. The film is like a remake of *Uptown Saturday Night* with Geechie Dan Beauford and Silky Slim as the heroes. Newman and Redford ended *The Sting* (1973) with winks and smiles. Murphy and Pryor ended *Harlem Nights* with bloody dismembered body parts.

See No Evil, Hear No Evil (1989)

Production and Distribution: Tri-Star Pictures.
Producer: Marvin Worth.
Director: Arthur Hiller.
Screenplay: Earl Barret, Arne Sultan, Eliot Wald, Andrew Kurtzman and Gene Wilder (story by Earl Barret, Arne Sultan, and Marvin Worth).
Photography: Victor J. Kemper.
Editor: Robert C. Jones.
Music: Stewart Copeland.
Release date: May 12, 1989.
Running time: 103 minutes.
Cast: Richard Pryor (Wally), Gene Wilder (Dave), Joan Severance (Eve), Kevin Spacey (Kirgo), Alan North (Braddock), Anthony Zerbe (Sutherland), Louis Giambalvo (Gatlin), Kirsten Childs (Adele).

On May 16, 1978, NBC aired the pilot to a sketch comedy show called *Windows, Doors & Keyholes*. Here is a review from the *Pittsburgh Post-Gazette*: "On the prowl for a decent comedy show, NBC offers this pilot, written by Leonard Stern, Arne Sultan and Bill Dana, an hour of sketches and blackouts. Most of the sketches are too long, but the opening bit about a blind man and his deaf partner running a newsstand is effective."[1] The newsstand sketch, written by Sultan and Earl Barrett, featured John Schuck as the blind man, and Hamilton Camp as the deaf man. The sketch was so well-received that Sultan and Barrett expanded it into a feature film script.

Wilder was forwarded the script from TriStar Pictures. He had been told about the plot, which he thought was "wonderful,"[2] but he read through the script and thought the overall writing was awful. The studio asked if he could rewrite the script to make it more to his liking. "I kept the plot the same, but not the junk that was in it," he said.[3] Additional writing was done by a couple of *Saturday Night Live* writers, Andrew Kurtzman and Eliot Wald. Like *Silver Streak* and *Stir Crazy*, *See No Evil, Hear No Evil* was set up as a comedy-thriller in which innocent men are wrongly accused of a crime and must capture the real criminals to prove their innocence. Wilder greatly improved the script by generating sympathy for the two main characters.

Dave Lyons (Wilder), a deaf man who owns a newsstand, is too proud to accept help from others and does everything he can to hide his affliction. Wally Karue (Pryor), a blind man, applies for a job at the newsstand. He, too, is proud and hides his affliction. Dave and Wally are testy with each other at first, but Dave sees Wally as a kindred spirit and offers him the job.

Dave and Wally go to a bar to celebrate. A beefy man gets mad at Dave for inadvertently standing on his jacket. Wally comes forward to defend him. The man becomes insulting, which prompts Wally to challenge him to a fight. What follows is an entertaining set piece in which Dave guides Wally through the fight. Dave helps his blind friend to

Wilder guides Pryor through a bar fight in *See No Evil, Hear No Evil* (1989).

connect his punches by using the aviation method of clock positions to pinpoint the man's whereabouts.

A bookie, Mr. Scotto, arrives at the newsstand and drops a unique gold coin in Dave's change box. Eve, a tall, lovely woman, comes along and shoots the bookie. She drops the gun and takes his suitcase before leaving. Dave and Wally are the only ones present for the shooting. Wally notices the smell of Eve's perfume and Dave gets a glimpse of the woman's long, beautiful legs as she flees. Dave picks up the gun just as the police arrive. He and Wally are promptly arrested and taken to the police station for interrogation.

Captain Braddock, impatient and tactless, starts barking questions at Dave and Wally before they can explain to him that they are disabled. Dave doesn't answer the police captain's questions because he has his back to Braddock and cannot read his lips. Wally doesn't answer his questions because he can't see that Braddock is addressing him. Braddock, convinced they are evading his questions, becomes increasingly frustrated with them. But, in the end, it doesn't matter what they have to say because Braddock has sufficient evidence to arrest them. To start, he has gone through Scotto's wallet and found a marker that shows Wally owed Scotto $2,800 in gambling debts. Even worse is the fact that the gun, which forensics has conclusively identified as "the death weapon," has Dave's fingerprints. As far as Braddock is concerned, Scotto threatened to harm Wally if he didn't pay his debt and Dave shot him to protect his friend.

(The biggest flaw of the script is the way it depicts the police. The writers rely on the police behaving moronically to move the story forward. It seems that Alan North was cast as Braddock to essentially reprise his role as Captain Ed Hocken from the 1982 television series *Police Squad!*. But that was an absurd spoof of cop shows. A comedy-thriller needs its characters to have a degree of believability to generate tension.)

Eve tells her accomplice, Kirgo, that she had to murder Scotto at the newsstand. Kirgo, unaware of Dave and Wally's disabilities, insists that they must kill the men before they are able to identify her. The killers show up at the police station pretending to be Dave and Wally's lawyers, but Wally immediately smells Eve's perfume and knows she is not there to help them. The men insist to Braddock that Eve is the killer, but he doesn't believe them. Dave and Wally escape from the police station and get lost in a crowd of protesters.

Kirgo and Eve catch up to Dave and Wally and take the coin from them. Wally reads Eve's lips as she uses a pay phone to make arrangements with their employer, Mr. Sutherland. Kirgo gets ready to escort Dave and Wally into an alley to shoot them. Wally figures to knock out Kirgo with a quick punch, but he needs to know where he is standing. He remembers that Dave calling out clock positions worked out for him earlier, in the bar. He casually asks Dave to tell him the time. Dave understands. "It's twelve o'clock!" he exclaims. Wally moves quickly and lands a punch. This gives the men the opportunity they need to escape. Dave and Wally elude Kirgo and Eve by stealing a police car. Wally steers while Dave gives him directions. Wally ends up driving through a warehouse, crashing through a wall, and landing the car on a garbage barge.

Dave knows from reading Eve's lips that she and Kirgo are on their way to the Great Gorge resort. The men contact Wally's sister, Adele, to help them pursue the killers. The hotel is fully booked due to a medical convention, but Dave, Wally, and Adele overhear a desk clerk tell a man she is holding reservations for a German doctor and a Swedish doctor. Dave poses as the German; Wally, as the Swede.

In the parking lot, Adele crashes her car into Kirgo's to create a distraction while Dave breaks into the killer's room to recover the coin. Kirgo and Eve eventually figure out Adele's ruse. They kidnap her and take her to Sutherland's estate.

Dave and Wally hurry to the estate to rescue Adele. They meet Sutherland, who happens to be blind. Sutherland reveals that the coin is a room-temperature superconductor, a scientific breakthrough he expects to sell for $8 million. Kirgo is angry because Sutherland led him to believe that he was simply bringing him a rare coin. He insists that they renegotiate their contract. Sutherland shoots Kirgo. Eve enters the room and shoots Sutherland.

(The film needed a villain as menacing as Patrick McGoohan. Kevin Spacey is too clownish as a villain. Anthony Zerbe is not on screen long enough to make an impact. Severance, however, makes a thoroughly menacing and alluring villain.)

Once in possession of the superconductor, Eve rushes towards Sutherland's helicopter pad to escape. Dave and Wally pursue Eve by creating a makeshift zip-line. Dave waits until he is above Eve to let go of the line. He falls on top of the assassin, thereby incapacitating her. The police arrive and arrest Eve.

Arthur Hiller, the director of *Silver Streak*, was called back to direct Pryor and Wilder in the film. Hiller's most recent film, *Outrageous Fortune*, was a comedy-thriller (much in the style of *Silver Streak*). The fact that *Outrageous Fortune* had been a hit at the box office was bound to boost everyone's confidence.

Hiller liked Wilder's draft of the script, as he said:

Wilder and Pryor are booked for murder in *See No Evil, Hear No Evil* (1989).

One of the writers [Arne Sultan] had passed away. The other one was the producer, but he felt somebody fresh should do it. And so Gene wrote a draft, and I was nervous because I thought, "Yes, we discussed a sort of story and that," but I thought, "You know, he's an actor. Will he be writing for himself?" No. He wrote for Richard. It was amazing. He knew Richard could do a Scandinavian accent. He wrote the scene of Richard pretending he was a Scandinavian doctor when he's checking into the hotel and that sort of thing. And it just all worked out so wonderfully, so wonderfully well.

Wilder said Pryor was "an angel"[4] on the set. "He made up things and I made up things, and it went well," he said.[5] He wrote in his autobiography, "[T]he experience on *See No Evil* was the happiest [of his collaborations with Pryor]. Richard was sane and clearheaded and filled with good humor."

Wilder was under great stress at the time because his wife, Gilda Radner, was in a battle for her life against ovarian cancer. Pryor was considerate of his co-star's feelings. He worked with Wilder to make Radner laugh on her regular visits to the set. This is clear proof that Pryor was a changed man. The comedian could not have been expected to be so unselfish during the making of *Stir Crazy*. He was downright mean in those days. When he got mad at Campus during the shooting of *The Mack*, he had no problem spewing insults about Campus's mother, even though the woman had died recently. Brashler said that Pryor could be "instantly cruel, goading, unmerciful." He quoted an associate of Pryor, who said, "[W]hen the vodka and drugs take hold … he will go for your soul, just personally assassinate you."[6] It was indeed a kinder version of Pryor that showed up on the set of *See No Evil, Hear No Evil*.

Hiller said, "My hardest job on directing *See No Evil, Hear No Evil* was to get [Richard] to believe in himself. He had lost faith in himself." He knew that Pryor could still be funny if he could just "get him up there." "And," he added, "Gene was very helpful."[7]

Pryor admitted that, before heading off to the set, he made time to sneak into the bathroom and shoot up. It wasn't until the next year that he made a complete break from drugs. He said that he only got off drugs when he no longer had the money to support his habit.

Upton wrote: "From this point Pryor's decline became much more pronounced. His ex-wife Jennifer had visited him on the *See No Evil* set in 1988 and was alarmed to see him 'walking like an old man.'"[8] Pryor wrote in his autobiography, "[E]ach day I was forced to confront the disease…. One day I would be able to get around using a cane. The next I wouldn't have the strength to even hobble."[9]

Pryor expresses fear and uncertainty as a blind man in *See No Evil, Hear No Evil* (1989).

Pryor and Wilder create a tender scene together on a park bench. Their characters talk about the way they have coped with their disabilities. Wally recalls sitting on a beach and crying. He says that he decided at the time that he wasn't going to "piss [his] life away" because of his blindness. Dave tells Wally that he was working as an actor when he went deaf. He had to give up acting because his lip-reading skills couldn't keep him from missing cues. He expresses bitterness that his wife abandoned him because she didn't want to be married to a deaf man. It would have been a better film if this relationship was the focus rather than the murder or the superconductor.

It cannot be denied that Pryor's performance in the film is stilted compared to his earlier, manic performances. But a blind man who must be cautious to make his way down a busy city street is going to behave in a stilted manner. Regardless, Pryor is charming and funny throughout the film.

Pryor was hired to perform voice-over work for *Look Who's Talking Too* (1990), but he was too ill to continue with the project and was replaced with Damon Wayans.

Another You (1991)

Production and Distribution: Tri-Star Pictures.
Producer: Ziggy Steinberg.
Director: Maurice Phillips.
Screenplay: Ziggy Steinberg.
Photography: Victor Kemper.
Editor: Dennis M. Hill.
Music: Charles Gross.

Release date: July 26, 1991.
Running time: 110 minutes.
Cast: Richard Pryor (Eddie Dash), Gene Wilder (George), Mercedes Ruehl (Elaine/Mimi Kravitz), Stephen Lang (Rupert Dibbs), Vanessa Williams (Gloria), Phil Rubenstein (Al), Peter Michael Goetz (Therapist), Billy Beck (Harry), Jerry Houser (Tim), Kevin Pollak (Phil), Craig Richard Nelson (Walt), Kandis Chappell (Gail).

The plot of *Another You* is difficult to follow at times. George (Wilder), a pathological liar in custody at a psychiatric hospital, is happy when his psychiatrist tells him he's been cured and discharges him from the hospital. Rupert Dibbs, a business manager, has hired a group of actors to pretend that George is a missing brewery heir, Abe Fielding. His plan is to eventually kill George and take control of Fielding's brewery and fortune. Eddie Dash (Pryor), an out-of-work con man, is assigned by a job placement counselor to be George's caretaker. The con man admits that he can learn a lot about "bullshitting" from a pathological liar. Dibbs tries to convince Eddie to be the one who murders George, but Eddie has come to like George and devises a way to fake his new friend's death. Eddie and George manage in the end to expose Dibbs.

In March 1990, Pryor suffered a heart attack. Despite being ill, he agreed to team with Wilder again for *Another You*. He arrived on the set wobbly on his feet and in great pain. He had his doctor shoot him up with cortisone and steroids to keep him working. He said, "It was the beginning of me not being able to do shit any more. The MS took over."[1]

Peter Bogdanovich had shot scenes for several weeks when Columbia/Tri-Star fired him. It was reported at the time that he was fired for being behind schedule and over budget. The director later claimed that the studio let him go over "creative differences."[2] He said: "I was making one film, the studio wanted another. In many ways, it's the best thing that could have happened. I was never really comfortable with the project. I should never have taken it in the first place."[3]

Another You was a critical and financial failure. Box-office receipts dropped nearly 80 percent from the first week to the second. Box Office Mojo determined from available data that, at the time of its release, *Another You* experienced the worst second weekend drop for a film in wide release. The film currently stands at number 13 in this category. (*Collide*, which experienced an 88.5 percent second weekend drop, tops the list as of this writing.)

Upton wrote:

Pryor in *Another You* (1991).

Wilder and Pryor in *Another You* (1991).

Another You has to be one of most distressing and dispiriting experiences any Richard Pryor fan will ever have to sit through. Not only is it a wretched mess of a movie, full of pointless asides and stillborn scenes, but also the sight of Pryor's deterioration is jarring from the get-go. He is not just physically awkward but patently disabled—stick-thin, rigid-stiff, looking almost desperately weak. Just before filming, the comedian's condition was such that he spent two weeks "learning how to walk again," which clearly didn't bode well for the comic potential of the movie.[4]

Another You became a Wilder film. The film's set pieces include Wilder pretending to be a tough guy at a restaurant, Wilder yodeling a love song to Ruehl at a nightclub,

Pryor in *Another You* (1991).

and a chase through a beer factory that ends with Wilder falling into a vat of beer suds. Still, Wilder had time to interact with Pryor. Michael Wilmington of the *Los Angeles Times* wrote:

> Pryor and Wilder do have something special when they interact—though, maddeningly, they rarely get to exploit it fully. Here, their roles are thin but tailor-made. Pryor plays a funky street con artist and Wilder a gentle but obsessive pathological liar who's just out of the asylum, two fantasists plunged into a bizarre Beverly Hills swindle.
> It's a plot full of double meanings, double appearances, lies upon lies and it climaxes with Wilder hugging his co-lead for a snapshot while holding up a sign that reads "Partners Forever." Obviously, this moment has little to do with the story. It's a kind of public statement of affection and allegiance from Wilder to Pryor and there's something almost touching about it: a little charge of emotion that the movie itself hasn't really earned.[5]

The team's chemistry and timing is off. A con man is smooth. Pryor is not smooth. A con man is a fast-talker. Pryor is no fast-talker. He talks slowly and walks in an unsteady manner. Wilder makes a joke about Pryor's emaciated appearance, which may have been a way to relieve the audience's tension about the comedian's poor condition.

Wilmington wrote: "Still, there's something appealing about the interplay between the stars: Pryor's frailer but still potent hipsterism and Wilder's cadenzas of neurosis. That's their chemistry. In the classic schema of movie comedy teams, Pryor is the smoothie and Wilder is the hysteric."[6]

This was the last teaming of Pryor and Wilder. There should have, and could have, been more. Mike Ryan of Uproxx wrote: "In an alternate universe, maybe we get seven or eight of these movies with Wilder and Pryor in their prime."[7]

The Three Muscatels (1991)

Production and Distribution: Paramount Pictures.
Producer: Betty Spruill.
Director: Romell Foster-Owens.
Screenplay: Flynn Belaine Pryor and Cal Wilson, from the novel *The Three Musketeers* by Alexandre Dumas.
Photography: John L. Demps Jr.
Editor: John David Allen.
Release date: November 1991.
Running time: 90 minutes.
Cast: Flynn Belaine (Donna/Dorian), Cal Wilson (Victor Langford), Reynaldo Rey (King Alberto Nacho), Joe Torry (Andre Squire), Roy Fegan (Puablo, the Traitor), Richard Pryor (Narrator/Wino/Bartender), Ron Goss (Squeeky Lopsider), Todd C. Burnette (Spanish Bandit), Jen Harper (Brothel Wench), Nicole Hodges Persley (Bean Dip Dancer), Eric L. Morton (Dungeon Guard).

Flynn Belaine, Pryor's wife, wrote the screenplay. Belaine starred in the film as a college student who falls asleep while reading Alexandre Dumas's *The Three Musketeers* and dreams that she is part of a zany version of the novel. Pryor narrates the film, shows up in the framing scenes as a wino, and appears in Belaine's dream as a bartender.

Pryor as a wino in *The Three Muscatels* (1991).

In 1995, Pryor was approached about doing a Mudbone movie. His then-wife, Jennifer, thought that it was a good idea. She said, "I think Richard *is* Mudbone now."[1] But the movie never happened.

Mad Dog Time (1996)

Production: Skylight Films, Dreyfuss/James Productions and Bruin Grip Services.
Distribution: United Artists.
Producer: Judith Rutherford James.
Director: Larry Bishop.
Screenplay: Larry Bishop.
Photography: Frank Byers.
Editor: Norman Hollyn.
Music: Earl Rose.
Release date: November 6, 1996.
Running time: 93 minutes.
Cast: Ellen Barkin (Rita Everly), Gabriel Byrne (Ben London), Richard Dreyfuss (Vic), Jeff Goldblum (Mickey Holliday), Diane Lane (Grace), Larry Bishop (Nick), Gregory Hines (Jules Flamingo), Kyle MacLachlan (Jake Parker), Burt Reynolds ("Wacky" Jacky Jackson), Henry Silva (Sleepy Joe Carlisle), Michael J. Pollard (Red Mash), Angie Everhart (Gabriella), Billy Idol (Lee Turner), Christopher Jones (Nicholas Falco), Paul Anka (Danny Marks), Rob Reiner (Albert the Chauffeur), Joey Bishop (Mr. Gottlieb), Richard Pryor (Jimmy, the Grave Digger), Juan Fernandez (Davis), Billy Drago (Wells), Réal Andrews (Clarke), Jon Ingrassia (Young).

Mad Dog Time centers on a simple and mundane gang war. Vic, a gangster boss, has been locked up in a psychiatric facility to be treated for paranoid schizophrenia. During his absence, Vic's operations were taken over by Ben London. Now that Vic has been released from the hospital, Ben expects him to retire and stay out of his way. Ben welcomes Vic back with a party at Vic's nightclub. Entertainment is provided by Paul Anka, who is joined on stage by Ben for a duet of "My Way." Vic, who has no intention of retiring, sets out to kill all of the rivals that have come forth while he was away.

Pryor, who plays Jimmy, the Grave Digger, shows up in a wheelchair in one scene. He has a few lines, which he struggles to deliver. Jedadiah Leland of Unobtainium 13 wrote: "Vic has to kill all of his other rivals, all of whom are played by actors like Michael J. Pollard, Billy Idol, Kyle MacLachlan, Gregory Hines, and Burt Reynolds. The bodies start to pile up but Jimmy, the Undertaker (Richard Pryor, looking extremely frail in one of his final roles) is always around to make sure that everyone gets a proper burial."[1]

The film reunited Pryor with Christopher Jones and Larry Bishop, both of whom acted with the comedian in *Wild in the Streets*. After *Wild in the Streets*, Jones received lead roles in a number of prestigious films, including *Three in the Attic* (1968), *Ryan's Daughter* (1970), and *The Looking Glass War* (1970). But then, suddenly, he left acting and became a recluse. In 1996, he was willing to talk about his early retirement. He explained that his experience as a film star became overwhelming. To start, he became disillusioned after a manager stole his money. Then, he had a tumultuous affair with Sharon Tate, who was married to Roman Polanski at the time. In 1969, Tate was murdered by members of the Manson family. Jones said, "I'd had a nervous breakdown over Sharon Tate's death."[2] And the work, itself, was hard for him. He said, "I had done three pictures in a row in Europe and had so many love affairs I was exhausted. I was tired, man."[3]

Leland wrote: "Remember how, in the 1990s, every aspiring indie director tried to rip off Quentin Tarantino by making a gangster film that mixed graphic violence with quirky dialogue, dark comedy, and obscure pop cultural references? That led to a lot of terrible movies but not a single one ... was as terrible as *Mad Dog Time*.... Almost every poorly paced scene in *Mad Dog Time* plays out the same way. Three or more men confront each other in a room. Hard-boiled dialogue is exchanged for an interminable length of time until someone finally gets shot. You would think, at the very least, it would be watchable because of all the different people in the cast but none of the actors really seem to be into it."[4]

Ken Tucker of *Entertainment Weekly* described the film as "jaw-droppingly incoherent."[5]

Roger Ebert and Gene Siskel voted this the worst film of 1996. Ebert wrote: "*Mad Dog Time* is the first movie I have seen that does not improve on the sight of a blank screen viewed for the same length of time. Oh, I've seen bad movies before. But they usually made me care about how bad they were. Watching *Mad Dog Time* is like waiting for the bus in a city where you're not sure they have a bus line."[6]

Lost Highway (1997)

Production and Distribution: October Films.
Producers: Deepak Nayar, Tom Sternberg, and Mary Sweeney.
Director: David Lynch.
Screenplay: David Lynch and Barry Gifford.
Photography: Peter Deming.
Editor: Mary Sweeney.
Music: Angelo Badalamenti.
Release date: February 21, 1997.
Running time: 135 minutes.
Cast: Bill Pullman (Fred Madison), Patricia Arquette (Renee Madison/Alice Wakefield), Robert Blake (Mystery Man), Balthazar Getty (Pete Dayton), Robert Loggia (Mr. Eddy/Dick Laurent) and Marilyn Manson (Porno Star No. 1).

Michael Rose of Mysterious Universe wrote: "[*Lost Highway*] seems entirely like David Lynch running on instincts. Brave, bold, disorienting and uncompromising, its mobius-strip-like structure is an experiment that largely paid off."[1]

It is difficult to describe the brave, bold, disorienting and uncompromising plot.

Fred Madison is buzzed by his intercom. He presses the "Listen" button and hears a man say: "Dick Laurent is dead." The man says nothing else. Fred looks out the window, but he cannot see anyone.

The next day, Fred receives a package that contains a video shot outside his home. He is understandably disturbed by the strange gift. Days later, he receives a second video that was shot *inside* his home. The video provides a view of the living room and then moves inside the bedroom, where Fred and his wife, Renée, are asleep.

At a party, Fred meets with The Mystery Man, an odd little fellow whose face is heavily caked with white powder makeup. He maintains a wide-eyed stare and a creepy grin. A strange conversation ensues.

THE MYSTERY MAN: We've met before, haven't we?
FRED: I don't think so. Where was it you think we met?

THE MYSTERY MAN: At your house. Don't you remember?
FRED: No, no, I don't. Are you sure?
THE MYSTERY MAN: Of course. As a matter of fact, I'm there right now.

The Mystery Man hands Fred his phone and instructs him to call his home. Fred calls. Someone picks up the phone. It is the Mystery Man's voice. "I told you I was here," he says.

The next day, Fred receives a final video, which shows him drenched in blood and kneeling beside his wife's dismembered corpse. Fred is convicted of murdering his wife and sentenced to death. A prison guard is baffled when he looks inside Fred's cell and discovers that he has been inexplicably replaced by a young mechanic, Pete Dayton. The warden has no choice but to release him.

At the garage where he works, Pete is visited by a gangster named Mr. Eddy, who trusts only Pete to work on his Cadillac. He says his car is making a noise and that he wants Pete to take a drive with him. Mr. Eddy becomes upset with a driver who is tailgating him. He lets the driver pass him and then runs him off the road. But he's still not satisfied. He drags the driver out of his car and brutally beats him. He brandishes a gun as he lectures the sobbing driver on the road fatalities caused by drivers who don't follow the rules. He instructs the man to read a driver's manual. "Tell me that you're gonna get a manual!" he bellows. The driver, whose face is bloodied and his eyes rolling back, promises to do so. Mr. Eddy composes himself. He apologizes to Pete for the violence, but explains that he is unable to tolerate tailgating.

Pete starts an affair with Alice Wakefield, Mr. Eddy's mistress. Alice resembles Renée Madison. Renée has, in effect, transformed into Alice as mysteriously as Fred transformed into Pete.

Alice is worried that Mr. Eddy suspects them of having an affair. She comes up with a plan to rob a wealthy friend, Andy, so they'll have enough money to leave town. Pete breaks into Andy's home and bludgeons him with a bronze figurine. Pete thinks Andy is out cold, but he suddenly springs to his feet and charges at him. Pete shoves Andy away, inadvertently causing him to fall onto a coffee table. The glass edge of the table slices through Andy's head, instantly killing him.

Pete and Alice flee to a cabin in the desert. There, Pete suddenly transforms back into Fred. The Mystery Man, who is filming him with a hand-held video camera, pays a visit. Fred drives off to the Lost Highway Hotel, where he finds Alice having sex with Mr. Eddy. Fred, enraged, forces Mr. Eddy by gunpoint out of the room. He shoves him into the trunk of his car, pistol-whipping him before closing the trunk. He drives out into the desert and opens the trunk. Mr. Eddy leaps out at Fred and scuffles with him. But the Mystery Man arrives and helps Fred murder Mr. Eddy.

Fred drives to his old house, buzzes the intercom and says: "Dick Laurent is dead." The film ends with detectives in pursuit of Fred on a dark, desolate highway. Fred's face violently changes back and forth between Pete's face and his own. Fred, pained by the unstable metamorphosis, screams horribly.

The film, which introduces transformations, doppelgängers, and surreal symbolism, has been perplexing viewers for decades. Anthony Leong of Media Circus wrote: "Love it or loathe it, *Lost Highway* is what I would call an 'intellectual puzzle,' with its many layers of subtlety and meaning told in an unconventional manner, begging for discussion and interpretation."[2]

The most interest surrounds a single character: The Mystery Man. He is, as described by Frederick Szebin and Steve Biodrowski, a "ghostly figure who may (or may not) have supernatural powers."[3] The presence of the Mystery Man makes it seem that Fred is, according to Rose, the "target of some sort of sinister campaign."[4]

Lynch has been cryptic about the meaning of the film. "I had been thinking about identity," he said.[5]

The film's co-writer, Barry Gifford, has offered an explanation that ties up everything simply. Fred Madison, he said, is suffering a psychological fugue, a condition in which a person who has suffered a traumatic event creates another identity as a means of coping. It makes perfect sense for Fred, who has been shattered by guilt and grief over having murdered his wife, to develop a split personality. Simply, he has become Pete to avoid reality. In this scenario, the Mystery Man is likely a part of his subconscious that is forcing him to confront reality. But Gifford's rational explanation has been opposed by Lynch, who is resistant to a single intellectual interpretation of the film. He said:

> Barry may have his idea of what the film means and I may have my own idea, and they may be two different things. And yet, we worked together on the same film. The beauty of a film that is more abstract is everybody has a different take. Nobody agrees on anything in the world today. When you are spoon-fed a film, more people instantly know what it is. I love things that leave room to dream and are open to various interpretations. It's a beautiful thing. It doesn't do any good for Barry to say, "This is what it means." Film is what it means. If Barry or anyone else could capture what the film is in words, then that's poetry.[6]

He added, "Intuitive thinking where you get a marriage of feelings and intellect lets you feel the answers where you may not be able to articulate them."[7]

On another occasion, Lynch suggested that Fred's logic has gone wonky and that he is experiencing hallucinations. But, again, the director was quick to withdraw from any explanation of the film. "I don't want to say too much,"[8] he said. His reasoning on the matter was simple: "I love mysteries. To fall into a mystery and its danger ... everything becomes so intense in those moments. When most mysteries are solved, I feel tremendously let down. So I want things to feel solved up to a point, but there's got to be a certain percentage left over to keep the dream going."[9]

A bigger mystery for some is the reason that Lynch cast Pryor as Arnie, the owner of a garage where Dayton works. David Foster Wallace wrote:

> Richard Pryor's infirmity is meant to be grotesque.... Pryor's painful to watch, and not painful in a good way or a way that has anything to do with the business of the movie, and I can't help thinking that Lynch is exploiting Pryor the same way John Waters exploits Patricia Hearst, i.e., letting an actor think he's been hired to act when he's really been hired to be a spectacle.... And yet at the same time Pryor's symbolically perfect in this movie, in a way: The dissonance between the palsied husk onscreen and the vibrant man in our memories means that what we see in *Lost Highway* both is and is not the "real" Richard Pryor. His casting is thematically intriguing, then, but coldly, meanly so.[10]

Lynch's films are known to feature dwarves and amputees. In 1997, Dominic Wells asked the director if he used Pryor to expand his gallery of grotesques. Lynch replied, "Now why should I want to make fun of Richard Pryor? And why *shouldn't* he be in the film? Richard Pryor is a great guy. He's in a wheelchair, and he can play a huge role, but I really wanted to work with him. I saw him on a show, and I fell in love with him. He was just talking about himself and his life, and I said I really wanted to work with this guy."[11] Lynch strongly rejected the accusation that he was trying to humiliate Pryor. He said, "That's the kind of thinking ... it's really sick and twisted. It's really them that are imagining these things, so they're the sick and twisted ones just to come up with that concept."[12]

The script includes a stage direction that simply reads: *Arnie waves to Mr. Eddy from the office.*[13]

Lynch got the idea on the set to have Pryor pick up the phone and improvise a conversation. He shot Pryor talking on the phone for nine minutes. Lynch said, "He was amazing. A fragment of that is in the film."[14]

Epilogue

Towards the end of his life, Harvey Korman said, "I'm getting more mail now than I ever have. That I really have impacted people's lives, that I have made people happier. That I have brought families together. That I have made a difference in their lives. I think that's maybe the most important."[1]

In 1992, Pryor was interviewed by Jane Pauley for *Dateline*. Pauley asked him how he would like to be remembered. He said, "I like for people to see my picture and laugh. I like to bring joy. That's how I'd like to be remembered."[2] That was the pure comedian within Pryor speaking. The pure comedian has no greater desire in his heart than to make people laugh. It was the same desire Danny Kaye had when he was doing voices and making faces, which are the very antics that inspired George Carlin to become a comedian. It was the same desire that Jonathan Winters had when, to Pryor's delight, stood on stage pretending to be an outlandish hayseed or a ribald old woman.

Pryor's roiling rage, which he harbored for himself and others, is not something that nurtured him as a comedian. Comedy is about connecting to other people and bringing joy to them. Rage brings gloom, destruction, and alienation. It is a poor comic tool, which Pryor learned too late in his life.

In 1998, Pryor was awarded the first Mark Twain Prize for American Humor from the John F. Kennedy Center for the Performing Arts. The following year, he performed his final acting role on the television sitcom *Norm*. The series star, Norm MacDonald, said that people on the set were shocked by the comedian's nearly complete paralysis. "Everyone was crying," said MacDonald. Jennifer told him that her husband was really nervous and it would help if he said something to reassure him. Pryor had great difficulty speaking and MacDonald told him it would be fine if he backed out of the role. In the end, Pryor's brief scene went on as planned.[3] Pryor celebrated his 65th birthday on December 1, 2005. Nine days later, he died of a heart attack at his home. A small group of close friends gathered for his funeral at Hollywood's Forest Lawn Cemetery.

Notes

Introduction

1. Eugene Robinson, "Richard Pryor: Preacher of Truth," *Washington Post* (December 13, 2005). https://www.washingtonpost.com/archive/opinions/2005/12/13/richard-pryor-preacher-of-truth/e2be5310-69a1-4977-a39c-3e56bb90a2cf/?utm_term=.2d1e53f517de.
2. Lily Tomlin, "Lily Tomlin Remembers Richard Pryor," *Entertainment Weekly* (December 23, 2005). http://ew.com/article/2005/12/23/lily-tomlin-remembers-richard-pryor/.
3. Sharon Waxman, "Richard Pryor's Rage for Life; Drugs and Pain Once Fueled the Comic's Raw Humor. Now, It's Locked Inside," *Washington Post* (October 20, 1998).
4. "George Carlin on Becoming a Comedian, Influences, Language, Humor, Las Vegas, Religion. UCLA," May 31, 1972. https://www.youtube.com/watch?v=KL5MplXhaE8.
5. Sam Merrill, "Playboy Interview: George Carlin," *Playboy* (January 1982).
6. Kliph Nesteroff, *The Comedians: Drunks, Thieves, Scoundrels, and the History of American Comedy* (New York: Grove Press, 2015), 258.
7. Mitch Broder, "Today's top comics salute their idols," *Chicago Tribune* (January 21, 1979), 87.
8. Richard Pryor, with Todd Gold, *Pryor Convictions* (New York: Pantheon Books, 1995).
9. David Henry and Joe Henry, *Furious Cool: Richard Pryor and the World That Made Him* (Chapel Hill: Algonquin Books, 2013).
10. Wayne Federman, "Why Richard Pryor Marks the Beginning of the Modern Comedy Era," *Vulture* (February 5, 2016). http://www.vulture.com/2016/02/on-richard-pryor-and-the-modernization-of-comedy.html.
11. Merrill.
12. Scott Saul, *Becoming Richard Pryor* (New York: Harper, 2014).
13. Henry and Henry.
14. Joan Acocella, "Richard Pryor, Flame-Thrower," *The New Yorker* (March 4, 2015). http://www.newyorker.com/culture/cultural-comment/richard-pryor-still-burning.
15. Scott Cohen, "Richard Pryor," *High Times* (December 1977), 61.
16. Letter from Harry Northup (June 25, 2017).
17. Federman.
18. Colin Beckett, "The Uses of Richard Pryor," *The Brooklyn Rail* (February 5, 2013). http://brooklynrail.org/2013/02/film/the-uses-of-richard-pryor.

The Busy Body

1. Fred Fitch, "Mr. Westlake and The Nephews," *The Westlake Review* (June 26, 2016). https://thewestlakereview.wordpress.com/2014/06/26/mr-westlake-and-the-nephews/.
2. Donald Westlake, *The Busy Body* (New York: Lancer Books, 1966).
3. Fitch.
4. *Ibid.*
5. *Ibid.*
6. *Ibid.*
7. Kaspar Monahan, "Caesar Praised as America's Peter Sellers," *Pittsburgh Press* (February 24, 1967), 12.
8. Fitch.
9. *Ibid.*
10. Westlake.
11. *Ibid.*
12. Fitch.
13. *Ibid.*
14. Henry and Henry.
15. Pryor, with Gold.
16. Monahan.
17. *Time* (June 9, 1967).
18. *Ibid.*
19. Barbara Bladen, "The Marquee," *San Mateo Times* (February 3, 1967).
20. *Ibid.*
21. *Ibid.*
22. Ken Barnard, "The New Trim Sid Caesar," *Detroit Free Press* (June 24, 1967), 24.
23. Dick Cavett, "Dick Cavett Remembers Sid Caesar's Brilliant Career and Chaotic Life," *New Republic* (December 20, 1982). https://newrepublic.com/article/116600/dick-cavett-remembers-comedian-sid-caesar.
24. Sid Caesar, *Where Have I Been? An Autobiogra-*

phy (New York: Crown, 1982). https://www.amazon.com/Where-Have-I-Been-Autobiography/dp/0517547945.

25. David Zurawik, "Appreciating Sid Caesar, the real father of TV sketch comedy," *Baltimore Sun* (February 12, 2014). http://www.baltimoresun.com/entertainment/tv/z-on-tv-blog/bal-sid-caesar-the-real-father-of-tv-sketch-comedy-20140212-story.html.

26. Kliph Nesteroff, *The Comedians: Drunks, Thieves, Scoundrels, and the History of American Comedy* (New York: Grove Press, 2015).

27. Jeff Simon, "Sid Caesar burned brightly but only briefly," *Buffalo News* (February 12, 2014).

28. Cavett.

29. Mervyn Rothstein and Peter Keepnews, "Sid Caesar, Comedian of Comedians from TV's Early Days, Dies at 91," *New York Times* (February 12, 2014). https://www.nytimes.com/2014/02/13/arts/television/sid-caesar-comic-who-blazed-tv-trail-dies-at-91.html.

30. Gerald Nachman, *Seriously Funny: The Rebel Comedians of the 1950s and 1960s* (New York: Pantheon Books, 2009), 120.

31. Dennis McLellan, "Sid Caesar dies at 91; comedy giant of the small screen," *Hartford Courant* (February 12, 2014). http://www.courant.com/breaking-news/la-me-sid-caesar-20140213-story.html.

32. Cavett.

33. Monahan.

34. Barnard.

35. Norma Lee Browning, "…and Sid Caesar Goes Mod," *Chicago Tribune* (October 6, 1966), 33.

36. Monahan.

37. Barnard.

38. Simon.

39. Cavett.

40. *Ibid.*

41. Bailey.

42. Nachman.

43. Richard Zoglin, *Comedy at the Edge: How Stand-up in the 1970s Changed America* (London: Bloomsbury, 2008).

44. Jason Bailey, *Richard Pryor: American Id* (Raleigh: The Critical Press, 2015).

45. *Ibid.*

46. Zoglin.

Wild in the Streets

1. Pauline Kael, *The Age of Movies: Selected Writings of Pauline Kael* (New York: Penguin Group, 2011).

2. *Ibid.*

3. *Ibid.*

4. *Ibid.*

5. Erich Kuersten, "Fourteen or Fight! *Wild in the Streets* (1968) or 'The Day It All Happened, Baby,'" *Acidemic* (May 20, 2011). https://acidemic.blogspot.com/2011/05/day-it-all-happened-baby.html.

6. *Ibid.*

7. Kael.

8. Glenn Erickson, "Wild in the Streets," *DVD Savant* (August 21, 2016). https://trailersfromhell.com/wild-in-the-streets/.

9. Alan Moore, "The League of Extraordinary Gentlemen, Volume III: Century #2 1969," *Top Shelf Productions* (August 9, 2011).

10. Sam Tweedle, "PCA Retro Review: *Wild in the Streets* (1968)," *Confessions of a Pop Culture Addict* (July 11, 2010). http://popcultureaddict.com/pca-retro-review-wild-in-the-streets-1968/.

11. Peter Winkler, "Whatever Happened to Christopher Jones?" *World Cinema Paradise* (February 24, 2014). http://worldcinemaparadise.com/2014/02/24/whatever-happened-to-christopher-jones-part-1/.

12. Henry and Henry.

13. Saul.

14. *Ibid.*

15. Aaron Hillis, "Interview: Larry Bishop on 'Hell Ride,'" *IFC* (August 7, 2008). http://www.ifc.com/2008/08/larry-bishop-on-hell-ride.

16. Erickson.

17. Greg Ferrara, "Wild in the Streets," *TCM*. http://www.tcm.com/this-month/article/1206422%7C0/Wild-in-the-Streets.html

18. Tweedle.

Uncle Tom's Fairy Tales

1. Saul.

2. Henry and Henry.

3. *Ibid.*

4. Saul.

5. Henry and Henry.

Carter's Army

1. Poseidon-3 from Cincinnati, OH, "Reviews & Ratings for Carter's Army (TV)," *Internet Movie Database* (July 11, 2006). http://www.imdb.com/title/tt0064135/reviews.

2. Pryor, with Gold.

3. Hilton Als, "A Pryor Love: The Life and Times of America's Comic Prophet of Race," *The New Yorker* (September 13, 1999), 68–81. http://www.newyorker.com/magazine/1999/09/13/a-pryor-love.

4. Saul.

The Phynx

1. Henry and Henry.

2. Nathan Rabin, "Rock stars rescue faded actors (and Colonel Sanders) in the Austin Powers lead-up The Phynx," *A.V. Club* (December 17, 2012). http://www.avclub.com/article/rock-stars-rescue-faded-actors-and-colonel-sanders-89931.

3. Bailey.

4. Jeff Rovin, *Richard Pryor: Black and Blue: The Unauthorized Biography* (New York: Bantam Books, 1983), 87.

You've Got to Walk It Like You Talk It or You'll Lose That Beat

1. *Box Office Booking Guide* (October 11, 1971).
2. *Filmfacts* (1971), 684–685.
3. A. H. Weiler, "You've Got to Walk It…, Genial Put-Down of Establishment," *New York Times* (September 20, 1971). http://www.nytimes.com/movie/review?res=9C05E2DC1338EF34BC4851DFBF66838A669EDE.
4. *Filmfacts*.
5. Judith Crist, "Been Away So Long It Looks Like Great to Me," *New York Magazine* (September 27, 1971), 75.
6. *Ibid*.
7. Weiler.
8. *Ibid*.
9. *Ibid*.
10. *Ibid*.
11. *Ibid*.
12. *Variety* (September 1, 1971), 26.
13. Rovin, 69.
14. Ann Guarino, *Daily News* (September 20, 1971), 44.
15. Constance Clarke, *Applause* (October 6, 1971), 12.
16. *Variety*.
17. Leo Mishkin, *Morning Telegraph* (September 22, 1971), 3.
18. *Ibid*.
19. Archer Winsten, *New York Post* (September 20, 1971).

Lady Sings the Blues

1. Jesse Hamlin, "Billie Holiday's bio, 'Lady Sings the Blues,' may be full of lies, but it gets at jazz great's core," *San Francisco Chronicle* (September 18, 2006). http://www.sfgate.com/entertainment/article/Billie-Holiday-s-bio-Lady-Sings-the-Blues-may-2469428.php.
2. Hamlin.
3. David Margolick, *Strange Fruit: Billie Holiday, Cafe Society, and an Early Cry for Civil Rights* (Philadelphia: Running Press, 2000).
4. Billie Holiday and William Dufty, *Lady Sings the Blues* (New York: Doubleday, 1956).
5. Pryor, with Gold, 141.
6. Daniel Kremer, *Sidney J. Furie: Life and Films* (Lexington: University Press of Kentucky, 2015).
7. Bailey.
8. Jay Weston, "Diana Ross Discusses Lady Sings the Blues on *Oprah*," *Huffington Post* (May 25, 2011). http://www.huffingtonpost.com/jay-weston/diana-ross-on-oprah-with-_b_829674.html.
9. Pryor, with Gold, 142.
10. Kremer.
11. *Ibid*.
12. *Ibid*.
13. Hamlin.
14. *Ibid*.
15. *Ibid*.

The Mack

1. Richard Harland Smith, "The Mack," *TCM* (2015). http://www.tcm.com/this-month/article/1118208%7C0/The-Mack.html.
2. *Ibid*.
3. *Ibid*.
4. Commentary track for *The Mack* (New Line DVD, 2004).
5. Tavis Smiley, "Michael Campus—'The Mack' Is Back," *Tavis Smiley Radio Show*. http://www.tavissmileyradio.com/michael-campus-the-mack-is-back/.
6. Commentary track for *The Mack*.
7. Smiley.
8. Saul.
9. Susan King, "'The Mack' is back after 40 years," *Los Angeles Times* (September 25, 2013). http://articles.latimes.com/2013/sep/25/entertainment/la-et-mn-the-mack-lacma-20130925.
10. Saul.
11. *Ibid*.
12. *Ibid*.
13. Commentary track for *The Mack*.
14. Saul.
15. *Ibid*.
16. *Ibid*.
17. *Ibid*.
18. *Ibid*.
19. King.
20. *Ibid*.
21. Commentary track for *The Mack*.
22. King.
23. Saul.
24. John A. Williams and Dennis A. Williams, *If I Stop I'll Die: The Tragedy and Comedy of Richard Pryor* (New York: Thunder's Mouth Press, 1991).

Some Call It Loving

1. Jonathan Rosenbaum, "Some Call It Loving," *Sight & Sound* (Autumn 1975).
2. Nick Pinkerton, "Interview: James B. Harris," *Film Comment* (April 3, 2015). https://www.filmcomment.com/blog/interview-james-b-harris/.
3. A. H. Weiler, "The Screen: 'Some Call It Loving' Is Diffuse Fantasy," *New York Times* (November 17, 1973).
4. Miriam Bale, "You May Say I'm a Dreamer, But I'm Just Trying to Buy Sleeping Beauty: Some Call it Loving," *The L Magazine* (February 13, 2013). http://www.thelmagazine.com/2013/02/you-may-say-im-a-dreamer-but-im-just-trying-to-buy-sleeping-beauty-some-call-it-loving/.
5. Bale.
6. Martin Wilson, "Some Call It Loving," *MUBI's Notebook* (June 17, 2012). https://mubi.com/films/some-call-it-loving.

7. Pinkerton.
8. Rosenbaum.
9. Nathaniel Drake Carlson, "Fantasies End: An Examination of James B. Harris' 'Some Call It Loving,'" *Pinland Empire* (July 15, 2015). http://www.pinnlandempire.com/2015/07/fantasies-end-examination-of-james-b.html.
10. Bale.
11. Weiler.
12. Danny King, "On the Hunt: The Films of James B. Harris," *MUBI's Notebook* (April 8, 2015). https://mubi.com/notebook/posts/on-the-hunt-the-films-of-james-b-harris.
13. Brandon. "Dream Castle/Sleeping Beauty (1973, James B. Harris)," *Deeper Into Movies* (June 3, 2011). http://deeperintomovies.net/journal/archives/6217.
14. Henry and Henry.

Hit!

1. Henry and Henry.
2. Kremer, 188.
3. *Ibid.*
4. *Ibid.*
5. Henry and Henry.
6. Kremer.

Uptown Saturday Night

1. Peter Golden, "You Want to be a What?" *New Jersey Monthly* (December 20, 2007). https://njmonthly.com/articles/jersey-living/you_want_to_be_a_what/.
2. David Rosen, "When He Was King: Ali's Comeback in Atlanta—A Lost Moment in American History," *Black Star News* (August 29, 2017). http://www.blackstarnews.com/sports/boxing/when-he-was-king-ali's-come-back-in-atl-a-lost-moment-in-american.
3. Golden.
4. Novotny Lawrence, "No Shafts, Super Flys, or Foxy Browns: Sidney Poitier's 'Uptown Saturday Night' as Alternative to Blaxploitation Cinema," *Poitier Revisited: Reconsidering a Black Icon in the Obama Age*, edited by Ian Gregory and Mia Mask (New York: Bloomsbury Academic, 2015), 244.
5. Als.
6. Donald Bogle, *Toms, Coons, Mulattoes, Mammies, and Bucks: An Interpretive History of Blacks in American Films (Fourth Edition)* (New York: Bloomsbury Academic, 2001), 175.
7. Bailey.
8. Goudsouzian, 346.
9. Vincent Canby, "Poitier in 2 Roles: Stars in and Directs 'Uptown' Comedy," *New York Times* (June 17, 1974). http://www.nytimes.com/movie/review?res=9B0DE1DD123DE73ABC4F52DFB066838F669EDE.
10. Bob Thomas, "Cosby Piqued by Criticism of 'Uptown Saturday Night,'" *Gettysburg Times* (July 11, 1974), 8.
11. *Ibid.*

12. Mark Anthony Neal, *Soul Babies: Black Popular Culture and the Post-Soul Aesthetic* (New York: Routledge, 2002), 29.

Adiós Amigo!

1. Germaine William, "Interview with Michael Schultz," *Black Bottom Film Festival* (February 25, 2017). https://www.youtube.com/watch?v=TVE1kGpYXIY.
2. Rovin, 105.
3. Martin Weston, "Richard Pryor: Every Nigger Is a Star," *Ebony* (September 1976), 56.
4. Pryor, with Gold, 143.
5. Henry and Henry.
6. Bryan Thomas, "'Adios Amigo': Fred 'The Hammer' Williamson and Richard Pryor are two sharp dudes taking turns with chicks and tricks," *Night Flight* (April 3, 2016). http://nightflight.com/adios-amigo-fred-the-hammer-williamson-and-richard-pryor-are-two-sharp-dudes-taking-turns-with-chicks-and-tricks/.
7. Rovin, 105.
8. *Ibid.*
9. Thomas.
10. Weston, 57.
11. *Ibid.*
12. *Ibid.*
13. Rovin, 120.
14. Thomas.
15. *Ibid.*
16. Roger Ebert, *Chicago Sun-Times* (June 16, 1980).
17. Tayvis Dunnahoe, "Adios Amigo/Review," *The Grindhouse Cinema Database* (April 14, 2017). https://www.grindhousedatabase.com/index.php/Adios_Amigo/Review.
18. Henry and Henry.

The Bingo Long Traveling All-Stars & Motor Kings

1. Hal Barwood, "RE: The Bingo Long Traveling All-Stars & Motor Kings," email to author, May 12, 2017.
2. William Brashler, *The Bingo Long Traveling All-Stars & Motor Kings (first paperback edition)* (Champaign: University of Illinois Press, 1993).
3. *St. Louis Post-Dispatch* (July 6, 1980), 109.
4. Barwood.
5. Pryor, with Gold.
6. *Ibid.*
7. Brashler.
8. James Earl Jones and Penelope Niven, *Voices and Silences* (New York: Scribner, 1993).

Car Wash

1. Tony Norman, "The wretched, venal life of Rev. Ike," *Pittsburgh Post-Gazette* (August 4, 2009).
2. Audrey T. McCluskey, *Richard Pryor: The Life*

and Legacy of a "Crazy" Black Man (Bloomington: Indiana University Press, 2008), 175.

3. Pryor, with Gold.
4. *Ibid.*
5. Nathan Rabin, "Random Roles: Margot Kidder," *A.V. Club* (March 3, 2009). http://www.avclub.com/article/random-roles-margot-kidder-24554.
6. Scott Simon, "Box Set Showcases Richard Pryor's Difficult, Spontaneous, Hilarious Life," *NPR* (June 8, 2013). http://www.npr.org/2013/06/08/189255421/box-set-showcases-richard-pryors-difficult-spontaneous-hilarious-life.
7. Roger Ebert, "Car Wash," *Chicago Sun-Times* (January 1, 1976). http://www.rogerebert.com/reviews/car-wash-1976.
8. *Ibid.*

Silver Streak

1. Ronald Bergan, "Jill Clayburgh obituary," *The Guardian* (November 7, 2010). https://www.theguardian.com/film/2010/nov/07/jill-clayburgh-obituary.
2. *Ibid.*
3. *Ibid.*
4. Jim Hemphill, "Conversations at the Cinematheque: Arthur Hiller" (February 4, 2010). https://www.facebook.com/notes/aero-theatre/conversations-at-the-cinematheque-arthur-hiller-for-the-in-laws-and-silver-strea/409361029827/?sw_fnr_id=3766842758&fnr_t=0.
5. Roger Ebert, "Hanging Out with Wilder and Pryor," *Chicago Sun-Times* (December 23, 1976).
6. *Ibid.*
7. "Gene Wilder on first working with Richard Pryor," *YouTube*, uploaded on February 24, 2011. https://www.youtube.com/watch?v=14ptlrpLuks.
8. Rovin, 131.
9. Ron Underwood (interviewer), "Visual History with Arthur Hiller," *Directors Guild of America*. https://www.dga.org/Craft/VisualHistory/Interviews/Arthur-Hiller.aspx?Filter=Full%20Interview.
10. Rovin, 133.
11. Hemphill.
12. Rovin, 135.
13. Terry Gross, "Actor Gene Wilder: 'Kiss Me Like a Stranger,'" *Fresh Air/NPR* (December 29, 2005). http://www.npr.org/templates/story/story.php?storyId=4537395.
14. *Ibid.*
15. Rovin, 135.
16. *Ibid.*
17. James Braxton Peterson, ed., *In Media Res: Race, Identity, and Pop Culture in the Twenty-First Century* (Lewisburg: Bucknell University Press, 2014), 196.
18. Colin Higgins, "'Silver Streak' Script, Revised Draft" (March 26, 1976), 74.
19. *Ibid.*
20. *Ibid.*
21. Peterson, 196.
22. Vincent Canby, "'Silver Streak' Tarnishes on a Tiring Film Trip," *New York Times* (December 9, 1976). http://www.nytimes.com/movie/review?res=9E0DE0DB123EE334BC4153DFB467838D669EDE.

Greased Lightning

1. Wendell Scott, *Wikipedia*. https://en.wikipedia.org/wiki/Wendell_Scott.
2. Kenneth Vose, "Re: Greased Lightning," email to author, August 31, 2017.
3. Laurence Dukore, "Re: Greased Lightning," email to author, May 20, 2017.
4. Dukore.
5. *Ibid.*
6. Vose.
7. Dukore.
8. Tommy Tomlinson, "Wendell Scott, Hall of Famer," *Tommy Tomlinson Blog* (May 24, 2012). http://tommytomlinson.com/?p=384.
9. Pryor, with Gold, 160.
10. *Ibid.*, 161.
11. *Ibid.*
12. Vose.
13. "Substitutions," *Los Angeles Times* (August 16, 1976), 68.
14. McCluskey.
15. Lee Grant, "Acting's No Laughing Matter," *Los Angeles Times* (January 19, 1977), 83.
16. Dukore.
17. Jean-Claude Bouis, "Richard Pryor goes like 'Greased Lightning,'" *San Bernardino County Sun* (September 18, 1977), 47.
18. *Ibid.*
19. Rovin, 142.
20. *Ibid.*, 143.
21. Janet Maslin, "Pryor Is Serious (and Fine)," *New York Times* (August 4, 1977).
22. Brian Donovan, *Hard Driving: The Wendell Scott Story* (Hanover, NH: Steerforth Press, 2008).
23. *Ibid.*
24. Bouis.
25. Tomlinson.
26. Rovin, 143.
27. Donovan.
28. Rovin, 144.
29. McCluskey.
30. Marshall Fine, "Pryor, Strong Acting Saves 'Lightning,'" *Clarion-Ledger* (Jackson, MS) (July 27, 1977), 24.
31. Justin Bozung, "Interview: Writer/Director Robert Boris on 'Doctor Detroit' and working with Richard Pryor," *TVStoreOnline Blog* (April 30, 2015). http://blog.tvstoreonline.com/2015/04/interview-writerdirector-robert-boris_30.html.

Which Way Is Up?

1. Lee Grant, "Acting's No Laughing Matter," 83.
2. *Ibid.*
3. Letter from Harry Northup, June 25, 2017.
4. *Ibid.*

5. Carl Gottlieb, "'Which Way Is Up?' Revised Final Draft Screenplay," 10.
6. Northup.
7. *Ibid.*
8. *Ibid.*
9. Grant.
10. Donna Brown Guillaume, "Visual History with Michael Schultz," *The Directors Guild of America* (April 3, 2002). https://www.dga.org/Craft/VisualHistory/Interviews/Michael-Schultz.aspx.
11. Mike Smith, "Interview with Carl Gottlieb," *Media Mikes* (April 29, 2010). http://www.mediamikes.com/2010/04/interview-with-carl-gottlieb/.
12. *Ibid.*
13. Saul.
14. Smith.
15. *Ibid.*
16. Guillaume.
17. *Ibid.*
18. *Ibid.*
19. Benson, 58.
20. *Ibid.*
21. Carson Calvin (interviewer), "Margaret Avery: Leading Man—Favorite," *Dialogues* (April 2, 2013). https://www.dialogues.org/interview/04/02/2013/margaret-avery-leading-man-favorite/1465814364.
22. Gideon Bachmann, "Gideon Bachmann Talks with Lina Wertmüller," *Film Quarterly* 30, no. 3 (Spring 1977), 7. https://archive.org/stream/Interview_with_Lina_Wertmüller/Interview_with_Lina_Wertmüller_djvu.txt.
23. Grace Russo Bullaro, *Man in Disorder: The Cinema of Lina Wertmüller in the 1970s* (Leicester: Troubadour, 2006), 1.
24. Bullaro, 24.
25. Budd E. Wilkins, "To Each His Own Bastard: A Viewer's Guide to 'The Seduction of Mimi,'" 2010.
26. Bullaro, 2.
27. *Ibid.*, 114.
28. *Ibid.*, 82.
29. Stuart Galbraith IV, "The Seduction of Mimi (Blu-ray)," *DVD Talk* (June 19, 2012). http://www.dvdtalk.com/reviews/55046/seduction-of-mimi/.
30. Wilkins.
31. Generoso Fierro, "Michael Schultz's 'Greased Lightning' Starring Richard Pryor: The One That Got Away," *Forces of Geek* (August 10, 2015). http://www.forcesofgeek.com/2015/08/michael-schultzs-greased-lightning.html.
32. Shelia Benson, "Who Is Co-Starring with Richard Pryor & Richard Pryor in Michael Schultz's New Film?" *Mother Jones* (July 1977), 56.
33. Saul.
34. Mike Smith, "Interview with Carl Gottlieb," *Media Mikes* (April 29, 2010). http://mediamikes.com/2010/04/29/interview-with-carl-gottlieb/.
35. Galbraith.
36. "'Which Way Is Up?': Movie Detail," *AFI Catalog of Feature Films.* http://www.afi.com/members//catalog/DetailView.aspx?s=&Movie=56093.
37. Saul.
38. Vincent Canby, "Comic Film 'Which Way Is Up?' Loses Way," *New York Times* (November 5, 1977).
39. Gottlieb, 3.
40. Joseph Jon Lanthier, "The Seduction of Mimi," *Slant Magazine* (June 11, 2012). http://www.slantmagazine.com/dvd/review/the-seduction-of-mimi.
41. Peter Biskind, "Lina Wertmüller: The Politics of Private Life," *Film Quarterly* 28, no. 2 (Winter 1974–1975), 10–16.
42. Wilkins.
43. *Ibid.*
44. *Ibid.*
45. Bullaro, 73.
46. R. C. Dale, "Review: 'The Seduction of Mimi,'" *Movietone News*, Volume 38 (January 1975). http://parallax-view.org/2015/07/20/review-the-seduction-of-mimi/.
47. Biskind.
48. Gottlieb, 73.
49. *Ibid.*, 87.
50. *Ibid.*, 88.
51. *Ibid.*, 87.
52. Lanthier.
53. Grant, 83.

Blue Collar

1. Grant, 83.
2. *Ibid.*
3. Ben Sachs, "Blue Collar, Black Mark," *Chicago Reader* (April 7, 2011). http://www.chicagoreader.com/chicago/blue-collar-film-review-paul-schrader-richard-pryor/Content?oid=3553732.
4. Frederic and Mary Ann Brussat, "Blue Collar," *Spirituality and Practice.* http://www.spiritualityandpractice.com/films/reviews/view/7275.
5. Gregg Kilday, "Writing His Way to the Top," *Los Angeles Times* (April 6, 1977), 104.
6. Brecht Andersch, "Hardcore: Paul Schrader in the 70's," *Open Space* (August 29, 2010). https://openspace.sfmoma.org/2010/08/hardcore-paul-schrader-in-the-70s-2/.
7. Andersch.
8. Maitland McDonagh (moderator), "Paul Schrader interviewed by Maitland McDonagh," commentary track for *Blue Collar* (Anchor Bay DVD, 2000).
9. Northup.
10. *Ibid.*
11. *Ibid.*
12. *Ibid.*
13. *Ibid.*
14. *Ibid.*
15. *Ibid.*
16. *Ibid.*
17. *Ibid.*
18. Sergio, "Rare Screening of 'Blue Collar' with Richard Pryor and Yaphet Kotto in Chicago Area," *IndieWire* (December 6, 2012). http://www.indiewire.

com/2012/12/rare-screening-of-blue-collar-with-richard-pryor-and-yaphet-kotto-in-chicago-area-139619/.
19. Rovin.
20. Northup.
21. *Ibid.*
22. Pryor, with Gold, 32.
23. *Ibid.*
24. Saul.
25. Cecil Brown, *Pryor Lives! Kiss My Rich, Happy Black ... Ass! A Memoir* (CreateSpace, 2013).
26. Greg Tate, *Vibe Q: Raw and Uncut* (New York: Kensington, 1995), 76.
27. Sue Reilly, "Richard Pryor's Ordeal," *People* (March 13, 1978).
28. Paul Schrader, *Norton & Friends* (October 18, 2016). https://www.youtube.com/watch?v=q8pFCWVlb9s.
29. Geoffrey McNab, "Raging Bull: 'Taxi Driver' screenwriter Paul Schrader on the perils of DIY cinema and surviving Lindsay Lohan," *The Independent* (February 15, 2014). http://www.independent.co.uk/arts-entertainment/films/features/raging-bull-taxi-driver-screenwriter-paul-schrader-on-the-perils-of-diy-cinema-and-surviving-lindsay-9126293.html.
30. Schrader.
31. McDonagh.
32. Pryor, with Gold, 127.
33. *Ibid.*
34. Sara Hutchison (producer), *Richard Pryor: Omit the Logic*, Fresh One Productions and Tarnished Angel, BBC Worldwide and Showtime Networks (July 31, 2013).
35. McDonagh.
36. Rovin, 152.
37. McDonagh.
38. Andersch.
39. Mark Cousins, *Scene by Scene*, BBC (April 25, 1998). https://www.youtube.com/watch?v=QBCw-tLfKec.
40. Schrader.
41. McCluskey, 178.
42. *Ibid.*
43. Rovin, 152.
44. Roger Ebert, "Yaphet Kotto: 'Blue Collar,'" *Chicago Sun-Times* (February 8, 1978). http://www.rogerebert.com/interviews/yaphet-kotto-blue-collar.
45. McDonagh.
46. Vincent Canby, "Film: On the Auto Front: The Assembly Line," *New York Times* (February 10, 1978). http://www.nytimes.com/movie/review?res=9903E5DC1430E632A25753C1A9649C946990D6CF.
47. McDonagh.
48. Brown.
49. *St. Louis Post-Dispatch.*
50. Christiansen, Richard, "Yaphet Kotto: When it comes to acting, he's for details, not labels," *Chicago Tribune* (August 24, 1980), 85.
51. Matthew Field and Ajay Chowdhury, *Some Kind of Hero: The Remarkable Story of the James Bond Films* (Stroud: The History Press, 2015).
52. *Ibid.*
53. James M. Tate, "Yaphet Kotto: The One and Only," *Cult Film Freak.* http://www.cultfilmfreak.com/yaphetkotto/.
54. Field and Chowdhury.
55. Tate.
56. *Ibid.*
57. Brown, 220.
58. The Playlist Staff, "Retrospective: The Directorial Career of Paul Schrader," *The Playlist* (August 5, 2013). http://theplaylist.net/retrospective-the-directorial-career-of-paul-schrader-20130805/.
59. Jefferson Cowie, *Stayin' Alive: The 1970s and the Last Days of the Working Class* (New York: The New York Press, 2010), 336.
60. Abby Ferla, "Putting the new GM-UAW contract in historical context," *Remapping Debate* (September 21, 2011). http://www.remappingdebate.org/map-data-tool/putting-new-gm-uaw-contract-historical-context.
61. John Barnard, *American Vanguard: The United Auto Workers During the Reuther Years* (Detroit: Wayne State University Press, 2004).
62. Canby.
63. Julius Kassendorf, "Film on Disc: Blue Collar," *The Solute* (February 22, 2017). http://www.the-solute.com/film-on-the-disc-blue-collar/.
64. Brussat.
65. *Ibid.*
66. *Ibid.*
67. Jesse Hassenger, "Richard Pryor takes on the man," *A.V. Club* (September 22, 2014). http://www.avclub.com/article/richard-pryor-takes-man-209376.
68. Jamie Kitman, "Blue Collar is the Closest Hollywood Got to the Factory Floor," *Trunkworthy* (October 23, 2014). http://www.trunkworthy.com/blue-collar-richard-pryor/.
69. Peter Biskind, *Gods and Monsters: Thirty Years of Writing on Film and Culture from One of America's Most Incisive Writers* (New York: Nation Books, 2004).
70. Stanley Rogouski, "Blue Collar (1978)," *Writers Without Money* (June 20, 2016). https://writerswithoutmoney.com/2016/06/20/blue-collar-1978/.
71. Brown.
72. Andersch.
73. Biskind.
74. "Take a ride with Harry Northup," *Retro Lady-Land* (February 11, 2015). https://retroladyland.blogspot.com/2015/02/take-ride-with-harry-northup.html.
75. Vincent Canby, "On the Auto Front: The Assembly Line," *New York Times* (February 10, 1978).
76. Dave Zurawik, "Pryor: 'Don't Take Away My Words…,'" *Detroit Free Press* (November 6, 1977).
77. *Ibid.*

The Wiz

1. Joanna E. Rapf, ed., *Sidney Lumet: Interviews* (Jackson: University Press of Mississippi, 2006), 78.
2. *Ibid.*

3. *Ibid.*
4. Tom Shone, *Blockbuster: How Hollywood Learned to Stop Worrying and Love the Summer* (New York: Simon & Schuster, 2004).
5. Tom Hischak, *Through the Screen Door: What Happened to the Broadway Musical When It Went to Hollywood?* (Lanham, MD: Scarecrow Press, July 8, 2004).
6. Charles Henry Harpole, *History of the American Cinema* (New York: Charles Scribner & Sons, 1990).
7. Reilly.
8. *Ibid.*

California Suite

1. Bob Thomas, "Cosby Gets His Chance in 'California Suite,'" *Santa Cruz Sentinel* (June 15, 1978), 32.
2. *Ibid.*
3. Brown.
4. *Variety* Staff, "Review: 'California Suite,'" *Variety* (December 31, 1977).
5. David Kehr, "California Suite," *Chicago Reader*. https://www.chicagoreader.com/chicago/california-suite/Film?oid=1072956.
6. Pauline Kael, *5001 Nights at the Movies* (New York: Picador, 1982), 115.
7. Bob Thomas, "What color is the devil?" *Associated Press* (June 25, 1980).
8. *Ibid.*
9. David Felton, "Richard Pryor's Life in Concert," *Rolling Stone* (May 3, 1979). http://www.rollingstone.com/culture/features/richard-pryors-life-in-concert-19790503.
10. *Pittsburgh Press* (August 28, 1979), 11.
11. Pryor, with Gold, 184–185.

The Muppet Movie

1. Nathan Rabin, "Austin Pendleton," *A.V. Club* (July 29, 2009). http://www.avclub.com/article/austin-pendleton-31009.
2. *St. Louis Post-Dispatch* (July 6, 1980), 109.

Wholly Moses!

1. "Wholly Moses!" *Wikipedia*. https://en.wikipedia.org/wiki/Wholly_Moses!
2. Rena Fruchter, *Dudley Moore: An Intimate Portrait* (London: Ebury Press, 2004).
3. *Ibid.*

In God We Tru$t

1. "Alan Spencer on 'The Last Remake of Beau Geste,'" *Trailers from Hell* (December 10, 2012). https://www.youtube.com/watch?v=8tZvCi4SolA.
2. Jim Clark, *Dream Repairman: Adventures in Film Editing* (London: Landmarc Press, 2010).
3. *Ibid.*
4. *Ibid.*
5. *Ibid.*

6. *Ibid.*
7. Spencer.
8. *Ibid.*
9. *Ibid.*
10. Clark.
11. *Ibid.*
12. Gary Arnold, "Hollywood Breaks Out Laughing," *Washington Post* (April 22, 1979).
13. Clark.
14. Gary Arnold, "Fumbling Feldman," *Washington Post* (October 2, 1980). https://www.washingtonpost.com/archive/lifestyle/1980/10/02/fumbling-feldman/9570bc64-8245-47f1-9bc5-ef723ea1b645/?utm_term=.1ec3929463bf.
15. Arnold.

Stir Crazy

1. Bruce Jay Friedman, "When Gene Wilder Went 'Stir Crazy,'" *Tablet* (September 1, 2016). http://www.tabletmag.com/jewish-arts-and-culture/212301/when-gene-wilder-went-stir-crazy.
2. Gene Wilder, *Kiss Me Like a Stranger: My Search for Love and Art* (New York: St. Martin's Press, 2005).
3. Friedman.
4. Chris Summers, "The demons that drove Richard Pryor to make us laugh," *BBC News* (August 25, 2013). http://www.bbc.com/news/entertainment-arts-23724276.
5. *Ibid.*
6. Henry and Henry.
7. Simon Barrett, "'Stir Crazy' 1980—What You Do Not Know About the Film," *Blogger News* (March 17, 2012). http://www.bloggernews.net/127885.
8. *Ibid.*
9. "Wilder and Pryor: Big Time in the Big House," *Stir Crazy: Merchandising and Advertising Manual*, 2.
10. Greg Ferrara, "Stir Crazy," *TCM*. http://www.tcm.com/this-month/article/461229%7C193994/Stir-Crazy.html.
11. "Richard Pryor Talks About Richard Pryor (The Old, The New), Rejection That Led to Loneliness and Drugs, God, Prayer, 'Nigger,' and How He Was Burned," *Ebony* (October 1980), 36.
12. Pryor, with Gold, 196.
13. John Meroney and Sean Coons, "The 'Flickering, Fragile Flame' of Richard Pryor," *The Atlantic* (November 21, 2013). https://www.theatlantic.com/entertainment/archive/2013/11/the-flickering-fragile-flame-of-richard-pryor/281515/.
14. Bailey.
15. Rovin, 189.
16. Elahe Izadi, "Remembering Gene Wilder and Richard Pryor, a magical and complicated comedy duo," *Washington Post* (August 30, 2016).
17. Wilder, 184.
18. Mike Ryan, "The Unlikely Comedy Genius of Gene Wilder and Richard Pryor," *Uproxx* (August 30, 2016). http://uproxx.com/movies/gene-wilder-and-richard-pryor/.

19. *Ibid.*
20. *Ibid.*
21. *Ibid.*
22. *Ibid.*
23. Bailey.
24. Wilder, 183.
25. Ferrara.
26. David Felton, "Pryor's Inferno," *Rolling Stone* (July 24, 1980). http://www.rollingstone.com/culture/news/pryors-inferno-19800724.
27. Wilder, 184.
28. *Ibid.*
29. "Comedy Teams: United They Fly," *Stir Crazy: Merchandising and Advertising Manual*, 1.
30. Rovin, 217.
31. Bruce Jay Friedman and Charles Blackwell, "'Stir Crazy' Final Script" (February 12, 1980), 32.
32. David Denby, *New York* (June 8, 1981), 51.
33. Mike Sacks, *Poking a Dead Frog: Conversations with Today's Top Comedy Writers* (London: Penguin, 2014).
34. Friedman.
35. Richard Rushfield, "Take Two: Revisiting 'Stir Crazy,'" *Uproxx/Hitfix* (March 26, 2015). http://uproxx.com/hitfix/take-two-revisiting-stir-crazy/.
36. Vincent Canby, "Pryor and Wilder Inside in 'Stir Crazy,'" *New York Times* (December 12, 1980). http://www.nytimes.com/movie/review?res=9904EED81238F931A25751C1A966948260.
37. Sacks.
38. "Comedy Teams: United They Fly," 1.
39. David Taylor, Phone conversation with author, June 30, 2017.
40. Gene Siskel, "'Hanky Panky' is, surprise, a hunky-dory comedy," *Chicago Tribune* (June 7, 1982). http://archives.chicagotribune.com/1982/06/07/page/62/article/hanky-panky-is-surprise-a-hunky-dory-comedy.
41. Aram Goudsouzian, *Sidney Poitier: Man, Actor, Icon* (Chapel Hill: University of North Carolina Press, 2004), 360–361.
42. Taylor.
43. Dick Lochte, "Book Notes," *Los Angeles Times* (June 14, 1981), 340.
44. "'Deep Trouble' Is Next," *Cincinnati Enquirer* (September 11, 1981), 46.
45. Marilyn Beck, "Wilder not making film this fall," *Sante Fe New Mexican* (September 17, 1981), 31.
46. "Carol Channing first Dolly: TV Q & A," *Ithaca Journal* (October 22, 1981), 50.
47. Bruce Jay Friedman, phone interview with the author, July 13, 2017.
48. Rovin, 182.

Bustin' Loose

1. Roger L. Simon, *Turning Right at Hollywood and Vine: The Perils of Coming Out Conservative* (New York: Encounter Books, 2011).
2. Marilyn Beck, "Burt Reynolds hopes to work with Sophia," *Morning News* (December 24, 1979), 9.
3. Helaine Head (interviewer), "Visual History with Oz Scott," *Directors Guild of America*. https://www.dga.org/Craft/VisualHistory/Interviews/Oz-Scott.aspx?Filter=Full%20Interview.
4. *Ibid.*
5. Pryor, with Gold.
6. K. C. Wright, "8 Acting Techniques (and the Stars Who Swear by Them)," *Backstage* (August 26, 2014). https://www.backstage.com/advice-for-actors/resources/8-acting-techniques-and-stars-who-swear-by-them/.
7. Simon.
8. *Ibid.*
9. Head.
10. Simon.
11. Head.
12. Simon.
13. *Ibid.*
14. *Ibid.*
15. Roger L. Simon and Lonne Elder III, "Family Dream Script" (1979), 109.
16. Vernon Scott, "The Trouble with Richard…," *Ottawa Journal* (July 4, 1980), 25.
17. Rovin, 220.
18. Simon and Elder, 75.
19. Vincent Canby, "'Bustin' Loose' stars Richard Pryor Gone Softy," *New York Times* (May 22, 1981). http://www.nytimes.com/1981/05/22/movies/bustin-loose-stars-richard-pryor-gone-softy.html.
20. Bailey.
21. Julian Upton, "Extinguishing Features: The Last Years of Richard Pryor," *Bright Lights Film Journal* (December 10, 2016). http://brightlightsfilm.com/extinguishing-features-last-years-richard-pryor/#.WQY7F8a1uUk.
22. Hassenger.
23. "Richard Pryor's Tragic Accident Spotlights a Dangerous Drug Craze: Freebasing," *People* (June 9, 1980).
24. Susanne Babbel, "Fear of Success," *Psychology Today* (January 3, 2011). https://www.psychologytoday.com/blog/somatic-psychology/201101/fear-success.
25. Zoglin, 63.
26. Bailey.
27. *Ibid.*
28. "Richard Pryor, Bo Derek and Alan Alda," *The Barbara Walters Special*, ABC News (August 3, 1980).
29. Beckett.
30. *Ibid.*
31. *Ibid.*
32. *Ibid.*
33. David Denby, *New Yorker* (June 8, 1981), 51.
34. Pryor, with Gold, 68.
35. Zoglin. 47.
36. Jonathan Lyons, "Some notes about Angry Birds," *Comedy for Animators* (May 22, 2016). http://comedyforanimators.com/2016/05/22/some-notes-about-angry-birds/.
37. Kerry Levielle, "Watch: It's More Than Just Red-Faced Yelling; Jack Nicholson Has Mastered the Art of

Anger," *IndieWire* (April 6, 2017). http://www.indiewire.com/2017/04/jack-nicholson-master-of-anger-1201802778/.

38. "Father Goose," *Time Out Film Guide*. https://www.timeout.com/london/film/father-goose.

39. Rob Wile, "It's the 30-Year Anniversary of the Greatest Wall Street Movie Ever Made: Here's the Story Behind It," *Business Insider* (June 27, 2013). http://www.businessinsider.com/an-oral-history-of-trading-places-2013-6.

40. Sandi Davis, "'Trading Places' screenwriter speaks on craft at OU," *Oklahoman* (March 12, 2013). http://newsok.com/article/3764787.

41. Kevin Avery, ed., *Conversations with Clint: Paul Nelson's Lost Interviews with Clint Eastwood, 1979 to 1983* (New York: Bloomsbury Academic, 2011).

42. Jon Zelazny, "Walter Hill: Last Man Standing," *Diary of a Screenwriter* (June 6, 2014). http://diaryofascreenwriter.blogspot.com/2014/06/walter-hill-last-man-standing.html.

Some Kind of Hero

1. Bozung.
2. *Ibid*.
3. *Ibid*.
4. *Cincinnati Enquirer* (November 14, 1981), 26.
5. Bozung.
6. Peter Lester, "Margot the Mom," *People* (August 24, 1981).
7. Bozung.
8. Lee Grant, "Meteoric success baffles Richard Pryor," *Los Angeles Times* (April 1, 1982), 162.
9. *Ibid*.
10. *Palm Beach Post* (January 25, 1982), 16.
11. Lois Armstrong, "Through the Fire," *People* (June 29, 1981). http://people.com/archive/cover-story-through-the-fire-vol-15-no-25/.
12. *Ibid*.
13. Rabin.
14. Lester.
15. *Ibid*.
16. *Ibid*.
17. *Ibid*.
18. *Ibid*.
19. Pryor, with Gold, 216.
20. "Interracial Ardor Cooled on Screen," *New York Magazine* (December 14, 1981), 15.
21. Lester.
22. *Ibid*.
23. Maureen Callahan, "Tortured in notorious 'Hanoi Hilton,' 11 GIs were Unbreakable," *New York Post* (February 15, 2014). http://nypost.com/2014/02/15/tortured-in-vietnams-worst-prison-11-us-soldiers-were-unbreakable/.
24. John S. McCain, "Prisoner of War: A First-Person Account," *U.S. News and World Report* (January 28, 2008). https://www.usnews.com/news/articles/2008/01/28/john-mccain-prisoner-of-war-a-first-person-account.

The Toy

1. "Richard Pryor Second Look at Life," *Los Angeles Times* (April 1, 1982), 1, 162.
2. Bailey.
3. Vincent Canby, "'Toy' A Comedy with Pryor and Gleason," *New York Times* (December 10, 1982). http://www.nytimes.com/movie/review?res=9C01E3DB103BF933A25751C1A964948260.
4. Odie Henderson, "For Rent: One Negro, As Is," *Big Media Vandalism* (February 16, 2013). http://bigmediavandal.blogspot.com/2013/02/for-rent-one-negro-as-is.html.
5. Jack Matthews, "Richard Pryor pulls laughs out of thin air in 'The Toy,'" *Detroit Free Press* (December 10, 1982), 21.
6. Rabin.
7. Ed Blank, "Crude Clowning Mars Richard Pryor's 'The Toy,'" *Pittsburgh Press* (December 10, 1982), 39.
8. Henry and Henry.
9. *Ibid*.
10. David Elliott (Gannett News Service), "Here Comes the Christmas Movies," *Journal News* (December 3, 1982), 63.
11. Jim Calio, "After 53 Years in the Limelight, Jackie Gleason Revels in How Sweet It Still Is," *People* (November 3, 1980).
12. Grant.
13. Pryor, with Gold, 219.
14. Rovin, 236.
15. *Ibid*.
16. Rovin, 235.
17. Phil Cornell, "So you want to be a movie star," *Courier-News from Bridgewater* (May 3, 1982), 8.
18. "Scott Schwartz talks with TV Store Online about A Christmas Story and The Toy," *TVStoreOnline Blog* (May 16, 2013). http://blog.tvstoreonline.com/2013/05/scott-schwartz-talks-with-tv-store.html.
19. *Ibid*.
20. Rovin, 244.
21. Pryor, with Gold, 218.
22. Pryor, with Gold, 221.
23. George Anderson, "Pryor, Gleason are wasted in 'The Toy,'" *Pittsburgh Post-Gazette* (December 10, 1982), 32.
24. Gary Minich, "Broken toy: Laughs lost in clutter of messy film," *Herald and Review* (December 18, 1982), 16.
25. Blank.
26. Betas Marsh, "Pryor's 'The Toy' Just Simply Doesn't Work," *Cincinnati Enquirer* (December 10, 1982), 29.
27. Gene Siskel, "A trend hits the screen: Black is back in films—but only for male actors," *Chicago Tribune* (December 5, 1982).
28. *Ibid*.
29. *Ibid*.
30. *Ibid*.
31. Bill Nichols, "'The Toy' isn't any fun, thanks to

Richard Pryor's sermonizing," *Clarion-Ledger* (Jackson, MS) (December 17, 1982), 55.

32. Bailey.

33. M. Enois Duarte, "The Toy," *High-Def Digest* (February 9, 2012). http://bluray.highdefdigest.com/5847/toy.html.

34. Blank.

35. Upton.

36. Saul Austerlitz, *Another Fine Mess: A History of American Film Comedy* (Chicago: Chicago Review Press, 2010), 263.

37. Gary Arnold, "'The Toy' Isn't Any Fun," *Washington Post* (December 11, 1982). https://www.washingtonpost.com/archive/lifestyle/1982/12/11/the-toy-isnt-any-fun/c57a37eb-6ad1-4838-abf0-db888c37ed8d/.

38. Bailey.

39. Henderson.

Superman III

1. David Newman and Leslie Newman, "Superman vs. Superman (Superman III)" [screenplay], revised April 1982.

2. Mike Ryan, "'Superman III': Rewatching 30 Years Later," *Huffington Post* (June 11, 2013). http://www.huffingtonpost.com/mike-ryan/superman-iii-30-years-later_b_3417466.html.

3. *Ibid.*

4. Bailey.

5. Ryan.

6. Roger Ebert, "Superman III," *Chicago Sun-Times* (June 17, 1983). http://www.rogerebert.com/reviews/superman-iii-1983.

7. Pauline Kael, *The New Yorker* (July 11, 1983), 90.

8. Eleanor Mannikka, *All Movie*. http://www.allmovie.com/movie/superman-iii-v47871.

9. Tate, 72.

10. Marilyn Beck, "Comedian shelves project to play role in 'Color Man,'" *Arizona Republic* (November 13, 1981), 159.

11. Bailey.

12. Bradford Evans, "The Lost Roles of Richard Pryor," *SplitSider* (September 1, 2011). http://splitsider.com/2011/09/the-lost-roles-of-richard-pryor/.

13. Richard Pryor, *Larry King Live*, 1987.

14. Als.

15. Rovin, 240.

16. Joe Pollack, "The Tamer Side of Gene Wilder," *St. Louis Post-Dispatch* (June 3, 1982), 61.

17. *Ibid.*

18. *Ibid.*

19. Taylor.

20. *Ibid.*

21. Gene Wilder, Jeffrey Price and Peter Seaman, story by Henry Rosenbaum, David Taylor and Gene Wilder, "Double Whoopee" [unproduced script], revised December 7, 1987, 2.

22. *Ibid.*, 3.

23. *Ibid.*, 4.

24. *Ibid.*, 5.

25. *Ibid.*, 3Z0.

26. *Ibid.*, 21.

27. *Ibid.*, 28.

28. *Ibid.*, 111.

29. "Richard Pryor To Star In World War II Comedy," *Jet* (February 7, 1983), 64.

30. Joe Baltake, "1 Piano, Slightly Out of Tune," *Philadelphia Daily News* (August 8, 1986).

31. Masco Young, "Color Red Foxx's Upcoming A. C. Gig Very Blue," *Philadelphia Daily News* (January 27, 1983), 41.

32. Pryor, with Gold, 226–227.

33. Tate, 71.

Brewster's Millions

1. Natsukashi Podcast, episode XLVI: "Brewster's Millions with writer Herschel Weingrod" (March 20, 2009). https://natsukashi.wordpress.com/2009/03/20/epxlvi-brewsters-millions-with-writer-its-herschel-weingrod/.

2. Amber Petty, "Rick of Time: 10 Best Rick Moranis Roles," *IFC* (August 22, 2016). http://www.ifc.com/2016/08/rick-moranis-roles.

3. Dover Publications, "Brewster's Millions." http://store.doverpublications.com/0486805301.html.

4. George Barr McCutcheon, *Brewster's Millions* (New York: Herbert S. Stone, 1902).

5. *New York Times* (October 12, 1906).

6. *Ibid.*, 1906), 9.

7. Dover Publications.

8. *Brewster's Millions*, Wikipedia (retrieved June 9, 2017). https://en.wikipedia.org/wiki/Brewster%27s_Millions.

9. *WTF with Marc Maron*, episode 805: Walter Hill (April 24, 2017). http://www.wtfpod.com/podcast/episode-805-walter-hill.

10. Stephen McMillian, "Q&A: The Legendary Lonette McKee," *Soul Train* (August 29, 2012). http://soultrain.com/2012/08/29/qa-the-legendary-lonette-mckee/.

11. *Ibid.*

12. *WTF with Marc Maron.*

13. Janet Maslin, "Film: Pryor in Remake of 'Brewster's Millions,'" *New York Times* (May 22, 1985). http://www.nytimes.com/movie/review?res=9E0CE3D9133BF931A15756C0A963948260.

14. *Ibid.*

15. *Ibid.*

16. *Ibid.*

17. Gene Siskel, "Pryor Not Worth A Million In 'Brewster,'" *Chicago Tribune* (May 22, 1985). http://articles.chicagotribune.com/1985-05-22/features/8502010676_1_richard-pryor-film-short-movie.

18. Vincent Canby, "Richard Pryor in Search of His Comic Genius," *New York Times* (June 2, 1985). http://www.nytimes.com/1985/06/02/movies/film-view-richard-pryor-in-search-of-his-comic-genius.html.

19. Bob Thomas, "Pryor's 'Brewster's Millions' never achieves potential," *Associated Press*, June 23, 1985.

20. Ron Cowan, "Time-tested plot returns in 'Brewster's Millions'" *Statesman Journal* (May 28, 1985), 29.

21. Ken Tucker, "'Brewster's Millions' has an often-repeated comedic plot," *Philadelphia Inquirer* (May 24, 1985), 100.

22. *WTF with Marc Maron*.

23. *Arkansas Democrat* (April 13, 1921).

24. Kent Jones, *Physical Evidence: Selected Film Criticism* (Middletown, CT: Wesleyan University Press, 2007).

25. *New York Times* (October 12, 1906).

26. Tucker.

27. Bailey.

Jo Jo Dancer, Your Life Is Calling

1. Pryor, with Gold, 226.
2. *Ibid.*
3. David T. Friendly, "Pryor Restraint," *Los Angeles Times* (May 5, 1986).
4. "Pryor says 'Jo Jo' isn't purely autobiographical," *Arizona Daily Star* (May 28, 1986), 6.
5. *Ibid.*
6. McDonagh.
7. Roger Ebert, "Richard Pryor Live on the Sunset Strip," *Chicago Sun-Times* (January 1, 1982). http://www.rogerebert.com/reviews/richard-pryor-live-on-the-sunset-strip-1982.
8. *Ibid.*
9. *Ibid.*
10. John H. Johnson, ed., "Richard Pryor Says 'Self-Deception' Is Like a Drug," *Jet* (April 28, 1986), 59.
11. Thom Mount, "No Regrets: Richard Pryor," *Interview Magazine* (March 1986).
12. *Ibid.*
13. Pauline Kael, "Jo Jo Dancer, Your Life Is Calling," *The New Yorker* (June 16, 1986).
14. Upton.
15. *Ibid.*
16. Henry and Henry.
17. David T. Friendly, "'Bottoming Out' And Learning How to Care," *St. Louis Post-Dispatch*, May 28, 1986, 82 [reprinted from *The Los Angeles Times*].
18. Canby, Vincent. "Screen: 'Jo Jo Dancer,'" *New York Times* (May 2, 1986). http://www.nytimes.com/movie/review?res=9A0DEFDC123EF931A35756C0A960948260.
19. Jennifer Lee, "Richard Pryor, Now Your Ex-Wife Is Calling," *People* (June 16, 1986). http://people.com/archive/richard-pryor-now-your-ex-wife-is-calling-vol-25-no-24/.
20. Upton.

Critical Condition

1. Denis Hamill, "Richard Pryor Was Funny and Real," *New York Daily News* (December 20, 2005). http://www.nydailynews.com/archives/boroughs/richard-pryor-funny-real-article-1.617039.
2. Denis Hamill, "Re: 'Critical Condition,'" email to author, November 2, 2016.
3. Hamill, "Richard Pryor."
4. Hamill, "Re: 'Critical Condition.'"
5. Hamill, "Richard Pryor."
6. Hamill, "Re: 'Critical Condition.'"
7. Michael Wilmington, "Pryor Fine, "Condition' Weakening," *Los Angeles Times* (January 16, 1987). http://articles.latimes.com/1987-01-16/entertainment/ca-3662_1_pryor.
8. Hamill, "Richard Pryor."
9. Hamill, "Re: 'Critical Condition.'"
10. *Ibid.*
11. Wilmington.
12. Upton.
13. *Ibid.*
14. Hamill, "Richard Pryor."
15. Wilmington.
16. *Ibid.*
17. Desmond Taylor, "Richard Pryor plays a con man playing a doctor," *Philadelphia Inquirer* (January 17, 1987), 37.
18. David T. Friendly, "Richard Pryor, Your Life Is Calling…," *Los Angeles Times* (April 27, 1986), 4.
19. Chris Hodenfield, "One Memorable Summer Night with Danny Kaye," *Los Angeles Times* (March 8, 1987). http://articles.latimes.com/1987-03-08/entertainment/ca-13287_1_danny-kaye.
20. Saul.

Moving

1. Andy Breckman, "Nobody Move! It's Richard Pryor!" *WFMU* (1997). http://wfmu.org/LCD/20/pryor.html.
2. Desmond Ryan, "Richard Pryor in comedy about moving," *Philadelphia Inquirer* (March 7, 1988), 29.
3. *Ibid.*
4. Michael Healy, "'Moving' van should take Pryor," *Los Angeles Daily News* (March 12, 1988), 32.
5. Dan Craft, "'Moving' out of line," *The Pantagraph* (March 25, 1988), 39.
6. *Ibid.*
7. Janet Maslin, "Film: 'Moving,' with Richard Pryor," *New York Times* (March 5, 1988). http://www.nytimes.com/movie/review?res=940DE7D61731F936A35750C0A96E948260.
8. *Ibid.*
9. David Edelstein, "Donkey Kongs," *Slate* (December 15, 2005). http://www.slate.com/news-and-politics/2017/08/clarence-thomas-legal-vision-is-becoming-a-trump-era-reality.html.

Harlem Nights

1. Pryor, with Gold, 247.
2. *Ibid.*
3. Upton.
4. Spike Lee, "Eddie! An exclusive interview with Eddie Murphy by Spike Lee," *Spin* (October 1990), 97.

5. *Ibid.*
6. *Ibid.*
7. Jason Bailey, "Eddie Murphy Is 'Never Gonna Be Richard Pryor': The Comedian's Widow on Pryor's Rivalries (And a Threesome)," *Flavorwire* (April 25, 2013). http://flavorwire.com/387151/eddie-murphy-is-never-gonna-be-richard-pryor-the-comedians-widow-on-pryors-rivalries-and-a-threesome.
8. Roger Ebert, "Harlem Nights," *Chicago Sun-Times* (November 17, 1989). http://www.rogerebert.com/reviews/harlem-nights-1989.

See No Evil, Hear No Evil

1. "Windows and Keyholes," *Pittsburgh Post-Gazette* (May 16, 1978), 29.
2. Eve Sullivan, "Wilder reflects on Pryor relationship at Avon," *Stamford Advocate* (October 17, 2013). http://www.stamfordadvocate.com/news/article/Wilder-reflects-on-Pryor-relationship-at-Avon-4905345.php.
3. *Ibid.*
4. *Ibid.*
5. *Ibid.*
6. William Brashler, "Berserk Angel," *Playboy* (December 1979).
7. "Interview with Arthur Hiller," *Archive of American Television*. http://www.emmytvlegends.org/interviews/people/arthur-hiller.
8. Upton.
9. Pryor, with Gold, 256.

Another You

1. Upton.
2. Andrew Yule, *Picture Shows: The Life and Films of Peter Bogdanovich* (New York: Limelight Editions, 1992), 251.
3. *Ibid.*
4. Upton.
5. Michael Wilmington, "Another You: Happy, Dopey, Snappy, Empty," *Los Angeles Times* (July 29, 1991). http://articles.latimes.com/1991-07-29/entertainment/ca-96_1_gene-wilder.
6. Wilmington.
7. Ryan.

The Three Muscatels

1. Tate.

Mad Dog Time

1. Jedadiah Leland, "Worst of the Worst: 'Mad Dog Time,'" *Unobtainium 13* (April 22, 2016). https://unobtainium13.com/2016/04/22/worst-of-the-worst-mad-dog-time-1996-directed-by-larry-bishop/.
2. Jan E. Morris, "Christopher Jones—Wild at Heart," *Cinetropic*. http://www.cinetropic.com/jones/bio.html.
3. *Ibid.*
4. Leland.
5. Ken Tucker, *Entertainment Weekly* (November 22, 1996).
6. Roger Ebert, "Mad Dog Time," *Chicago Sun-Times* (November 29, 1996). http://www.rogerebert.com/reviews/mad-dog-time-1996.

Lost Highway

1. Michael Rose, "'Lost Highway'—A Look at David Lynch's Cult Classic," *Mysterious Universe* (August 13, 2013). http://mysteriousuniverse.org/2013/08/lost-highway-a-look-at-david-lynchs-cult-classic/.
2. Anthony Leong, "Demystifying Lost Highway," *Media Circus* (1997). http://www.mediacircus.net/lh.html.
3. Frederick Szebin and Steve Biodrowski, "David Lynch On 'Lost Highway': A surreal meditation on love, jealousy, identity and reality," *LynchNet* (April 1997). http://www.lynchnet.com/lh/cinelh.html.
4. Rose.
5. Szebin and Biodrowski.
6. *Ibid.*
7. *Ibid.*
8. Mikal Gilmore, "David Lynch and Trent Reznor: The Lost Boys," *Rolling Stone* (March 6, 1997). http://www.rollingstone.com/music/news/david-lynch-and-trent-reznor-the-lost-boys-19970306.
9. *Ibid.*
10. David Foster Wallace, "David Lynch Keeps His Head," *Premiere* (1996).
11. Richard A. Barney, ed., *David Lynch: Interviews* (Jackson: University of Mississippi Press, 2009).
12. *Ibid.*
13. David Lynch and Barry Gifford, "'Lost Highway'—The Screenplay" (June 21, 1995).
14. *Ibid.*

Epilogue

1. "Harvey Korman Interview," *Archive of American Television* (April 20, 2004). http://www.emmytvlegends.org/interviews/people/harvey-korman.
2. Hutchison, *Richard Pryor: Omit the Logic*.
3. Greg Fitzsimmons, "Norm MacDonald and Mark McGrath," *Fitzdog Radio* (August 30, 2011). https://gregfitz.libsyn.com/norm-mac-donald-and-mark-mc-grath.

Bibliography

Books

Bailey, Jason. *Richard Pryor: American Id*. Raleigh: The Critical Press, 2015.

Bullaro, Grace Russo. *Man in Disorder: The Cinema of Lina Wertmüller in the 1970s*. Leicester: Troubadour, 2006.

Goudsouzian, Aram. *Sidney Poitier: Man, Actor, Icon*. Chapel Hill: University of North Carolina Press, 2004.

Henry, David, and Joe Henry. *Furious Cool: Richard Pryor and the World That Made Him*. Chapel Hill: Algonquin Books, 2013.

Kremer, Daniel. *Sidney J. Furie: Life and Films*. Lexington: University Press of Kentucky, 2015.

McCluskey, Audrey T. *Richard Pryor: The Life and Legacy of a "Crazy" Black Man*. Bloomington: Indiana University Press, 2008.

Nachman, Gerald. *Seriously Funny: The Rebel Comedians of the 1950s and 1960s*. New York: Pantheon, 2009.

Nesteroff, Kliph. *The Comedians: Drunks, Thieves, Scoundrels, and the History of American Comedy*. New York: Grove Press, 2015.

Pryor, Richard, with Todd Gold. *Pryor Convictions*. New York: Pantheon, 1995.

Rovin, Jeff. *Richard Pryor: Black and Blue: The Unauthorized Biography*. New York: Bantam Books, 1983.

Sacks, Mike. *Poking a Dead Frog: Conversations with Today's Top Comedy Writers*. London: Penguin Books, 2014.

Saul, Scott. *Becoming Richard Pryor*. New York: Harper, 2014.

Simon, Roger L. *Turning Right at Hollywood and Vine: The Perils of Coming Out Conservative*. New York: Encounter Books, 2011.

Wilder, Gene. *Kiss Me Like A Stranger: My Search for Love and Art*. New York: St. Martin's Press, 2005.

Williams, John A., and Dennis A. Williams. *If I Stop I'll Die: The Tragedy and Comedy of Richard Pryor*. New York: Thunder's Mouth Press, 1991.

Zoglin, Richard. *Comedy at the Edge: How Stand-up in the 1970s Changed America*. London: Bloomsbury, 2008.

Articles

Als, Hilton. "A Pryor Love: The Life and Times of America's Comic Prophet of Race." *The New Yorker* (September 13, 1999), downloaded from http://www.newyorker.com/magazine/1999/09/13/a-pryor-love.

Beckett, Colin. "The Uses of Richard Pryor." *The Brooklyn Rail* (February 5, 2013), downloaded from http://brooklynrail.org/2013/02/film/the-uses-of-richard-pryor.

Felton, David. "Richard Pryor's Life in Concert." *Rolling Stone* (May 3, 1979), downloaded from http://www.rollingstone.com/culture/features/richard-pryors-life-in-concert-19790503.

Fitch, Fred. "Mr. Westlake and The Nephews." *The Westlake Review* (June 26, 2016), downloaded from https://thewestlakereview.wordpress.com/2014/06/26/mr-westlake-and-the-nephews/.

Friedman, Bruce Jay. "When Gene Wilder Went 'Stir Crazy.'" *Tablet* (September 1, 2016), downloaded from http://www.tabletmag.com/jewish-arts-and-culture/212301/when-gene-wilder-went-stir-crazy.

Hamill, Denis. "Richard Pryor Was Funny and Real." *New York Daily News* (December 20, 2005), downloaded from http://www.nydailynews.com/archives/boroughs/richard-pryor-funny-real-article-1.617039.

Hamlin, Jesse. "Billie Holiday's bio, 'Lady Sings the Blues,' may be full of lies, but it gets at jazz great's core." *San Francisco Chronicle* (September 18, 2006), downloaded from http://www.sfgate.com/entertainment/article/Billie-Holiday-s-bio-Lady-Sings-the-Blues-may-2469428.php.

King, Susan. "'The Mack' is back after 40 years." *Los Angeles Times* (September 25, 2013), downloaded from http://articles.latimes.com/2013/sep/25/

entertainment/la-et-mn-the-mack-lacma-20130925.
Meroney, John, and Sean Coons. "The 'Flickering, Fragile Flame' of Richard Pryor." *The Atlantic* (November 21, 2013), downloaded from https://www.theatlantic.com/entertainment/archive/2013/11/the-flickering-fragile-flame-of-richard-pryor/281515/.
Rabin, Nathan. "Random Roles: Margot Kidder." *A.V. Club* (March 3, 2009), downloaded from http://www.avclub.com/article/random-roles-margot-kidder-24554.
Tate, James M. "Yaphet Kotto: The One and Only." *Cult Film Freak*, downloaded from http://www.cultfilmfreak.com/yaphetkotto/.
Thomas, Bryan. "'Adios Amigo': Fred 'The Hammer' Williamson and Richard Pryor are two sharp dudes taking turns with chicks and tricks." *Night Flight* (April 3, 2016), downloaded from http://nightflight.com/adios-amigo-fred-the-hammer-williamson-and-richard-pryor-are-two-sharp-dudes-taking-turns-with-chicks-and-tricks/.
Upton, Julian. "Extinguishing Features: The Last Years of Richard Pryor." *Bright Lights Film Journal* (December 10, 2016), downloaded from http://brightlightsfilm.com/extinguishing-features-last-years-richard-pryor/#.WQY7F8a1uUk.
Weston, Martin. "Richard Pryor: Every Nigger Is a Star." *Ebony* (September 1976).
Wilkins, Budd E. "To Each His Own Bastard: A Viewer's Guide to The Seduction of Mimi" (2010).

Periodicals

Chicago Sun-Times
Chicago Tribune
Detroit Free Press
Ebony
Jet
Los Angeles Times
New York Times
People
Philadelphia Inquirer
Spin

Index

Numbers in *bold italics* indicate pages with illustrations

Adiós Amigo (1976) 47
The African Queen 124, 135
Als, Hilton 23, 156
Another You (1991) 190
Apted, Michael 142, 173, 179
Avery, Margaret 73, *74*, 78, 85, 132
Aykroyd, Dan 135

The Bad News Bears 133
Bailey, Jason 13, 14, 24, 29, 46, 99, 118, 131, 142, 148, 149, 155, 156, 168
Barwood, Hal 52, 53
Beatty, Ned 58, 60, 142, 144, 146, 147
Beckett, Colin 3, 132
The Bingo Long Traveling All-Stars & Motor Kings (1976) 52
Blades, Rubén 173, *178*
blaxploitation 40–42, 50
Blazing Saddles 49, 50, 63
Blue Collar (1978) 85
Bogdanovich, Peter 167, 191
Boyd, Stephen *20*, 21
Boyle, Peter 85, 111
Brashler, William 52, 53, 56, 109, 189
Breckman, Andy 180, 181
Brewster's Millions (1985) 160
Bridges, Beau 65, *68*, 70–72
Brooks, Mel 12, 20, 49, 50, 63, 71, 108, 114, 134
Brown, Cecil 73, 77, 92–93, 95, 96, 99, 106
Brown, Jim 94, 151, 160
Bullaro, Russo 78, 79
Bustin' Loose (1981) 123
The Busy Body (1967) 5

Caddyshack 133
Caesar, Sid 2, 5, *6*, 8–13, 203, 204
California Suite (1978) 104
Canby, Vincent 46, 64, 81, 94, 98, 101, 120, 121, 131, 143, 166, 171
Car Wash (1976) 57
Carlin, George 2, 57, 201
Carter's Army (1970) 20
Castle, William 5, 8–13

Cavett, Dick 11–13
Chaplin, Charlie 1
Chase, Annazette 34, 142
Clayburgh, Jill 58–61
A Clockwork Orange 99
Coburn, James 108
Coleman, Marilyn 73, 84
Cosby, Bill 3, 42, *43*, 46, 102, 104, 106, 107, 182
Critical Condition (1987) 173

"Double Whoopee" (unproduced screenplay) 157
DuKore, Laurence 65–67, 70, 72

Eastwood, Clint 49, 136
Edwards, Blake 159, 160

Father Goose 135
Feldman, Marty 111–113
Fields, Chip 85, 89, 90
Fields, Verna 113, 124, 129
Fields, W.C. 132–134
Fitch, Fred 5, 6, 8, 9
Fonda, Jane 104, 106
48 Hrs. 135
Foxx, Redd 45, 46, 182, 185
Franklin, David 117, 119
Frazetta, Frank 10
Friedman, Bruce Jay 114, 116, 120–122, 160
Furie, Sidney 26, 28–30, 40, 42, 168

Galbraith, Stuart 79, 80
Giannini, Giancarlo 80, 82, 107–108, 159
The Girl Can't Help It 151
Gleason, Jackie 85, 142–147
Golonka, Arlene 5, 9
Gottlieb, Carl 25, 73, 77, 79–81, 83–85
Goudsouzian, Aram 122
Grant, Cary 135
Greased Lightning (1977) 65
Grier, Pam 65, 77
Grier, Rosey *20*, 21
Grizzard, George 106

Hamill, Denis 173, 175, 178, 179
Harlem Nights (1989) 182
Henry, David 2–3, 10, 17–19, 24, 39, 40, 41, 49, 51, 58, 116, 118, 145, 171
Henry, Joe 2–3, 10, 17–19, 24, 36, 39, 40, 41, 49, 51, 58, 116, 145, 171
Higgins, Colin 58, 59, 62
Hit! (1973) 40
Hodenfield, Chris 180
Holiday, Billie 27–30
Hope, Bob 132

In God We Tru$ (or Gimme That Prime Time Religion) (1980) 111

Jo Jo Dancer, Your Life Is Calling (1986) 168
Jones, Christopher 14, 16–18, 195
Jones, James Earl 49, 52, 56, 57, 67
Julien, Max 18, 30, 32–36, 84

Kael, Pauline 14–16, 106, 155, 171
Kaufman, Andy 111, 113
Kaye, Danny 2, 180, 201
Keaton, Buster 9, 61, 148
Kehr, Dave 106
Keitel, Harvey 85, 86, 88–91, 93, 94, 96, 98, 100
Kidder, Margot 58, 136, 138–140, 144, 151, 157
King, Larry 156
King, Mabel 52, 84, 102
King, Zalman 25, 37–39
Knight, Ted 133
Korman, Harvey 201
Kotto, Yaphet 85, 86, 89–91, 93–96, 98
Krantz, Steve 70, 73, 77
Kuersten, Erich 15, 16

Lady Sings the Blues (1972) 26
Landis, John 135
Lemmon, Jack 46, 62
Lewis, Jerry 2, 141, 146
Little, Cleavon 50, 65, *67*, 69
Live and Let Die 95
Lost Highway (1997) 196

Index

Lynch, David 196, 198, 199
Lyons, Jonathan 132

The Mack (1973) 30
Mad Dog Time (1996) 195
Matthau, Walter 46, 85, 104, 133, 135
McGoohan, Patrick 58–61, 188
McKee, Lonette 73, 161, 166, 167
McQueen, Steve 10, 24, 40
Modern Times 74
Moody, Lynne 136, 138, **139**
Mooney, Paul 17, 73, 123, 168, 169, 171
Moore, Roger 95
Moranis, Rick 161–163
Moreland, Mantan 46, 95
Morris, Garrett 173, **174**
Moving (1988) 180
The Muppet Movie (1979) 108
Murphy, Eddie 135, 136, 147, 148, 182–184

Newton, Huey 13, 19, 32, 33
North, Alan 186, 187
Northup, Harry 3, 73–75, 85, 90–92, 94, 96, 100

Pendleton, Austin 108
The Phynx (1970) 23
Poitier, Sidney 42–46, 50, 106, 114, 116–119, 121, 122, 157
Price, Jeffrey 157, 159
Price, Vincent 124
Pryor, Jennifer Lee 19, 58, 118, 137, 172, 179, 185, 190, 194

Rabin, Nathan 24
Reynolds, Burt 72, 159, 160, 195
Richard Pryor: Live in Concert 101
Richard Pryor: Live on the Sunset Strip 1, 170
Rosenbaum, Henry 121, 122, 157
Rosenbaum, Jonathan 37, 39
Ross, Diana **27**, 29, 102
Rovin, Jeff 24, 26, 50, 62, 63, 64, 71, 91, 118, 119, 122

Ryan, Robert 5, 10
Ryan, Mike 153, 155, 193

Saget, Bob 173, 178
Sandler, Adam 133–134
Saul, Scott 2, 17–19, 23, 32–36, 77, 79, 81, 92, 180
Schrader, Paul 85, 89–91, 93–100, 131, 148, 169, 170
Schultz, Michael 47, 49, 57, 58, 65, 70, 72, 73, 77–79, 81, 84, 89, 94, 123, 129, 130
Schumacher, Joel 57, 102
Schwartz, Scott 142, 145, 146
Scott, Oz 123–126, 128, 129
Scott, Wendell 65–73
Seaman, Peter 157, 159
The Seduction of Mimi 73, 77–79
See No Evil, Hear No Evil (1989) 186
Seems Like Old Times 121
Shaw, Stan 52, **53**, 116, 182
Silver Streak (1976) 58
Simon, Neil 11, 104, 106, 107, 121
Simon, Roger L. 123, 127–129, 131
Siskel, Gene 121, 131, 147, 148, 166, 196
Some Call It Loving (1973) 37
Some Kind of Hero (1982) 136
Spacey, Kevin 186, 188
Spelling, Aaron 20, 21, 23
Spencer, Alan 111, 113
Spheeris, Penelope 18, 19, 96
Spielberg, Steven 52, 55
Starkey, Ray 136, **137**
The Sting 75
Stir Crazy (1980) 114
Superman III (1983) 151
Swept Away 85, 108

Taylor, David 121, 122, 157
The Three Muscatels (1991) 194
Ticotin, Rachel 173, **177**
"Timmons from Chicago" (unproduced screenplay) 47, 57
Todd, Beverly 42
Tomlin, Lily 1, 85

Tomlinson, Tommy 68, 71
The Toy (1982) 142
Trading Places 135, 167, 168
Tweedle, Sam 16, 18

Uncle Tom's Fair Tales: The Movie for Homosexuals (1969) 18
Upton, Julian 131, 149, 171, 173, 179, 184, 190, 191
Uptown Saturday Night (1974) 42

Valdez, Luis 73, 74
Van Peebles, Melvin 65, 67, 69, 70, 72
Veber, Francis 134, 142, 149
Vose, Kenneth 65–67, 69, 72

You've Got to Walk It Like You Talk It or You'll Lose That Beat (1971) 25

Walston, Ray 58, 60, **61**
Wayans, Damon 1
Weingrod, Herschel 135, 161, 162
Weinstein, Hannah 65–67, 114, 115, 122
Wertmüller, Lina 73, 77–79, 81–85, 159
Westlake, Donald 5, 6, 8–10, 113
Weston, Jack 106
Weston, Jay 26, 29
Which Way Is Up? (1977) 73
Wholly Moses! (1980) 109
Wild in the Streets (1968) 14
Wilder, Gene 58–65, 114–122, 134, 135, 151, 156–158, 160, 186–193
Williams, Billy Dee 20, 27, 29, 30, 40, 52, 53, 56, 95
Williams, JoBeth 114
Williams, Robin 117, 150
Williamson, Fred 47, 50, 51
Winters, Jonathan 2, 13, 148, 201
Winters, Shelley 14, 16–18, 50
The Wiz (1978) 102

www.ingramcontent.com/pod-product-compliance
Lightning Source LLC
Chambersburg PA
CBHW081554300426
44116CB00015B/2878